Policing Public Opinion
in the French Revolution

Policing Public Opinion
in the French Revolution

THE CULTURE OF CALUMNY
AND THE PROBLEM OF FREE SPEECH

Charles Walton

OXFORD
UNIVERSITY PRESS

OXFORD
UNIVERSITY PRESS

Oxford University Press, Inc., publishes works that further
Oxford University's objective of excellence
in research, scholarship, and education.

Oxford   New York
Auckland   Cape Town   Dar es Salaam   Hong Kong   Karachi
Kuala Lumpur   Madrid   Melbourne   Mexico City   Nairobi
New Delhi   Shanghai   Taipei   Toronto

With offices in
Argentina   Austria   Brazil   Chile   Czech Republic   France   Greece
Guatemala   Hungary   Italy   Japan   Poland   Portugal   Singapore
South Korea   Switzerland   Thailand   Turkey   Ukraine   Vietnam

Published by Oxford University Press, Inc.
198 Madison Avenue, New York, New York 10016

www.oup.com

First issued as an Oxford University Press paperback, 2011

Oxford is a registered trademark of Oxford University Press

Library of Congress Cataloging-in-Publication Data
Walton, Charles, professor of history.
Policing public opinion in the French Revolution : the culture of calumny
and the problem of free speech / Charles Walton.
p.   cm.
Includes bibliographical references and index.
ISBN 978-0-19-979580-2
1. Freedom of speech—France—History.   2. Censorship—France—History.
3. Civil rights—France—History—18th century.
4. France—History—Revolution, 1789-1799.   I. Title.
JC599.F8W35 2009
303.3'76094409033—dc22   2008008549

Printed in the United States of America
on acid-free paper

For Alice

ACKNOWLEDGMENTS

If this study succeeds in shedding light on the freedom of expression during the French Revolution, it is thanks to the ideas and opinions others have shared freely with me over the years. My greatest thanks go to Robert Darnton, my dissertation advisor, who has followed the progress of this project from its earliest stages. His incisive comments and support, not to mention his own work, have been immensely helpful. I also owe many thanks to David Bell, who has read several drafts of this study, offering useful insights each time. Phil Nord and Peter Lake read this work in its form as a dissertation and provided valuable suggestions. I am indebted to them both.

I would also like to convey my gratitude to my undergraduate mentors, Carla Hesse and Susanna Barrows, who inspired my interest in French cultural history at the University of California, Berkeley. Unsurprisingly, it was in Berkeley—a place where controversies and struggles over free speech never seem to exhaust themselves—that I became interested in the issue. It was mostly in France, however, that this project developed, and I owe Paul Cohen—cohort from Princeton, *camarade* in Paris—enormous thanks for his frequent and careful readings of my work. Stephen Clay deserves thanks for alerting me to the importance of calumny during the Revolution and for sharing his archival expertise when I was still trying to figure out how to read an inventory. I am grateful to Alan Forrest and Dena Goodman for their kindness and generosity in helping me get past some obstacles early on in the project.

Several friends and colleagues have read and commented on earlier drafts of all or parts of this book, and I would like to express my gratitude to them all: Julia Abramson, David Andress, Mihaela Bacou, Ariane Chebel d'Appollonia, Charly Coleman, Jennifer Heuer, Russell Jacoby, Andrew Jainchill, Lucien Jaume, Colin Jones, Nina Kushner, Thomas Kaiser, Laura Mason, Anne McCall, John Merriman, Joel Migdal, Cristina Nehring, Jeremy Popkin, Robert Post, Allan

Potofsky, Jeffrey Ravel, Neil Safier, Jennifer Sessions, Todd Shepard, Francesca Trivellato, and David Troyanski. I would also like to thank those who have shared their ideas and advice with me over the years: Hilary Bernstein, Gregory Brown, Jonathan Cole, Danielle Haase-Dubosc, Annie Duprat, Arlette Farge, Amy Freund, Bernard Gainot, Bryan Garsten, Glenda Gilmore, Jeff Horne, Michael Kwass, Herman (Gene) Lebovics, James Livesey, Kenneth Loiselle, Jill Maciak Walshaw, Jean-Clément Martin, Anne McCall, Renaud Morieux, Samuel Moyn, Gerald Neuman, Brian Ogilvie, Thierry Rigogne, Cliff Rosenberg, Terry Whiteside, Pierre Serna, Patrick Weil, and Isser Woloch. Several colleagues at Sciences Po, Paris, the University of Oklahoma, Norman, and Yale University have pushed me to think about the problem of calumny and free speech beyond the context of the French Revolution, among them, James Cane-Carrasco, Joanne Freeman, Lillian Guerra, and Melissa Stockdale. I have also learned much from the students enrolled in my seminar on the history of free speech in the Atlantic World, which I taught at Sciences Po and Yale. Their passionate interest in the subject served as a motivating reminder of why I chose this topic in the first place.

Several of the events discussed in chapter 6 grew out of conversations with the late Edna Lemay, who shared her extensive knowledge about the early revolutionary National Assemblies with me. Daniel Roche provided me with his transcriptions of the unpublished parts of Jacques Ménétra's journal, and I extend my thanks to him. Philippe de Carbonnières deserves thanks for the generous time spent helping me find appropriate illustrations for this book. Thanks go to my friend and neighbor in Paris, Daniel Laberthonnière, for the many hours—days, really—assisting me in formatting my data on the *cahiers de doléances*. I would like to thank my editor, Susan Ferber, for taking on this project shortly after I had completed my dissertation and for her unflagging support in seeing the project through. I also appreciate the valuable comments of OUP's anonymous readers of this manuscript.

Research for this book has been generously funded by the Social Science Research Council, the Center for International Studies and the Council on Regional Studies of Princeton University, the Hilles Fund and the European Studies Council of Yale University, and the Oklahoma Humanities Council. I appreciate their support.

Finally, I would like to express my gratitude to my parents as well as to friends and family in France who offered me their help and have kept my motivation from flagging: Jean-Marc Commun, Soria Hafed, Rebecca Walton and Jean-Christophe Giron, Smain Benouahlima, and the Gineste family. Ariane Chebel d'Appollonia and Michael Montgomery offered me their sympathetic ears and intelligent reflections over the years. One of my greatest debts is to Joseph Gonzalez, a historian of early modern Europe and longtime friend, who inspired my interest in history at a very early stage. Lastly, I owe warm thanks to Yacine Khezzari.

Contents

ABBREVIATIONS

AN   Archives nationales de France

AP   *Archives parlementaires: Recueil complet des débats législatifs et politiques des Chambres françaises imprimé par ordre du corps législatif,* ed. Jérôme Mavidal and Émile Laurent, 1st series, 82 vols. (Paris: P. Dupont, 1867–1990)

BNF   Bibliothèque nationale de France

BP   Bibliothèque de la Poste

ACP   *Actes de la Commune de Paris pendant la Révolution,* ed. Sigismond Lacroix, 1st and 2nd series, 19 vols. (Paris: L. Cerf, 1894–1955)

APP   Archives de la Préfecture de police, Paris

AMB   Archives municipales de Bordeaux

AMM   Archives municipales de Marseille

ADHG   Archives départementales de la Haute-Garonne

ADR   Archives départementales du Rhône

Société des Jacobins   Alphonse Aulard, *La Société des Jacobins: Recueil des documents pour l'histoire du club des Jacobins de Paris,* 6 vols. (Paris: Presses de Jouaust, 1889–1897)

Encyclopédie   Denis Diderot and Jean Le Rond d'Alembert, eds., *Encyclopédie ou dictionnaire raisonné des sciences, des arts et des métiers,* 17 vols. (Paris and Neuchâtel: 1751–1765).

Moniteur   *Réimpression de l'ancien* Moniteur, *seule histoire authentique et inaltérée de la Révolution française depuis la réunion des États-généraux jusqu'au Consulat (mai 1789–novembre 1799),* 32 vols. (Paris: Plon Frères, 1850–1854)

PV   *Procès-verbaux de l'Assemblée nationale* (Paris: Baudouin, s.d.). 75 vols.

Policing Public Opinion
in the French Revolution

Introduction

By spring 1793, as France edged toward the Terror, even Tom Paine's patience with free speech began wearing thin. In a letter to Georges Danton, deputy to the French National Convention and founding member of the Committee of Public Safety, Paine expressed his alarm about the relentless insults and slander plaguing revolutionary politics. A deputy himself, Paine urged Danton to take repressive measures. "Calumny," this champion of civil liberties insisted, "is a species of treachery that ought to be punished as well as any other kind of treachery."[1] He explained why: "[It] is a private vice productive of public evil, because it is possible to irritate men into disaffection by continual calumny who never intended to be disaffected." In other words, calumny weakened the bonds between citizens and their political system, fomenting agitation or, worse, civil war. "The danger increases every day of a rupture between Paris and the departments," he presciently warned. "The departments did not send their deputies to Paris to be insulted, and every insult shown to them is an insult to the departments that elected and sent them." A month later, sixty departments went into rebellion against Paris.

Paine's letter is historically ironic. Just months earlier, the former American revolutionary and British radical had been tried in absentia by a special court set up by William Pitt in London. He was convicted for his *Rights of Man*, declared to be seditious libel and an insult to the English monarchy.[2] Paine's election to the French National Convention allowed him to evade Pitt's wrath with dignity in Paris. It was there, though, that he saw calumny consume his cherished democratic politics. He watched as it inflamed factions in the Convention and poisoned relations between local and national authorities. Tensions culminated on May 31, 1793, when armed sans-culotte radicals in Paris surrounded the National Convention, forcing legislators to arrest twenty-two Girondin deputies, "the calumniators of the citizens of Paris."[3] Shortly before the purge, Paine expressed optimism that the Girondins would remain in office. "Calumny [against the Girondins] becomes harmless and defeats itself when it attempts to act upon too large a scale. Thus the denunciation of the [Paris] sections against the twenty-two deputies falls to the ground."[4] Events proved him wrong. The Terror was just beginning to build momentum. Later that year, several leading Girondins were guillotined, and Paine was arrested for his ties to them. He languished in prison until the fall of Robespierre in July 1794.

Perhaps the greatest irony about Paine's letter is that the Terror enacted precisely what he had demanded: the repression of calumny. Beginning with the Law of Suspects (September 17, 1793), revolutionaries criminalized a wide range of calumnious speech, from insults and defamatory remarks against authorities to the disparagement of patriotism, republicanism, and the Revolution.[5] Over the next ten months, thousands throughout France were arrested for crimes of expression. In Paris, more than one-third of the indictments brought before the revolutionary tribunal involved crimes of speech and opinion.[6] But the revolutionary government did not stop at repression. It also created a nationwide network of agents responsible for monitoring public opinion and spreading revolutionary propaganda. It embarked on an extravagant campaign to morally regenerate society, spreading patriotism, republican virtue, and enlightenment throughout France. Little more than four years after having proclaimed the freedom of expression in the Declaration of the Rights of Man and of the Citizen, revolutionaries appear to have turned their backs on their own principles. In the terms often used during the Cold War, the Revolution, it seems, had slid from freedom to totalitarianism.

This study examines the many reasons for the tragic reversal in freedom of expression between 1789 and the Year II (1793–1794). It is worth noting at the outset one of the most important reasons, namely, that most contemporaries did not view the repression of calumny as a violation of free-speech principles. For them, press freedom (which was the kind of free speech they insisted on most often) was not incompatible with restrictions and regulations. In the months leading up to the passage of the Declaration of Rights, contemporaries demanded only the abolition of prepublication censorship, that is, the require-ment to submit book and pamphlet manuscripts to royal censors for approval prior to publication. (Some wanted the principle to be extended to the news-paper press, which was heavily regulated and censored.) At the same time, they insisted on maintaining, even reinforcing, old laws against offensive writings. Attacks on religion, moral values, honor, and social and political hierarchy were all considered criminal forms of calumny. This conception of press freedom was prominent among the advocates of press freedom in all three orders, or Estates, of France—the clergy, the nobility, and the third estate (commoners).

Recognizing the distinction contemporaries made between prepublica-tion censorship (which they opposed) and ex post facto punishment for cal-umny (which they supported) is crucial for understanding the chronology of the Revolution and how the problem of free speech figured in it. In most accounts of the revolutionary press, historians contrast an early liberal phase of unlimited freedom with a subsequent, repressive phase.[7] In explaining how the Revolution passed from the one to the other, they stress the outbreak of war or the rise of Jacobins to power, both of which occurred in 1792.[8] The tendency to divide the Revolution into "liberal" and "repressive" phases stretches back to the rise of French liberalism in the early nineteenth century. In her attempt to salvage parts of the Revolution at a time of conservative backlash near the end of Napoleon's reign, Madame de Staël, novelist and political commentator, idealized its early years, distinguishing them from the horrors that followed once Jacobins—"that dreadful sect"—came to power. In her *Considerations of the Principal Events of the French Revolution*, she asserted, "Not only does the Constituent Assembly [1789–1791] claim the gratitude of the French people for the reform of the abuses by which they were oppressed; but we must render it the further praise of being the only one of the authorities which have governed France before and since the revolution, which allowed, freely and unequivocally, the liberty of the press."[9]

De Staël paints a glowing but inaccurate portrait of the Revolution's early years. Efforts to repress injurious speech—oral and printed—occurred in the Constituent Assembly as at all levels of politics between 1789 and the Terror. Nor were these efforts uniquely Jacobin. Punitive demands came from all quarters. Although few were convicted for speech crimes before the Terror, this was due to legal and judicial chaos, not to rising tolerance thresholds.[10] To the contrary, tolerance thresholds dropped precipitously in the Revolution's early years, com-pelling leaders—despite nascent libertarian views espoused by some Jacobins in 1791—to repress calumny by 1793. At the same time, many leaders, distressed by the escalation of calumny, sought to counter the deteriorating situation by promoting moral regeneration. They hoped that spreading "public spirit" would curb calumny and quell rampant vengeance. Engineering civic consciousness was not, for them, antithetical to free speech. It was the precondition for its enjoyment.

French revolutionaries were not the first to tether free speech to legal limits and moral regulation. Although the French tradition of freedom is often criticized for being inherently illiberal—favoring state authority over civil liberties—revolutionaries' notions about the nature and limits of free expression were neither new nor peculiarly French. In ancient Greece, the principle of *parrhesia*, translated today as "free speech," involved numerous social, intellectual, and moral prerequisites. To legitimately exercise it, one had to be free from all social dependencies, guided by a desire to speak truth to power, and, for the Epicureans at least, trained in the art of "educating the soul."[11] These conceptions were revived and modified in early modern Europe. In early Stuart England, freedom of speech was thought to be not a negative liberty opposed to censorship (as it is generally understood today), but a positive liberty through which virtue could be realized.[12] This helps explain why John Milton, who called for repealing the Licensing Act in his celebrated 1644 tract *Areopagitica*, could elaborate on the benefits of press freedom even as he denied this freedom to "papists" (Roman Catholics), heretics, and the vulgar, that is, individuals he deemed incapable of demonstrating virtue. "No law," he insisted, "can permit that which is impious or evil absolutely, either against faith or manners."[13] These ideas crossed the Atlantic to New England, where they found expression in the Puritan imperative to "govern the tongue." As historian Jane Kamensky has shown, Puritan obsessions with the spiritual and moral implications of speaking freely led on occasion to extreme measures, notably banishments and witch burnings.[14]

The rise of the secular Enlightenment in the late seventeenth and eighteenth centuries did nothing to alter the belief that moral and intellectual regulation should accompany the freely spoken or written word. Baruch de Spinoza, arguably the most radical free-speech philosopher of the Enlightenment, declared that only speech inspired by a desire to think rationally was to be free. Words inspired by the passions or intended to undermine authority assumed the status of an action, and actions could be subject to constraints. "[A man] can speak against [authorities], provided that he does so from rational conviction, not from fraud, anger, or hatred"—calumny, in other words—"and provided that he does not attempt to introduce any change on his private authority."[15] A century later, Immanuel Kant built upon Spinoza's ideas. In his "An Answer to the Question: What Is Enlightenment?" (1784), he, like Spinoza, distinguished between speech and action. "Argue as much as you want and about what you want, but obey!"[16] To the question "Which restriction [on speech] hinders enlightenment and which does not, but instead actually advances it?" he responded, "The public use of one's reason must always be free.... The private use of reason may, however, often be very narrowly restricted, without otherwise hindering the progress of enlightenment."[17] "Public" speech, for Kant, involved speaking as a disinterested scholar to other disinterested scholars in an effort to advance knowledge and the collective good. It did not encompass speech deployed in the service of particular interests or passions.

Thus, French revolutionaries were hardly novel or unique in imagining moral and legal limits on free speech. Nor did the Anglo-American legal tradition give them any reason to modify their views. Press freedom had existed in England since the expiration of the Licensing Act in 1695, but as the jurist William Blackstone explained in his popular *Commentaries on the Laws of England* (1765–1769), it consisted in "laying no previous restraints upon publications, and not in freedom from censure for criminal matter when published."[18] Although historians of the early American republic disagree on whether the framers of the Constitution embraced Blackstone's definition in drafting the First Amendment, there can be little doubt that press freedom was, at the very least, ambiguous, leading Benjamin Franklin to remark, "Few of us [have any] distinct Ideas of its Nature and Extent."[19] For his part (and in what is still another irony), Paine continued adhering to Blackstone's definition of press freedom even after the Terror and the repeal of the U.S. Sedition Act of 1798.[20]

However, unlike the framers, who made no mention of limits in the First Amendment, French revolutionaries alluded to them in the Declaration of the Rights of Man and of the Citizen of 1789. Article 10 reads, "No one shall be disquieted on account of his opinions, even religious, *provided their manifestation does not disturb the public order established by law.*"[21] This qualification may seem trivial; after all, most liberal governments prohibit such speech as crying out "Fire!" in crowded theaters. But contemporary notions of "public order" were much broader than those commonly held today. "Public order" encompassed a religious, moral order, which is why the defenders of religious freedom lamented its inclusion. Similarly, Article 11 reads, "The free communication of ideas and opinions is one of the most precious of the rights of man. Consequently, every citizen may speak, write, and print freely, *subject to responsibility for the abuse of such liberty in the cases determined by law.*"[22] But what constituted an abuse? And how were abuses to be dealt with?

Revolutionaries' responses to these questions were greatly informed by what I refer to as the culture of calumny and honor. Inherited from the Old Regime, this culture involved the contradictory habits of expressing contest through calumny and of treating calumny as a criminal offense, even treason if it attacked the honor of sovereign authority or the moral values that authority was thought to embody and protect. For revolutionaries as for contemporaries of the Old Regime, honor and morality were the sine qua non of stable society. Without mechanisms for avenging wounded honor and without institutions for reinforcing moral consciousness, society, they feared, would succumb to anarchy and strife. This is precisely what many thought was happening after 1789. Not only was the Revolution destroying the institutions that had formerly regulated honor and morality; it was also overturning the principles upon which honor and morality had been based, namely, social hierarchy and religious orthodoxy.

The advent of free speech and civil equality in 1789 had a profound impact on social and political relations. It threw into question the norms governing patterns of esteem and deference and exacerbated antagonisms hitherto contained by Old Regime customs and institutions. Madame de Staël, though she may have exaggerated the Constituent Assembly's commitment to unlimited free speech, keenly understood the antagonistic nature of hierarchy and honor in Old Regime society. Her insights merit quoting at length.

> As the different classes of society had scarcely any relations with each other in France, their mutual antipathy was of course the stronger....In no country have the men of birth been so completely strangers to the rest of the nation: they came into contact with the second class only to bruise it.... The elegance of the French nobility increased the envy which they inspired. To imitate their manners was as difficult as to obtain their prerogatives. The same scene was repeated from rank to rank; the irritability of a nation, lively in the extreme, inclined each one to be jealous of his neighbor, of his superior, of his master; and all, not satisfied with ruling, labored for the humiliation of each other.[23]

Two decades ago, historian François Furet saw in de Staël's observations a source of the Revolution's radicalization. Better known for attributing the Terror to Enlightenment egalitarianism, he briefly speculated in his essay "The Terror" that the legacy of Old Regime privilege may have also contributed to the Revolution's tragic course. "Aristocratic society, composed of castes created by the monarchy and fiercely jealous of their privileges, left the embers of its violence to the Revolution, which fanned them into conflagration."[24]

The chapters ahead explore this conflagration. They show how the transition from aristocratic privilege to civil equality unleashed the systemic violence of the Old Regime. The problem, I argue, was not the principle of civil equality; rather, it was the abruptness of the transition. The sudden democratization of honor unleashed a sudden democratization of vengeance. Meanwhile, contemporaries continued to view calumny as a criminal offense. In the absence of stable courts, calumniated individuals tried to stir up the public's outrage by conflating their individual honor with the honor of sacred totems of authority and collective identity. While for revolutionaries injurious attacks amounted to attacks on the honor of the nation, for royalists they constituted assaults on the honor of the throne (lèse-majesté) and the sacredness of the altar. As the Revolution progressed, affairs of calumny thus took on increasingly eschatological dimensions, making tolerance and compromise increasingly unlikely. Clearly, it was one thing to declare free speech and civil equality, quite another to raise tolerance thresholds and secure the principle of loyal opposition.

In exploring how the culture of calumny and honor radicalized revolutionary politics, this study engages with debates on the origins of the Terror, the thorniest issue in the study of the French Revolution. Many explanations have been advanced over the past two centuries, but three broad interpretations have taken prominence. According to the first, the Terror grew out of revolutionaries' ideological commitments to equality, collective sovereignty, and moral regeneration. These "utopian" ideals, often attributed to the influence of Jean-Jacques Rousseau's writings, are said to have set the bar too high, leading disillusioned revolutionaries to blame and kill each other for the failure to realize them.[25] The second explanation emphasizes resistance and counterrevolution. Its defenders stress the destabilizing role of those who refused to accept the freedom of religion, the abolition of privileges, and the curtailment of monarchical authority and who sought to reverse the Revolution by any means possible, including arms.[26] The third explanation stresses circumstances. Its proponents believe that early revolutionary reforms might have been consolidated had it not been for contingent, unforeseen events, such as the outbreak of war in 1792 and the king's failed attempt to flee France in June 1791—the famous flight to Varennes.[27]

My thesis reinforces aspects of these interpretations and ties them together. It points to a polarizing dynamic at the heart of revolutionary politics—one that began by exacerbating enmities between revolutionaries and counterrevolutionaries and continued by exacerbating enmities among revolutionaries themselves. The culture of calumny and honor, as an explanation for the Revolution's radicalization, sheds light on key events, notably the king's flight. Insofar as the king's honor demanded unwavering esteem and deference, relentless affronts to it did much to turn royalists against the Revolution and compel the king to flee. Indeed, Louis XVI said as much before and after the flight. On the eve of it, he deplored the "thousands of calumniating newspapers and pamphlets" of rebels who "labor to present the monarchy under the most false and odious colors." Upon his return, he attributed his reasons for fleeing to the "insults [that] have gone unpunished."[28]

In addition to explaining the origins of the Terror's repression of speech, this study offers an alternative perspective on moral regeneration. Scholars have been largely unsympathetic to "utopian" attempts to remake the moral foundations of society, viewing them as naive, illiberal, even totalitarian. Yet early revolutionaries were hardly naive or utopian in the way they initially invoked morality to legitimize the new regime. Despite Edmund Burke's assertion in 1790 that they were nothing but "atheists and madmen," most French legislators shared Burke's assumption that religion constituted the only viable moral foundation for the new order.[29] If revolutionaries were naive about anything, it was in thinking that they could count on the existing moral infrastructure—the Church—after having declared religious freedom, expropriated Church property to pay the monarchy's debt, and imposed on the clergy an oath of allegiance to the new regime. It was only after three years of failing to win the clergy's support that revolutionaries embarked on the radical project of inventing a secular religion, turning churches into temples of reason, erecting altars to the nation, and creating a new calendar based on nature. The fervor with which they pursued these endeavors sprang from their alarm over spiraling civil strife. Moral regeneration, they hoped, would curb calumny, a major source of their troubles, by inspiring unity and restraint. By 1793, revolutionaries had indeed become schizophrenic, calumniating, killing calumniators, and moralizing all at the same time. This state of affairs, I show, owed to the collapse of institutions and norms that used to regulate honor and the failure of new ones. The Terror may have exhibited traits common to modern totalitarian regimes—rampant denunciation, fanaticism, purges—but it emerged from conditions commonly found in weak or failed states.[30]

Since the Terror's policing of public opinion had origins in Old Regime customs and practices, our study begins there. Part I, "The Old Regime," begins with a chapter on eighteenth-century beliefs about the need to "police," or manage, collective values. From devout absolutists to secular philosophes, there was widespread consensus that the state should maintain and reinforce moral values, customs, and manners, what the French called *mœurs*. Chapter 1 also identifies the police practices that would persist after the abolition of prepublication censorship in 1789, specifically, repression, surveillance, and the diffusion of moral propaganda. Finally, this chapter points out the tensions within an increasingly self-conscious and expanding "public opinion," specifically, between democratic and disciplinary tendencies. These tensions would become explosive in 1789, once institutions that had regulated them collapsed. Chapter 2 analyzes the Old Regime culture of calumny and honor. It stresses how honor figured as a basis of social hierarchy and political legitimacy and, consequently, why contemporaries so frequently resorted to calumny in the course of social and political conflict. I also review the institutional and social practices governing the economy of esteem and deference in Old Regime society, focusing particularly on dueling and the jurisprudence on injurious speech. Chapter 3 traces how philosophes and administrators imagined legitimate limits on press freedom during the Enlightenment. Tensions among their views foreshadow revolutionary clashes over free expression. Finally, chapter 4 examines how demands for press freedom evolved between the drafting of *cahiers de doléances* (formal demands for reform) throughout France in the winter and spring of 1789 and the Declaration of the Rights of Man and of the Citizen promulgated in August. Although the majority of cahiers demanded press freedom, they also insisted on maintaining Old Regime laws against verbal and written attacks on authority, religion, mœurs, and honor. In promulgating the Declaration of Rights, the National Assembly made no mention of these desired restrictions, deferring the matter to subsequent legislation, which was not forthcoming. The stage was thus set for widespread conflict over limiting free speech and determining core values.

Part II, "The French Revolution," examines the struggle to define and enforce limits on free speech between 1789 and the Terror (1793–1794, or the Year II according to the revolutionary calendar). Chapter 5 focuses on efforts to pass press laws. It analyzes the shifting tactical stances of revolutionaries on the issue of free speech. I show the emergence of a new, quasi-libertarian position on free speech that rejected the notion of seditious libel.[31] Trumpeted by radical and reactionary minorities, the position had no impact on legislation. More prominent was the belief that calumny constituted a criminal offense. As early as July 1789, revolutionaries began translating the Old Regime crime of lèse-majesté (treasonous activity, including calumnious speech against monarchical authority) into the new crime of lèse-nation. Special courts were established to deal with such crimes, and several affairs involving speech were put on the dockets, but judicial instability and amnesties prevented them from being treated. Shortly after the overthrow of the monarchy in August 1792, the lèse-nation court was abolished. Affairs of calumny shifted to the National Convention, where they were more vulnerable to political pressure. Punitive demands intensified, culminating in the legislation of the Terror, which made calumny a capital offense.

Chapter 6 focuses on four instances of arrest or exclusion of deputies in the National Assembly for speech offenses in the year 1790, the supposedly "peaceful" year of the Revolution's "liberal phase."[32] These case studies reveal the interplay between popular agitation and high Assembly politics, showing how struggles over honor and religion generated punitive, exclusionary impulses. In the absence of libel laws, embattled parties invoked sacred principles to justify punishment, thereby infusing affairs with eschatological stakes. Chapter 7 examines this "will to punish," as historian Georges Lefebvre referred to it, more broadly. Drawing on police records in Paris and the provinces, I trace how punitive impulses radicalized politics at all levels between 1789 and the Terror. Several affairs involving "speech crimes" on the revolutionary tribunal's docket in the Year II, I show, began as local squabbles over honor, though convictions were often justified on ideological grounds. This chapter also reveals that despite the Terror's harsh laws against calumny, revolutionary tribunals frequently cited earlier ones passed during the so-called "liberal phase" of the Revolution (1789–1791).

Finally, chapter 8 returns to the issue of morality and the "policing" or state management of public opinion. It shows how leaders, alarmed by escalating calumny and vengeance, tried to inspire civil restraint by reinforcing morality. At first, they expected clerics to assist them in this task. But sharp divisions within the Church—exacerbated, though not caused, by the Civil Constitution of the Clergy of 1790—led revolutionaries to abandon traditional religion altogether and create a new one based on patriotism and secular civic morality. In 1792, a Bureau of Public Spirit was established within the Ministry of the Interior, and its agents were sent into the provinces to spread republican propaganda and monitor public opinion. The work of these agents and the polarizing impact they had will be discussed in this chapter, along with the numerous proposals for civil censorship put forth in 1793. I argue that the authors of these proposals, mostly deputies, sought to channel the punitive impulses generated by calumny into mild, pedagogical forms of censure. Finally, I show that moral regeneration efforts continued after the Terror. They were espoused and theorized by a former royal censor, Dieudonné Thiébault, the very individual who had defended prepublication censorship in 1789. Thiébault's ideas about the importance of "public spirit" persisted through the nineteenth century, eventually leading to the creation of universal, compulsory education during the Third Republic, as I suggest in the conclusion.

To argue, as I do, that revolutionaries remained attached to Old Regime habits, that the early years of the Revolution were not as "liberal" as often portrayed,

and that the problem of free speech contributed to the repressive and regenerative practices of the Terror is not to deny the Revolution's achievements. This
study in no way refutes the view that the Revolution contributed to advancing
human rights, democratic institutions, and civil equality, at least in the long run.[33]
It does, however, explain why the Revolution produced lethal repression and
moral fanaticism in the short term. In doing so, it aims to broaden the problems
and expose the pitfalls encountered when hierarchical, authoritarian reflexes mix
with liberal aspirations—especially under the strains of abrupt regime change.

Part I

The Old Regime

CHAPTER ONE

Policing in the Old Regime

Can there exist a more reasonable and incontestable relationship than the one between policing and the science of mœurs?
—J. Peuchet, "Discours préliminaire," *Jurisprudence, Encyclopédie méthodique*, 1791

Virtue and Terror

Standing before the National Convention on February 5, 1794 (17 Pluviôse, Year II), Maximilien Robespierre delivered his most famous speech, "On the Principles of Political Morality." "The moral force of popular government in times of revolution," he declared, "is both virtue and terror." Few statements express so succinctly the pathological spirit of the Terror. For historian R. R. Palmer, the speech constitutes "one of the most notable utterances in the history of democracy."[1] Indeed, from the perspective of stable liberal democracies today, it reads like a blueprint for totalitarianism. Put in context, however, the speech can be understood as a tactical response to the revolutionary predicament. As a leading member of the Committee of Public Safety, which held executive power, Robespierre found himself pinched between those who wanted to dismantle the Terror (the Indulgents) and those who wanted to push it further (the *hébertistes*). He felt compelled to justify the Terror, aware that repudiating it would leave too many revolutionaries who had blood on their hands—not least himself—vulnerable to countervengeances. At the same time, he recognized that rampant vengeances were threatening to consume the whole Revolution. Thus, even as he presided over efforts to channel them into judicial institutions, he tried to inspire civil restraint by invoking virtue. Finally, he felt obliged to pay lip

17

service to the principle of popular sovereignty, which Jacobins had used so effectively in wresting executive power from the monarchy in 1792 and from certain Girondin ministers in 1793.

In short, factions had to be defanged, the state's monopoly on punishment had to be secured and legitimized, and society had to be both empowered and restrained. Translating these tasks into a convincing political program was not easy. But since "virtue" and "terror" struck chords with idealistic and vengeful revolutionaries, Robespierre wove them into his rhetoric. Propounding on virtue, he insisted that the duty of legislators was to "inspire patriotism, purify mœurs, elevate spirits and minds, and steer the passions of the human heart toward the public interest."[2] Under ordinary circumstances, he explained, virtue would suffice to sustain democracy. In the throes of revolution, however, virtue would have to be accompanied by terror. "Without virtue," he warned, "terror is calamitous; without terror, virtue is impotent." For Robespierre, the Terror was "nothing other than prompt, severe, and inflexible justice."[3] For many historians, it was a brutal police state, one that made a mockery of the civil liberties declared in 1789, especially the freedom of expression and of opinion. Indeed, by 1794, the revolutionary government was actively monitoring, repressing, and manipulating public opinion.

How did Robespierre, a strident advocate of press freedom at the Revolution's outset, end up leading such a ruthless, propagandistic regime? Why did he think "virtue" and "terror" were compelling justifications for policing opinion? Some scholars point to the influence of Jean-Jacques Rousseau. In *The Social Contract*, Rousseau imagined democracy as a moral project involving constraints on individuals for the sake of the "general will." Individuals, he theorized, achieve true freedom only by putting the community's interests before their own. The community thus has the right and responsibility to compel all members to submit to the general will, by force if necessary. "Whoever refuses to obey the general will shall be constrained to do so by the whole body; which means nothing else than that he shall be forced to be free."[4] For Rousseau, the individual who attacks the general will "becomes by his crimes a rebel and a traitor to his country.... The judgment [stands as] proof ... that he has broken the social contract, and consequently that he is no longer a member of the State.... He ought to be cut off from it by exile as a violator of the compact, or by death as a public enemy; for such an enemy is not a moral person, he is simply a man."[5]

Robespierre's speeches echoed *The Social Contract* in many respects. According to the "incorruptible" deputy from Arras, virtue consisted in "the sublime sentiment that imagines the priority of the public interest over the interests of individuals," and terror was to be directed against "the oppressors of humanity" who undermined this sentiment. Such similarities have led some scholars to see *The Social Contract* at the origins of the French Revolution, particularly the Terror. This *faute à Rousseau* thesis stretches back, in fact, to the period of the Revolution itself. Fulminating across the English Channel in 1790, Edmund Burke criticized French revolutionaries for spending too much time pondering Rousseau.[6] Several nineteenth-century historians, picking up on Burke's refrain, traced the Terror's origins back to Rousseau.[7] During much of the twentieth century the *faute à Rousseau* thesis was overshadowed by interpretations stressing circumstances and class friction, but with the linguistic turn in the 1970s, it began making a comeback among historians (it had flourished among political theorists between the 1950s and 1970s). It figured in much of the scholarship inspired by François Furet in the years leading up to the Revolution's bicentennial.[8] By the mid-1990s, however, historians began challenging this explanation. Some argued that few national deputies had read, much less understood, *The Social Contract* when they arrived in Versailles for the meeting of the Estates-General in 1789.[9] Others insisted that even if revolutionaries had read it, they rejected crucial parts of it, especially its insistence on unmediated popular sovereignty.[10] By the mid-1990s, even Furet rejected the thesis. "In the final analysis," he concluded in one of his last essays, "there is not much of *The Social Contract* in the French Revolution."[11]

Rousseau's influence on revolutionaries continues to be debated, and recent work suggests that the pendulum may be swinging back in the affirmative direction.[12] In any case, I believe that the Terror—and Rousseau's ideas—can be better understood by situating them within Old Regime and Enlightenment culture more broadly. While the next chapter examines the origins of the Terror's violence, tracing it back to the Old Regime culture of calumny and honor, this chapter considers the origins of the Terror's policing of opinion and moral regeneration, relating them to longstanding concerns with religion and mœurs.

Policing Religion and Mœurs

As the Bourbon state expanded during the Old Regime, its policing became increasingly theorized. For contemporaries, *la police* referred to "the order or regulations established in a city for all that concerns the security and utility of inhabitants."[13] As scholars have noted, the term was often conflated with Eurocentric notions of "civilization." To be "well policed" meant to be "polished, refined, cultivated, and advanced," and societies lacking police were considered uncivilized.[14] Antoine Furetière's dictionary of 1690 stated, "In general, [*la police*] is opposed to barbarism. The savages of America had neither laws nor police when they were discovered."[15] Throughout the eighteenth century, absolutists, philosophes, and revolutionaries all agreed that security and prosperity depended on competent administration and the improvement of mœurs. They differed, though, on how to accomplish this improvement, especially in the second half of the century. While some considered Catholic orthodoxy to be indispensable for securing good mœurs, others stressed the benefic effects of refined sociability and the development of the arts, sciences, and commerce. Still others thought that good mœurs depended on universal ethics; although the Church might be useful in spreading ethical precepts, those precepts were ultimately rooted in Nature and accessible to all religious sects.

The issue of mœurs was much less complicated at the beginning of the eighteenth century, or at least it seems so in Nicolas Delamare's *Traité de la police*. Released in several editions between 1705 and 1738, this multivolume treatise anticipated the scientific approach to governing that philosophes would later develop. Although the treatise dealt with many practical administrative matters (health, roads, public order, subsistence, construction, and sanitation), religion and morality took precedence. Delamare stated, "Religion is without a doubt the first and principal [object of policing]…one might even say the only object if we were wise enough to perfectly fulfill the duties religion prescribes."[16] Religion instilled, he explained, the morality needed to maintain good mœurs.[17] The religion Delamare had in mind was, of course, Catholicism, and he devoted many pages to refuting the claims of paganism, Judaism, and the "heresies" (Calvinism and Jansenism). But Delamare was ultimately a bureaucrat, not a theologian. Hence, he employed quasi-secular reasoning—the same kind of reasoning, in fact, that philosophes and revolutionaries would later employ. According to him, heresy was immoral not because it offended the heavens, but because it elevated individual passions and interests over the well-being of the community. In terms anticipating revolutionaries' condemnations of counterrevolutionaries, Delamare referred to heretics as "blind and corrupt, substituting their particular interests for the truth."[18]

Before the high Enlightenment of the mid-eighteenth century, conventional wisdom held that the ultimate source of morality and good mœurs was religion. In his 1688 *Les mœurs de ce siècle*, for example, Jean de La Bruyère reflected on the mœurs of various societies throughout the world. Like Montaigne and other early modern writers, he credited "uncivilized" societies for possessing the simple virtues that many Europeans lacked. In the final analysis, though, the absence of Christianity in these societies deprived them of "truth," rendering them inferior. For La Bruyère, truth inhered only in Christian mœurs, and he counseled European travelers not to overexpose themselves to foreign ones. Alien manners, he warned, would rub off and corrupt their own.[19] But by the mid-eighteenth century, enlightened philosophes were seeking to displace Christianity as the ultimate source of morality and good mœurs. For them, the improvement of mœurs required scientific inquiry, not theological exegesis or blind faith. The 1740s and 1750s saw a flurry of tracts on mœurs: François-Vincent Toussaint's *Les mœurs* (1748), Montesquieu's *De l'esprit des lois* (1748), Charles Duclos's *Considérations sur les mœurs de ce siècle* (1751), and Voltaire's *Essai sur les mœurs* (1756). Although religion was not entirely absent from these works, these authors tended to treat it as, at best, a convenient instrument for propagating the tenets of a moral system grounded in Nature, at worst, a fanatical force capable of destroying mœurs and unleashing sectarian violence.

In his *De l'esprit des lois*, Montesquieu had little to say about the necessity of religion for the maintenance of good mœurs. Developing a comparative sociological perspective, he analyzed the relationship between positive law, moral principles, and mœurs (as manners) in various types of societies. He argued that positive law, rather than standing apart from mœurs, should be situated within them, constituting their declarative and coercive aspects. If authorities wanted to be obeyed, their laws needed to resonate with the customs and values already present in society. Although Montesquieu's sympathies with republicanism are discernible, he did not announce a universal basis for morality and mœurs. Laws were to be considered good or bad according to how well they reinforced the moral principles needed to maintain the type of society in question. In monarchies, good mœurs were to be reinforced through the moral principle of honor; in republics, through virtue (through public spirit in democratic republics); in despotisms, through fear.

Montesquieu's moral relativism was not embraced by all contemporaries— and certainly not by Jansenists and Church authorities in France. The latter came close to condemning the work, but the Vatican took care of the task, putting *De l'esprit des lois* on the Index in 1751.[20] Yet, even many philosophes eschewed his relativism, preferring a universal basis for good mœurs. According to Voltaire, this basis lay in the development of the arts, sciences, and commerce. In his *Essai sur les mœurs*, which recounted world history from the Ancients to the reign of Louis XIV, Voltaire attributed Europe's "superior" mœurs to precisely this development. Although all societies, including European, were prone to fits of fanaticism and war, Europe's unmatched progress in the arts, sciences, and commerce placed it ahead of others in the evolution from barbarity toward civilization.[21]

In the 1770s, philosophes began grafting the norms of civility in the Republic of Letters onto Voltaire's notion of universal history. Politeness in exchanges was no longer a matter of mere courtesy.[22] Nor was it simply an expedient for maintaining harmony within the expanding Republic of Letters, as it had been at the turn of the century.[23] Polite sociability and refined mœurs were now bound up with the progress of civilization.[24]

Some philosophes doubted that the arts, sciences, and sociability would lead to moral progress. In numerous essays beginning with his celebrated *Discourse on the Arts and Sciences* (1750), Rousseau argued famously that, to the contrary, they undermined it. In cultivating desire for status and luxury, the arts, sciences, and polite sociability increased social inequalities and corrupted individuals, making them slaves to the perceptions of others.[25] Although few philosophes rejected civilization so roundly, many shared Rousseau's misgivings about the capacity of the arts, sciences, and sociability to improve mœurs without the help of morality. In his *Les mœurs*, for example, Toussaint argued that good mœurs depended on proper moral principles, ones rooted in Nature, not religion.[26] "This study is about mœurs," he announced in the preface; "religion figures in it only in so far as it contributes to mœurs." Virtue, for Toussaint, was the universal moral principle prescribed by Nature. It transcended religions, appealing to "Mohammedians" and Christians alike. Toussaint believed that by advancing knowledge of universal morality and cultivating sentimental attachments to it, mœurs could be improved. "What are good mœurs?...They are behavior regulated by the knowledge and love of virtue."[27]

In *Considérations sur les mœurs de ce siècle* (1751), Charles Duclos also stressed the moral foundations of good mœurs. Like Toussaint, he believed that neither religion nor polite sociability sufficed for their improvement. "Religion," Duclos asserted, "is the perfection of morality, not its basis."[28] As for manners, he thought it "desirable that the politeness of gentle manners be united with the politeness that comes from the heart."[29] Without good intentions, polished manners were nothing but hypocritical varnish concealing immoral egoism. "The most polite people are not the most virtuous. Simple and austere mœurs find themselves among people guided [*policé*] by reason and equity....Well-policed people are better than polite ones [*les peuples policés valent mieux que les peuples polis*]."[30] For Duclos, policing involved governing consciences according to moral guidelines, specifically, "[the] seeking of personal advantages within the project of the general good." Good mœurs required "being a patriot" and "considering men in relation to humanity and one's country."[31] "Let us teach people to love each other, and prove to them that doing so will bring them happiness. We can demonstrate to them that their own glory and interest can only be secured in exercising their duties."[32]

Duclos reflected on the links between morality, reputation, and public opinion. He was aware that in a society in which status and opportunities turned on honor and reputation, opinions mattered immensely. "Public opinion," he observed, "is both judge and punishment. It never fails to be severe toward what it condemns."[33] For Duclos, public opinion was as important in society as subsistence. "It is not only material needs that bind people together; men also have an existence that depends on the reciprocal opinions they have of each other."[34] Hence, opinions, like the distribution of resources, needed to be based on the ethical principle of the general interest. "It is the general interest that dictates the laws and fixes virtue; it is the particular interest that commits crimes when it is opposed to the general interest. In fixing the general opinion, public interest becomes the measure of esteem and respect."[35] Duclos's ideal economy of esteem stood apart from the actual one, and his pronouncements must be read against the backdrop of a world in which respect and deference depended greatly on proving oneself capable of avenging wounded honor. As we shall see in subsequent chapters, these two economies of reputation—an ideal one based on commitment to the general interest and the actual one based on individual honor and the ability to defend it—coexisted in revolutionary politics. In their effort to protect their reputations from calumny, revolutionaries would waver between the two, preaching the virtues of the general interest while resorting to whatever means possible—including terror—to punish calumniators.

Other philosophes shared Duclos's belief that sound morality consisted in contributing to the general interest, being patriotic, and basing public esteem on those values. In a republican idiom, these values constituted public spirit.[36] In his *Morale universelle* (1776), for example, Paul-Henri Thiry, baron d'Holbach, wrote, "What is called public spirit refers to the general interest of society....Spread throughout the nation, public spirit heralds good government and citizens who seek to earn the esteem of their fellow citizens."[37] This esteem was to be grounded in "a most sensible morality [that] makes it a duty for all citizens to contribute to public utility."[38] Under tyranny, Holbach theorized, social bonds break down. With individuals pursuing only their particular interests, "public spirit does not exist." In *Histoire philosophique et politique des deux Indes*, the abbé Raynal (or one of his collaborators, which included Holbach) attributed the decline of republicanism in Holland to the weakening of public spirit. "How much have mœurs degenerated there! Private interests that purify themselves in their union have become entirely isolated."[39] Lacking patriotism, Holland "no longer has any public spirit."[40] Raynal claimed that the Dutch conquest of Indonesia was fraught with problems because the Dutch East India Company relied on mercenaries rather than citizen-soldiers. Mercenaries, he observed, were motivated solely by the promise of plunder. Having no stake in the common interest of the nation that recruited them, they were prone to corruption. Citizen-soldiers, on the other hand, possessed public spirit since they were motivated by the quest for their country's glory and the prospect of sharing collectively the material benefits of colonization. To reinforce public spirit, Raynal recommended that all citizens be given stock in the East India Company.[41]

Although the Old Regime offered many theoretical paths to good mœurs, it offered few institutional vehicles for reaching them. Much of the literature promoting sociability and the arts and sciences was written by participants of salons, royal academies, and *sociétés savantes*. In practice, the salons hardly lived up to the moral, egalitarian ideals that their literary participants propounded; they could be as divisive, petty, and hierarchical as any other Old Regime institution. In any case, salons touched the lives of few.[42] The royal academies and *sociétés savantes* involved the participation of more individuals, both in terms of membership (though women were excluded) and the publics attending open meetings. And as Daniel Roche has shown, the proportion of meetings devoted to *la morale* increased in function of the size of the public attending them—a clear sign that elite members felt a civic duty to spread their scientific findings on morality with the population.[43] Still, these institutions hardly constituted universal education. Nor was there consensus that the masses should be educated, in the broad sense of being enlightened. With the notable exception of Condorcet, the philosophes opposed teaching the laboring masses how to reason critically. At most, the masses were thought to need instruction in rudimentary skills, such as reading, writing, counting, and basic morality (to inculcate discipline and respect for hierarchy). Voltaire wrote, "It is not the working man who should be educated, but the worthy bourgeois."[44]

Yet, moral education was on the decline in eighteenth-century France. In his study of educational reform in the Old Regime, Harvey Chisick shows that "those most ready to see the people broadly educated and even enlightened were pious Christians," not secular-minded philosophes and administrators.[45] But the Church's ability to educate the masses was weakened by the expulsion of the Jesuits from France in the early 1760s and by the overall secularization of society during the latter half of the eighteenth century. Chronic fiscal strains throughout the century precluded any effort on the part of the state to support mass education, despite promises to do so stretching back to the reign of Louis XIV.[46] What Duclos concluded in his *Considérations sur les mœurs* in 1751 remained true through to the end of the Old Regime: "Today we find many forms of instruction but not a [moral] education. We train savants and artists of all kinds, but we have not yet undertaken to make men, that is, to instill a sense of mutual respect for each other."[47]

By 1789, then, there were many theories about mœurs and high expectations for their improvement but few institutional mechanisms for realizing this improvement. Steeped in a culture prone to conceiving social and political problems in moral terms, revolutionaries and counterrevolutionaries drew upon these theories after 1789. Ending the Revolution, they believed, would require a regeneration of mœurs. Yet, the diversity of views they had inherited led to clashing approaches on how to do so, notably between devout Catholics and moderate Christians in favor of religious freedom. The Civil Constitution of the Clergy of 1790 was an attempt at compromise. It gave the Church a central public role in educating the masses in exchange for swearing an oath of fidelity to the principles of the Revolution. But the compromise failed. Chronic tensions over reconciling religion and the Revolution eventually led revolutionaries to put Catholicism aside altogether and establish a new, secular cult, one based on virtue, patriotism, and the general interest, that is, on public spirit.

Policing Opinion

If the Old Regime had few institutions for improving mœurs, it had a battery of them to police opinions. Royal censors, inspectors of the Book Trade, the Council of State, the Church, the Lieutenant General of Police in Paris, the intendants in the provinces, the local courts, and the parlements all tried to regulate public opinion. They monitored, suppressed, and punished. They also spread opinions of their own, officially through publicized bans and condemnations, secretly by manipulating texts and planting rumors. Yet, state control over public opinion was hardly monolithic. Governing institutions often worked at cross purposes and sought to undermine each other. In this, they were quite successful. By 1789, none of them had much credibility left; consequently, their ability to control the force they helped create—public opinion—was greatly diminished.

Recent studies of royal censorship reveal the complexity of institutional struggles over regulating public opinion.[48] The censorship bureau was part of the Administration of the Book Trade, which was situated within the monarchy's *Chancellerie*. The censors inspected manuscripts prior to publication and, when they did not reject the work outright, accorded various kinds of official approbations: *privilèges*, *permissions simples*, and *permissions tacites*. These attributions conferred various degrees of rights, or rather privileges, over texts. Censors often worked with writers to modify texts in accordance with the press laws of 1723, 1728, and 1727, which prohibited attacks on religion, mœurs, and authorities. Although there was much consensus on these prohibitions, they were defined so broadly that altering texts often boiled down to tactical maneuvers to advance the interests of particular institutions, Court factions, or clientele networks. Although censorship might enervate writers, it could also lead them through political minefields, shielding them from more threatening forces. Indeed, writers did not merely "put up" with censorship. Many embraced it, taking the censors' approval for success and legitimacy within the world of letters.[49]

As the print industry expanded in the eighteenth century, so too did the censorship bureau. Although it banned only 10–30 percent of submitted manuscripts over the course of the eighteenth century, its arbitrariness and ineffectiveness provoked criticism, not only from authors and printers, but from the Church, Court factions, and parlements as well.[50] By the late 1750s, the shortcomings of censorship had become obvious even to the Director of the Book Trade himself, C.-G. Lamoignon de Malesherbes. For Malesherbes, the main problem was how to reconcile religious and political orthodoxy with the commercial interests of the French publishing industry, whose profits were increasingly going to foreign printers who managed to smuggle works banned in France across the border. In his unpublished *Mémoires sur la librairie* (1758–1759), Malesherbes justified the expanded use of *permissions tacites*—authorizations which did not bestow as many benefits as *privilèges* but which conveyed official tolerance.[51] With this more relaxed policy, which lasted through to the end of the Old Regime (though with periodic suspensions and crackdowns), Malesherbes tried not only to create a more tolerant environment for writers and greater profits for French publishers; he also tried to spare the censors the embarrassment of seeing the books they approved subsequently condemned by the Parlement of Paris.

Unlike other forms of policing public opinion, censorship did not figure in the course of the French Revolution. Curtailed by the monarchy in 1788, abolished by the National Assembly in 1789, censorship vanished from the literary landscape in 1790 when the bureau finally closed its doors.[52] More important for their legacy on the Revolution were the practices of seizing print and punishing writers, printers, and booksellers. During the Old Regime, these actions were conducted at times discreetly, at other times spectacularly. The discreet suppression of texts before they were printed or distributed had the advantage of not attracting the public's attention to the work. As many contemporaries observed, nothing increased demand for a book more than burning it on the steps of the Palais de Justice. Among the more discreet means, authorities might thwart the spread of "bad books" through intimidation, unpublished bans, and *lettres de cachet. Lettres de cachet* usually resulted in the imprisonment of printers and authors without trial.[53]

With discreet means at their disposal, why would authorities ban and condemn books with great fanfare? According to historian Barbara de Negroni, publicized condemnations were less about preventing a work from being read (though condemnations might make books prohibitively expensive) than about gaining political leverage over rival institutions, embarrassing them for having failed to protect mœurs, religion, and authority. During the Old Regime as during the Revolution, condemnations served as vehicles for asserting power and conveying values. An official who denounced or condemned an allegedly bad work might win public esteem, not to mention deference from other authorities who, though chafing at being upstaged, might feel pressured into going along. For example, when the Parlement of Paris condemned Claude-Adrien Helvétius's atheistic *De l'Esprit* in 1759, burning it on the steps of the Palais de Justice, the magistrates managed to humiliate the royal censors who had approved it, forcing Malesherbes to revoke its *privilège*.[54] The Parlement thus demonstrated that it was more vigilant than the monarchy in protecting religion and mœurs. It also proved that it was capable of transcending longstanding struggles against the monarchy over its supposed Jansenist sympathies by positioning itself as the protector of all Christianity from the "atheistic" assault of *la philosophie*.

Public condemnations of printed works might also serve to undermine certain patronage networks. When Parlement banned Rousseau's *Émile*, it struck not only at the monarchy's "lax" censorship bureau but also at Rousseau's protectors, notably, the extremely powerful Madame Luxembourg and Prince de Conti.[55] Condemnations may have been arbitrary—works more impious than *Émile* managed to circulate unmolested by Parlement—but they had a political logic: in the name of protecting religion, mœurs, and authority, public condemnations were political weapons. Revolutionaries, we shall see, were no less conscious of the political value of public condemnations, even if the principles they claimed to protect were different from those of their predecessors.

Print was not the only target of Old Regime policing. The theater, a notably contentious site of public opinion throughout the eighteenth century, also drew the attention of authorities.[56] At the turn of the century, the itinerant acting troupes of the seasonal fairgrounds appeared and disappeared in the wake of erratic rulings over the monopolistic privileges held by the Comédie-française.[57] The Comédie-française itself was subject to the intervention of authorities. Although the actors had a great deal of control over their repertoire, numerous institutions (or clientele networks working through those institutions) might intervene, prohibiting performances and banning publications of scripts.[58] Meanwhile, authorities also policed audiences. It was not uncommon for parterres to be hemmed in by troops and permeated with spies. Spectators who misbehaved (and in the eighteenth century authorities were highly concerned with political agitation) might find themselves brought before police courts or community-based bourgeois commissions who occasionally imposed punishments.[59]

Speech and singing were also targets of surveillance and repression during the Old Regime, especially during political crises.[60] The power to police speech was greatly enhanced in 1708 when a network of undercover agents was established under the authority of the Lieutenant General of Police.[61] These agents roamed the public spaces of Paris, eavesdropping on conversations and initiating arrests for seditious speech and song.[62] Historian Alan Williams estimates that the number of spies on the police payroll in Paris varied between 350 and 500 in the years 1730 to 1785. These spies, in turn, relied on informers who were recruited on a contingent basis.[63] The number of informers is unknown, but one can well imagine, as Williams does, that given the mass of poor Parisians, information might easily be obtained for a beer or a ticket to the opera.[64]

Old Regime policing institutions not only monitored and repressed opinions; they spread opinions as well. Covert propaganda was sometimes circulated with the connivance of key officials who would tolerate, even facilitate, the sale of unapproved works. In 1760, for example, Malesherbes surreptitiously sent Voltaire's *Pierre le Grand*, which had been seized by the inspectors of the book trade and denied a permission by the dauphin and the king's chancellor, to a bookseller in the Palais-Royal, who sold copies discreetly.[65] Ministers and high-ranking officials had many means to spread news, rumors, and calumny that suited their interests. In addition to its official newspaper, *Gazette de France*, the government maintained a *bureau des nouvelles*, which regulated the flow of information and opinions in Paris with the help of hired hacks.[66] Robert Darnton claims that future revolutionaries Jacques-Pierre Brissot de Warville and Honoré-Gabriel-Riqueti, comte de Mirabeau were on the Old Regime police payroll, "writing bulletins and circulating them throughout the public to contradict false stories and anecdotes."[67] Arlette Farge shows how the police tried to manipulate opinion during the Cartouche affair in 1721. Leader of a network of thieves in Paris, Cartouche was a hero to many. To garner public support for executing him and disbanding his network, the police actively diffused moralizing propaganda.[68]

The Parisian public was aware of the government's efforts to monitor and manipulate its opinions. In his *Tableau de Paris*, Louis-Sebastien Mercier refers to the presence of undercover agents in public places, such as cafés, as common knowl-edge.[69] State surveillance and propaganda were so well known that they could be mocked in an anonymous pamphlet published in early 1789, *Les mânes de M. Métra ou ses réflexions posthumes pour guider ses confrères les gobe-mouches des Tuileries, du Luxembourg et du Palais-Royal, sur les reformes à proposer aux États-généraux.* The narrator of this pamphlet was the ghost of the notorious and now deceased purveyor of rumors, François Métra.[70] In small print on the first page, the author reminded readers who Métra had been: "Everyone knows or should know that M. Métra was one of the most solid supports of the Cracow tree [a rumor mill in the Luxembourg Gardens]."[71] In the text, Métra confesses to his prior involvement in spreading rumors and explains that he has been instructed by his fellow deceased Frenchmen to convey their pro-posals for the upcoming meeting of the Estates-General. "After having spent the better part of my life listening to and spreading a great deal of nonsense, it is about time that I listen to and spread news which is interesting and reasonable."[72] His talents as an informer and propagandist were now summoned for the more dignified tasks of serving as a reporter and representative. "[My dead compatriots] thought that it was important for their descendents that there be a deputy in Paris in charge of communicating their ideas about the nation, and to inform them about all that goes on at the Estates-General."[73] Press freedom was among the many reforms Métra was instructed to propose. "It will be necessary to take care of the first and foremost freedom, that upon which all others are assured, in a word, the freedom to think, which must be founded on the freedom of the press."[74]

Revolutionaries would, indeed, declare the freedom of the press in August of 1789. But in doing so, they abolished only prepublication censorship. State sur-veillance, repression, and manipulation of opinion would persist. But unlike the political institutions of the Old Regime, which had a certain degree of legitimacy to police public opinion, those of the Revolution—the monarchy, the National Assembly, the Church, the new municipalities, local clubs, and sectional assem-blies—attempted to do so without clearly defined laws and without sufficient legitimacy. Clashes ensued, contributing to the Revolution's radicalization.

Public Opinion: Discipline and Empower

A vast historical literature on the rise of public opinion in eighteenth-century France has sprung up in recent decades, much of it inspired by Jürgen Habermas's *Structural Transformation of the Public Sphere* and new readings of Alexis de Tocqueville's classic *The Old Regime and French Revolution*.[75] Habermas argued that a "bourgeois" public sphere emerged in response to, and in tandem with, the development of capitalism and the absolutist state in the late seventeenth and eighteenth centuries. Less concerned with the origins of the French Revolution, Habermas's aim was to show how eighteenth-century public opinion was relatively open (at least to the bourgeoisie), governed by reason, and resistant to the manipulation of governments and clientele networks. Tocqueville's view of public opinion was less rosy. According to this nineteenth-century writer and statesman, authors during the Old Regime, excluded from formal positions of authority, came to wield political influence through writing. Their abstract "literary politics," which reflected a lack of practical experience in governing, led to catastrophe. After contributing to the demise of the Old Regime, their ideas accelerated the recklessness of the new one. In seeking to make the world conform to their utopian principles—notably, equality—revolutionaries broke with all tradition and abandoned all restraint.

Although Habermas and Tocqueville presented public opinion in different lights—as an ideal model of democratic communication on the one hand, as a harbinger of dangerous revolutionary politics on the other—both saw it as independent of state control before 1789. This view has been overturned by a large body of recent scholarship that shows how Old Regime institutions contributed to the rise of public opinion, both as a rhetorical construct and sociological force. According to Keith Baker, the monarchy and the Parlement of Paris began in the 1750s to erect "public opinion" as a final court of appeals in struggles against each other.[76] Focusing on the content and diffusion of opinions, Robert Darnton argues that the proliferation of political libels, some of which became best-sellers, eroded the legitimacy of the Old Regime. Like Baker, Darnton sees Old Regime institutions and power brokers as influential in the development of public opinion. By the 1770s, he notes, many of the great philosophes had managed to work their way into the regime's administrative and cultural institutions. Writers of the next generation, largely denied access to these privileged precincts, ended up offering their services to notable public figures and officials, who used them in waging libel wars against each other.[77] Although they earned their living as the mouthpieces of powerful insiders, these hack writers expressed the rage and frustration of oppressed outsiders. They turned the "victim of despotism" trope into a veritable leitmotif for politics in the last two decades of the Old Regime. Their messages, Darnton suggests, eroded the legitimacy of the Old Regime.

If state institutions and elite insiders contributed to the rise of public opinion, by the end of the Old Regime, public opinion had taken on a life of its own, outstripping their control. But how did public opinion figure in the course of the Revolution? Few studies have explored this question. For their part, Baker and Darnton attribute the Revolution's radicalization to other factors; while Baker stresses revolutionaries' commitment to Rousseauian notions of collective will, Darnton points to contingent circumstances, notably the outbreak of war in 1792.[78] One might argue, as Daniel Mornet did in *Les origines intellectuelles de la Révolution française*, that 1789 was so cataclysmic that little in the Old Regime is relevant for understanding the Revolution.[79] Yet there is much in the recent literature on public opinion in Old Regime France that helps make sense of the Revolution's course. Taken together, this literature reveals contradictory dynamics in the public sphere. On the one hand, public opinion enlarged, ideologically and sociologically, who was to be included in the public. Expansive conceptions of the public tended to be invoked in efforts to outflank entrenched authority or political rivals. Those who employed this inclusive logic may not have espoused democratic sovereignty, but their arguments nevertheless had democratic implications. On the other hand, the expansion of the public sphere spawned concerns about indiscriminate inclusion. Such worries prompted the creation of moral, intellectual, and social criteria for deciding who should be admitted into the ranks of the legitimate public.

Several historians have underscored the increasing inclusiveness of public opinion in the eighteenth century. In her study of the popular underground Jansenist newspaper, *Nouvelles ecclésiastiques*, Arlette Farge notes how its popular, informal tone reached out to a broad public, encouraging "the participation of lay people" as early as 1728.[80] By the time that "public opinion" implied a right and a duty to know and judge in the 1750s, there had already been nearly three decades of struggle between the police and the organs of popular opinion, the effect of which was to sensitize the people to the power of their views. The *Nouvelles ecclésiastiques* was not the only cultural vehicle for popularizing and politicizing the public in the early eighteenth century. The subaltern troupes of the seasonal fairground theaters drew the public into their battles against the Comédie-française. At times when the troupes were forbidden to speak on their makeshift stages (the Comédie-française's privileged monopoly covered spoken performance), they put on plays depicting their political-legal struggles, calling upon spectators to read out the lines that actors carried on placards. In this way, spectators became politicized, drawn into affairs involving privileges and the state.[81]

While spectators were breaking into the ranks of the public despite efforts to exclude them, subaltern art critics began challenging the tight grip elites had on aesthetic judgment. These "low-life" critics contributed to the formation of an oppositional public, one that would eventually work its way into artistic representation itself, appearing in the paintings of Jacques-Louis David's *Brutus* and the *Oath of the Horatii* in the 1780s.[82] Meanwhile, spectators at the Comédie-française and in many provincial theaters began asserting themselves as sovereign publics—the voice of the nation—toward the end of the Old Regime. This self-proclaimed status made efforts to repress unruly audiences politically charged; it was one thing to repress rabble, quite another to repress "the public" and "the nation."[83]

On yet another front, trial-brief writers increasingly incorporated "the people" in their well-publicized trial briefs in the 1770s and 1780s. Exploiting the trope of "simple virtue victimized by aristocratic cunning and despotism," these writers legitimized popular indignation, implicitly fusing it with public opinion. Moreover, in trying to reach as many readers as possible, trial-brief writers sought to enlarge the public.[84]

The democratizing dynamics of public opinion were, to some degree, countered by disciplinary ones. Enlightened elites such as Kant, Malesherbes, and Condorcet often went to great lengths to distinguish public opinion from popular opinion.[85] The tribunal of public opinion was, according to these theorists, limited to the abstract world of print; it did not extend to the agitated world of assembled individuals. Even Condorcet, the most republican of the three, expressed misgivings about popularizing "the public."[86] A member of the French Academy, Condorcet was steeped in a milieu that valued (in theory at least) civility and reason, considering them prerequisites to participating legitimately in the public sphere. Indeed, these criteria were brought to bear in appointments to the royal academies.[87] Before being appointed, candidates had their morality, reputation, and talent scrutinized. Civility—as a concept and as a set of "polite" practices—held a preponderant place in other sites where public opinion was produced, notably, the salons and the Republic of Letters. To gain access to these cultural precincts, philosophes and playwrights had to demonstrate good morals and manners.[88] Meanwhile, efforts to "civilize" unruly spectators took place in the official theaters in the 1780s. While audiences were trying to elevate themselves into empowered publics with the right to balk at bad plays and even determine playbills, authorities were trying to get them to sit still and be silent. The installation of benches in the parterres of the Comédie-française and Comédie-Italienne was an attempt—one that failed—to discipline theatergoers and to transform the theater into a kind of school.[89]

The emergence of public opinion in eighteenth-century France thus bequeathed two sets of dynamics, democratizing and disciplinary. Both would persist after 1789. While authorities stressed the latter, oppositional forces exploited the former. The politics of the Year II are interpretable in light of these twin dynamics. Once in power, Jacobins sought to discipline an unruly society through moral regeneration and policing. But since they had risen to power by exploiting democratic impulses within the public sphere, they could hardly abandon the principle of empowered inclusion. Rhetorically at least, sovereignty had to reside in the people; in practice, the people had to be morally restrained and their opinions policed.

Legacies

The French Revolution inherited much from Old Regime policing: theories, practices, and perhaps even personnel. In Paris, many of the Châtelet's commissioners, the former police inspectors working for the Lieutenant General of Police, and a part of the *guet* police force were invited to work for the newly established policing committee of the municipality in the fall of 1789.[90] Although personnel records for the *comité de police, sûreté et tranquillité* of Paris during the early years of the Revolution no longer exist, the frequent visits to print shops and seizures of publications conducted by police in this period suggest a continuity of tactics, at the very least.[91] We do know that the permanent staff of General Lafayette's National Guard in Paris (founded in July 1789) comprised many former *gardes de la prévôté de l'Hôtel* and *sergents à pieds et à cheval*, with the more radical elements of those forces confined to the Guard's volunteer contingents and sectional battalions. National Guard units throughout France would partake, as we shall see, in the policing of public opinion after 1789. At the same time, the Revolution initially upheld the monarchy's *police générale*; assigned to departmental administrations, its attributions included the maintenance of the physical and moral order of the realm. But the *police générale* existed alongside new municipal police forces, a situation not without tensions.[92] Indeed, the multiplicity of policing institutions in the early years of the Revolution, together with the lack of legal guidelines, generated confusion and a good many jurisdictional disputes.

If Old Regime police practices (and perhaps personnel) persisted after 1789, so too did Old Regime notions about what constituted legitimate policing. Revolutionaries may have denounced the "despotism" of the old police system—and they certainly decried the ongoing use of spies in the new one—but new authorities upheld the view that opinions and mœurs needed to be policed.[93] In 1790, Louis Pierre Manuel wrote a scathing, though skewed, two-tome work exposing the arbitrariness of the Old Regime police, *La police dévoilée de Paris*. He was quite familiar with the prior system, having spent three months in the Bastille in 1783 for his *Coup d'œil philosophique sur la règne de Louis*. His position in the new municipal government gave him access to police archives, which he culled diligently, if selectively, revealing the corruption of the old system. In well-documented detail, he showed how the Lieutenants General of Police had become the arbitrary referees of clashes within the Republic of Letters. In one set of correspondence, he discovered Rousseau corresponding with Antoine de Sartine, the Lieutenant General of Police in 1772. Rousseau had tried to persuade Sartine to investigate the source of malicious rumors against him, and he even provided Sartine with the names of those whom he suspected. Manuel expressed dismay that the very writer whom revolutionaries so admired could have stooped to the level of a paranoid snitch; "it is always the [all too human] man who betrays the philosophe!"[94] This anecdote was one of many such incidents recounted in *La police dévoilée*. Indeed, the Lieutenant General of Police was so frequently solicited that one wonders why Manuel limited the title of his work to "exposing" only the police; it reads like a general indictment of Old Regime society.

Although Manuel criticized Old Regime policing in practice, he did not reject its theoretical principles. In many respects, he shared Delamare's early eighteenth-century views, though with some modification. Whereas religion was the sole source of good mœurs for Delamare, for Manuel "the great force on our mœurs is opinion."[95] Like Delamare, though, Manuel believed that good mœurs required state tutelage. Anticipating the public-instruction policies of the Ministry of the Interior in 1792, Manuel suggested that the National Assembly appoint "a man of letters…in each city" of France. This "instructor" would be responsible for dispelling old prejudices and "teaching the people, sovereign as they are, deference for those whom they choose as their…municipal officers."[96] Thus, the new regime was to be as committed to securing good mœurs as the old one should have been, had it lived up to its own principles, advancing that "great art of policing" by "managing and forming public opinion through Enlightenment and mœurs."[97]

In the volume of the *Encyclopédie méthodique* devoted to jurisprudence, policing, and municipal government published in 1791 (written in 1789), Jacques Peuchet sang the praises of the Old Regime police. "The police of Paris, separated from its abuses and deformities, is without doubt one of the most perfect that exists, and one that can be reasonably presented as a [good] model."[98] Like Delamare, Peuchet believed that morality was the chief object of policing. Again, whereas Delamare conceived of morality in exclusively religious terms, Peuchet conceived of it in terms of universal ethics. Still, Peuchet found religious sentiments useful for reinforcing civic values. Distancing himself from theological dogmatism, he wrote, "I won't bother examining whether those who are raised with the values of morality and honor…can forgo religion; I only want to say that, whatever reasoning one employs, it is impossible to prove that the masses can go without religious sentiments which conduct them in the exercise of their [civic] duties." He added, "All that alters these sentiments, or makes one forget or spurn them…merits public hatred and repression."[99] Peuchet warned that curtailing religious authority would lead to undue reliance on secular authority, which, in the absence of a shared secular morality (revolutionary moral regeneration had not yet begun), would become arbitrary and repressive. "It is indisputable that anywhere [religious] authority over consciences is destroyed, it will be necessary to replace it with another authority and increase the means of constraint and force within families and society.…It is an error to vote for the destruction of religious administration and increase the excessive powers of arbitrary authority."[100]

For all its reliance upon religion to cultivate civic discipline, Peuchet's *police* was nevertheless grounded in philosophical principles that transcended any particular sect. Like many philosophes, he claimed that "public morality is born within the general order.…[It stems] from the relationship that men, living closely with each other, perceive between their duties [on the one hand] and their interests, their happiness, and the happiness of the community [on the other]." Conceding that morality, like religion, could be perverted and used as a pretext for social intolerance, he nevertheless believed it was indispensable for securing virtue and social bonds. "Public morality makes men see their particular interests in the social union and the preservation of the fundamental principles of society."[101]

If public morality served as society's guiding principle, public opinion served as its guiding force. Like his enlightened predecessors, Peuchet believed that public opinion exerted a salutary influence on authority, "extending all the way up to the ministers and even the sovereign himself." But opinion needed tutelage, and it was the task of writers, he insisted, to enlighten the public through moral reflection. Through their mediation, discord in the public sphere could be avoided and public spirit would flourish. "Public spirit…this temperament of the national character, is maintained and, in a sense, assured by writers. They are respected by the nation, they modify public opinion, and alter it in the long term; their ideas fuse with popular ideas, purifying, improving, and civilizing them." It is worth stressing that, for Peuchet, public opinion was influential, not sovereign, and its policing was needed to encourage the progress of "gentle mœurs, polite manners, generosity, and humanity."[102]

There is an ambivalent tension in Enlightenment theories of policing and public opinion, from Montesquieu to Peuchet. It is difficult to determine whether the state, as a moral tutelary agent, or society, through the authority of its opinion, was supposed to have the final say. Vectors of command and influence seemed to point back and forth between state and society, with writers sometimes emerging as mediators between the two. In most of these tracts, disciplinary and democratic drives seem to be operating simultaneously, with little clarity about their respective limits. But whereas most philosophes were content to envisage a loose, mutually reinforcing relationship between mœurs and opinion—between state and society—Rousseau collapsed them. In *The Social Contract*, all these elements are fused and frozen in the constitutive moment of democracy. "It is pointless to distinguish the mœurs of a nation from the objects of its esteem [its opinions and laws], since they all adhere to the same principle," that is, to the general will.[103] But Rousseau's melding of mœurs, opinion, state, and society into the general will does not, I believe, sufficiently account for the Revolution's radicalization. Neither, though, should the loose, imprecise way these elements interacted with each other in the theories of other philosophes be seen as responsible for it. The theoretical tension between the disciplinary and democratic discourses that accompanied the rise of public opinion in the eighteenth century was not necessarily bound to produce the anarchy and authoritarianism of the Revolution's radical phase. To the contrary, by accommodating positions of command and resistance, this tension provided the Old Regime with checks and balances—not republican checks and balances, of course; these discourses were less about formal constitutional arrangements and the rule of law than about *rapports de forces*. Still, they provided rationales for contingently working out daily struggles between competing forces. They helped authorities justify policing opinion for the sake of mœurs while offering contesting forces the leverage of public opinion as an authoritative voice.

Once the Old Regime fractured in 1789, no institution—old or new—had sufficient power or legitimacy to mediate between the disciplining and democratic currents animating the public sphere. While disciplinary efforts were denounced as "despotic," democratic drives were branded "anarchic." Again, the problem was not an inherent incompatibility between those drives; after all, both have been present in democratic political culture for centuries. The problem, rather, was the weak legitimacy of institutions that tried to regulate them.

The imperative incumbent upon revolutionary leaders to manage disciplinary and democratic impulses in the public sphere helps explain why they would try, rhetorically at least, to base the regime's legitimacy on both. It sheds light on why Robespierre, in his speech on political morality, would stress virtue (to satisfy demands for discipline) and collective sovereignty (to satisfy demands for democracy). In doing so, he drew on rationales and dynamics deeply rooted in the Old Regime.

If the legacy of Old Regime policing goes a long way in accounting for the Revolution's policing of public opinion, it does not explain the Terror's lethal brutality. It is one thing to monitor and manipulate opinions, quite another to send individuals to the scaffold for them. What, then, drove revolutionaries to kill each other for speech and opinions?

CHAPTER TWO

The Culture of Calumny and Honor

A good reputation is all the more necessary to a prince in that he who enjoys one can do more with his name alone than those who are not esteemed can do with armies.
—Cardinal de Richelieu, *Testament politique*, 1640

A well-timed libel can produce a revolution. It can change and govern minds and irremediably destroy a man....We are surprised that the famous Naudé said nothing about it in his book on *Les coups d'États*.
—Simon-Nicolas-Henri Linguet, *Théorie du libelle, ou, l'art de calomnier avec fruit*, 1775

To be injured by speech is to suffer a loss of context, that is, not to know where you are....Exposed at the moment of such a shattering is precisely the volatility of one's "place" within the community of speakers; one can be "put in one's place" by such speech, but such a place may be no place.
—Judith Butler, *Excitable Speech*, 1997

The Meaning of Calumny

"There is no greater crime than calumny." Thus wrote the author of *Le véritable tableau de la calomnie* in 1649 during the Fronde, expressing a view held widely in Old Regime France.[1] In his treatise on injurious speech in 1776, the jurist François Dareau declared, "All that is the worst in crime can be found in calumny."[2] The jurist Daniel Jousse had already claimed in 1771 that it constituted "a kind of murder to attack the honor and reputation of someone, which are held to be dearer than one's life."[3] Further, the Church believed that one's individual reputation, like one's physical life, was so sacred that it withheld the sacrament of Communion to calumniators and murderers alike.[4] Indeed, calumny was frequently equated with murder and often said to be more egregious. The author of *Le véritable tableau de la calomnie* argued, "Ruining a man's reputation is more evil than taking bread out of a pauper's mouth. In the latter case, it is merely a question of one's body. In the former, it is a question of one's soul, which is more precious."[5]

The Enlightenment may have secularized the way people thought about honor—viewing it as worldly property rather than "a true spiritual possession"— but the idea that one's reputation was equal to, or even greater than, one's life persisted.[6] The author of *Traité sur la calomnie*, published during the libel war within the Republic of Letters in 1769, insisted that "calumny deserves neither more pity nor more indulgence [than murder]."[7] The view was repeated on the eve of the Revolution. In *De la morale naturelle suivie du "Bonheur des sots"* (falsely attributed to Necker!), calumny is described as "more cruel than the daggers of assassins."[8] Similarly, the author of a tract responding to the duc d'Orléans's call for press freedom in 1789 maintained that "to dishonor a citizen through scandalous writings is to bring about his civil death."[9]

What, precisely, was calumny to contemporaries of the Old Regime? Definitions varied. According to a seventeenth-century jurisprudential dictionary, "to calumniate is to maliciously and knowingly propagate or maintain a judgment which is false, without evidence, or contrary to reason; [it is] to falsely accuse someone of a crime or to denounce a crime that has not occurred."[10] The author of *Le véritable tableau de la calomnie* treated it together with *médisance*, or malicious gossip. "As there is no crime worse than calumny, it would be unjust of me to remain silent about the vice of *médisants* who, with their malicious tongues, seek to ruin the reputation of their brethren."[11] The jurist Dareau distinguished between the two. Whereas calumny referred to the maliciously false imputation of a crime, *médisance*, or maligning, entailed impugning one's moral integrity. Both kinds of injurious speech, Dareau emphasized, were reprehensible. Although calumny was punished more severely than maligning, the latter could, in fact, do more damage. The concreteness of calumnious imputations allowed victims to disprove the charge, but the vague doubts and suspicions generated by *médisance* were much harder to refute.[12] In any case, such fine distinctions were absent from common notions of calumny, which tended to lump it together with *médisance*. As the *Encyclopédie* defined it, "One commits calumny when one imputes to someone faults or vices [i.e., not only crimes] that the person does not have."[13]

There were many ways to spread calumny in Old Regime France. Print, rumor, public singing, and private correspondence all served as effective vehicles for tarnishing and destroying reputations. According to the author of *Traité sur la calomnie*, epistolary slander was particularly effective, especially when such letters were sent to one's enemies or protectors. The author insisted that the writers of such letters should be prosecuted, and he proposed requiring all letters going through the state's postal system to carry the names of senders: "[Such letters] can destroy the most established fortunes, tear asunder the most sacred bonds, and deprive fathers and heads of enterprises the support necessary for their activities."[14] An opponent of the Enlightenment, the author went on to air his suspicions about the philosophes, whom he accused of calumniating through their disingenuous use of reason. "The reputation [of a writer] and his work is often sacrificed through the malignity of a calumniator who is almost always skilled in the art of conveying opinions about the author's character and mœurs by criticizing his work."[15]

For all of its perceived turpitude, some who reflected on calumny expressed ambivalence about it. The author of *Le véritable tableau de la calomnie*, after ranting for pages about its evils, encouraged readers to refrain from knee-jerk indignation. One could even be thankful to calumniators; since friends and loved ones were often too polite to point out one's shortcomings, the tongue of one's enemies could be "extremely useful for helping us realize our own faults, to become aware of our own maladies which might otherwise remain hidden from us."[16] The entry "calomnie" in the *Encyclopédie* suggested that those who claim to be the victims of calumny are often themselves guilty of distorting the truth. It depicted calumny as a fact of life and a world without it as pure fantasy.

> Take flight in some *imaginary* world where you assume that words are always the faithful expression of sentiments and thought...where one lives without suspicion and distrust, sheltered from deception, perfidies, and calumnious denunciations: what wonderful commerce [would prevail] among the men who would people this happy globe![17]

These views about calumny—that it exposed faults, that its alleged victims were often its perpetrators, and that a world without it is too much to hope for—would resurface in debates on press freedom after 1789. Although the desire to punish calumniators predominated, some legislators and journalists insisted on the benefits of calumny in crafting new, quasi-libertarian conceptions of free speech.

In *La philosophie dans le boudoir* (1795), the marquis de Sade parodied these arguments by pushing them to extremes. In a fictionalized political pamphlet read by one of his characters, arguments about the benefits of calumny were marshaled into a full-blown republican apology of it. The pamphlet, *Français, encore un effort si vous voulez être républicains*, argued that although calumny might exaggerate one's flaws, it ultimately deters bad individuals from perpetrating evil by holding up those individuals' character to public scrutiny. Calumny thus curbed bad impulses. Honest people, on the other hand, had nothing to fear from calumny, for it provided occasions for them to demonstrate their integrity. In combatting calumnious assertions, righteous individuals were spurred on to even greater heights of virtue. "I ask you, then, for what reasons should calumny be feared, especially in a [republican] regime in which it is essential to identify the bad people and increase the virtuous energy of the good?"[18]

Honor

Sade's irony underscores how reprehensive calumny was thought to be in eighteenth-century France. Indeed, contemporaries had good reason to worry about it. In a society in which advancement and influence depended upon honor and reputation, calumny could threaten social, economic, and political interests, at all levels of society. The stakes of honor were, of course, high at Court, where favors, privileges, and access to the king depended upon it. Injurious speech—regardless of whether it contained any truth—could turn courtesans into pariahs, disgrace ministers, and even rock the economy and jeopardize royal coffers. The economic importance of honor extended into the countryside. Despite the *Annales-School* image of subsistence farmers concerned with little more than eking out an existence, recent research on the early modern French countryside reveals the presence of a vigorous market and credit system. Even poor farmers and domestic servants depended upon credit. Access to it, however, necessitated a good reputation, which could be compromised by jealous or vengeful neighbors with malicious tongues.[19]

City dwellers had much the same reasons to worry about the impact of calumny on their honor. As historian David Garrioch observes in his study of neighborhood life in Paris, the values on which a good reputation was based were "essentially those that were necessary for survival in the particular social and economic context in which people found themselves." Garrioch adds that preoccupations with honor stemmed more from the symbolic charge of injurious speech than from the verity of the statements uttered. Contemporaries did not always take such speech literally but interpreted it as a challenge necessitating a response. "[*Injures*] were a symbolic casting-out of the victim, individual expressions of rejection and contempt which if left unpunished could affect the attitude of other people."[20] The perceived scarcity of opportunities and resources in society was reflected in the economy of honor, esteem, and deference. Indeed, there was something quasi-mercantilist about Old Regime conceptions of honor—as if contemporaries believed there was a fixed quantity of honor in the world and that securing one's portion of it had to be at the expense of others.

In any case, the importance of honor is reflected in the high proportion of affairs involving injurious speech on the dockets of local courts and of high courts of appeals (the parlements). The records of the *petit criminal* chamber of the Châtelet, the *prévôtal* court of Paris, show that, after petty theft, injurious speech constituted the most frequently treated crime, accounting for approximately one-third of affairs on the docket—nearly two-thirds if one includes speech offenses accompanied by violence.[21] In her study of the towns and countryside of Languedoc, Nicole Castan uncovers similar proportions for speech offenses brought before the Parlement of Toulouse.[22]

The culture of honor in the Old Regime involved lofty ideals and pitiless pragmatism. Ideally, honor consisted in courage, integrity, civility, and respect for superiors and for sacred collective values (especially religion and patriotism). Pragmatically, it involved the ability to command esteem and deference and to avenge attacks on one's reputation. Honor and vengeance were inseparable, as the authors of the entry "honneur" in the *Encyclopédie* ruefully noted: "In some European countries today, people still honor the most shameful and odious of vengeances; and almost everywhere—despite religion, reason, and virtue—people still honor vengeance."[23] The authors clearly thought that religion, reason, and virtue were supposed to curb societal vengeances. So, too, did revolutionaries who strove to morally regenerate society in order to curb the vengeances fueling the Terror.

Honor in the Old Regime depended on objective criteria, such as birth, titles, and privileges, as well as subjective ones, notably, the opinions of others. Navigating between the two sets of criteria was challenging and often fraught with dilemmas. Social and political changes in the eighteenth century further complicated matters. The expansion of the absolutist bureaucracy and venal office holding, the growth of professional armies, the spread of commercialization and credit, urbanization, the development of "civility" and elite sociability, and the rise of the public sphere all impinged upon the rules of honor, producing anxieties about one's standing and how to assert and defend one's honor.[24] The expansion of the public sphere was a particularly vexing development for the culture of honor; for in broadcasting calumny to ever greater numbers of people, the public sphere raised the stakes in honor-related affairs.

One reason contemporaries worried so much about calumny had to do with the belief that wounded honor could never be fully healed. In his entry "scar" (*cicatrice*) in the *Encyclopédie*, the chevalier Jaucourt compared surgical scars to the scars left by calumny: "The mark is ineffaceable. . . . It resembles the effect of calumny: even after the wounds have been closed, the scars forever remain."[25]

This view was of a piece with early modern European conceptions about victimization, which tended to view the targets of crimes—objects or people—as irremediably damaged or contaminated. In his *Commentary on the Law of Prize and Booty* (1604), the Dutch jurist Hugo Grotius criticized the "superstitious scruples" of privateers who physically separated violently seized goods from commercially exchanged ones for fear that the former would somehow contaminate the latter.[26] It was also believed that the intervention of the courts might exacerbate the infamy suffered by victims, even when judgments were favorable to them. For in adjudicating scandals, the courts confirmed their existence in a solemn and sovereign voice, thereby reinforcing the shame associated with them.[27] Under the entry "infamie" in *Le Dictionnaire des cas de conscience* (1740), the theologians of the Sorbonne observed, "Infamy is the stain imprinted on the honor and reputation of a person which can never be removed."[28] They cited a Roman emperor, "We impose the punishment [for the crime] but we can never erase the infamy [attached to it]." Later in the article, the theologians softened this view but still insisted that damaged honor was difficult for the courts to repair. Distinguishing between legal and social infamy, they noted that the former (*infamie de droit*) was more permanent than the latter (*infamie de fait*), that is, a victim whose violation was established through a legal decision carried a more indelible stain on his or her honor than the victim whose dishonor was apperceived only by the community. "A man who has against him only *infamie de fait* can reestablish his reputation by altering his conduct and improving his mœurs....[On the other hand, *infamie de droit*] can only be effaced with great difficulty, through the grace of a Prince or through a solemn judgment that reestablishes the defamed person to his original reputation."[29] Lest one think that the theologians were referring to the perpetrators of crimes, the example they give clearly demonstrates that they had victims in mind as well. They referred to the hypothetical case of a raped woman who succeeds in getting a conviction against her rapist. To the question "Has the woman thereby restored her honor?" the theologians responded, "Her infamy is even greater and more certain because of the sentence than it was before."[30]

In a world in which victims had little to gain (and perhaps more to lose) from the judicial treatment of calumny, there was much incentive to avenge oneself outside of court, especially if one had the resources to do so. The fact that local courts so often dealt with such offenses anyway in the eighteenth century suggests either that society was shedding itself of the early-modern notion that judicial intervention tarnished the honor of the victim or, as I suspect, that such offenses were so common that court records represent only a fraction of them.

Dareau understood the risks to individual honor in the courtroom, which is why he downplayed the importance of discovering the truth of alleged calumnies in his treatise on injurious speech. "In addition to the fact that the effort to prove the truth of the claims asserted through calumny leads to more *injures* being aired…if truth can serve as an excuse, it will open the way everyday for new *injures* to be made, which it is always prudent to avoid."[31] Dareau encouraged magistrates to focus on, first, determining the fact of the statement (was it made and was it made by the defendant?) and, second, the relative status of the parties involved. Social hierarchy, not truth, was the animating principle of Old Regime jurisprudence on injurious speech. Hierarchy shaped the categories used to classify injurious speech, assessments of egregiousness, and the kinds of punishments to be meted out.

Dareau began his *Traité sur les injures* distinguishing between private [*particulier*] and public affronts. The latter included attacks on public figures and the collective, sacred values, notably, religion and mœurs. Surprisingly, Dareau had little to say about public speech offenses; defining them took fewer than forty pages of his nearly five-hundred-page treatise. Not that he found these offenses trivial. To the contrary, like Jousse, Dareau believed that injurious speech against religion and sovereign authority constituted two of the greatest crimes recognized by the law: *lèse-majesté divine* and *lèse-majesté*.[32] But he and Jousse devoted the better part of their respective treatises to explaining the intricacies of the sociopolitical hierarchy. At the top of Dareau's hierarchy, one finds God and the king, followed by ecclesiastics, gentlemen of the court, military officers, robins, judges, administrators, and even writers (*gens de lettres*). (Jousse's list put God and the saints on top, followed by the king, the pope, cardinals and bishops, priests, magistrates, and military officers.) Toward the bottom, one finds simple bourgeois, *gens du peuple*, and women.[33] One detects the habitual disregard of magistrates for affairs concerning the modest classes in Dareau's exhortations that they take these cases seriously. He insisted that, even if such cases were tedious, it was important to demonstrate that the rule of law would avenge the victims of offenses among the lower orders. Otherwise, he warned, individuals might take vengeance into their own hands, thereby threatening public order.[34] The honor of those from the modest classes was one thing, the honor of the indigent and despised quite another. Jousse made the point succinctly and unequivocally: "People of base or infamous status [*vils* or *infâmes*] cannot turn to the courts for injurious speech."[35]

The relative status of the parties involved in affairs of injurious speech helped determine how offenses were to be classified. According to Dareau, an *injure* could be atrocious, serious, or mild [*atroce, grave,* or *légère*]. (Jousse recognized only *graves* and *légères* offenses.) Whereas mild offenses could be treated as either civil or criminal affairs, those that were serious—*atroces* or *graves*—were to be treated as strictly criminal affairs. This is an important fact to keep in mind. It helps explain why revolutionaries tended to inflate insults directed at individual honor into calumny against sovereign authority or collective values. Doing so justified treating the affair as high crime. And although a victim's honor could never be entirely restored through a criminal conviction, the punishment was greater and more honorable for the victim, since what was being avenged was not merely an attack on individual honor but an attack on the sacred foundations of authority and community values.

According to Jousse, the foremost juridical consideration in affairs of speech was "the status of the person who makes the injurious statement and the status of the person receiving it."[36] Dareau concurred, "Although verbal or written offenses might not be atrocious in themselves, they are considered such when made by someone of base status against someone in authority."[37] Dareau and Jousse said that in cases involving close-knit power relationships, the dependent party had fewer or no rights. Thus, a bailiff could not seek redress for the verbal offenses made by a judge, a son by his father, a wife by her husband, or a domestic or artisan by his or her master. "Otherwise," Dareau explained, "it would not be possible to teach anyone a lesson," as if insulting reprimands were indispensable for obtaining good discipline![38] A close-knit power relationship between the two parties also justified inflating the offense into a public crime, due to the risk to authority involved. Included in Jousse's list of sixteen of the most serious speech offenses—after lèse-majesté divine and lèse-majesté—one finds *injures* made by wives against their husbands, children against their parents (this offense could merit death if accompanied with violence), vassals against their lords, and domestic servants against their masters.[39] Dareau illustrated the hierarchical nature of the jurisprudence, "A speech offense by a domestic servant against his master might be considered serious, whereas the same offense made by the master against a domestic servant might not be considered at all."[40]

Even sentencing was shot through with hierarchical considerations. Jousse instructed his readers, "If a speech offense is committed by someone of lowly condition against someone of higher rank, it is punished more severely."[41] If, however, a person of higher status slanders someone beneath him, the offense might not be punished at all, since "the distinguished status of an offender renders the offense pardonable."[42] In affairs concerning only individuals (rather than political, guild, or familial authority), the law provided for two kinds of reparations: monetary and symbolic. Monetary reparations were intended to cover court costs and any damages the insult may have caused the victim. Symbolic reparations might involve apologizing in a public place, usually the site where the offense was committed or the victim's home. Reparations *en personne* applied only to offenders of the same or inferior social rank as the victim. "If, on the other hand, a distinguished man offends someone beneath him," Dareau wrote, "the outrage must be extreme for him to be subject to reparations *en personne*."[43] The same logic applied in cases concerning elite commoners insulted or calumniated by individuals of lower status. However, among the modest classes, reparations *en personne* were to be avoided, for fear that they might provide occasions to renew hostilities.[44] If, however, institutional authority—and this included familial authority—was undermined by speech, the offense was to be considered a public crime. In such cases, perpetrators were sentenced to public apologies to the king, God, and the community and could be condemned to banishment, the galleys, even death.[45]

For Dareau and Jousse, protecting authority and social hierarchy was more important than determining whether the alleged calumny had any truth. It is astonishing that neither author explained how judges were to assess the verity of allegedly calumnious statements. Jousse raised the problem in passing, acknowledging it to be a "grande question," but then dismissed it, concluding that even if the injurious statement were true, "the verity of it never excuses the author."[46] Clearly, what mattered in such affairs were the lesions of honor suffered by elites.

With so much effort put into safeguarding sociopolitical hierarchy, what would it mean when the Revolution introduced the principles of free speech and civil equality? How would elites, accustomed to their privileged status in the Old Regime economy of esteem and deference, respond to slander after 1789? How much could even the most tolerant revolutionary leader allow insults and calumny to go unpunished before his authority was compromised? The Revolution not only threw the ideological basis of political legitimacy into question. It shook the sociological foundations of social and political legitimacy as well.

Managing Honor in a Hierarchical World

There were many ways to get even for calumny in the Old Regime beyond the courts. Responding in kind was common, as the libel wars, which intensified throughout the century, suggest. If the parties in an affair of honor were of the same social standing, they might opt to duel or brawl. For elites with the right connections, *lettres de cachet* could bring about the imprisonment of an alleged calumniator without the protracted scandal of a court case; the Bastille, among other prisons, housed many such detainees in the eighteenth century.[47]

Voltaire's career illustrates many of the tactics individuals adopted in trying to manage their honor. It also reveals the limits of these tactics and the risks involved. According to Frantz Funck-Brentano, Voltaire's first lettre de cachet in 1717 was not, as often believed, issued in response to the appearance of *J'ai vu*, a tract attacking the government. This error reinforces the mythic image of the philosophe as a heroic critic of arbitrary government. In fact, Voltaire was arrested for vulgar insinuations of incest between the regent and his daughter in *Puero regnante*, a verse sung in the streets of Paris.[48] He spent nearly a year in the Bastille. His next stay in the Bastille occurred nine years later. By that time, he had become the frequent guest of Parisian nobles, whom he amused with his biting wit. When the chevalier de Rohan became the target of his ridicule, the nobleman avenged himself by unleashing his thugs, who beat up Voltaire in the street while his hosts looked on. According to historian Peter Gay, Voltaire's hosts "found him even more amusing as a victim than as a dinner companion."[49] Although lesions of honor might be avenged through dueling, this ritual form of combat was to be carried out between social equals. Voltaire demanded a duel with the chevalier, but the latter's cousin, the Cardinal de Rohan, succeeded in getting a lettre de cachet issued against him.[50] In the aftermath of the affair, Voltaire's noble friends turned their backs on him. As Gay concludes, one was not to "break class barriers by talking back to a nobleman," for in "conflicts between rank and justice, it was justice, not rank, that gave way."[51] It should be noted, however, that there was no conflict between rank and justice. Rank *was* just in the Old Regime, and the chevalier and Voltaire's noble friends undoubtedly thought that punishing a bourgeois calumniator was in the natural order of things.

Aside from lettres de cachet and duels, one might seek redress for calumny through the courts. Voltaire pursued this option in 1746. He had just been appointed royal historiographer in 1745 and had further ambitions of becoming a *gentilhomme de la chambre* and a member of the *Académie française*. His adversaries tried to block his advancement by spreading libels against him. Aware that he could not remain idle without sacrificing his reputation, Voltaire requested a police investigation. Charges were filed against Louis Travenol, a violinist at Court, and his father. The affair dragged on for several years, wending its way from the Châtelet to the Parlement of Paris. In the end, neither party was satisfied with the verdict, which turned out to be a forced compromise. Voltaire never turned to the courts again. Instead, he found yet another way of engaging in battles over honor: writing. In the following decades, Voltaire attacked his enemies through correspondence and print, safely from his home in Ferney, a stone's throw from the Swiss border.

In recounting the Voltaire-Travenol incident thirty years later, Dareau praised Voltaire for having chosen litigation over the venomous pen. The jurist deplored the fact that too many writers did not do likewise. (He failed to recognize that Voltaire did, in fact, libel enemies thereafter.) "If a great master like Voltaire, whose genius and talent would have furnished him with superior weapons had he chosen to strike against [his enemies] through injurious writing, did not reject the idea of turning to the courts...this is all the more reason that offended writers should follow his example."[52] Alarmed by the proliferation of libels at the time he wrote his treatise in the 1770s, Dareau suggested that a special tribunal should be established to deal with them. (As we shall see, revolutionaries would also propose establishing special courts—civil censorship tribunals—to deal with calumny in 1793.)

Whereas elites turned to duels, lettres de cachet, and libels to get even for calumny outside the courts, the modest classes, especially young men, took affairs of honor into the streets. Dareau's exhortation to magistrates to pay more attention to such affairs suggests that they were common, and indeed, the records of the Châtelet contain a high proportion of cases involving *injures* accompanied by violence.[53] The journal of Jacques-Louis Ménétra, a master glazier reflecting back on his years as a shiftless young man in the 1770s, provides numerous examples of affairs of honor being settled through fisticuffs, swords (despite their restricted use to nobles), even broomsticks.[54] By the time the Revolution broke out, Ménétra was settled into a mastership in Paris. But the culture of calumny and honor that had structured and animated Old Regime neighborhood life spilled over into local revolutionary politics, as we shall see in coming chapters.

Calumny, Honor, and the French Revolution

It is not surprising that Dareau's treatise on injurious speech appeared when it did (1775). By that time, the culture of calumny and honor, vexed and amplified by an expanding public sphere, had spread to all corners of public life. Battles within the Republic of Letters, resistance to the Maupeou coup (1771–1774), outrage over the liberalization of the grain trade and abolition of the guilds (1774–1776), speculation wars, fiscal crisis, and corruption scandals (1780s) all contributed to a surfeit of calumny.[55] The culture of calumny was so pervasive, it served as the leitmotif of Pierre-Augustin Caron de Beaumarchais's box-office hit, *Le barbier de Séville*, staged the very same year, incidentally, that Dareau's treatise was published. Controversy surrounding the opening of Beaumarchais's subsequent box-office hit, *La folle journée ou le mariage de Figaro* (1784) was itself animated by calumny. As for Beaumarchais, he became a central figure in calumny affairs throughout the rest of the decade, as victim and perpetrator.[56] By the 1780s, as Robert Darnton has shown, powerful men in finance and politics had writers working for them (Beaumarchais worked for Calonne), churning out propaganda and libels in efforts to win over the public. And as the public sphere expanded in the last decades of the Old Regime, calumny spiraled.

Whether the culture of calumny, and, specifically, printed libels, brought down the Old Regime is a matter of debate among historians.[57] What is certain is that when revolutionaries declared free speech in the Declaration of the Rights of Man and of the Citizen in 1789, they remained steeped in that culture. They continued expressing contest through calumny even as they continued viewing calumny as a highly criminal offense, even treason when it attacked sovereign authority or sacred moral values. And although there was much consensus on abolishing mandatory prepublication censorship, contemporaries had not yet worked through—legally or psychologically—the implications of free speech for their reputations, not to mention for the economy of esteem and deference upon which political legitimacy was based.

Setting legal limits on free speech would become a pressing and quarrelsome issue in the early years of the Revolution. The stakes in securing esteem and deference were, of course, high. In their efforts to distinguish liberty from license—dissent from calumny—contemporaries were guided by more than contingent concerns about their honor. They were also influenced by the legacy of Enlightenment ideas about legitimate limits on free speech.

CHAPTER THREE

Imagining Press Freedom and Limits in the Enlightenment

To God, would I maintain that men might insolently spread satire and calumny against their superiors or their equals.

—Denis Diderot, "Libelles," *Encyclopédie*, 1765

Freedom and Limits

On December 27, 1788, Louis XVI's Director General of Finances, Jacques Necker, announced the agenda for the upcoming meeting of the Estates-General. Among the many reforms to be discussed, Necker included press freedom, in these terms: "Your Majesty is impatient to receive the opinions of the Estates-General concerning the *just measure of freedom* that the press should be accorded for works or the publicity of works concerning public administration, government, or any topic of public concern."[1] Approved by the king, the report was printed up and distributed throughout France. With little more than four months to go before the meeting, the government was turning over the question of press freedom to the nation for reflection.

But the floodgates had already burst open. The monarchy's attempt to abolish the parlements the previous May provoked a torrent of unauthorized pamphlets. On July 5, 1788, when Louis tried to resolve the crisis by agreeing to summon the Estates-General to discuss reforms, it was believed that he suspended censorship, and the outpour continued.[2] But an explosion of print and temporary reprieve from censorship did not amount to legitimate freedom. As Necker saw it, the task ahead was to set new legal and regulatory parameters for the publishing industry.

Thinking through freedom and limits raised a number of questions. Why should the press be free? What risks did this freedom involve? And how should abuses be defined and limits enforced in order to secure benefits while avoiding drawbacks? In reflecting on these issues, revolutionaries drew from a wide range of Enlightenment ideas. This chapter examines this legacy. It begins by showing how conceptions of a self-regulating public emerged. Beleaguered by censorship and repression in the late 1750s, philosophes tried to outflank authorities by spreading the idea of a self-policing "public"—a public inherently immune to the influence of bad books and more effective than the state in punishing their authors. Later, once the philosophes had secured positions in the social, cultural, and political institutions of the Old Regime, they adopted less expansive notions of press freedom. They no longer maintained that public opinion was sufficiently capable of repressing abuses of this freedom. As calumny proliferated, contemporaries began meditating on the laws and regulations needed to deal with injurious print. In the final year of the Old Regime, the issue of press freedom became imbricated in political struggles among competing factions and institutions. Although nearly everyone agreed that the press should be free and that calumny should be punished, they disagreed on who should have the authority to define and enforce new laws governing free expression.

There may well have been a widespread desire for press freedom by 1789, but contemporaries were not naive about the power of publicity. They recognized that the outcome of their struggles depended greatly on the ability to control the policing of public opinion.

The Oppositional View: A Self-Regulating Public Opinion (1750s–1760s)

There was no coherent campaign for press freedom in the French Enlightenment. The story of an epochal struggle between freedom-seeking philosophes and a repressive state, depicted in many histories of the Enlightenment in the twentieth century, has recently given way to a more complex picture—one of complicities and compromises between writers, the Court, the royal administration, the parlements, and the Printers' and Booksellers' Guild.[3] The philosophes did, to be sure, seek greater toleration for their ideas, if not for those of their adversaries. And although they sometimes criticized prepublication censorship and police repression, they rarely called for abolishing both at the same time.[4] On the whole, they tended to be prudent and tactical in discussing press freedom, aware that courting, rather than castigating, authorities better served their interests, whether those interests involved the protection of their own works or the suppression of those of their enemies.

By midcentury, the philosophes had influential sympathizers at Court and in the royal administration.[5] Support was provided licitly and illicitly. Licitly, the Directors of the Book Trade expanded the use of *permissions tacites* and *permissions simples*. Although these authorizations did not confer exclusive privileges and thus did not protect publishers from counterfeiting or prosecution for libel, books receiving them were usually, though not always, spared judicial repression.[6] Illicitly, authorities sometimes abetted the underground market of unauthorized books.[7] Even the Directors of the Book Trade and Lieutenants General of Police (the positions overlapped after 1763) occasionally conspired to circumvent their own system of licensing and surveillance, sending manuscripts abroad to be printed and protecting them when they came back as books into France.[8]

Yet, complicity between the philosophes and authorities should not be overstated. Directors of the Book Trade and Lieutenants General of Police were subject to pressure from many sides, and their efforts to help the philosophes sometimes encountered formidable resistance. Enemies of the Enlightenment at Court, in the Church, and in the parlements tried to drive the philosophes out of existence.[9] Although they did not succeed, their efforts led to not a few condemnations, book seizures, and lettres de cachet. Individuals involved in the book trade, including authors, found themselves thrown into the Bastille and other such prisons with increasing frequency in the decades between 1750 and 1780.[10] Thus, even as the Enlightenment gained increasing legitimacy in society, the personal and financial risks of writing and publishing remained high.[11]

The vicissitudes of official tolerance for the philosophes helps explain their ambivalent, tactical pronouncements about press freedom. With the sympathetic Malesherbes at the helm of the Book Trade and authorization to publish the *Encyclopédie* in the late 1740s and early 1750s, they had little reason to complain. The situation changed abruptly in the wake of the Damien Affair of 1757. In the aftermath of the assassination attempt on Louis XV, the *Conseil d'État* declared all writings attacking religion or the state to be punishable by death. Two years later, the Parlement of Paris condemned the *Encyclopédie*, and the project went underground.[12] The magistrates also condemned Helvétius's materialist and sacrilegious *De l'Esprit*, burning it on the steps of the Palais de justice, thereby humiliating the royal censors for having approved it.[13] Five years later, the Parlement passed a Law of Silence prohibiting public discussion of administration and royal finances.

It was in this "dark period," as Robert Darnton calls it, that the philosophes honed their most radical ideas on press freedom.[14] They employed two arguments. First, they denied that books could provoke sedition. In his 1764 *Dictionnaire philosophique*, Voltaire quipped, "I know of many books that bore; I know of none that have caused real harm."[15] A year later, he seems to have taken a page from Hume's 1742 "Of the Liberty of the Press," expounding on the peaceful progress that comes only through reading.

> Each citizen can speak to the nation through writing, and each reader can examine leisurely and dispassionately what his compatriot submits to him through the press. Our assemblies can sometimes be tumultuous: it is only in the contemplation of the reading room that one can do good.[16]

The article "presse" in the clandestinely published volume of the *Encyclopédie* repeated this view, asserting that readers were "immune from contracting passions."[17] In his 1764 *Refléxions sur les avantages de la liberté d'écrire et d'imprimer sur les matières de l'administration* (it was not published until 1775), André Morellet wryly dismissed Parlement's concerns that a free press would stir up the people: "It is strange that one opposes the advantages [of press freedom] with such vague fears."[18] According to Morellet, if troubles occurred in the wake of a publication, it was the fault of authorities, not writers and publishers. "It is false that public tranquility can be disturbed [by writings] in any state where authorities know how to attain respect"—that is, where authorities know how to govern respectably since the public, Morellet assumed, was reasonable and of one mind in its judgments.[19]

Another argument for press freedom advanced during this "dark period" held that public opinion was inherently self-regulating and that, consequently, it was useless, even counterproductive, for authorities to obstruct the circulation of ideas. Borrowing freely from Montesquieu's *De l'esprit des lois*, the authors of the article "libelles" in the *Encyclopédie* claimed that libels and satire were unknown in the East where despotism hampered the intelligence and wit needed to write them—a roundabout way of flattering the French for indulging in the vice. In a thinly veiled dig at authorities, they argued that in aristocracies, libels were punished severely because magistrates were "as little sovereigns not strong enough to dismiss insults." And while democracies tolerated libels, which served as a check on authority, "enlightened monarchies" treated them as mere misdemeanors, punishing them through mild "correctional policing."[20] The *encyclopédistes* departed from Montesquieu's views, however, in positing the notion of a self-regulating "public opinion," one that was sufficiently capable of punishing scandalous writers. Glossing over how the public did so, they, like Morellet, blamed authorities for disturbances, believing that as long as sovereign authorities did nothing reproachable, they need not worry about the impact of libels. "Decent people embrace the party of virtue and punish calumny with contempt."[21]

These were provocative assertions, but the encyclopédistes (or their meddlesome editor) tempered them with conventional appeals to the law. It is worth citing their argument in full, for it appears neither in *De l'esprit des lois*, which inspired most of the article, nor in Diderot's more radical (but unpublished) tract *Lettre sur le commerce des livres* of 1763.

> To God, would I maintain that men might insolently spread satire and calumny against their superiors or their equals. [Apparently, social inferiors were fair game.] Religion, morality, the right of truth, the necessity of subordination, order, peace, and tranquility of society all conjoin to detest such audacity; but in a [well-regulated] state, I would not want to repress such licentiousness through means which would destroy all freedom. *One can punish abuses through wise laws, which in their prudent execution unite justice with the greatest happiness of the people and the preservation of the government.*[22]

The concession lent an air of conventionality to what was otherwise a radical stance. Still, the article said nothing about what "wise laws" were to consist in.

The next article appearing in the volume, "libelles diffamatoires," was unequivocally conventional. While readers of the previous article may have relished the idea that authorities should be held accountable to them (the public), they would have been comforted to know that their own reputations would not be brought before this court. The authors summarized the Old Regime jurisprudence on injurious speech, stressing its hierarchical aspects. They observed that punishments were set according to the status of the person attacked and the conditions under which the libel was produced. If the defamation involved calumny, "the author is punished and sometimes sentenced to death." Executions for calumny were rare in the eighteenth century, but not unheard of.[23] In any case, the fact that the article conveyed no criticism about such conventions suggests that the encyclopédistes, or their squeamish editor who often mutilated their articles, accepted the status quo or felt that readers needed to be assured that they did.[24]

Diderot's 1763 *Lettre sur le commerce de la librairie*, which was not published until 1861, advanced what was arguably the most radical position on press freedom during the French Enlightenment. The Printers' and Booksellers' Guild had hired Diderot to propose new regulations to the new Royal Administrator of the Book Trade and Lieutenant General of Police, Antoine de Sartine, but his tract turned out to be too radical for the guild, which gave it a thorough overhaul and a new title before submitting it.[25] Most studies of the tract situate it within complex struggles over privileges and literary property, and indeed, those issues are central in the text.[26] But Diderot also advanced quasi-libertarian views about how press abuses should be handled. In calling for *permissions tacites à l'infinie*—permission for all publications regardless of content—he stressed the futility of both prepublication censorship and postpublication repression. He assured that a truly bad book—one so dangerous that no author or printer would dare submit it to the censors, even for a *permission tacite*—would meet with the public's wrath. He made no mention of the "wise punitive laws" alluded to in the *Encyclopédie*. Apparently, there was no need for them. For should a truly dangerous book appear, the public would be so outraged, it would express its choler in the form of "public vengeance."[27] "Public vengeance" is certainly more severe than "public contempt," the term used in the *Encyclopédie*, and it might be considered nothing more than rhetorical excess. But if there was an exaggerated concept at play in Diderot's argument, it was not "public vengeance." Rather, it was the notion of a reasonable public—a uniform body of opinion capable of discerning truth from calumny and of punishing the latter. As we have seen, the public sphere in eighteenth-century France defied the sanitized portraits the philosophes made of it. When stakes were high, dispassionate reason often gave way to vindictive libel, and the public sphere became a battlefield for struggles over honor and esteem—the prerequisites for power.

The philosophes were well aware of this. When Voltaire wrote scandalous tracts in the name of Rousseau to compromise the "citizen of Geneva" in the Republic of Letters, he counted on the public's inability to discern truth from dissimulation.[28] Diderot's and d'Alembert's lack of confidence in public opinion prompted them to go running to the Lieutenant General of Police when a libel cut too close to the bone. In 1772 the abbé Antoine Sabatier, a former philosophe, published a scathing indictment of the encyclopédistes in *Trois siècles de notre littérature*. Diderot and d'Alembert begged Sartine to suppress the work. Sartine asked them if it impugned their mœurs or private conduct. They insisted that it did, since it predicted the greatest calamities as a result of their principles. Sartine rejected their argument. Turning their own principles back on them, he told them to take their complaint to the public.[29]

Clearly, there were limits to how far the *encylopédistes* would go in erecting public opinion as the supreme tribunal over the printed word. Still, the notion of public opinion as such persisted, taking on a life of its own in the course of political struggles during the Old Regime's final decades. As Keith Baker has shown, magistrates—notably Malesherbes, who, after resigning as Director of the Book Trade in 1763, devoted himself to judicial functions in the *Cour des aides*—viewed

it as a legitimate restraint on sovereign power once the parlements were abolished in the Maupeou coup of 1771.[30] So, too, did Jacques Necker after he was
dismissed as Director General of Finances in 1781.[31] Both men, we shall see,
would temper this view on the eve of the Revolution. If the "tribunal of public
opinion" was a powerful notion, it was essentially an oppositional one—readily
abandoned when the alienated or ousted managed to secure (or resecure) power.

The Law Is the Limit: Condorcet's *Fragments sur la liberté de la presse* (1776)

By the 1770s, the philosophes' situation had changed. They were working their
way into the establishment, holding influential posts in the administration and
cultural institutions.[32] From such elevated positions, the problem of press freedom and limits looked different. Erecting public opinion as the final word on
taste, morality, and politics seemed less important than establishing legal, institutional, and moral parameters for the world of print. And given the cultural and
political battles raging in the 1770s and 1780s, there were compelling reasons
to be thinking about such parameters. In the wake of the grain crisis of 1768,
Ferdinando Galiani, a Neapolitan diplomat and man of letters in Paris, wrote a
controversial tract attacking the philosophical foundations of physiocracy. The
tract, *Dialogues sur le commerce des bleds*, also criticized the philosophes' mode of
disputation in promoting the new economic policy, sending shock waves through
the Republic of Letters. In the bitter pamphlet war that ensued, aggrieved parties
sought the support of Sartine, then Director of the Book Trade and Lieutenant
General of Police.[33] The Republic of Letters was further divided by the Maupeou
coup of 1771. While Voltaire supported the radical judicial reforms, other philosophes defended the parlementary magistrates, their erstwhile repressors.[34]
Finally, contested appointments to the Académie française and the Académie des
sciences where the encyclopédistes were gaining strength had the effect of pitting
members against each other and stirring up debate over the need to censor the
Academies' own (calumnious) publications.[35]

Marie-Jean-Antoine-Nicolas Caritat, the marquis de Condorcet was in the
thick of these struggles. His appointment as assistant secretary to the Académie
des sciences in 1773 was a highly contentious affair.[36] He became an advisor
to Anne-Robert-Jacques Turgot, Controller General of Finances between 1774
and 1776. An enthusiastic supporter of press freedom himself, Turgot appointed
Condorcet *inspecteur des Monnaies* in 1775, around the time when his liberal economic

reforms were stirring up violence and published protest.[37] It was in this context that Condorcet wrote his *Fragments sur la liberté de la presse*. The text marks the most thorough contemplation of the "wise laws" that were to accompany the abolition of prepublication censorship. Condorcet's ideas on press freedom are worth investigating, not because they served as a blueprint for revolutionaries but because they shed light on the tensions surrounding the issue in late eighteenth-century France. They give insight into the tolerance thresholds that Condorcet assumed his readers shared.

According to Condorcet, the most serious print crime was sedition. Absolutists would have agreed, of course, but Condorcet erected a mountain of criteria for determining guilt. First, proof had to be furnished that the accused not only wrote the work in question but also engaged in having it circulated.[38] Second, it had to be demonstrated that the work in question contributed to a wrongdoing and that this wrongdoing resulted necessarily from the publication. Finally, it had to be demonstrated that the author intended this wrongdoing.[39] Clearly, Condorcet's plan would have made indictments for sedition next to impossible to obtain. Yet, he included a backdoor clause. In periods of unrest, such as war or civil strife, press freedom could be suspended. He gave historical examples of times when authorities proscribed, rightly in his view, certain forms of expression. "It was in this way," he wrote,

> that Queen Elizabeth could, without tyranny, ban for a time unauthorized preaching....The act of preaching is itself irrelevant. Every man has the right to preach to those who want to listen to him; every man has the right to be preached to by whomever he wants. But since this freedom can stir up unrest, Elizabeth had the right to justifiably suspend this law for a fixed period of time.[40]

Condorcet thus built a "state of exception" into his plan; press freedom could be sacrificed for the sake of preserving the general order.

For Condorcet, speech offenses against public figures (officials, guild leaders, and authors all shared "public" status in his plan) were to be treated differently from those against private individuals (*particuliers*). He identified three kinds of speech violations: calumny, defamation, and insults or vague accusations (see table 3.1). The worst was calumny, which referred to the malicious and false imputation of a criminal or dishonorable action to someone. The perpetrators of calumny against public and private figures were to undergo the same punishment that the victim would have undergone had the denunciation been determined to be true. Matters became more complicated in cases of defamation and insult.

Table 3.1 The Place of Intentions in Assessing Press Abuses according to Condorcet

	Intentional Calumny: False imputation of criminal activity or a wrongdoing that incurs loss of honor	Defamation: Nonmalicious denunciations of criminal or reprehensible activity or accusations not involving loss of honor	Insults, Vague Accusations
Against private individuals	*Criminal offense.* For calumnious criminal accusations, the perpetrator receives the punishment the accused would have; for other calumnies: humiliation by pillory; short-term imprisonment; temporary exile; reparations.	*Punishable offense (délit).* For disproved imputations of criminal activities or for imputations of non-criminal activities (regardless of their truth), the Court imposes reparations and damages. Even if imputation is true, the publicized imputation is still an offense: the accuser should have gone to the authorities.	*Minor offense.* Civil reparations.
Against public authority, writers, corporate bodies	*Criminal offense.* Same as above.	*Encouraged.* The right to publicize suspicions about criminal and/or immoral activities serves as a salutary check on authority; distinguished from calumny not by verity but by the accuser's intentions.	*Punishable offense (délit).* Insults undermine respect and authority of officials. In cases of vague allegations, the author is punished only if s/he does not substantiate claims with evidence.

Defamation was defined as the nonmalicious (in intent) public accusation of criminal or reprehensible activity. According to Condorcet, defamation against a private individual was to be treated as a serious offense, even if the accusation turned out to be true, since the denunciator should have submitted the matter to authorities.[41] Inversely, defamation against public figures was to be tolerated and even encouraged. Indeed, the very purpose of press freedom was to empower the public to censure and monitor authorities. If writers had to worry about reprisal for voicing suspicions or for hazarding accusations that, after further investigation, turned out to be false, the chilling effect would hamper public opinion's function as a check on authority.[42]

These guidelines posed a potential problem: how were the courts supposed to distinguish between punishable calumny and virtuous defamation if "truth" was irrelevant? The jurists Dareau and Jousse, we have seen, emphasized the importance of determining the relative social status of the parties involved. For Condorcet, however, culpability depended upon the author's intentions. His position on this point is worth highlighting; for I believe it helps explain judicial practices during the Terror. In the highly polarized climate of revolution when truth was too difficult (or contentious) to ascertain and social status no longer mattered, tribunals sought to uncover the moral and political consciences of suspects. "What were your true sentiments on August 10, 1792, when the monarchy fell?"[43]

Condorcet also proposed employing different criteria in assessing insults, or vague accusations, against public and private figures. Whereas such speech was to be treated as a minor offense when it concerned private individuals, it was to be treated as a serious crime when directed at public figures. This reasoning differs from the views of Montesquieu and the encyclopédistes, who believed that the attribution of lèse-majesté should not pertain to such speech. In *De l'esprit des lois*, Montesquieu stated, "Nothing renders the crime of high treason more arbitrary than declaring people guilty of it for indiscreet speech."[44] Disrespectful criticism, the Bordeaux magistrate argued, could even be salutary, especially in monarchies where it served as a kind of collective psychological release valve. "[It] consoles the disgruntled, diminishes jealousies, gives the people the patience to suffer, and makes them laugh at their own sufferings."[45] The harshest treatment that satire or libels merited in a monarchy, according to Montesquieu, was correctional policing, which, in the Old Regime, tended to involve relatively modest fines or short stays in prison.[46] Condorcet, on the other hand, stressed the political dangers of disrespect. "Each citizen has the right to judge the conduct of the employees of the nation; but no one has the right to take away public esteem [from a public official] through vague imputations."[47] As for insults, he believed they were even more dangerous than calumny. Since calumny imputed a concrete crime, it could be disproved. Insults, however, deprived officials of the respect the community invested in them, respect that was needed to exercise authority and maintain the community's well-being.

Condorcet's legal framework for press freedom thus narrowed the range of permissible speech. Of the three kinds of injurious speech—calumny, defamation, and insult—only defamation, that is, an accusation made in good faith of criminal or reprehensible actions, was to be tolerated and only in cases in which public figures were the targets. But distinguishing the permissible from the punishable—civic denunciations from calumny—required assessing authorial intentions. Condorcet offered no guidelines for how to do so.

Condorcet's proposal also narrowed the role of public opinion. Whereas earlier philosophes depicted public opinion as sufficiently discerning and self-regulating to pass judgment on all public matters, Condorcet believed that this "tribunal" should have limited jurisdiction. It was to be the final court of appeals only for affairs concerning violations of mœurs, such as pornography.[48] He insisted that it was as ignoble for the state to punish such offenses as it was for someone to engage in them. Circumscribing public opinion still further, he distinguished between public opinion and *publicized* opinions, holding that the public's censure of mœurs violations should be restricted to casual conversation and banned from print, copied manuscripts, and songs. While he recognized the salutary influence of an opprobrious "public opinion" on mœurs, he emphasized that the *publicity* of its judgments could be disruptive.

Thus, in Condorcet's schema, public opinion figured as an abstract repository of censorious sentiments. But he wanted it to remain abstract, depriving it of the means to compete with state institutions. He reiterated this argument again in 1789, a time when notions about public opinion were becoming mixed up with discussions about more democratic forms of sovereignty. In an open letter to deputies to the Estates-General, he wrote, "Public opinion exerts over us a nearly irresistible force; it is a useful instrument, but one to which no external force should be added, in giving its decisions a solemnity which would allow no possibility to resist it."[49] He discouraged the idea, which must have been circulating at the time, that public approbation and disapprobation of deputies' actions should be institutionalized as a form of civil censorship. In the spirit of his 1776 tract, he feared that giving censorious expression an institutional base would undermine law and authority, leading to divisiveness and anarchy. Deputies would become the slavish agents of local factions and be inhibited from exercising authority through their individual conscience and reason. He concluded, "A virtuous man can withstand a dispersed public opinion; but the strength to withstand it once it is consolidated…into a respected organ is almost beyond human capabilities."[50]

Condorcet's insistence on the law as the ultimate regulator of speech presupposed a neutral, disinterested application of it. Judicial neutrality, however, was too much to expect in the final decades of the Old Regime, when the judicial order itself was at the center of political struggles. It is quite possible that Condorcet drafted *Fragments* sometime between 1771 and 1774, when the parlements had been abolished and enlightened administrators were trying to establish a new legal-judicial system. In the late 1780s, when the monarchy again tried, but failed, to dispense with the parlements, the magistrates would resist, provoking a political crisis that brought the Old Regime to a grinding halt. In the new regime of press freedom that opened up, legislative and judicial institutions could not be counted on to be sufficiently impartial in defining and enforcing press laws.

Censorship as Check-and-Balance: Rereading Malesherbes and Thiébault (1789)

Tracts on press freedom proliferated in the months before the meeting of the Estates-General, and even royal officials got in on the act. Those by a former censor, Malesherbes, and a current one, Dieudonné Thiébault, are exceptional in their length and depth of reflection. After stepping down as Director of the Book Trade in 1763, Malesherbes worked on and off for the government and magistracy and had just resigned from his position as Royal Minister in the summer of 1788 when the government asked him to submit his ideas on press freedom. Although he repeated many of the suggestions he had made in his 1758 *Mémoires sur la librairie*, he now took into account the new political landscape, notably, the political position of the parlements and the imminent abolition of mandatory censorship. Thiébault's tract, which bore the same title as Malesherbes's manuscript, considered these issues even more rigorously. Unlike Malesherbes's memoir, Thiébault's *Mémoire sur la liberté de la presse* was published. It figured in debates on press freedom in 1789.

Historians have tended to see Malesherbes's and Thiébault's texts in different lights. While views on Malesherbes vary (he is seen as either a champion of liberalism within an oppressive regime or a moderate conservative), there has been more consensus that Thiébault was an outmoded defender of the Old Regime and that his tract was little more than a half-hearted, roundabout call for maintaining censorship.[51] Yet, these two men conveyed similar views, and they were quite innovative and astute in their reflections. Even if neither called for the outright abolition of censorship, they drew upon Enlightenment ideas in proposing ways to extend freedom to writers while protecting them from arbitrary, postpublication repression. Both authors envisaged protecting writers and empowering public opinion by establishing a system of checks and balances between the administration and the courts.

Malesherbes knew much about the difficulties in trying to establish such a system. Dismissed in 1771 from his post as first president of the *cour des Aides* in the Maupeou coup, he wrote remonstrances over the next several years in which he insisted on the benefits of press freedom as a check on absolute monarchy.[52] In 1787, he accepted a position as Royal Minister, though not without hesitation. A year of working for the monarchy was enough to have cultivated in him a distrust of the parlements. Whereas he had defended the magistracy against royal "despotism" in the early 1770s, on the eve of the Revolution he presented royal censorship as a salutary check on the despotism of the parlements.[53]

Malesherbes's background helps explain what appears to be a curious contradiction in his *Mémoire sur la liberté de la presse*: he called for both press freedom and censorship. The censorship he envisaged differed from the one practiced until then. He proposed that authors choose to either submit their works to the censors with the guarantee that, if approved, they would receive judicial immunity, or bypass the censors at their own "risk, peril, and fortune."[54] For Malesherbes, there was no doubt that writers and printers should be held accountable for abuses of press freedom, such as calumny, breaches of *bonnes mœurs*, and attacks on religion and sovereign authority. But it was the unchecked authority of the parlements that Malesherbes regarded as the greatest threat to press freedom.

In a letter to the Controller General of Finances, Étienne-Charles de Loménie de Brienne, in 1788, Malesherbes observed that the parlements now had a monopoly on speaking for the nation.[55] He wrote this when it appeared that the public was encouraging the Parlement of Paris to challenge the crown's attempt to abolish the parlements.[56] But by winter 1789, when Malesherbes completed his manuscript, the situation had changed. The public was now suspicious about the Parlement's stated commitment to equitable reforms, and he feared that if the magistrates continued exercising exclusive punitive authority over the world of print, they would soon become despotic. While conceding that royal censors could sometimes be tyrannical, he held up royal censorship as the lesser of two evils.

> The principles of censorship are arbitrary [according to Enlightenment writers]… but if books are deemed reprehensible by the judicial system, it will no longer be the whims of a single man on which [the fate of] a book will depend; rather, it will depend on [the whims] of all the councilors of the Parlement and Châtelet, who, if displeased with a book, will find it appropriate to denounce it.[57]

Malesherbes based his misgivings about the French magistracy on several factors. First, unlike their English counterparts, French judges formed a self-interested corporation and conducted certain proceedings secretly.[58] Second, French magistrates did not have the expertise to adjudicate affairs concerning complex subjects, such as theology and metaphysics. Judges were often moved by the eloquence of plaintiffs seeking to protect their intellectual fiefdoms.[59]

In a footnote, Malesherbes deviated from his general reflections to slip in his suspicions about the Parlement's recent *arrêté* in favor of press freedom. He warned,

> Nothing better reveals the arbitrariness of the rules…that the Parlement proposes to follow as soon as it obtains what it calls "the freedom of the press" than the terms of its recent *arrêté* which, in calling for this freedom, excepts "reprehensible works, whose authors will be held to account."[60]

He added that if seventeenth-century writers like Molière and La Bruyère had lived under such a free-press regime, they would have spent most of their time in court.[61] The *arrêté* that Malesherbes was referring to had been issued on December 5, 1788. In many ways it prefigured Article 11 of the Declaration of the Rights of Man and of the Citizen. The Parlement called for

> the lawful [*légitime*] implementation of the freedom of the press, the only prompt and sure means for good people [to combat] the licentiousness of the wicked, excepting reprehensible writings for which authors are answerable according to the law.[62]

"Lawful" implied legal limits, a qualification that amounted to asserting the Parlement's exclusive authority to determine and punish press abuses. Malesherbes's suspicions were not unfounded. In an earlier passage of the *arrêté*, the Parlement signaled its intention to punish its opponents, referring to

> the maneuvers practiced in the realm by ill-intentioned people to deprive the nation of the fruit of its magistracy's efforts by substituting the fire of sedition and the horrors of anarchy for the desirable success of a generous and wise freedom.[63]

In a single strike, the Parlement of Paris presented itself as the stalwart defender of press freedom, arrogated to itself the authority to define and pursue abuses, and warned its opponents that it regarded them as seditious.

It is in this political context that Thiébault's *Mémoire sur la liberté de la presse* should be reappraised. This ex-Jesuit has been depicted as sailing against the prevailing currents, the sole conservative defender of a system under inexorable collapse. Many of his proposals and commitments, however, did not differ from those of Malesherbes. Both suggested reforms that would extend more freedom to authors while avoiding the drawbacks that they thought unlimited press freedom might engender. For Thiébault and Malesherbes, press freedom meant freedom from the tyranny of the parlements and from *mandatory* royal censorship. However, the best way to avoid the former, they believed, was to submit *voluntarily* to the latter.[64]

Like Diderot and Malesherbes, Thiébault believed it was impossible to stop the circulation of bad books. "Abuse is inseparable from the common use of things, as long as there remains an ounce of freedom."[65] He reasoned that just because guns could be used to kill people, governments should not start banning them.[66] Still, abuses were to be punished, and Thiébault proposed that if writers declined to submit their works to the censors, they, along with the printer and distributors, could be held legally accountable for offenses in print. If, however, submitted works were approved, they were to be immune from all prosecution,

FIGURE 3.1. Dieudonné Thiébault. Courtesy of the Carnavalet Museum.

DIEUDONNÉ THIÉBAULT
Père du général Thiébault
d'après une miniature de Sicardy

except in cases of calumny and defamation.[67] (He thought that since slander could be subtle and go undetected by the censors, authors should always be held responsible for such offenses.)[68] Thiébault added that a writer whose work was submitted but refused an approbation should also be immune from prosecution, unless, of course, the author chose to have it published and circulated anyway. This immunity was justified because the author had demonstrated good faith in submitting the work in the first place.[69]

Thiébault shared Malesherbes's distrust of the parlements. He argued that, without the protection of the censors' approbation, authors would become vulnerable to the whims of the magistrates. Whereas under the old system, printers and distributors were held responsible for bad books more often than were authors, under a free-press regime, more would be printed, but "the number of guilty authors will necessarily increase."[70] If the courts' arbitrariness could not be avoided (and he doubted that it could), the magistrates would end up exercising "the most encompassing, absolute, and formidable influence over public opinions, the doctrines of the Nation, and people's minds."[71] Alluding to the monarchy's current struggle against the parlements, he pointed out a contradiction on the part of those who demanded unlimited press freedom while decrying the tyranny of the parlements.

> You fear aristocracy, yet you are about to establish the most complete aristocracy in the name of freedom! You say that your magistrates have exercised too much influence over your laws, yet you are going to give them authority over the very ideas upon which the laws themselves are to be based. You complain about speech restrictions, yet you are [now] going to open yourselves up to the most severe inquisitions! You do not want to be held back any longer from doing wrong, yet you yourselves are about to authorize a law which will inevitably strike at your property, happiness, freedom, and life.[72]

Thus, Thiébault and Malesherbes thought in terms of checks and balances. Voluntary censorship run by the royal administration, they believed, would serve as a check on parlementary tyranny. Furthermore, since neither the administration nor the parlements would exert exclusive control, the press would become more responsive to demands from below. The victims of oppression would feel freer to air grievances, knowing that complaints against the monarchy would not be pursued by the parlements and that complaints against the parlements would be protected by the legally binding approbation of royal censors.[73]

Still, the right to denounce through print did not, according to Thiébault, exempt authors from responsibility for calumny. Like most enlightened contemporaries, he thought that press abuses were punishable. For Thiébault and Malesherbes, abuses were those already defined by Old Regime law: attacks against mœurs, government, religion, and the honor of citizens. In discussing these matters, Malesherbes exuded more tolerance, though less rigor, than did Thiébault. He dismissed concerns about threats to the "principles of government," pointing to the fact that the king had already suspended censorship requirements for tracts dealing with reforms. As for religion, he believed that controversies over Jansenism, so tumultuous in the past, were now over. In his view, therefore, "fears about the threat of press freedom for religion and government have often been exaggerated."[74] For Malesherbes, "the censor should watch over all that concerns public order and do no more than that."[75]

Whereas Malesherbes had little to say about attacks on religion, except that they might provoke trouble and should be repressed if necessary, Thiébault expounded on their danger.[76] He viewed them in much the same way as Montesquieu and Rousseau had viewed attacks on mœurs: the sign of society on the brink of self-destruction.

> And who could ignore the terrible havoc that metaphysical sophisms have wreaked among weak minds! We cannot deny that among all Peoples, in all centuries, and under all systems [of government], men's respect for religion has never been altered without public corruption ensuing quickly thereafter along with the dissolution of social bonds![77]

According to Thiébault, an entirely unrestricted press would not only destroy mœurs and honor; it would also undermine the state's (unwritten) constitution and legitimate authority.[78]

Clearly, Thiébault was no radical. And it might even seem that he was insincere about the freedom he was proposing. Whereas other proponents of press freedom trumpeted its virtues while ignoring the question of limits, Thiébault assumed that limits were necessary and stressed the importance of cultivating the *sentiment* of freedom, that is, the notion one has about the will she or he exerts.

> It is the sentiment of freedom and not freedom itself which raises us up and ennobles us.... He who were a slave without knowing it would still be capable of virtue.... It is better, from the political point of view, to give the Nation the true sentiment of press freedom rather than the real thing in its unlimited form.[79]

Although Malesherbes and Thiébault agreed on much, they differed on some points. Malesherbes condoned anonymous writings, seeing them as necessary for society to confront despotism without risk of reprisal. He mentioned

Montesquieu's aversion to anonymous denunciations but dismissed it.[80] Thiébault, however, thought that the names of authors and publishers should appear on all publications. In the case of works approved by the censors, the name of the author would already be registered. But what about works not submitted voluntarily to the censors? Thiébault suggested that a copy of all publications, approved or not, be submitted to a public depository, each page signed by the author and printer along with a declaration of responsibility for the content. This formality, he argued, would protect authors from subsequent changes that printers might make—a chronic nuisance of eighteenth-century literary life—and ensure legal accountability.[81] In addition, Thiébault believed that writers should furnish a cautionary sum to ensure that, in the case of libel, injured parties would be compensated.[82] Thiébault's readers may have wondered how "the weak," whom his free-press regime was supposed to empower, might afford this. In any case, such concerns are entirely absent from Malesherbes's tract.

Unlike Malesherbes, Thiébault recommended maintaining censorship of newspapers and almanacs. Newspaper licensing, he insisted, was to be obligatory and the number of licenses limited. Why? He followed a tortuous path in arriving at this conclusion. At first, he considered putting newspapers under the same kind of voluntary censorship as books. But he believed that the celerity with which newspapers circulated and the immediacy of their widespread impact rendered them more bound up with the public interest than books.[83] (It should be noted that such rationales inspired regulations on radio and television in the twentieth century.) Thiébault was also concerned about the financial interests of subscribers who might lose substantial sums should a newspaper operating without a *privilège* be shut down.[84] As for almanacs, Thiébault considered their information too important to leave to the open market. He believed that errors could have grave consequences for an agricultural society highly dependent on this information.[85]

Malesherbes did not treat the issue of newspapers. In fact, he ignored or glossed over many of the implications of press freedom that Thiébault took seriously. The most significant problem Malesherbes overlooked was how press offenses against the public were to be handled, particularly threats to public order, religion, *bonnes mœurs*, or principles of government. While he recognized that such abuses could exist and should be dealt with, he offered no criteria for assessing them and no guidelines for bringing "bad" authors and printers to justice. Malesherbes's tolerant, liberal tone was achieved by simply skirting thorny issues.

Thiébault gave abuses of press freedom deliberate consideration. He proposed establishing a bureau of censors, not at all related to the censors who issued approbations for books. These censors would form an academy independent of the government. They would comb newspapers for announcements of new books not approved by the royal censors. Embodying public opinion, the censors would read these books, informing the administration about dangerous ones so that advertisements could be suppressed.[86] At this stage, the work could still be circulated. If the censors determined that the work in question was extremely dangerous, the Public Minister would intervene. The Minister could stop the circulation of an allegedly dangerous book only for a short time and would have to bring the affair before a court. If the court did not adjudicate within a specified period, the book would be permitted to circulate.[87]

With what criteria were the Public Minister and the courts supposed to assess a denounced book? And if it were determined to be seditious or calumnious, what punishment was to be be imposed? After raising these questions, Thiébault modestly admitted that he did not have answers. For calumny against individuals, he saw little difficulty in calculating punishment; like Condorcet, he thought that it should be in proportion to the risks and/or suffering to which the victim had been exposed.[88] But for crimes against society, the risks and injury were difficult to measure. Like Condorcet, Thiébault believed that the degree to which a bad book was criminal depended, at least in part, on the circumstances in which it appeared.[89] He urged enlightened citizens to give these matters further reflection in order "to give us the penalty which we lack and which alone can thwart arbitrary judgments."[90]

Of all his concerns, Thiébault worried most about the unchecked power of the parlements. Like Malesherbes, he feared that repression would be far more arbitrary if left solely to the discretion of the sovereign courts, which held both legislative and judicial powers. Voluntary censorship run by the royal administration, he believed, would serve as a check on the parlements. Summing up the options to his readers, Thiébault asked, "Do you prefer the power that prevents wrongdoing or the power that punishes it?"[91]

The Revolutionary Position: Brissot and the Exception to the Separation-of-Powers Principle (1789)

At least one revolutionary journalist responding to Thiébault's tract insisted that he preferred punishment. Gabriel Feydel, editor of the newspaper *L'Observateur*, scoffed at Thiébault's arguments. In an issue appearing in August 1789, Feydel wrote, "Don't ever forget that the law must act through punishments, and not through prohibitions."[92] A week later, he criticized Thiébault's tract. "In vain M. Thiébault objects that the freedom of the press might have drawbacks."[93] He continued, "We respond to M. Thiébault that prohibition is the arm of despotism, punishment the arm of the law."[94]

Feydel was not alone in extolling the virtues of a legal, ex post facto punitive regime over a regulatory one. In a pamphlet appearing in June 1789 shortly before the third estate declared itself to be the National Assembly, Jacques-Pierre Brissot de Warville demanded the abrogation of all Book Trade regulations. Still fuming over the *arrêt du Conseil* of May 6–7, which shut down his newspaper, Brissot urged the Estates-General to declare press freedom, pass new press laws, and establish a new court to try censors for having violated this freedom. He conceded that press abuses needed to be dealt with but insisted that preventative censorship had no legitimate role. "It is necessary to prevent licentiousness, libels, etc....[This is] a valid principle, for which the application of censorship is wrong....Without doubt, it is necessary to prevent offenses, but [this should be done] through laws and not through arbitrary regulations."[95]

What laws? Brissot was vague on this point, admitting that "it is difficult to reconcile [press] freedom with the desire to punish calumniators."[96] Indeed, a press regime based entirely on law raised several complicated issues: "To what degree should the public have the right to censure its representatives and executive power? When does censure amount to libel? These questions pose great difficulties, and I dare to say that they have not been sufficiently discussed in any Constitution, not even in England."[97] Brissot encouraged the Estates-General to take time to reflect carefully before passing the appropriate legislation. In the meantime, he proposed a temporary, working definition. To "outrage" or "calumniate" a member of the Estates-General, according to Brissot, involved attributing to that member speech, opinions, or actions that would "dishonor" him before the Assembly.[98] Thus, just as during the Old Regime, honor and hierarchy mattered more than truth.

Brissot urged deputies to pass a temporary law authorizing the Estates-General to censure and imprison those found guilty of libel against deputies, "for to insult [them] is to insult the Nation itself."[99] If a deputy were to write such a libel, he was to be expelled from the Estates-General. Given Brissot's enthusiasm for Anglo-American constitutionalism with its separation of legislative and judicial powers, explaining how legislators could justly adjudicate affairs of honor involving themselves required creative argumentation. He conceded that the Estates-General could not preside over *all* criminal affairs without falling into despotism.[100] However, allowing them to adjudicate affairs involving political libel would give them absolute authority over just one small part of the law. And in any case, as he assured his readers, such cases were rare in the United States and Britain.[101] To this rather weak argument, he added that the Estates-General's jurisdiction over such affairs was justified because of their supremacy over all other institutions. He warned that if rival institutions had this jurisdiction, they would try to undermine the Estates-General by letting *libellistes* off the hook.[102]

Brissot's proposal was clearly designed to advance the cause of the Estates-General, which, at the time of publication, was being dominated by the third estate. Abolishing censorship would loosen the monarchy's already tenuous grip on publicity; giving the Estates-General exclusive jurisdiction over political libels would neutralize the parlements; and with provisional laws maintained at the discretion of the Estates-General (soon to become the National Assembly), why hurry to define speech offenses? As it turned out, legal limits would not be defined until summer 1791.

Ultimately, then, all political camps but the Church had reasons for demanding press freedom in 1789. (And as we shall see, even much of the clergy supported it.) Yet, all camps also had reasons to keep the authority to enforce limits within their own sphere of control. Indeed, the stakes were too great and the influence of publicity too strong to leave the setting and enforcing of limits to adversaries. In the short term, it appears that Brissot's views prevailed. The National Assembly successfully navigated between the Scylla of censorship and the Charybdis of the courts, emerging as the sole legitimate authority to determine limits on press freedom, even if it did not get around to defining them for two years. Meanwhile, old and new authorities would police political expression on their own initiative. And as this chapter and the previous ones have shown, the Old Regime and the Enlightenment bequeathed practices and principles to guide them in doing so.

CHAPTER FOUR

From the Cahiers de doléances
to the Declaration of Rights

Individual freedom of thought must remain in accordance with the morality and
manners of a people.

—*Réponse aux instructions envoyées par S. A. S. monseigneur le duc d'Orléans, à ses chargés de
procuration dans ses bailliages, relativement aux États-généraux,* 1789

Press Freedom on the Eve of the Revolution

The turbulent conditions that Condorcet believed would justify restricting press
freedom in his 1776 *Fragments sur la liberté de la presse* were precisely those reigning in
France when this freedom was declared. Futile assemblies of intractable notables,
an unbridled speculation war accompanied by a vicious libel war, pitiless calumny
campaigns directed by and against ministers, the impending bankruptcy of the
monarchy, and highly contested judicial reforms were rocking the Old Regime at
its foundations, paralyzing government and sparking popular violence.[1] Yet, amid
the storm, calls for press freedom were made across the political spectrum, from
the crown, clergy, and parlements to the most progressive elements of the nobility and third estate. Indeed, desire for this freedom was so widespread in 1789
that it is difficult to find signs of outright opposition to the principle.

But the devil was in the details. Demands for press freedom were often accompanied by demands for regulations and restrictions on it. We have seen that most
philosophes and progressive royal administrators during the Old Regime were
rarely naive in conceptualizing this freedom. Whether they saw it as a means for
spreading enlightenment or regarded it as a pragmatic solution to an unstop-
pable clandestine print market, they nearly always envisaged limits. But what did
communities throughout France think about press freedom on the eve of the

meeting of the Estates-General, especially now that the monarchy had requested their opinion on the matter?[2] How did local views trickle upward, if at all, in the series of meetings that began with local parish assemblies, corporations, and town councils, continued with primary assemblies where the general cahiers de doléances were drafted, and culminated in the National Assembly, which promulgated the Declaration of the Rights of Man and of the Citizen in August 1789? Finally, what do the presence of limits on press freedom in the cahiers and their absence in the Declaration of Rights suggest about the problems revolutionaries later encountered in implementing this freedom?

The Cahiers de doléances

In *The Old Regime and the French Revolution*, Alexis de Tocqueville expressed astonishment at having discovered in the cahiers de doléances a general desire to bring down the Old Regime. "I realized with something like consternation that what was being asked for was nothing short of the systematic, simultaneous abolition of all existing French laws and customs."[3] Tocqueville added that the drafters should have recalled the old dictum "Claim too great freedom, too much license, and too great subjection shall befall you!"[4] However fitting this adage may have been for other demands, it was not warranted for free-press demands. Abuses of this freedom were precisely what a good many authors of cahiers sought to have punished, and they envisioned the reinforcement of Old Regime laws to do so.

Take, for example, the cahier drafted by the clergy of Villefranche-de-Rouergue. It called for "la liberté indéfinie de la presse" as a means to spread and advance enlightenment. Yet it also demanded that the names of publishers and authors appear on publications so that they could be held liable for works violating "the dominant religion, the general order, public decency, and citizens' honor."[5] The nobles of Lille also expressed themselves in this forward- and backward-looking manner, calling for "the indefinite freedom of the press" by the "suppression of censorship," followed by the requirement that the names of authors and printers appear on works so that they could be punished for statements contrary to "religion, the general order of things, public decency, and the honor of citizens." They also demanded corporal punishment for distributors of foreign works containing reprehensible content.[6] The third estate of Châtillon-sur-Seine touted the enlightened benefits of a free press but then coupled the demand for it with a call for the courts to punish writers and printers for publications contrary to "religion, mœurs, and the Constitution of the state."[7]

Although historians have noted the great frequency of demands for a free press—indeed, such demands figure in over 80 percent of the general cahiers—they have tended to ignore the widespread desire for limits.[8] Yet, not only did the vast majority of cahiers express desire for limits, the limits that were specified came straight from Old Regime press laws, the very laws historians often cite as proof of the lack of press freedom before 1789. The Book Trade Code of 1723, for example, threatened to punish "according to the rigor of ordinances" anyone involved in the production and distribution of "libels against religion, the service of the King, the good of the state, the purity of mœurs, and the honor and reputation of families and individuals."[9] The excessively repressive ordinance of 1757 imposed capital punishment on anyone involved in writing or distributing works that "attack religion, agitate spirits, undermine our authority, or disturb the order and tranquility of our states."[10] Restrictions on published statements attacking religion, mœurs, honor, the general order, and state authority—though absent from most of the pamphlet literature dealing with press freedom in spring 1789—appeared frequently in the cahiers.

Desire for regulations and restrictions on press freedom is expressed in 89 percent of the general cahiers that mention the press. I consulted the available 531 general cahiers of the three orders: the clergy (165 cahiers), the nobles (165), and the third estate (201).[11] General cahiers refer to those drafted by primary assemblies at the bailliage level.[12] These assemblies also elected representatives who were responsible for carrying the general cahier to the meeting of the Estates-General in Versailles in May 1789. I also consulted the initial, lower-level (or local) cahiers of four densely populated areas: Paris, Rouen, Marseilles, and Aix-en-Provence.[13] These local cahiers were drafted by corporations and parishes of the third estate (by *bailliages secondaires* in the case of Aix-en-Provence) and handed to representatives who subsequently convened in primary assemblies. What follows is a content analysis of the general cahiers of the three orders drafted by primary assemblies at the bailliage level and the preliminary, local cahiers of several cities or densely populated bailliages. In addition to calculating the frequency of demands for press freedom, I classified and counted demands for regulations and restrictions. Often, regulations and content restrictions were specified. In some cases, however, the cahiers expressed desire for them but deferred the task of determining them to the Estates-General, the king, or both. (See table 4.1 and figure 4.1.)

Although the question of limits on press freedom has not been overlooked by all historians of the cahiers de doléances, it has tended to be treated in passing or impressionistically.[14] In her *Le régime de la presse pendant la Révolution* (1901), Alma Söderhjelm offered the most thorough discussion of limits to date.[15] She read much

Table 4.1 Frequency of Demands concerning the Press

	Total	%	Clergy	%	Nobles	%	Third	%
Available cahiers	531		165		165		201	
Press mentioned	427	80.5%	128	77.5%	139	84.2%	160	79.6%

into the differences in tone among the three orders' demands. She saw the third estate out in front with the most radically formulated demands, the nobles following closely behind but trailing in enthusiasm, and the clergy divided on the matter. To illustrate the boldness of the third estate, she underlined the appearance in several of their cahiers of demands for "unlimited freedom of the press" (*liberté illimitée de la presse*), claiming that this phrase appears more frequently in the bourgeois cahiers than in those of the nobility (which is not true).[16] Söderhjelm seems to have conflated *unlimited* with other superlative qualifiers such as *absolute* and *indefinite* since *unlimited* appears in only four documents.[17] Moreover, whereas she construed *unlimited* to mean the absence of all restrictions and regulations, the nobles and third estate used all these superlative qualifiers—*unlimited, indefinite,* and *absolute*—in a temporal sense. This explains her puzzlement as to why such demands (appearing in 61

FIGURE 4.1 Kinds of free press demands

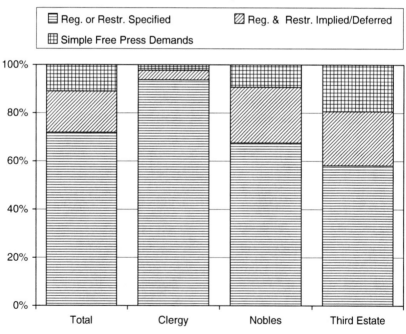

cahiers, by my count) frequently specified regulations and restrictions (appearing in 37 of the 61).[18] She attributed this (apparent) contradiction to contemporaries' inexperience with the concept: "People before the Revolution did not yet have a precise notion of what unlimited freedom of the press meant."[19] That may have been true, but they did have meanings that made sense to them, and a temporal interpretation of these qualifiers makes these demands intelligible. Given the monarchy's provisional suspension of censorship in July 1788 for the sake of the upcoming meeting of the Estates-General, these qualifiers expressed a desire to prolong this suspension indefinitely. One can surmise this interpretation from the cahier by the nobles of Vitry-le-François, who called for "the most severe punishments against violators of the restrictions which must be legally applied to the *indefinite* freedom of the press."[20] Similarly, the nobles of Châlon-sur-Saône called for "the establishment of press freedom, indefinitely through the abolition of censorship, on the condition nevertheless that printers put their names on the works they publish and are held responsible, alone or with the author, for anything contrary to the dominant religion, the general order, public honor, and the honor of all citizens."[21]

Many cahiers expressed an awareness that press freedom already existed and that the issue at hand was how to restrict and regulate it.[22] The nobles of Châtillon-sur-Seine, for example, called for the abolition of all laws concerning censorship in their cahier. They observed, "This law, which is as pointless as it is impracticable, has consequently become entirely obsolete."[23] The clergy of Clermont-Ferrand asked the king to renew old regulations governing the press, "rather than legally authorize press freedom, which, in fact, already exists all too much and is degenerating into license."[24] Likewise, the clergy of Dôle seemed to view this freedom as a sad reality when it requested that "the police watch over the freedom of the press with more circumspection."[25]

Of the three orders, the clergy was, as Söderhjelm noted, least enthused about press freedom (see table 4.2). They railed against the "prodigious quantities of scandalous works, the unfortunate fruit of a love of independence."[26] They bemoaned the underground market of "perverse" works, convinced that it was "altering all religious and political principles" and "delivering fatal blows to faith and mœurs."[27] Some complained that bad books were "poisoning" the countryside, "corrupting morals, spreading discord within families, provoking tensions between the different estates, and causing divorces to multiply."[28]

Yet for all the clergy's alarm about press freedom, only 17 of their cahiers explicitly opposed it (see table 4.2). Twenty-six clerical cahiers, in fact, demanded it, sometimes singing its praises.[29] Only 8 clerical cahiers, along with 1 noble cahier and 1 by the third estate, insisted on censorship.[30] Even in these cases, they

Table 4.2 Dispositions toward Press Freedom

	Total	%	Clergy	%	Nobles	%	Third	%
Press mentioned	427	100%	128	100%	139	100%	160	100%
Free press mentioned								
Yes	368	86.2%	69	53.9%	139	100.0%	160	100.0%
No	59	13.8%	59	46.1%	0	0.0%	0	0.0%
Free press supported								
Yes	319	86.7%	26	37.7%	134	96.4%	159	99.4%
Ambivalence	32	8.7%	26	37.7%	5	3.6%	1	0.6%
No	17	4.6%	17	24.6%	0	0.0%	0	0.0%
Censorship demanded	10	2.3%	8	6.3%	1	0.7%	1	0.6%

Percentages in the top half are based on the number of cahiers mentioning the press. Percentages in the bottom half are based on the number of cahiers mentioning the freedom of the press.

envisaged significant reforms. For example, the clergy in Amiens called for the establishment of a committee of three censors composed of an honest magistrate, an incorruptible man of letters, and a rigorous theologian. The clergy of Le Mantes pressed for postpublication censorship by Church officials, demanding that they be authorized to conduct random inspections of print shops and that they be in charge of reading all new publications, denouncing bad ones to the Public Ministry, which would be responsible for bringing the affair before the courts. In the only third-estate cahier calling for censorship, the bourgeoisie of Libourne supposed that the Provincial Estates would assume the responsibility of authorizing publications. Only three of the ten general cahiers that called for censorship did not propose significant changes to the old system.[31] This is an eloquent indication that for prerevolutionaries, Old Regime censorship was dead.

Among the 427 general cahiers mentioning the press, there are two that, despite their exceptional length, exemplify the way Enlightenment optimism about press freedom could be combined with demands for regulations and restrictions. These cahiers give extended articulation, I believe, to widespread notions about legitimate limits. None went further than the nobles of Châtillon-sur-Seine. They began their cahier praising the press for having spread a spirit of critical reflection and enlightened ideas about justice.[32] They underlined how the press helped inform and guide administrators in carrying out their duties but believed that censorship discouraged many individuals with useful knowledge from publishing it. Administrators, they argued, often received this information only when it became imperative to obtain it, if at all. By definitively abolishing prepublication censorship and facilitating the flow of information, press freedom, these nobles insisted, would improve the functioning of government.

The nobles of Châtillon-sur-Seine then outlined regulations and restrictions. They recommended that writers register their manuscripts with royal notaries in the districts where they intended to have their works published (an idea that appears in three other noble cahiers as well).[33] The printers of registered works were not to be held responsible for criminal content. (This also appears in several other cahiers.) The author alone was to bear responsibility, a measure that would have satisfied not only Voltaire, who believed that authors should be free to have their works published at their own profit and risk, but Malesherbes as well, as we have seen. If, however, the printer chose to publish an unregistered work, he and the author would be held jointly responsible. Finally, after the printing of the manuscript, the author and printer were to sign a declaration asserting that the printed version conformed to the original manuscript.

These were already elaborate regulations. But there was more. The nobles of Châtillon-sur-Seine insisted that any writer found to have insulted religion, the law, the king, or the nation or whose works provoked divisions among the people was to be punished according to "the rigor of laws which already exist or that the Estates-General chooses to modify or create." Thus, this cahier not only called for maintaining the harsh jurisprudence for injurious speech; it authorized the Estates-General to make it harsher if they so desired.

The cahier of the third estate of Vézelise also combined Enlightenment optimism with Old Regime restrictions, though with less stress put on punishment. They asserted that press freedom was necessary for a people to be truly free.[34] The interests of the king and the people, they believed, would be advanced by the truth that a free press would bring to light. After several lofty paragraphs about the virtues of press freedom, the authors began slinging mud at the king's ministers, declaring that truth is only disadvantageous to such men who amass personal fortunes on the ruins of the state. Man's dignity, they insisted, requires that he be free to act against ministerial corruption.[35] After lambasting ministers, the bourgeoisie of Vézelise turned their attention to libels. They called for "the erection of barriers against this torrent of scandalous writings that cultivates a taste for libertinage…leading men away from their responsibilities as citizens." In this, they sounded much like the clergy. They also sounded like the many midcentury philosophes who believed that good mœurs were the sine qua non of stable, flourishing societies. Once mœurs were corrupted, so they believed, only state force could prevent society from sliding into anarchy.[36]

All this appeared in the preamble to concrete demands, the first of which was quite typical: "the freedom of the press, except for libels and obscenities that will be dealt with by the law." Subsequent articles, however, departed from cahier norms in proposing the establishment of provincial committees in charge of monitoring all books concerning mœurs, history, philosophy, ethics, and fiction. The authors of good books were to be rewarded; those of bad ones were to be declared "bad citizens." The proposal clearly smacks of censorship, but not of the prepublication kind. It chimed with Thiébault's recommendations, as well as with the civil censorship described by Montesquieu and Rousseau. Unlike the nobles of Châtillon-sur-Seine, though, the bourgeoisie of Vézelise called for gentle punishment for press abuses. In the spirit of Rousseau's *Lettre à d'Alembert*, they called for bad authors to be publicly humiliated rather than banished, imprisoned, or executed.

Most cahiers, however, did not envisage mitigated punishment for criminal expression. To the contrary, many insisted on harsh sentences. Explicit punitive language can be found in sixty-six cahiers (15.5 percent of those mentioning the press), slightly more than the number of cahiers containing enlightened arguments about the benefits of a free press (11 percent).[37] The third estate of Orléans, for example, urged the Estates-General to fix "a solemn law prohibiting, with the most rigorous of punishments, writings attacking religion, mœurs, the respect due to the sacred person of the King and the honor of citizens."[38] With the reticence characteristic of a good many clerical cahiers, the clergy of Nancy urged that, if the Estates-General decide that press freedom is a measure necessary for political liberty, they should nevertheless "take severe precautions to prevent abuses by imposing grave punishments."[39] Especially harsh, the third estate of Monteuil-sur-Mer and the nobility of Lille demanded corporal punishment for offenses.[40] Most cahiers, though, were vague about punishment, calling simply for "due punishment."

What abuses were the authors of the cahiers most concerned about? Mœurs figured most frequently among all three orders (see figure 4.2). Among the clerical cahiers, mœurs was mentioned even more often than religion! Religion, though, was the second most frequently stated concern for the clergy and third estate, although it ranked third among the nobles, who expressed more concern about attacks on individual honor. Such attacks ranked third on the list of limits demanded by the third estate. In contrast, the clerical cahiers hardly mentioned honor at all. After mœurs and religion, the clergy's most frequently cited concern was libels against the government and the constitution—or, more generally, political authority. This concern appeared in roughly 40 percent of their cahiers that discussed the press. Political authority was much less frequently mentioned by the nobility (8 percent) and the third estate (11 percent). This suggests that the latter two orders viewed press freedom as a vehicle for challenging traditional institutions of authority. (See table 4.3 and figure 4.2 for the relative frequencies of cited restrictions for each order.)

The only novel restrictions appearing in the cahiers were "the rights of other individuals" (*les droits d'autrui*), which appeared in three cahiers, one from each estate, and "respect for the nation," also found in three cahiers, one by the nobles and two by the third estate.[41] All but two of these six cahiers combined these categories with Old Regime restrictions. Of the two cahiers that contain only these new content restrictions, one was written by Condorcet and is frequently cited in studies of the cahiers.[42] Clearly, though, it was not representative of the spirit of the general cahiers.

The reason historians have so often overlooked the widespread desire for limits on press freedom on the eve of the Revolution may have to do with the fact that such limits hardly appear in the cahiers they most often cite, namely, those of the third estate of the most densely populated bailliages in France: Paris, Marseille,

Table 4.3 Regulations and Content Restrictions

	Total	Total %	Clergy	%	Nobles	%	Third	%
Mœurs	202	47.3%	111	86.7%	42	30.2%	49	30.6%
Religion	175	41.0%	104	81.3%	37	26.6%	32	20.0%
Political authority	82	19.2%	53	41.4%	11	7.9%	18	11.3%
Individual honor	78	18.3%	10	7.8%	38	27.3%	30	18.8%
General order	55	12.9%	16	12.5%	25	18.0%	14	8.8%
New restrictions	6	1.4%	1	0.8%	2	1.4%	3	1.9%
Total specified restrictions	236	55.3%	117	91.4%	58	41.7%	61	38.1%
Restrictions implied/deferred	80	18.7%	5	3.9%	35	25.2%	40	25.0%
Total restrictions specified, implied, or deferred	316	74.0%	122	95.3%	93	66.9%	101	63.1%
Total regulations specified, implied, or deferred (names of authors/printers, registration of publication, inspection of works, etc.)	380	89.0%	125	97.7%	126	90.6%	129	80.6%

Percentages are based on the number of cahiers mentioning the press for each order.

FIGURE 4.2 Proportions of Restrictions in Demands for Press Freedom

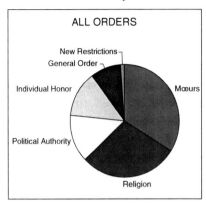
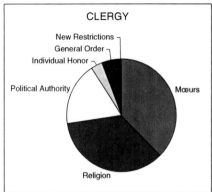
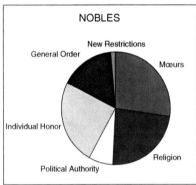
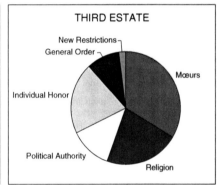

Rouen, Lyon (*ville*), Bordeaux, and Aix-en-Provence. One might suppose that, given the prominence of the press in these areas, the public had become inured to abuses and did not worry about them. Close inspection of the preliminary cahiers drafted at the level of parishes and corporations in these cities, however, suggests otherwise.

Consider Rouen. The fifth largest in France, the city had a particularly active bourgeoisie in the spring of 1789.[43] Of the sixty-two corporations that drafted cahiers, only twelve demanded a free press, five of which came from the legal professions.[44] Formulations ranged from straightforward (the *procureurs au parlement* requested simply "the freedom of the press") to cautious (the *notaires* added restrictions to protect citizens' honor and public order). Five of the twenty-eight artisans' guilds (watchmakers, grocers, stockings fabricants, small-wares makers, and mirror makers) demanded press freedom. Surprisingly, their demands were often more elaborate than those made by the legal corporations. For example, none of the legal corporations came close to phrasing a demand as developed as the one by the watchmakers' guild.

The burdens placed on printers make us dependent on foreign works. The sums of money...sacrificed to procure forbidden books would be better spent reward- ing acts of virtue or encouraging manufacturing....[Our] mœurs gain nothing from the more or less spectacular prohibition [of books]. The nation is gratu- itously deprived of the enlightenment that press freedom would spread concern- ing aspects of administration and notably, concerning the virtues of each of its members in whom this enlightenment has been entrusted.[45]

For their part, the stocking fabricants adopted a more punitive tone, calling for rigorous prosecution of writers, printers, and distributors who abused press free- dom. They also proposed ecclesiastical censorship of texts concerning religion.[46]

Among the parishes on the outskirts of Rouen, free-press demands were made far less frequently, appearing in 4 of 153 cahiers. Yet, these cahiers express more originality and frankness than those drafted by higher assemblies. The small farming village of Duclair outside Rouen wrote, "We're no longer worried about the freedom of the press; abuses exist, of course, but prohibitions have done nothing to stop bad books anyway, and they've done much to stop good ones."[47] The other three cahiers were explicit about restrictions, especially on works threatening public order. The cahier of Saint Paul, which had only 271 inhabit- ants, called for press freedom but warned that it might be imprudent to grant it without restrictions; its authors underscored the current climate as proof: "The effervescence of the present revolution attests to the dangers [of unrestrained libels]."[48] In the spring of 1789, then, peasants saw themselves already swept up in the excesses of a revolution! This cahier also confirms what the clergy bemoaned—the spread of "philosophie" into the countryside.

How were all of these formulations synthesized in the general cahier of Rouen? Both the city of Rouen (which was accorded exceptional general-cahier status) and the bailliage proclaimed, "The freedom to communicate ideas is an essen- tial aspect of personal freedom....All citizens are permitted to have their works printed without having to submit to censorship...excepting the qualifications and modifications that the Estates-General chose to impose."[49] Thus, the con- crete regulations and restrictions that were specified in the cahiers drafted at lower levels were omitted and the task of defining them left to the Estates-General.

Limits on press freedom were also omitted from the general cahier of Marseilles. Eight of fifty-one corporations in that city demanded press freedom with great diversity in tone and specified restrictions. Yet, the general cahier demanded "the freedom of the press, except for restrictions that the Estates-General might impose."[50] In Paris, free-press demands were made in many district cahiers.[51] Again, formulations range widely, from tepid assent to bold insistence. In a curious and radical departure from cahier norms, the district of Théatins claimed that press freedom would be jeopardized if printers were held responsible for content and authors were required to declare their names. The district assured that there were "already enough means to track down and punish the authors of libels."[52] In any case, like the general cahiers of Rouen and Marseilles, specific restrictions were left out of the general cahier of Paris (*intro muros*), which insisted only on holding authors and printers responsible "for the consequences of their writings."[53] The general cahiers of Bordeaux, Lyon (*ville*), and Nantes also avoided specifying regulations and restrictions in their demands for press freedom.[54]

It appears, then, that in densely populated places where demands went through a succession of assembly debates before being inscribed in a final general cahier, limits were omitted. Why? One might suppose that the plethora of published pamphlets at the time—notably, the many instructions, memoranda, and model cahiers—had influenced the primary assemblies of densely populated areas. These pamphlets rarely mentioned limits in demanding press freedom, and even when they did, their authors (mostly noble) were concerned about protecting honor more often than religion or mœurs. Writers in the spring of 1789 knew that a world was opening up in which they might exert political influence. They therefore had little interest in limits. Why insist on restrictions that might be turned against oneself?

This is precisely what happened to Alexandre de Lauzières de Thémines, Bishop of Blois. In calling for limits on press freedom, he put himself in the predicament that most writers avoided. His model cahier, *Instructions et cahier du hameau du Madon*, dealt with, among other issues, fiscal reforms. It was above all a scathing indictment of the Calonne ministry. Thémines took this occasion to outline his views on press freedom. He stated that the freedom to think should not be confused with the freedom to publish. "If each individual is master of his own opinion, this does not put him in charge of public instruction and policing." He offered an analogy:

> Imagine if a foreigner came to France to find as many philosophical systems, religions, and political agendas as there are people; if he found everywhere—even on the stairs of the palace of Versailles—the brochures and libels of the day; if he went to the location where a great number of people are [regularly] defamed under the noble pretext of patriotism; one would call the universe into question.... Property, life, and the honor of citizens should be under the protection of the law...in all well-administered [*policées*] nations there must be respected regulations of which the first article should be to punish all clandestine works.[55]

Thémines proposed establishing a system of surveillance within the Public Ministry office, not unlike the systems proposed by Rousseau and Thiébault.

This *aréopage*, or learned assembly, would keep an eye on publications and alert the minister to dangerous works so that judicial action might be taken. Slandered individuals would not have to suffer financial ruin from legal fees since the Public Minister would pursue affairs involving defamation.

Yet, defamation is precisely what Calonne, the disgraced former minister of Louis XVI, accused Thémines of spreading. In his published response, Calonne turned the Bishop of Blois's principles against him:

> You should be judged, Monsieur, by your own maxims. What would you say before the *aréopage* you insist on establishing to punish the authors of defamatory pamphlets? How would you respond to the Public Minister whose task, you propose, would be to avenge the honor of citizens?[56]

Most writers were more prudent than Thémines. They remained vague about limits on press freedom. With tensions so high and power not yet secured (the Bishop may have assumed he still had unquestioned authority), it was not wise to insist on regulations and restrictions.

Does the marked absence of demands for limits on press freedom in most of the pamphlet literature explain the marked absence of such demands in the general cahiers from densely populated urban areas? It is difficult to tell, but in reading hundreds of cahiers and nearly four dozen pamphlets deemed to have been influential in the spring of 1789, I have occasionally discovered strong textual similarities that suggest that the authors of the cahiers living in bailliages far from each other were inspired by the same pamphlets. For example, the nobles of Armagnac in the southwest, the nobles of Poitiers in the center-west, and those of Châlons-sur-Saône in the Burgundian center, together with the third estates of Metz in the northeast and Villers-Cotterets just east of Paris, all used the same syntax and lexicon to demand "the indefinite freedom of the press, absolute by the abolition of censorship."[57] (It is rare to find the abolition of censorship mentioned explicitly in the cahiers.) They all required the name of the printer on works and held the printer and author jointly responsible for content, and four of the five mentioned specified content restrictions using the same lexicon and sequence, desiring the repression of writings attacking "the dominant religion, the general order, public decency, and the honor of citizens." ("The dominant religion" and "the general order" were commonly mentioned restrictions in the cahiers but usually formulated differently.)

For all their textual similarities, subtle differences among these cahiers suggest that, even if the authors of these cahiers borrowed from the same pamphlet, they did so selectively. Of the five similar cahiers mentioned above, the one from Poitiers added two restrictions not found in the others: on writings that undermined "the constitution and the laws of the realm" and "respect for the king." Moreover, one cahier asserted that press freedom was rooted in individual liberty, a claim found in the instructions circulated in the name of the duc d'Orléans, but not in the other four cahiers of the group.[58] I also discovered lexical similarities between a widely circulated pamphlet and the cahier by the clergy of Autun. Both requested press freedom for discussions concerning administration, "because the affairs of the state are the affairs of each person."[59] A notable difference, though, is that unlike the pamphlet, the cahier added restrictions: "except for attacks on religion, mœurs, and the rights of others."

Clearly, then, the authors of most general cahiers did not allow themselves to be swept up by the more liberal formulations of press freedom found in the pamphlet literature. They wanted and expected limits. But why, then, did the general cahiers of densely populated bailliages such as Rouen, Paris, Marseilles, and others refrain from specifying limits? It is impossible to know for certain, but if what occurred in the National Assembly that summer during debates on the Declaration of the Rights of Man and of the Citizen sheds any light on the matter, the reason may have had to do with the inability of deputies in primary assemblies, particularly large ones, to agree on what limits should be implemented. The greater the political stakes and the greater the number of deputies assembled, the less likely it was that consensus on limiting press freedom would be reached.

The Declaration of Rights

Between May and August 1789, the freedom of the press went from being an item on the agenda for reforming the administration to becoming an inalienable and universal right of the citizen. Seeking to bolster its own legitimacy and determine the guiding principles for a new constitution, the National Assembly decided to issue a declaration of rights.[60] Debates on the final wording of Articles 10 and 11 of the Declaration of the Rights of Man and of the Citizen, which dealt with religious freedom and free expression, reveal the difficulty involved in reaching compromise. Rhetorically strident, these articles show that deputies hedged their bets, tempering bold principles with precautionary clauses. These clauses were vague, however, since national deputies could not agree on how to reconcile free speech with the protection of other core values, particularly religion and mœurs.

The ambivalence of deputies on the issue of limiting press freedom in August had been preceded by months of ambivalence on the part of the monarchy. Since the spring, the crown had been giving mixed signals about its tolerance threshold. In April, it renewed all prior laws and ordinances governing the press.[61] A month later, the king's *Conseil d'État* ordered the shutdown of Brissot's and Mirabeau's unauthorized newspapers and increased police surveillance. Still, press freedom remained on the official agenda, and on May 19 the *garde des sceaux*, ceding to public pressure, authorized journalists to cover the meeting of the Estates-General, provided they withheld commentary.[62] On June 23, just days after the Estates-General transformed itself into the National Assembly, deputies reminded the king during his royal session with them that the problem of press freedom still needed to be resolved.[63]

In July and August, the problem became imbricated in the larger issue of a declaration of rights. The first proposed declaration in the National Assembly was made by Gilbert du Motier, marquis de Lafayette, on July 11. Drawing inspiration from certain state constitutions of the United States, Lafayette avoided mentioning restrictions.[64] He asserted that certain rights were inalienable, among them the freedom of opinion and of communication "by any available means."[65] Over the next month and a half, dozens of other proposals streamed into the National Assembly, which set up several committees to review them and to draft model declarations that would be discussed and voted on by the whole Assembly.

How did these proposals envision press freedom? Like the cahiers, they advanced a variety of formulations. Among the 32 proposals assembled by Antoine de Baecque, Wolgang Schmale, and Michel Vovelle, 14 mentioned Old Regime restrictions: 5 invoked religion, 4 mœurs, 7 public order and tranquility, 6 the honor of citizens, and 3 respect for political authority. However, whereas only 3 general cahiers from all over France had mentioned "the rights of other individuals" (*les droits d'autrui*), 16 model declarations did so. Clearly, this marks an important shift in how limits were being conceived; rather than framing them in terms of traditional collective values, such as morality and religion, *les droits d'autrui* suggested a more liberal approach, focusing on the individual. Though novel and clearly modern, the concept of *les droits d'autrui* would not work its way into a declaration of rights until June 1793.[66]

Taken together, specified regulations and restrictions appeared in 21 of the 32 proposals. In addition to these, 6 proposals said nothing about the press, including, ironically, the one proposed by future radical journalist Jean-Paul Marat. Another 3 proposals did allude to limits but deferred defining them to the Constitution.[67] Aside from Lafayette's proposal, there remains an anonymous one that called simply for the author's name to appear on published works.

A noteworthy difference between the cahiers de doléances and declaration proposals was the position of specified limits in the overall document. While many of the rights proposals sounded more stridently liberal than the cahiers in articulating press freedom, restrictions often crept into adjacent articles. For example, Article 13 of Jérôme Pétion de Villeneuve's proposal seems unambiguous: "Each individual may write and publicize his thoughts; one should no more obstruct the development of intellectual faculties than the development of physical faculties." In a prior article, however, he stated that individual freedom could be limited by the law, and indeed, he called for laws to repress religious opinions that disturbed "public tranquility."[68] Étienne-François Sallé de Choux (who, like Pétion, would eventually sit on the left in the National Assembly), in his proposed article on press freedom, invoked only *les droits d'autrui*. However, in an earlier article, he called for the law to specify duties as well as rights. "Given the clash of passions fueled by particular interests that can disturb society and even overthrow it, laws are necessary to determine the rights and obligations of all members, to put restraints on those who refuse to respect them."[69] He warned about secret transgressions that might elude the law and stressed the need for religion, "which alone can repress such crimes by ruling over hearts." Similarly, under the rubric "the rights of citizens," the future left-wing deputy Arnaud-Raymond Gouges-Cartou called for the freedom of ideas and their communication, the sole restriction being attacks on *les droits d'autrui*. However, in a subsequent article under "the rights of societies," he referred to "secret crimes" on the moral level that only religion and moral instruction could prevent.[70] Although such qualifications do not amount to legal restrictions on speech, they suggest that these deputies expected religious and moral institutions to discipline thoughts and speech as a prior condition to enjoying freedom responsibly.

Two other proposals also viewed religion and mœurs as prior to positive law.[71] Preceding an article declaring the right to communicate and publicize ideas freely for any subject "not proscribed by the law," the future Girondin J. M. A. Servan insisted on the importance of religion in shaping opinion, even as he tried to define religion in broad, confessionally neutral terms.

> Religious laws conform to civil liberty when, in prescribing moral actions beneficial to all, they impose a cult and dogma only to the degree that is necessary to secure the [more universal] principles of morality.... Laws [those prior to positive law], and especially the law of opinion, secure civil liberty when, for actions that positive law does not prescribe, each individual directs his actions toward the public good defined by the law of opinion which chastises through shame and rewards through esteem.[72]

Like many midcentury philosophes concerned with civic morality, Servan thought that religion encouraged people to consider the general good. Alongside religion figured a second source of morality: public opinion. Servan viewed public opinion not just as a well of ideas from which authorities would draw to make policy, but as a moral regulating force as well. His ideas reveal the strains involved in trying to reconcile the preservation of civic mœurs through religion on the one hand and the granting of religious freedom on the other.

On August 4, the day feudal privileges were abolished, the National Assembly voted against a declaration of duties. Whereas before, restrictions on free speech had fallen neatly into the "duties" column of proposals, they were now inserted into articles on the right to freedom of opinion and of expression. On August 19, the comte de Mirabeau presented a draft on behalf of the *comité du cinq*. It called for limits on expression that violated the rights of other individuals.[73] The National Assembly rejected it. According to Marcel Gauchet, deputies criticized the draft for not protecting religion. It did not call for the establishment of a public cult, failed to declare religion the guarantor of mœurs, and did not even acknowledge God as the inspiration for the declaration's principles.[74] Pressed for a new model, deputies chose an obscure one written earlier that month by one of the Assembly's thirty bureaus, the *sixième*. Contrary to the *comité du cinq*'s draft, this one was infused with religion.

Debate on the freedom of opinion and of religious expression began on Saturday, August 22, and quickly became tumultuous.[75] Despite pleas by the National Assembly's president at the start of the session to remain calm, deputies were at each other's throats, and the president threatened twice to step down. By the end of the day, the Assembly had reached no agreement. On the twenty-third, the duc de Castellane presented a more liberal and laconic article than those discussed the day before. He proposed that "no one be disturbed for his religious opinions or bothered in the exercise of his cult."[76] The proposal stirred up a storm of opposition, and the "public order" clause was put back on the table. Mirabeau opposed the clause. He insisted that religious cults should not be policed, even if, he added bitingly, the Roman emperors Nero and Domitian had done so to crush the nascent Christian movement. Mirabeau's sarcastic point was reinforced by the more sober arguments of Jean-Paul Rabaut Saint-Étienne who, speaking on behalf of his many Protestant constituents in Nîmes, called for the absolute freedom to express any religious opinion. But the majority insisted on maintaining the "public order" clause, which clearly implied the maintenance of orthodox religion.[77] Many worried that extending civil equality to Protestants would provoke sectarian strife, observing that the specter of the sixteenth-century Wars of Religion still haunted contemporary imaginations.[78]

By the end of the day on August 23, the National Assembly agreed to declare the freedom of religious opinion but stopped short of approving the freedom of public worship. Article 10 read, "No one should be disturbed for his opinions, even religious ones, provided that their manifestation does not disturb public order as determined by the law."[79] Ultimately, the article did not advance the cause of religious minorities much further than the 1787 edict recognizing Protestant property and marriage rights. Like the edict, the article did not grant full civil status to Protestants or the right to hold administrative offices and teaching positions.[80] Many deputies were dissatisfied with the article, and it was criticized in the press.[81] Still, the final formulation of the article was a good deal more tolerant than the *sixième bureau*'s original proposal. Although the bureau had been quite progressive with regard to press freedom, calling for limits only on violations of *les droits d'autrui*, it had approached religious freedom with less verve, qualifying this freedom in three articles, none of which exuded religious tolerance. The first article insisted on the necessity of religion in order to strike down "secret crimes" occurring in one's moral conscience that might otherwise remain beyond the grip of the law and undermine the "good order" of society. The second declared Catholicism the official national cult. The third protected alternative religious opinions from repression, provided they did not disturb the public order. In the end, the National Assembly approved only the third proposition.

It was clear to religious pluralists, of course, that the "public order" clause was sufficiently vague to be pressed into the service of Catholic hegemony, especially if legislators were to subsequently declare Catholicism the official religion of France.[82] The next day, August 24, a deputy tried to reverse the situation by proposing to replace the *ordre public* clause with *les droits d'autrui*, but modifications to articles already adopted were not permitted. The discussion then turned to Article 11, the freedom of expression. Again, the *sixième bureau*'s proposal served as a starting point for discussion: "The free communication of ideas being a right of the citizen, it must not be restricted in so far as it does not infringe on the rights of others."[83] This qualification—*les droits d'autrui*—which had been rejected the day before by conservative deputies in the article concerning the freedom of religious opinion, now served as the starting point for debate on free expression. It would be rejected again.

The National Assembly reached consensus on the first part of the article, which concerned the freedom to communicate ideas. The latter part, which concerned limits, sparked intense debate. François-Alexandre-Frédéric, duc de la Rochefoucauld-Liancourt proposed altering it, making authors accountable "for the abusive use of this freedom, as prescribed by the law." Rabaut Saint-Étienne warned that the clause was too vague and would lead to inquisitions and censorship. He tried to recover the *droits d'autrui* clause. Another deputy suggested the inclusion of both clauses, but the majority squawked. A few deputies questioned whether restrictions should even be included in a declaration of rights. Robespierre thought that all restrictive limits should be confined to the Constitution.[84] "Abuses pertain only to penal law.... All restrictions, all exceptions to the exercise of rights must be taken up in the Constitution."[85] This suggestion polarized the Assembly further. Mirabeau then intervened and reframed the whole debate. Rather than argue about whether limits should be mentioned in the declaration of rights, he questioned whether they should be treated as restrictions (which, he warned, would lead to new forms of censorship) or, as he preferred, repression, applied after publication in cases of criminal content. Like other progressives at the time, Mirabeau conceived of press freedom as compatible with ex post facto punishment. "We give you a desk to write a calumnious letter, a press for a libel; you must be punished once the crime is committed: it is a matter of repression, not restrictions; it is the crime one punishes, and the freedom of men should not be hampered under the pretext that they might want to commit crimes."[86] The discussion now moved toward consensus. Despite two final attempts to pull the article in conservative and liberal directions, Mirabeau prevailed. The article on free expression passed in the following terms: "The free communication of ideas and opinions is one of the most precious rights of man. Each citizen may therefore speak, write, and print freely, while nevertheless being held accountable for abuses of this freedom in such cases as are determined by the law."[87]

In the end, then, the National Assembly opted to authorize punishment for abusive, criminal speech. But it postponed defining what constituted an abuse. Would abuses be limited to attacks on the rights of other individuals (*les droits d'autrui*)? Or would they encompass attacks on collective moral and religious values, as so many cahiers had insisted and a good number of deputies still wished?

The Primacy of Religion and Mœurs

In his 1788 book, *De l'importance des idées religieuses*, Jacques Necker, a Protestant and Louis XVI's Director General of Finances, defined the aims of legislation: "Wise laws should have two major objectives: maintaining public order and the happiness of individuals; but to achieve them, the aid of religion is absolutely necessary."[88] For Necker, Christianity preceded positive law and was even more important than public opinion, whose authority he had done so much to promote in recent years.[89]

Unlike laws or public opinion, religion, he now argued, had the advantage of being able to "reach into the secrets of our hearts."[90] "By their influence on mœurs," he continued, religious opinions "produce an infinite number of good acts."[91] Necker was not alone in thinking so. As we have seen, this view was common during the eighteenth century, even among many enlightened philosophes.

Similar views, though less confessionally elastic, were propounded by the Bishop of Nancy, Anne-Louis-Henri de La Fare. In his opening sermon at the meeting of the Estates-General on May 4, 1789, La Fare insisted that religion was the basis of happiness and urged that it remain the sacred foundation of the reformed state. (La Fare would head the *sixième bureau* that proposed establishing Catholicism as the exclusive national cult, and he would later become an active counterrevolutionary.) Apparently, La Fare's views were enthusiastically received by the monarchy, clergy, third estate, and newspaper press. (The response of nobles was mixed.)[92] As the preponderant mention of religion and mœurs in demands for press freedom in the cahiers de doléances suggests, the importance Necker and La Fare gave to religion chimed with public sentiment.

In the summer of 1789, conservative and progressive deputies in the National Assembly advanced declaration proposals that included restrictions on free expression to protect religion and the general order. Particularly revealing about the widespread nature of such concerns, three of the four proposals that emphasized the important role of religion in shaping civic values were written by deputies who would later sit on the left (Servan, Gouges-Cartou, and Sallé de Choux; the fourth was anonymous). The belief that religion and mœurs constituted the mutually reinforcing twin pillars of a stable order underwent its first serious challenge in discussions on the Declaration of Rights, just as factions were beginning to form in the National Assembly. The division was discernible in debate over Article 10. Although the supporters of religious orthodoxy failed to get their views inscribed in the Declaration of Rights, the "public order" clauses in Articles 10 and 11 left open the possibility that "public order" would later be defined as a Catholic moral order. Attempts to declare Catholicism the national cult were indeed made over the next year. The defenders of religious freedom worried, not without reason, that Catholic hegemony over public morality would favor the forces seeking to reverse the Revolution. Still, like their adversaries, progressives believed that good mœurs required tutelage. The problem was that they had no alternative moral paradigm to Catholicism and no institution other than the Catholic Church to rely upon.

Thus, a raw nerve in revolutionary politics stretched across religion and mœurs. If Jacobins would later become obsessed with morally regenerating society through new secular principles, it was clear from the outset that many wanted to keep society under the moral sway of the Catholic Church. And there were compelling reasons for keeping it there, especially as privileges were being abolished and feudal documents, not to mention châteaux, were going up in smoke. But what would happen once clerics began using religion to stir up popular opinion against the Revolution over the next two years—against policies that extended citizenship to non-Catholics, deprived the Church of its vast wealth, and blocked the creation of an official national religion? As we shall see, revolutionaries would eventually detach mœurs from religion and seek new secular moorings for them. They would invoke public spirit, the law—even the Revolution itself—as the bases of their new civil religion. Fighting fire with fire, they would spread these values with evangelical fervor, invoking them to justify their efforts to consolidate punitive authority in the state. But as the cahiers de doléances of 1789 suggest, the repression of bad mœurs was already deemed legitimate and necessary by much of French society.

In any case, the war over the sacred underpinnings of the new order would break out later, beginning in the spring of 1790. For now, in August of 1789, revolutionaries managed to reach a compromise on free speech. They abolished what was widely held to be an inefficient and arbitrary, though essentially defunct, press regime. But even as they drove nails into the coffin of prepublication censorship, they tempered their bid for freedom—and ultimately undermined it—calling for the repression of abuses that they failed to define.

Part II

The French Revolution

CHAPTER FIVE

From Lèse-Nation to the Law of Suspects

Legislating Limits

To punish calumny without violating the freedom of the press is the most difficult problem to resolve in politics.

—Jacques Pierre Brissot, *Patriote français*, 1790

The Explosion of Calumny

On October 5, 1789, as hungry Parisians marched to his palace at Versailles, Louis XVI signed the Declaration of the Rights of Man and of the Citizen. Free speech was thus ratified, representing one of the most important achievements of the French Revolution. But deputies in the National Assembly had no time to celebrate. France was seething with calumny, and pressure to work on the fine print of Articles 10 and 11—defining abuses—mounted quickly.

Only days after drafting the Declaration, deputies confronted the kind of political speech that would proliferate in coming months. On August 31, as they deliberated on whether to accord the king absolute veto powers, they received an anonymous letter warning them that "two thousand letters are ready to be sent to inform the provinces about the conduct of their deputies."[1] The letter, *Motion faite au Palais-Royal, pour être envoyée aux différents districts et aux provinces*, was read aloud in the Assembly. Its authors asserted their right to circulate their opinions, citing Article 11, after which they urged voters to immediately "revoke all ignorant, corrupt, and suspect deputies."[2] A subsequent letter from the Palais-Royal, where crowds were preparing to march on Versailles, went further. It counseled deputies against approving the royal veto, warning that "fifteen thousand men are ready to 'enlighten' your châteaux."[3]

Scandalized, the Paris municipal assembly published an *arrêté* the next day condemning these "atrocious calumnies," which sought "to terrorize the National Assembly" and "desecrate the palace of a prince so cherished and honored by the nation."[4] Arrests followed. On September 1, Eugène-Eléonore Gervais, a cook and leader of a movement of workers and domestic servants seeking political enfranchisement, was apprehended by the National Guard in the Palais-Royal for seditious speech. The Châtelet court sentenced Gervais to nine years in the galleys.[5] On September 2, the Assembly of Representatives of the Commune of Paris ordered the arrest of the marquis de Saint-Huruge. A National Guard commander and former prisoner of the Bastille (one nineteenth-century historian described him as "sedition incarnate"), Saint-Huruge was suspected of having penned the letter threatening to circulate the *Motion*.[6] He denied the charge but remained imprisoned for over a month, despite the lack of incriminating evidence.[7] Waves of public indignation rippled through Paris, exacerbating tensions between the districts, the municipal government, the National Guard, and the courts.[8]

Affairs of calumny began piling up. On October 7, the commune persuaded the Châtelet to issue another arrest warrant, this time against radical journalist Jean-Paul Marat, for allegedly slandering a municipal counselor, Étienne-Louis-Hector de Joly. Relying on an unnamed source, Marat accused Joly of mishandling official documents.[9] A week later, news from Brittany reached the National Assembly that Augustin-René-Louis Le Mintier, Bishop of Tréguier, was calumniating the National Assembly, railing against revolutionaries' bad mœurs.[10] In one of its first decrees after moving from Versailles to Paris, deputies charged Le Mintier with lèse-nation and authorized the Châtelet to handle this and all subsequent lèse-nation affairs, many of which involved political expression.

But legal limits on free speech remained undefined, and this silence in the legislation produced a storm of political contention. In the National Assembly, deputies fulminated regularly at the podium, demanding the punishment of calumniators and rakes.[11] They also read from the relentless stream of complaints about speech crimes from the provinces. For their part, writers and journalists who were denounced often took up press freedom as their shield. In doing so, they began expanding the meaning of the principle. Not only did it entail the abolition of prepublication censorship; it now started to encompass the prohibition of ex post facto repression and punishment. This new, quasi-libertarian position was advanced only partially and tactically in clashes over calumny in the first two years of the Revolution. Since most believed that abusive speech should be punished, alleged "calumniators" wavered between demanding tolerance for themselves and punishment for their adversaries. Still, a quasi-libertarian position on free speech started to take shape in this period, eventually coalescing into a coherent, Jacobin position by summer 1791. Jacobins failed, however, to impose their views in the drafting of the Constitution of 1791, which specified speech crimes. As the Revolution radicalized in 1792 and 1793, the quasi-libertarian position collapsed. Its erstwhile defenders, notably Robespierre, began adopting a more demagogic, punitive stance regarding calumny. By the Year II, widespread obsessions with calumny and desire to see calumniators punished found expression in the laws and judicial machinery of the Terror.

Calumny Is Good: The Emergence of a Quasi-Libertarian Position (1789–1791)

Although elements of what would eventually become a quasi-libertarian position on press freedom appeared early in the Revolution, they rarely came together coherently or consistently before 1791. Until then, contemporaries alternated between tolerant and punitive positions, depending on the circumstances.

A closer look at the affairs of Saint-Huruge, Le Mintier, and Marat in the fall of 1789 reveals a great deal of inconsistency on the legitimate limits of free speech. In a pamphlet defending Saint-Huruge, who had been incarcerated for allegedly signing the *Motion faite au Palais-Royal* and drafting the letter menacing deputies' châteaux, the radical journalist Camille Desmoulins argued that imprisonment was unjust for several reasons, none of which involved libertarian principles. He insisted that the Châtelet court, which practiced outdated secret procedures, had no business handling the affair. He believed that Saint-Huruge belonged with the lèse-nation suspects who were being held in the prisons of the Abbaye and Brie-Comte-Robert awaiting the National Assembly's decision on what to do with them.[12] (The Assembly would soon assign temporary jurisdiction over lèse-nation affairs to the Châtelet.) Desmoulins defended the *Motion*, which he himself had signed. As for the letter threatening to burn down deputies' châteaux if they supported the royal veto, Desmoulins's arguments became slippery. He reasoned that either Saint-Huruge had signed the incendiary letter or he had not. If he had not signed it, he could obviously not be held accountable. If he had signed it, he must have thought it was not criminal. His innocent intentions thus exonerated him.[13]

Another of Saint-Huruge's defenders, the sieur "Samoht" (Thomas), also made his case without recourse to libertarian logic. He pleaded for leniency, urging the court to "punish [Saint-Huruge] as a crazy man," not a seditious one.[14] Shifting focus from the incendiary letter toward secret, sinister plots, he warned, "Be careful not to confuse the crazy person who signs his name to a threatening letter with the real villain who keeps his dagger hidden."[15] Even Saint-Huruge, in his own defense, did not invoke the right to free speech. Denying the charges against him, he claimed to share others' indignation. He urged authorities to track down the real authors of the letter and impose a "striking example of punishment" to avenge the honor of the nation and its august Assembly.[16]

The controversy over the Saint-Huruge affair subsided, but the affairs of Le Mintier (Bishop of Tréguier) and Marat in October kept the problem of calumny alive in public debate. In a pastoral letter distributed throughout Brittany, Le Mintier assailed revolutionary achievements, including the freedom of speech and opinion. "Through a deplorable abuse of freedom, [revolutionaries] want all citizens to be allowed to think and write whatever they want."[17] Revolutionaries soon disabused the bishop of this view. Municipal authorities from Tréguier and surrounding villages convened to draft a denunciation of the pastoral letter, which they sent to the National Assembly. They declared the letter to be "the most dangerous writing that has yet appeared...a string of contagious errors concerning morality, politics, and administration...censure at once choleric and calumnious of the nation and its representatives."[18] The National Assembly agreed. After reading a few passages, the deputy Charles-Jean-Marie Alquier asked, "What right do you [the bishop] think you have to slander the august representatives of the nation?"[19] Some deputies defended Le Mintier but failed to convince the majority, which, in a decree a week later, accused him of lèse-nation and sent the affair to the Châtelet.[20]

Even Robespierre, who would later adopt a quasi-libertarian stance, felt that incendiary sermons and pastoral letters were crimes. During debate on whether the National Assembly should judge lèse-nation affairs itself or delegate the task to an independent court, Robespierre insisted, "These crimes can only be judged by the nation, by its representatives...incendiary pastoral letters are published, the provinces are in a state of unrest.... We must listen to the *comité des rapports*, the *comité des recherches* and crush conspiracies [in order to] establish a Constitution worthy of the nation."[21] Elisée Loustalot and Louis-Marie Prudhomme of the patriot newspaper *Révolutions de Paris*, later renowned for advancing a libertarian conception of press freedom, boiled down the Tréguier affair to this: did the pastoral letter constitute a crime of lèse-nation? They had no doubt. "One only has to read it to be convinced of this."[22]

In early 1789 and 1790, few disputed the attribution of lèse-nation for political libel. Yet when the threat of repression loomed over their own heads, journalists and their defenders often invoked Article 11 of the Declaration of Rights. Ignoring its vague qualification concerning abuses of press freedom, they advanced quasi-libertarian arguments. Loustalot, for example, despite his intolerant stance on the Le Mintier affair, offered an apology for calumny that would be further developed in the coming two years. Defending Marat in the Joly affair of October 1789, Loustalot wrote that although he did not have enough information to confirm Marat's accusation,

> for the well-being of individuals and the maintenance of the constitution and freedom there must be an irreconcilable war between writers and executive power; the moment that the judiciary throws itself into the arms of the executive against the press, the equilibrium is broken and the people become slaves; *ministers and administrators are, by right, exposed to calumny,* and this necessary inconvenience is sufficiently offset by their status and power. Virtuous men who hold public functions do not fear calumny; calumny only brings down the corrupt.[23]

This defense of calumny was clearly one-sided. As Loustalot defined it, the good war was the one between writers and royal and local administrations, not between writers and the National Assembly. This distinction helps explain why he condemned Le Mintier's attack on the National Assembly while insisting on Marat's right to accuse a government official, perhaps even wrongly.

Right-wing journalists were also prone to double standards in discussing legitimate limits on press freedom. In late December 1789, the royalist Barnabé Farmian de Rozoi of the *Gazette de Paris* applauded a recent ordinance banning the distribution of libels. The ordinance was passed at a municipal meeting during which a member complained that libels were "insulting mœurs, religion, and the respect all good citizens should have for their sovereign."[24] The actual language of the ordinance shifted attention away from religion and monarchy, condemning the "mass of incendiary and calumnious writings which tend to compromise the honor of citizens and the character of the nation."[25] Among its many restrictions, the ordinance forbade colporteurs from selling unsigned works. In his elation, Rozoi overlooked this clause; he failed to put his name on the *Gazette de Paris* until June 1792.[26] Moreover, for all his outrage about the "calumnious" patriot press—a leitmotif in his newspaper—Rozoi readily invoked the Declaration of Rights when authorities accused him of calumniating. Under fire from authorities in Paris and Brest, Rozoi asserted, "If all municipalities about which we have made some observations denounce us, what will become of this RIGHT TO EXPRESS ONE'S OPINION, EVEN ON RELIGIOUS MATTERS?"[27]

Most writers during the early years of the Revolution did not envisage press freedom without ex post facto punishment for abuses. When they sought to defend themselves or their allies from repression, they rarely advanced libertarian arguments. More often they asserted that limits on press freedom, though necessary in the long run, were impossible to enforce during revolutionary upheaval. The Cordeliers district in Paris made this argument in June of 1790 when they sent a pamphlet to the other districts, encouraging them to join the Cordeliers in protesting the recent arrest of Louis-Marie Stanislas Fréron, journalist of *L'Orateur du peuple*. The Cordeliers wrote, "If, in this moment of inevitable, even *salutary anarchy* the august representatives of the nation have thought it wise to not make a law that the clash of great interests would no doubt subvert anyway, what right do the municipal police have to think they can erect themselves as legislators?"[28]

Writers often accused authorities of arbitrariness. An anonymous pamphlet of 1790, for example, reproached the National Assembly's *comité des recherches* for ordering the arrests of two individuals involved with the reactionary journal *Le Père Duchesne* (not to be confused with the better-known radical journal by the same title). The author juxtaposed incendiary passages excerpted from the radical press (specifically, Fréron's *L'Orateur du peuple* and Marat's *L'Ami du peuple*) with passages from the crass but better reasoned *Le Père Duchesne*. The author insisted that, despite its "buggers," "fuckers," and *sacrediés*, *Le Père Duchesne* inspired "peace, tranquility, and respect for public order," unlike the radical newspapers that urged readers to kill royalists. The author concluded, "To all those who really know what liberty means I denounce both incendiary journalists who go unpunished and the public functionaries who apply double standards, persecuting the innocent and absolving the guilty."[29]

Radical journalists accused authorities of arbitrariness as well. Several inveighed against the decree of July 31, 1790, which, at the behest of the right-wing deputy Pierre-Victor Malouet, ordered the Châtelet to pursue as lèse-nation suspects any writer who incited "the people to revolt against the law, spill blood, and overthrow the Constitution."[30] In citing Desmoulins and Marat, Malouet may have been seeking to get even for the rebuff he received on June 17 when he had tried to prevent the National Assembly from summoning the authors of Catholic libels in the Midi, where sectarian violence had broken out. In any case, the decree of July 31 contained broad enough language to render it applicable to all seditious speech, radical or royalist. Despite this and despite the fact that the Châtelet had nearly as many cases against reactionaries as radicals on its docket, a National Guardsman from Soissons sounded the alarm: "The entire Assembly has become

FIGURE 5.1. Malouet denouncing Camille Desmoulins, July 31, 1790. Courtesy of the Bibliothèque nationale de France, cabinet d'estampes.

Malouet dénonçant C. Desmoulins.

royalist....Beware, all patriot writers, the Châtelet holds you in its prisons and will soon butcher you!"[31] Although the decree cited only Marat and Desmoulins as examples—and for passages that even a journalist belonging to the *Société des amis de la liberté de la presse* declared reprehensible—the guardsman urged other left-wing journalists, notably Prudhomme, Gorsas, and Hodey, to be on guard: "Your proscription is voted for along with all other good patriot writers!"[32]

Although writers could be as one-sided as deputies in demanding tolerance or punishment, they began developing arguments that would eventually coalesce into a more coherent quasi-libertarian position by 1791. One argument held that anonymous writings and calumny served as salutary checks on officials and elites. In a collection of essays on *Le pour et le contre sur la liberté de la presse, par un impartial*, a writer reasoned that "since the poor will always greatly outnumber the rich and since the latter's vexation of the former will always be greater and less well publicized, republican governments should tolerate anonymous writings which will keep the aristocracy in check through fear and thus maintain the rights of the people."[33] In conceiving of press freedom as a check on social and political power, this view radically inverted Old Regime jurisprudence, which held social inferiors more accountable for injurious speech than their superiors.

Others objected to allowing inferiors to slander anonymously those above them. Jean-Baptiste-Louis Billecocq, for example, referred to the vast quantity of cahiers de doléances which demanded that the names of authors and printers appear on publications so that they could be held responsible for bad content.[34] He believed that, however unfortunate social inequality may be, it was inevitable, and since inequality breeds jealousy, laws had to be passed to protect "citizens" (i.e., "active citizens," or those who met the necessary property requirements to vote) from calumny.[35] Only the "mediocre," Billecocq claimed, resorted to calumny, and he believed that, along with state finances, calumny was the nation's "greatest calamity" and the most pressing problem the Estates-General needed to tackle.[36]

The National Assembly failed to criminalize calumny in 1789. The first attempt to do so occurred in January 1790, when the abbé Sieyès and the marquis de Condorcet presented a press-law proposal on behalf of the *comité de constitution*. The plan was rejected outright and not even put to a vote. A close examination of it explains why. For all its overtures to the benefits of press freedom, it upheld many aspects of Old Regime jurisprudence. And although Old Regime attitudes and reflexes concerning honor persisted in the early years of the Revolution, maintaining the old jurisprudence in the wake of free expression struck many as intolerable. Articles 2 and 3 of the proposal amounted to sedition laws and provoked the most criticism. Not only did they proscribe works calling for opposition to the law; they also declared punishable any work appearing within a week of a revolt and containing false allegations—regardless of whether the work called explicitly for revolt—as long as the work's influence on those participating in the revolt could be shown. Article 4 upheld the principle of lèse-majesté, making injurious remarks toward the king punishable according to Old Regime jurisprudence—that is, potentially by death. Published attacks on mœurs were punishable by fines equivalent to half a year's salary and loss of civil rights for up to four years. Facing vehement opposition, Sieyès admitted that the proposal had some faults but insisted on the necessity of a provisional compromise until the Penal Code could be completed.

The Sieyès-Condorcet proposal encountered opposition from all sides. Some attacked its provisional nature. The former censor and now fervent revolutionary Louis-Félix Guynement de Kéralio wrote, "If press freedom is a great public benefit in one moment, it is so in all."[37] The conservative Mallet du Pan took a different tack, writing, "The provisional nature of the proposal suggests the half-heartedness of the legislator....The public will penetrate these sentiments, as will the executors of the law....Criminals will be half-certain of impunity."[38] Brissot inveighed against holding writers responsible for insurrections. "What? Because two mistaken or corrupt witnesses will attest that a [good] freedom-inspired work was misunderstood by the ignorant, misinterpreted by the ambitious, and excited the people to insurrection, you would condemn the writer to death?"[39] Brissot also criticized it for prohibiting sedition, bad mœurs, and calumny without ever defining those terms.[40] (Conservative deputies would later invoke the same reasoning in militating against the attribution of lèse-nation.) Marat hurled his habitual bile at the proposal, promising to provide more substantial criticism in a later issue, which he never did.[41]

In the storm over the Sieyès-Condorcet plan, one pamphlet stands out, not for its influence at the time—it was hardly noticed—but for its quasi-libertarian arguments, which would gain ground over the course of 1790 and 1791. In his eighty-page *Lettre de M. Loyseau à M. Condorcet*, Jean-René Loyseau boldly claimed that writing could never be seditious.[42] Distinguishing words from deeds, he insisted that sedition laws should pertain only to the latter. He conceded that individuals should be able to sue for calumny and defamation in civil courts, but he believed that public functionaries were fair game. The public had the right not only to accuse them but also to be informed about the functionary's public and private conduct. A calumniated official might defend himself before the public, but he was not to be permitted to sue or file charges against the alleged slanderer. Finally, Loyseau called for tolerating anonymous writings. "To expect authors and printers to reveal themselves is to undermine the freedom of the press."[43]

The failure of the Sieyès-Condorcet plan and the ongoing absence of legal limits on press freedom did nothing to prevent official and unofficial repression against the press in the spring and early summer of 1790. Courts, officials, and crowds tried to impose punitive limits on what they took to be abusive expression. The Châtelet continued to pursue lèse-nation affairs. In May, authorities in Paris shut down an aristocratic reading salon. That same month, Parisian crowds attacked the offices of several royalist newspapers and burned issues in the streets.[44] In November, patriots at the Café Procope issued their own *arrêté* and formed deputations to "convince" royalist journalists to mend their ways. The journalists may not have been cowed by these deputations, but they did become less critical of the municipality once Lafayette assigned National Guardsmen to protect them.[45]

The Malouet sedition decree of July 31, 1790, provoked more controversy over limiting press freedom. Loustalot of *Révolutions de Paris*, for example, accused the authors of the decree, notably Malouet, Lafayette, and Bailly, of conspiring to destroy the patriot press.[46] He claimed that the new regime's press policies were more insidious than those of the Old Regime. Back then, he explained, writers had been banned by censorship or pursued openly by the courts. Such actions may have been unfair, he conceded, but at least they were forthright. Now, writers were the victims of a hidden war "in which ruse and force have combined against both guilty and innocent writers."[47] He offered an example. During the anniversary celebration of the storming of the Bastille on July 14, the wife of a printer imprisoned on lèse-nation charges for having published a libel against Lafayette threw herself at the General's feet, begging for her husband's release. In a spectacular display of beneficence, Lafayette embraced her and pardoned her husband. Loustalot fumed,

> The printer had been arrested for crimes of lèse-nation, perhaps incorrectly, but he had been arrested nonetheless.... Had it only been for the crime of lèse-Lafayette, brought before the court at Lafayette's request [i.e., a civil suit initiated by Lafayette], the General could have legitimately ceded to the tears of a weeping wife and dropped the charges. But if he can annul a lèse-nation affair because some pretty woman jumps into his arms, I do not see any reason why a *free* man should admire or applaud this.[48]

Clearly, Loustalot did not question the attribution of lèse-nation for certain kinds of public expression. Rather, he protested the use of personal status to short-circuit the rule of law. Marat condemned the Malouet decree, insisting that writing could never be seditious. He did not elaborate on this libertarian principle, preferring, as usual, to demonize adversaries. For him, the need to punish counterrevolutionaries took precedence over the need to extend freedom of expression to all. "Let us conclude that the criminals of lèse-nation can never be found among *patriot* writers, who are the scarecrows of the real criminals."[49]

Criticism of the Malouet decree came from moderate and right-wing journalists as well. Like their left-wing counterparts, they, too, fell short of demanding absolute tolerance. An anonymous contribution to the *Journal de Paris* begins in quasi-libertarian spirit: "The citizen must be free to express his thoughts through speech, writing, and print....Any [press] law is an obstacle, and to seek to regulate this freedom is to restrict it."[50] But the author continued by insisting upon the importance of public order, claiming that words were indeed actions and therefore subject to sedition laws. "In no governed [*policée*] society is it permitted to raise the people against the sovereign, the judges, and the law, to conspire against the government and public liberty, to outrage citizens through libels and defamation....The mode of communication does not matter: the *intention* and the *effect* of the offense constitute the gravity of the crime."[51]

Brissot rejected this argument. In a long response appearing in *Patriote français*, he refuted the author's claim that no well-policed society allows writers to raise the people against the sovereign, observing that, "in the new politics, the people are the sovereign."[52] Countering the author's belief that "it is quite simple to punish calumny while maintaining the freedom of the press," Brissot remarked, "To punish calumny without undermining the freedom of the press is the most difficult problem to resolve in politics"—a view, by the way, that reflected his own dilemma in being simultaneously a public official and a journalist.[53] He criticized the Malouet decree as well but on grounds different from those of other critics. He argued that it addressed a particular problem—the recent writings of Desmoulins and Marat—rather than a general problem in a universal manner. But Brissot's argument was disingenuous. Although the decree referred specifically to the two radical journalists, it encompassed all seditious writings.

In a subsequent article, Brissot proposed the general outlines of press legislation. Drawing on libertarian arguments circulating at the time, he encouraged calumniated individuals, including deputies and public officials, to defend themselves before public opinion. If the results were not satisfactory, plaintiffs should then be permitted to sue in civil court—the public prosecutor should not be allowed to pursue the case on behalf of the alleged victim as a criminal affair.[54] This qualification, a central tenet of all quasi-libertarian arguments, is significant. Civil law suits for calumny, we have seen, were rare in the Old Regime. Even though the law accommodated such suits, they ran counter to the culture of honor since plaintiffs ran the risks of appearing self-interested and of being further humiliated in the course of the trial. Moreover, the condemnations of civil courts lacked the solemnity and striking force of criminal convictions, which expressed the vengeance of a divinely sanctioned hierarchical and moral order. Brissot departed from nascent libertarian arguments, however, in recognizing public libels as seditious and punishable. His definition of public libel resembled, in fact, Malouet's, which he claimed to oppose! He wrote, "A publication can harm society in a variety of manners: when it incites people to rise up against the law or against those in charge of making laws or executing them."[55]

Although Loustalot, Marat, and Brissot did not elaborate full-blown libertarian arguments, such arguments were expressed in 1790, especially in the wake of the Malouet decree. Loyseau's letter of January to Condorcet went into a second edition after the passage of the decree. His ideas were further developed by Michel Thomassin in *Réflexions sur la liberté de la presse*. Writing anonymously, Thomassin dismissed fears that press freedom would allow "calumny to empoison all that is respectable."[56] Quoting a "great publicist" of the century (André Morellet), he wrote, "One cannot disturb through writing a state that is well governed."[57] Like Loyseau, Thomassin insisted on complete tolerance (except for libels against private persons), asserting that ex post facto punishment of libels would be "more tyrannical than the [censorship] prohibitions it would replace."[58] He contested a proposed law requiring the names of authors and printers on works, warning, "So far, the courts have only burned publications; who knows if, soon, they will not start burning their authors as well?"[59] In his second, more developed pamphlet on the matter of press freedom, Kéralio urged that the requirement to put the names of authors and printers on publications was "ineffective, unjust, and oppressive."[60] He cited the Englishman Robert Pigot, whose unconventional views on press freedom in England were being discussed in France. Pigot thought that the English model of press freedom was precisely what the French should reject. He claimed that English journalists and writers were not as free as many in France believed. Despite the absence of censorship, the British government had formidable resources at its disposal to intimidate and repress writers. Kéralio also asserted that publications could never be seditious since writing was not an action, and he was suspicious of authorities who sought to punish calumniators. "It is not calumny they fear; it is light, it is truth."[61] The public, he believed, was capable of distinguishing truth from calumny and of punishing calumniators on its own, without state intervention.[62] Kéralio extended this reasoning to publications that violated mœurs as well. Conceding that such writings were reprehensible, he believed that regulation could do little to stop them. The only viable solution was to improve the nation's mœurs through education—a project that revolutionaries did little about until late 1792.

In summer 1791, as legislators were completing the Constitution and Penal Code, they finally defined limits on free speech. In debating the issue, Jacobin deputies adopted a quasi-libertarian stance, drawing on the ideas advanced the previous year—unevenly by journalists, more coherently by Loyseau, Thomassin, and Kéralio. Several reasons explain why Jacobins embraced these radical ideas. First, the club swung leftward in this period due to the exodus of constitutional-monarchist members. The split occurred after months of internal disputes over whether the club should support increasing demands for a republic. Suspicions about the king's loyalty to the Revolution, confirmed by his attempt to flee France in June, emboldened the republican movement. Yet, most deputies, including most Jacobins, rejected and feared the movement.[63] On July 16, the very day a majority of Jacobin deputies abandoned the club to found the Feuillant Club, the National Assembly exonerated the king. The next day, a massacre of republican petitioners took place on the Champs de Mars. The National Guard, under the command of Lafayette—himself, a Jacobin-turned-Feuillant—fired on republican petitioners gathered to celebrate the second anniversary of the storming of the Bastille. In an attempt to muzzle republican agitators in the aftermath of the event, the National Assembly outlawed "seditious" speech, thereby launching the *petite terreur*. In late July and August, several journalists, printers, and peddlers were arrested. In these critical months of 1791, then, Jacobins went from being the backbone of a formidable left-wing block in the National Assembly to a beleaguered minority increasingly aligned with a much feared popular movement. These conditions explain why Jacobin deputies and journalists sought to expand the scope of free speech to include their increasingly radical, republican position.

Between May and August 1791, quasi-libertarian arguments were advanced by three notable Jacobins: Maximilien Robespierre, François-Xavier Lanthenas, and Jérome Pétion de Villeneuve. Robespierre delivered a speech on the issue at the Jacobin Club in May, around the time the National Assembly began discussing the Penal Code. In June, when the provisions of the Penal Code concerning the press were being debated, Lanthenas's treatise on press freedom was published. Pétion delivered his speech on press freedom in the National Assembly during the *petite terreur* in August. Like Loyseau, Thomassin, and Kéralio the year before, these leading Jacobins argued that published opinions were not actions and could not, therefore, be treated as sedition.[64] Echoing Loustalot's "calumny is good" argument, Pétion told his colleagues,

> Public persons are necessarily exposed to censure and subject to opinion; nothing can shelter them from it: denounced at this tribunal, they must always be prepared to appear before it. It is only through irreproachable conduct that they can respond to calumnies. *The public interest demands that one be able to inculpate without fear.*[65]

Robespierre pontificated on the virtue of public opinion, contrasting it with the evil of authority. "The empire of public opinion is gentle, salutary, natural, and irresistible; the empire of authority is tyrannical, odious, absurd, and monstrous."[66] Any regulation or repression of the press, Robespierre warned, would weaken public opinion's ability to serve as a check on state power. Echoing Pigot, he worried that the mere threat of official repression would intimidate authors from airing suspicions. Like Condorcet in his *Fragments sur la liberté de la presse* of 1776, Robespierre claimed that accusations made by the press, even if not fully substantiated, served to pressure officials into launching investigations into potential conspiracies that might otherwise remain covered up. "The freedom of the press," as he put it, "must inspire a certain terror."[67]

The proposals of Robespierre, Lanthenas, and Pétion were largely, but not entirely, libertarian. Private individuals (and, in some cases, even public officials whose private conduct was attacked) were to be permitted to sue for libel in civil court. Beyond this concession, however, these Jacobins sought absolute tolerance for political speech. Pétion and Lanthenas were aware of the novelty of their position. The former told his fellow deputies,

> this doctrine contradicts Old Regime ideas which held the slightest attack on what was called "the honor of men in government" to be a serious offense that could not be too severely punished, whereas the offense made against a simple citizen hardly attracted the attention of the courts.[68]

Unlike the general cahiers de doléances, which called for maintaining regulations and restrictions on the press, Lanthenas called for the "complete abrogation of all Old Regime laws concerning injurious speech, calumny, blasphemy, religious cults, the theater, and the press," replacing them with "guidelines that consecrate the most unlimited freedom to communicate ideas."[69] Unlike Loyseau and Kéralio, who believed that Old Regime jurisprudence should be maintained in so far as injurious speech against ordinary citizens was concerned, Lanthenas called for new legislation in this domain as well. He believed that convictions should be based solely on the intentions of the alleged slanderer. If intentions were shown to have been malicious, punishment was to be proportional to the suffering intended.[70]

The quasi-libertarian views on press freedom advanced in 1790 and 1791 contained tensions and contradictions worth underlining, not because they had any impact on the degenerating political situation—there were more significant factors—but rather because they give insight into the dilemmas involved in implementing press freedom in a time of abrupt democratic transition. Robespierre, Pétion, and Lanthenas characterized public opinion as at once sovereign and immature. Robespierre declared that public opinion was the "only legitimate censor of writings. If it approves a publication, what right do you [fellow deputies] have to condemn it? If it does not, why bother condemning it yourselves?"[71] He claimed that an expressed opinion could never be the sufficient cause of disorder since, if it is invalid, it will be ignored; if it stirs up agitation, it must therefore conform to the people's interests and merely awaken preexisting desires.[72] Yet, Robespierre recognized that public opinion was still fallible, a fact he attributed to persistent prejudices. How would society overcome them? Through freedom itself, he believed. In a regime of free expression, individuals would get used to evaluating opinions, and their moral discernment would improve. They would learn to distinguish legitimate denunciations from calumny, taking into account "the circumstances, the facts, and the character of both the accuser and the accused."[73] Loyseau had conveyed similar optimism the year before, believing that press freedom would change the way people responded to libels. If libels were presently causing so much political agitation (and he conceded that they were), it was because people's skin was still thin: "Since we have not yet gotten used to freedom, we become unnerved easily."[74]

Lanthenas also wavered in depicting public opinion as unified and sovereign on the one hand, fractious and immature on the other. At one point in his treatise, he accused those who doubted the public's ability to discern good from bad writings of "insulting the human race," charging them with "lèse-humanité." In a later passage, he conceded that public opinion was still fallible, insisting that the solution was "not to erect laws but to improve mœurs through instruction."[75] For his part, Pétion did not deny that the recent explosion of libels had produced a factious public, but he opposed controls on the press, claiming that political disturbances were inherent in the very nature of revolution. In the transition from despotism to freedom, he explained, "there occurs necessarily a war between the outgoing tyrants...and the people trying to conquer their rights." Libels proliferate, and the only thing one can do is to "renounce useless [press] laws and let the storm pass."[76] To do otherwise, he warned, would lead to despotism.

Learning curves and transitional storms, then, were all that separated an immature, fractious public opinion from becoming enlightened and unified.

These optimistic arguments glossed over—even as they revealed—the problem revolutionaries confronted in dealing with widespread demands to punish calumniators. Quasi-libertarian ideals were clearly at odds with prevailing punitive attitudes and reflexes. Yet, the proponents of this progressive conception of press freedom were not altogether deaf to punitive demands. In seeking to secure legal tolerance for oppositional speech, they tactically assigned the task of punishing speech abuses to public opinion. Doing so offered a sanitized way to acknowledge punitive demands, since public opinion was ultimately abstract, unlike state repression and street vengeance.

In giving public opinion exclusive jurisdiction over speech affairs, the quasi-libertarian argument failed to explain how the public's judgments would be distinguishable from the myriad other instances of censure and calumny in the public sphere. Lacking a privileged organ or institution for deliberating and pronouncing judgments, would not the public's verdicts be subject to further scrutiny, not to mention charges of calumny? Robespierre and Pétion skirted this problem by projecting a unified, enlightened, and sovereign public opinion into the future. Lanthenas also portrayed a bright future for public opinion, but he reflected more rigorously on the institutional means of making the public unified and enlightened. I will say more about his civil-censorship proposal of 1793 in chapter 8, but already in 1791, he began imagining ways to channel punitive impulses into civic practices. He envisaged establishing locally elected juries to deal with speech offenses. These juries would contribute to public instruction since their verdicts would convey moral lessons. Because punishments were to be symbolic and not violent, this form of public censure would serve as a civilizing force, substituting moral regulation for vengeance. Lanthenas summed up his position, "To counter the disadvantages of indefinite press freedom, we need not pass [repressive] laws but rather measures to improve mœurs and spread instruction."[77]

Calumny Is Bad: Securing Respect for Authority (1789–1791)

Whatever tensions and flaws the quasi-libertarian argument may have had, the main reason its proponents failed to get their views inscribed in revolutionary legislation was that, quite simply, few shared them. Skin *was* still thin, and given the democratizing context, reputations were as important and vulnerable as ever. Most contemporaries were not prepared to accept a world in which calumniators would go unpunished, and few were disposed to hauling their wounded honor off to a civil court, much less to the court of public opinion.[78] Indeed, it was precisely in the realm of public opinion that, as Beaumarchais had observed and many feared, "calumny grows into a general chorus of hatred and proscription."[79] Nor was the claim that a virtuous individual need not worry about the influence of calumny very convincing. As Billecocq soberly noted, "It is often said that a good man...has his conscience as his witness and is not disturbed by calumniators....This language is very philosophical but unfortunately not true."[80]

We have seen how concerns with calumny, honor, and hierarchy infused Old Regime jurisprudence on injurious speech. Altar and throne served as the sacred foundations of authority upon which a socially hierarchical legal system was built. Punishments were meted out less according to the nature of the offense than according to the status of the parties involved. The Revolution threw a wrench into this system. The abolition of privilege and establishment of civil equality, together with the breakdown of institutional mechanisms for regulating the economy of esteem and deference, made managing reputations increasingly difficult, causing obsessions with calumny to intensify. Consequently, political elites—even the erstwhile champions of free speech—who sought to protect and defend themselves began grafting their individual honor onto sacred, collective totems of authority and justice: the monarchy, religion, the law, the nation, the people.

Disenchantment with free speech and obsessions with calumny appeared in a tract defending the duc d'Orléans. This rival cousin of Louis XVI had actively promoted press freedom in the prerevolutionary period. As we have seen, his model cahier, which included this demand, circulated widely. By spring and summer 1790, Orléans's reputation had become tarnished. Suspected of instigating the October Days in the hopes of toppling the king, Orléans was "invited" by Lafayette to go to London on a diplomatic mission. The invitation was really a dignified form of banishment.[81] In any case, libels against him proliferated in his absence. In an effort to defend the duke's reputation, a former barrister of the Paris Parlement wrote a pamphlet on his behalf, *Observations de M. Oudet*, in summer 1790. The clunky subtitle sums up the argument, "on the right to speak and print opinions and on the need to hinder and repress abuses and to punish the guilty and calumniators." After referring to widespread demands in the cahiers for legal limits on speech (ironically, Orléans's own model cahier had made no mention of them), Oudet offered guidelines for assessing the "good" or "bad" intentions of writers. Good writers, according to him, advance the arts and sciences, purify mœurs, and protect the nation from libels. Bad writers attack reputations and provoke civil strife. Grafting the honor of public figures (such as Orléans) onto the honor of the nation, Oudet wrote, "If [a writer], under the pretext of being useful to the nation, is shown to be a calumniator and seeks to stir up civil war, his punishment should avenge both the denounced citizen *as well as the entire nation, which the calumniator tried to immolate.*"[82] Oudet conceded that Orléans could have sued his calumniators as a private citizen in a civil court and perhaps should have, but he stressed the public prosecutor's responsibility to intervene. One senses that Oudet thought civil suits were beneath the dignity of a duke and that avenging his honor, restoring his reputation, and discouraging further libels required a solemn criminal conviction.

By the time Oudet got around to proposing press laws, he seemed to have entirely forgotten about the civil-suit option. Libels figured as strictly criminal affairs. He called for restricting press freedom to writers over the age of twenty-five; those younger would have to obtain a guarantor.[83] All publications were to be signed by the printer and the author and submitted to the court clerk. Authors suspected of writing calumnies that threatened public safety or "citizens in general" were to be charged with lèse-nation. If convicted, they were to be punished according to Old Regime jurisprudence, which imposed public apologies, payment for damages, fines, and rituals of public humiliation. If the calumny concerned the king, legislators, the nation, or public tranquility, guilty authors were to be put to death.[84] It is worth noting that, at the time this pamphlet appeared, the Châtelet had more than a dozen such lèse-nation cases on its docket.

The fact that Oudet, rather than the duc d'Orléans, wrote this pamphlet attests to the persistence of Old Regime patterns of honorable avenging. Defending one's own honor in court or in the public sphere was looked upon poorly. Virtuous vengeance involved defending the honor of superiors, the collectivity, or collective values. Such attitudes appear in the correspondence between provincial authorities and the National Assembly. For example, in demanding more rigorous repression of libels against the king, authorities of the department of Seine-Inférieure wrote, "In dismissing libels spewed against them, the dignified representatives of the nation prove they are most noble and generous; but these same sentiments should prompt them to exercise the greatest severity when the head of this same nation…is abused in odious writings."[85] The principle of selflessness in avenging honor was also expressed in the Malouet decree of July 31, 1790. Article 2, which did not pass, stipulated that "if injurious speech and calumnies are made against the King, reparations and punishment will be pursued in the name of the nation; if insults and calumnies are made against the Legislature, reparations and punishment will be pursued in the name of the King."[86] During debate on this proposal, Malouet distinguished libels attacking his personal honor from those attacking the honor of public authority. In the midst of his tirade against Desmoulins, left-wing deputies shouted, "Take your denunciation to the police."[87] Indignant, Malouet replied that the issue was not about calumnious attacks on his personal honor, and he claimed to have brushed off such attacks for more than a year. The calumnies spread by Desmoulins and Marat concerned the National Assembly as a whole and therefore constituted "public crimes" and, hence, lèse-nation."[88]

Local magistrates in Marseilles also expressed the greater importance of avenging calumnious attacks on authority or collective values over attacks on individuals. In a requisition to a district tribunal in April 1791, the public prosecutor justified the recent repression of libels written by an imprisoned lèse-nation suspect, Jean-François Lieutaud.

> If we have kept silent until now, it is because Lieutaud's writings have only attacked us personally…but today, there is a libel which compromises the honor of the Tribunal and public tranquility, and this scandal affects us as public men.…The freedom of the press was not declared to be used abusively against Justice and its ministers in such an outrageous manner.[89]

The quasi-libertarian view, we have seen, inverted this logic: it called for tolerating calumnies against officials, or at least officials' public conduct, though in some cases, it allowed officials to sue for calumnies concerning their private conduct. But the district tribunal in Marseilles seconded the public prosecutor's view, declaring that it would have been "blameworthy" and "cowardly" for local authorities to have done nothing "when the Law is scorned, respect due to Justice is violated, and public peace is compromised."[90]

Although this affair was settled (the National Assembly absolved Lieutaud of charges of collusion with Turin-based counterrevolutionaries in May 1791, despite much evidence), many such affairs were not. Among the outstanding cases that the Châtelet turned over to the new *arrondissement* courts of Paris in January 1791, one finds several involving speech. It may not be surprising to find among the list of alleged calumniators the names of polemical journalists such as Desmoulins (*Révolutions de France et de Brabant*), Marat (*L'Ami du peuple*), Loustalot (*Révolutions de Paris*), and the authors of the conservative *Journal de Paris*.[91] Nor is it surprising to find among the plaintiffs figures holding authority, such as the royal public prosecutor, de Joly (against Marat), numerous officials of the Parlement of Paris, and the administrators of the *Caisse d'escompte*, whom the press vilipended for the financial fiascos of 1788–1789. Calumny affairs undertaken by the royal public prosecutor on behalf of important public figures such as Moreau de Saint-Méry and Beaumarchais also figure. It is surprising, however, to find among these affairs one launched on behalf of the comte de Mirabeau. A champion of press freedom in the prerevolutionary period, Mirabeau holds a heroic place in the historical literature for having stoically withstood calumny.[92] On July 3, 1790, a prosecutor at the Châtelet accused Sébastien Brumeaux de Lacroix of calumny for his *Trahison découverte du comte de Mirabeau*. The author accused Mirabeau—rightly, as it turned out—of secretly colluding with the monarchy.[93] The author said that until now he had been scrupulous about distinguishing the private Mirabeau from the public one, ignoring the many excesses of his private life, such as his intimate relations with the wife of a close friend. But since Mirabeau had now proved to be corrupt as a public figure, his private character was legitimately open to scrutiny as well.[94]

Later that month, Mirabeau supported Malouet's effort to pass a press law and have Desmoulins arrested. The comte published his own denunciation of the radical journalist, which included calumnious excerpts from *Révolutions de France et de Brabant*, and forwarded it to the National Assembly's *comité des recherches*. Mirabeau claimed that he had been trying for quite some time to introduce press-limit legislation but that resistance in the Assembly prevented him from even getting the matter discussed. He deplored the fact that, under the present circumstances, one could do little to combat libels. The Châtelet's closure was imminent, the regular courts were not functioning, and the government had no means for dealing with the problem.[95] Whereas the quasi-libertarian view held that all denunciations of calumny should be submitted to the public, Mirabeau appealed to the public only because there were no institutional alternatives. Although the Châtelet continued to rule on criminal cases until December 1790, it generally avoided settling calumny affairs, which were often political dynamite. Already under fire, magistrates wanted to avoid making more enemies. In the last five months of its existence, the Châtelet completed only eleven cases of injurious speech.[96] The Mirabeau-Lacroix affair was among those left on the docket.

Many in France were becoming exasperated by the escalation of calumny in the press. Citizens, local officials, and political clubs inundated the National Assembly with letters denouncing libels and requesting press laws. The fact that deputies had established the *comité des recherches* to receive such denunciations only reinforced expectations that calumny would soon be punished. In denouncing calumniators to the National Assembly in 1789 and early 1790, plaintiffs tended to use respectful, deferential language to convey their desire for punitive press laws. A public prosecutor in Preuilly, for example, denounced Louis-Sébastien Mercier for disrespectful statements about the oath the king made in the National Assembly on February 4, 1790, "Certainly, in favoring the freedom of the press the National Assembly has wisely reserved the right to repress the abuses of journalists who, without limits, principles, or mœurs, don't know how to respect anything in their newspapers."[97] After failing to obtain a conviction against the royalist journalist Rozoi of the *Gazette de Paris* at the Paris police tribunal in March 1790, officials in Brest denounced him to the National Assembly's *comité des recherches*, ending their letter with the hopeful prospect that "the National Assembly will soon trace the limits in which press freedom must be circumscribed to prevent it from degenerating into license."[98] Even in Paris, where radicalism was much advanced, early denunciations expressed deference and respect. In October 1789, the commune of Paris denounced a libel that it found incendiary and calumnious, all the more so for being cheap and therefore intended for the "inferior classes." Municipal officials asked the president of the National Assembly to read it to his colleagues so that they might "take the necessary measures that their wisdom suggests against the authors, printers, and distributors of such libels."[99]

As time passed and legislators failed to pass press laws, denunciators adopted a bolder tone. In his denunciation of Rozoi, a postal director in Paris, Claude Le Comte, insisted, "You must eradicate this evil at its source to prevent the simple-minded from falling into [the journalist's] trap; you owe this to [the people] and to the law of which you are the creators."[100] In May 1790, the mayor of Tarbes wrote to the National Assembly, "We have satisfied our obligations in denouncing the seditious....We will follow the guidelines that the Assembly will soon trace....Our most sacred duty is to watch over the maintenance of the constitution and make [people] cherish and respect the law...and our courageous representatives."[101] In his denunciation of a local newspaper in Lyon in September, a grenadier warned the National Assembly of the dangers for "the new Constitution if the freedom of the press is exploited by those who say whatever they want, leading the people into a state of error and fear."[102] And whereas the municipal officials in Brest had been relatively reserved in denouncing Rozoi in June, by December they expressed exasperation in denouncing another royalist journalist, Jacques Mallet-du-Pan: "It is time, Sirs, that the author of this libel paid the price for his calumnies [against] our sacred Constitution, our august representatives, and our dignified Magistrates who work to defend our interests and ensure our safety."[103]

The contradictory and aborted efforts of the National Assembly to pass press laws sent mixed signals to the provinces, contributing to confusion and frustration. On June 17, 1790, the National Assembly debated on how to stop the spread of Catholic libels in the Midi, where sectarian violence had broken out. In the end, deputies could only agree on summoning the authors to appear before the Assembly and stripping them of their civil status until they did so.[104] Deputies also asked the monarchy, which held executive power, to instruct the local *présidial* court in Nîmes to take action. The relative restraint of these measures owed much to the deputies' recognition that the libels circulating in Nîmes and Uzès had been inspired by a protest declaration that right-wing deputies had published in April in response to a decree that closed all discussion on making Catholicism the official national religion (more on this in a later chapter). The Right's ongoing opposition to this decree, combined with Malouet's insistence on press freedom, prevented the Assembly from sending the authors of the Catholic libels to the Châtelet as lèse-nation suspects.[105] Deputies seemed to recognize that harsh measures might inflame the Midi, where the embers of sectarian strife were still smoldering.[106]

Despite the relative restraint of the June 17 decree, in Bordeaux, where insurrections were feared, authorities construed it as a green light to repress Catholic libels. In an *arrêté* posted throughout the city, the public prosecutor cited the decree, seeing it as the initial sign of an imminent press law.

> The [National Assembly] has recognized that these reprehensible writings attack its decrees as well as acts of executive power...that a judgment is necessary that will intimidate forever those who dare to mislead the simple people....This decree leads us to wait respectfully for the National Assembly to impose justice on these seditious writings and their authors on behalf of an outraged France.[107]

According to the prosecutor, repression was conceived not just as an expedient for restoring public order, but as vengeance on behalf of an indignant nation. The Bordeaux authorities banned the libels, threatened to treat all subsequent libels as sedition, and instructed citizens to turn in all copies to authorities and to denounce those who failed to do so. Meanwhile, the authors of the libels in Nîmes ignored their summons to appear before the National Assembly.[108]

The case of two distributors of libels in Valenciennes, "la femme Roch" and her son, also reveals how local authorities acted on the mixed cues they received from the National Assembly. Municipal officials had them arrested on

August 20, 1790. The suspects were still in prison three weeks later when the municipality sent a letter to the National Assembly asking what should be done with them. The authorities cited what they thought, wrongly, was the text of the Malouet decree of July 31. (They had never received an official copy and had learned about it through newspapers.) Whereas the actual decree called for treating as lèse-nation writings that "incited people to revolt against laws, spill blood, and overturn the Constitution," their version was stretched to include writings that "stir up trouble, undermine the promise of a new constitution which will make citizens happier, mar the respect and recognition due to their representatives...and undermine the attachment and loyalty so legitimately due to [the] monarch."[109] The Valenciennes officials said that they had received the August 2 decree that granted amnesty for all press-crimes committed prior to July 31 (except for Marat's *C'en est fait de nous*), but since this latter decree also ordered the *comité de constitution* to propose guidelines for implementing the July 31 decree, they thought it was still to be enforced.[110]

The misreading of the original July 31 decree by administrators in Valenciennes was not an isolated case of convenient extrapolation. Their interpretation reflected the kinds of limits many had been anticipating. Disrespect for the king, the National Assembly, authorities, and the law was often deemed to be criminal. The prosecutor of the district of Nantua denounced a libelous letter from Noyon that ridiculed the chaotic situation of finances and the bedlam reigning in the National Assembly. He declared the letter to be "contrary to the respect due to the representatives of the nation" and warned about its "dangerous effect on weak minds."[111] Departmental authorities in the Aube denounced a published letter that "ridiculed the homage and admiration that [administrators] express every day for their august representatives." They believed the letter aimed "to blacken the sublime sentiments of recognition [for the Assembly] that they share with 24 million men."[112] Even mere titles could be construed as sedition. The mayor of Gy in the Haute-Saône denounced a prospectus for a newspaper entitled *L'Ami de la clergé et de la noblesse* as "incendiary and seditious," and he called for prosecuting the author for abetting counterrevolution.[113]

For local officials, respect for authority was the sine qua non of political order. Writings that undermined such respect, they believed, could unleash civil unrest. Municipal authorities of Montbrison banned a libel that, they claimed, sapped "respect for, love of, and submission to [the Assembly's] decrees" and offended "a King so cherished and who only wants to rule over free men."[114] In an anonymous denunciation of right-wing newspapers appearing just after the king's flight to Varennes in June 1791, the author (probably a constitutional priest) said it was urgent that the Assembly arrest royalist writers. He believed that the queen was encouraging their efforts to pry the king's commitments away from the Revolution. The author added that a few "light reprimands" were in order for the antimonarchical slurs in Mercier's *Annales patriotiques et littéraires* published shortly after the king's flight, arguing, "Even though the King has committed a great wrong against the nation, he still merits respect."[115] The widespread purchase of such sentiments probably explains why the monarchy did not collapse sooner than it did.

In areas rife with factionalism, it is understandable that authorities, having little legitimacy, would be obsessed with protecting their honor. Statements impugning their integrity, intentions, or dignity were often considered calumnious and highly punishable. The philosophical distinction between speech and action was irrelevant to such men. They perceived a slippery slope between expressions of disrespect and outright insurrection. In debate on press limits in the National Assembly in 1791, Antoine-Pierre-Joseph-Marie Barnave, who was otherwise quite tolerant of press abuses, recognized the precarious situation of local officials. He said that although national deputies could easily dismiss calumnious attacks, "in a department or a district, a brazen calumniator who is determined to destroy a tribunal or an administration is absolute master if public authority can not find a law to refrain him."[116]

Barnave believed that punishment for press abuses should be "gentle." Local authorities thought otherwise. In their denunciation of a pastoral letter circulating in their department, the administrators of La-Tour-du-Pin declared the opening line "Times are bad" to be criminal. In informing the public about the denunciation they sent to the National Assembly, they exhorted, "May a prompt and terrible punishment strike anyone who dares mobilize religion for such dreadful [antirevolutionary] ends."[117] Administrators in the department of Aisne denounced a letter appearing in Rozoi's *Gazette de Paris* that they found to be injurious to the king and the National Assembly. They urged the Assembly to "use all the rigor of the law" to punish those implicated in producing and circulating such "seditious" writings. Since new laws against calumny did not yet exist when they made their denunciation in June 1790, one is led to believe that the administrators had harsh Old Regime laws in mind.

Many denunciations received by the National Assembly reveal the intense, widespread desire to see calumniators punished. In the Côte-d'Or, for example, as local National Guardsmen were commemorating the death of fellow Guardsmen at the hands of royal troops in Nancy, a sieur Rouard was heard making injurious statements against the Guard, the National Assembly, and the

Revolution. (National Guardsmen from many cities had been sent to Nancy to deal with a mutiny within the royal army.) Incensed, the Guardsmen told Rouard that although his comments "merited immediate death," they would refrain from dispatching him on the spot. They referred the matter to the municipality, which convened an extraordinary meeting to draft a formal denunciation of Rouard to the National Assembly. In the summer of 1790, the town of Boué in the department of Aisne denounced a laborer, Yves-Gabriel Rousseau, for disparaging "the nation, the municipality, and the National Guard."[118] They complained that Guardsmen were refusing service until Rousseau was punished for lèse-nation. In Toulouse, the National Legion became incensed about the "cruel and outrageous" statements against the king and National Assembly found in a libel distributed in the courtyard of the Palais de Justice. They complained to the city's public prosecutor, who identified the printer. A judge authorized the Legion to pay the printer a visit. The son of the printer answered the door and confessed to his father's responsibility. Although this visit must have been intimidating, it did not lead to judicial action. Worried that the affair might end there, a local individual denounced the printer to the National Assembly's president, "Since I am afraid this offense could go unpunished, and since I think it is urgent to stop such pernicious license, I beg of you to denounce this writing to the National Assembly so that it might follow through on the initial steps taken by my brave and faithful co-citizens."[119]

"Following through" often meant commencing lèse-nation procedures. Since the National Assembly had jurisdiction over lèse-nation indictments, declaring an affair to be lèse-nation offered local officials an easy way out of dealing with potentially explosive situations. In November 1790, the municipal officers of Grenoble denounced an antirevolutionary address that the sieur de Rival of the local royal militia was distributing to his fellow troops. They suspected Rival of having strong ties with the local "aristocracy of the robe and sword." Since the libel appeared to them to constitute lèse-nation and since as municipal officers they could only exercise authority over simple policing matters (milder forms of injurious speech fell within this domain), they claimed it was the National Assembly's responsibility to handle the affair.[120] They added that what appeared to be an "isolated crime" might actually be part of an organized counterrevolutionary publicity campaign. Although inflating such speech into lèse-nation and airing suspicions of counterrevolution helped justify sending the affair to the National Assembly, such conspiracies did, in fact, exist, as we shall see.

Sometimes, though, officials were prudent in denouncing libels published by local elites, probably to avoid exacerbating local tensions or to protect themselves from reprisals should the political situation be reversed. Officials in Castellane (Basses-Alpes) informed the National Assembly about the antirevolutionary sermon of a local bishop. "Although we remain persuaded of the bishop's good sentiments and are far from thinking he may have bad intentions, we would like to demonstrate to the National Assembly our zeal and our respectful allegiance to all the Assembly's decrees."[121] Authorities in Morlaix in the North also denounced their bishop but requested clemency. Despite the wrongs expressed in the bishop's recent circular, he was, they claimed, a good bishop, and his views should be seen as revealing nothing more than an obstinate attachment to old prejudices.[122]

Denunciations of speech and writing often served as occasions to renew civil oaths and reinforce loyalty and civic morality. In January 1790, officials in Massiac (Cantal) burned libels in the public square, after which they, along with the local National Guard, swore an oath to be faithful to "the law, the King, and the nation." They warned the community not to "profess openly" the "dangerous maxims" contained in these writings.[123] In some instances, writings were considered treasonous precisely because they violated oaths. In May 1790, a municipality in the Manche denounced *Adresse aux assembées primaires du département de Chaâlons*, insisting that its author be "punished as a traitor to his country and as a perjurer of the oath he most certainly must have taken to uphold the Constitution and to be faithful to the nation, the law, and the King."[124] In Perpignan in early May 1790, "patriotic citizens" blamed the proliferation of Catholic libels against the Revolution on local authorities who were not forcing local elites to swear the civil oath.[125] They hoped that the clamor of oaths would drown out the libels, or at least weaken their impact.

Public denunciations of libels, then, served many purposes. Like oaths, denunciations were speech acts intended to reinforce esteem, deference, and trust between local and national authorities. Denunciations anathematized values perceived to threaten the new order while giving vent to collective sentiments of outrage and indignation. Denunciations could also serve more mundane purposes, such as providing the occasion to seek favors. A schoolteacher from the Dordogne sent the National Assembly a long-winded denunciation of Thomas Marie Royou's *L'Ami du roi*, after which he requested jobs in the local gendarmerie for his son, "five-foot two inches tall," and his son-in-law, "five-foot six inches tall," both "literate" and quite skilled in math.[126]

Above all, denunciations of calumny served to convey where the legitimate limits of speech lay—or would lie once the National Assembly got around to legislating them. Two years went by before such laws were finally promulgated. In the meantime, unchecked calumny continued polarizing France and radicalizing revolutionary politics. It was in this context that deputies defined legal limits on free speech.

The Defeat of the Quasi-Libertarian Position and the Struggle to Control Policing (1791–1792)

In the clash between progressive and conventional positions on free speech in the summer of 1791, the former gave way. The quasi-libertarian view, hardly seconded outside of the Jacobin Club, was further hampered by the inflamed climate following the king's flight in June and the Champs de Mars massacre in July. Inaugurating the *petite terreur* on July 18, the National Assembly banned speech and writing calling explicitly for resistance to the law.[127] During debate, the right-wing deputy Regnaud de Saint-Jean d'Angély proposed criminalizing speech that "opposed the general will as expressed by its representatives." Pétion warned that such a law would undermine press freedom, but to no avail.[128] He managed, however, to persuade deputies to adopt less vague language. Only speech that "explicitly" encouraged resistance to the law would be banned. On the nineteenth, the National Assembly passed legislation concerning correctional policing. It, too, included repressive provisions sentencing anyone who insulted authorities with "fines of up to ten times their income tax" and "up to two years of imprisonment."[129]

Upon the passage of the July 18 law, authorities sprang into action.[130] The police and new district courts in Paris (notably the sixth *arrondissement* court) pursued individuals for seditious speech. At first they targeted radicals, but after complaints about one-sidedness were aired, they cracked down on right-wing journalists as well.[131] Some were arrested; others fled the city or went underground.[132] On September 14, all sedition charges were dropped when the king, cognizant of his weak legitimacy and undoubtedly eager to have royalist journalists get back to work, issued a general amnesty.[133]

The sedition law of July 18 and the subsequent *petite terreur* were temporary. The constitutional provisions passed by the National Assembly on August 22 and 23, however, had a more significant and enduring impact on press freedom. The concession Jacobins had succeeded in obtaining in July—namely, that only speech calling "explicitly" for resistance to the law would be considered criminal—was now jettisoned in favor of assessing authorial intentions. Article 17 in the section on judicial powers, presented by Jacques-Guillaume Thouret on behalf of the *comité de constitution*, prohibited writings that inspired resistance to the law or that degraded constituted authority. It also stipulated that the intentions of authors were to be assessed. It read:

> No man can be investigated or pursued for the writings he prints or has printed regardless of the subject matter unless he *intends* to provoke disobedience to the law, *to degrade constituted authorities*, to encourage resistance to their acts, or to promote any activity defined as a crime or offense by the law.
>
>   Censuring the acts of constituted authorities is permitted; but deliberate calumnies against *the probity of public functionaries and the rectitude of their intentions* in the exercise of their functions can be pursued by those who are targeted.[134]

The repressive scope of the Thouret provisions was great, and it provoked opposition. Robespierre urged his fellow deputies to adopt the phrasing of the Constitution of Virginia: "The freedom of the press, one of the greatest avenues of liberty, can only be limited by despotic governments."[135] Barnave praised the Americans for avoiding any mention of restrictions on free speech in the Bill of Rights. Most deputies, however, sided with Thouret, and the Assembly passed the constitutional provisions with these restrictions.[136]

The Thouret provisions gave radical journalists springing back from the *petite terreur* fresh reasons to fulminate. The August 26 issue of Marat's *L'Ami du peuple* was entirely devoted to the subject of its headline: "The Destruction of the Freedom of the Press." This law, he wrote,

> clearly undermines press freedom...for under the most despotic governments and the cruelest tyrannies, one persecutes political writers *only* for having intended to incite the people to disobey a law, to degrade constituted power and resist its actions, and one has never persecuted for any other reason than these.[137]

Marat found it "absurd and contradictory" to prohibit citizens from criticizing the probity of authorities and attacking their private conduct. "The first [prohibition] assumes that the agents of authority are saints who embezzle without ever meaning to; the second assumes that a man who is crooked in his private life is always pure in his public conduct."[138] Brissot, who had never been a full-blown libertarian on the question of press freedom and who had deftly managed to keep his newspaper going during the *petite terreur*, lamented the Thouret provisions. "The defeat of the patriots during yesterday's Assembly meeting...suggests that today there will no longer be a great advantage [to the freedom of the press]."[139]

Despite the repressive potential of the Constitution of 1791—and indeed, its provisions would be invoked during the Terror—the radical and royalist presses continued to thrive. Why? First, the Legislative Assembly never clarified how the provisions concerning the press were to be enforced. Second, lèse-nation remained undefined. Although the Penal Code contained a section defining "crimes against the *res publica*," it did not state whether these crimes constituted lèse-nation, for which a special high court was being established, the *Haute Cour nationale pour les crimes de lèse-nation*. The Penal Code also did not categorize kinds of speech offenses. Thus, it was not clear whether calumny was to be treated as an ordinary or political offense. Confusion over how to deal with lèse-nation affairs, together with factionalism, delays in establishing new courts, and conflicts between branches of government led to judicial paralysis.

Pressure to take action against the press increased as the political situation worsened after France declared war against Austria in spring 1792. In early May, the National Assembly charged Marat (*L'Ami du peuple*) and Royou (*L'Ami du roi*) with lèse-nation. The accusations were prompted by the murder of General Théobald Dillon by mutinous troops during a retreat near Lille. While Marat had been urging "patriot" soldiers to rid themselves of "treacherous" generals for months, Royou expressed elation about the arrival of Austrian troops on French soil. Deputies agreed on prosecuting both journalists but differed on how to proceed. Some believed that ordinary laws were sufficient and that the local justices of the peace should handle such affairs. Pursuing these affairs this way would favor the monarchy since its Ministry of Justice oversaw the work of justices of the peace. Others wanted the National Assembly to exercise its constitutional authority to indict for lèse-nation and send the two journalists before the Haute Cour nationale in Orléans.[140] The fact that the Minister of Justice had recently rebuffed a deputation demanding the arrest of Marat reinforced the arguments of those pressing the National Assembly to take action.[141]

Although Jacobins were finally being appointed to some ministries, they did not yet control the Ministry of Justice. They therefore had every reason to inflate speech crimes into lèse-nation, for doing so allowed the National Assembly, rather than the Ministry of Justice, to indict. Marguérite-Élie Guadet argued, "One must distinguish offenses that attack the honor … of individuals from those that affect society as a whole. … I ask whether or not writings that summon fire and the sword against our generals, the national representation, and constituted authorities are not national crimes?"[142] Other deputies, notably the more radical Pierre-Joseph Cambon, who would later sit on the Committee of Public Safety during the Terror, tried to temper the lèse-nation frenzy sweeping over many

Brissot-leaning Jacobins. He insisted that ordinary laws and ordinary judicial institutions sufficed to punish bad writers. Inflating these crimes into lèse-nation, he feared, would sound the death knell for press freedom. "We must refrain from passing a decree which will destroy the freedom of the press, which will throw into the prisons of Orléans [where lèse-nation suspects were held] all patriot writers."[143] (His concern for patriot rather than royalist writers bespeaks the partisanship and double standards often involved in struggles over press freedom.)

One would think, of course, that the responsibility for the mutiny near Lille lay with the mutinous troops. Prosecuting them did cross the minds of deputies, but Marc-David-Albin Lasource discouraged his colleagues from blaming them, for fear of provoking further mutinies. In his view, the troops were merely acting on the criminal ideas spread by the press. Better, then, to strike at the source of the problem by punishing seditious journalists. Reversing the logic of quasi-libertarians (and, for that matter, Spinoza and other Enlightenment advocates of free speech), which held that individuals should be held accountable for their actions but not for their speech, Lasource called for pardoning actions and punishing speech.[144] Bellowing with the will to punish, Lasource concluded, to resounding applause, "I demand that the National Assembly assume a great character of *vengeance*." Voices cut in, "of *justice*." Lasource clarified, "I speak of the vengeance of the law, a vengeance that you owe to the nation."[145]

In charging Marat and Royou with lèse-nation, the National Assembly did not solve the problem of an uncooperative royal administration. It was one thing to accuse, another to arrest, and the Assembly still depended on the Minister of Justice to bring culprits before the high court. After a month of inaction, the Minister of Justice, Antoine Duranthon, was summoned to the National Assembly. He explained that the principle of press freedom did not give him much latitude, and he feigned regret about having already violated the principle by sending a circular to district and departmental courts urging them to prosecute seditious writers. (His circular, by the way, only painted patriot and Jacobin writers as "seditious.")[146] He observed that local authorities were not cooperating. A deputy sympathetic to Duranthon boiled the problem down to confusion over the laws. "You have not even provided penal laws [regarding the press]; yet, the Constitution declares that [an abuse of] press freedom can be not only a capital offense for attacks on individuals, but also a crime of lèse-nation. How can we go another day without taking care of such a crucial law?"[147] Left-wing deputy Claude Basire refuted this and insisted that current laws were clear and sufficient. He blamed the justices of the peace for acting in a partisan manner, allowing certain libels to circulate. This was true in some instances, but it was also true that by summer 1792, all factions were colonizing parts of the state apparatus—police forces, administrations, even the Assembly's *comité de surveillance*—in order to facilitate the spread of their own libels and to thwart those of adversaries.

In the struggle over enforcing limits on free expression, the monarchy had certain advantages. The king's Minister of Justice oversaw the judicial system, from local justices of the peace to the workings (if not the rulings) of the Haute Cour nationale. This explains why left-wing deputies sought to attribute jurisdiction over speech crimes to municipal governments, many of which were loyal to the left wing of the Assembly. On May 30, 1792, the former public prosecutor and future Girondin deputy Armand Gensonné proposed creating a new "national-security" administration. Independent of the Ministry of Justice, it would stretch from the municipal, district, and departmental administrations up to the National Assembly's *comité de surveillance*, thus sidestepping entirely the royal administration. He also proposed expanding the Assembly's police intelligence and reinforcing its jurisdiction over "crimes against the nation," including speech crimes. Justifying the expansion of municipal jurisdiction over such crimes, he claimed that vagabonds were currently invading major cities, infecting them with "uncivic behavior, love for disorder, and hatred of the Constitution." To remedy this epidemic, Gensonné proposed allowing municipal police to repress speech considered injurious to the nation or the constitution.[148] (Even the sporting of nontricolored cockades was to be punished.)[149] If affairs were serious or involved orchestrated conspiracies, the municipalities were to send them to the National Assembly, which would consider making lèse-nation charges.

Brissot supported Gensonné's plan. Whatever misgivings he may have had about the Thouret provisions of the Constitution the year before, he now declared that "all who, through writing, speech, or actions, seek to degrade the National Assembly, seek its dissolution, incite the army against it, or seek arrangements counter to the dignity of the nation" were "enemies of the nation."[150] Responding to placards opposed to this new "Inquisition," Brissot complained that the plan was being too hastily "calumniated."[151] To reassure the apprehensive, he insisted that "nothing would be more ridiculous than to organize a great institution for national security only to use it to punish café comments or the excesses of a few obscure newspapers."[152] He maintained, however, that those who knew how to assess evidence and detect conspiracies recognized the need to extend local policing powers and to coordinate their efforts with the police committee of the Legislative Assembly. He lamented that the Constituent Assembly's police committees, the *comité des rapports* and the *comité des recherches*, and the current Legislative

Assembly's *comité de surveillance* had not been given sufficient policing authority.[153] He claimed that the justices of the peace and local courts, under the authority of the monarchy, could not be trusted to inform the Assembly about conspiracies. It was thanks to the patriotism of certain municipalities that the Assembly had any information about them at all.[154]

In the year following the monarchy's collapse, Gensonné's plan was implemented by Jacobins more radical than he. During the spring and summer of 1793, the National Convention created a national security administration, stretching from local surveillance committees up to the Convention's Committee of General Security and Committee of Public Safety. Justifying the repression of oppositional speech, authorities invoked vague, politically charged notions about what it meant to "calumniate" and "degrade constituted authority." Such speech, already considered a political crime by the Constitution of 1791, now met with the institutional efficacy of the Terror.

Obsessions with Calumny and the Law of Suspects (1792–1793)

With the collapse of the monarchy on August 10, 1792, punitive power shifted to the local level. On that very day, insurgents killed the royalist writer François Suleau, parading his head through the streets of Paris. Two weeks later, Rozoi was convicted by the Paris commune's extraordinary Tribunal du 17 août and promptly guillotined. In these stormy weeks, national authorities proved incapable of containing popular vengeance, as the prison massacres of early September so tragically demonstrated. The culture of calumny that had done so much to pit royalists against Jacobins now began poisoning relations among Jacobins themselves in the early months of the First Republic. A war between the Brissot-leaning members of the club (known as *brissotins*, *rolandistes*, and later, the Girondins) and others more sensitive to sans-culotte sentiment intensified. Accused of calumniating sans-culottes and the Paris commune, Brissot and Roland were expelled from the Jacobin Club in October and November.[155] The propaganda machines of both factions spread the calumny produced in Paris into the provinces, polarizing them as well. While the Girondins established a *bureau d'esprit public* (housed within the Ministry of the Interior) and subsidized the presses of Brissot and the Cercle Social with state funds, Jacobins mobilized the radical press and exploited the active correspondence they maintained with provincial clubs. Both factions sent agents into the provinces to diffuse propaganda, replete with calumnious denunciations and denunciations against calumniators.

Quasi-libertarian views on free speech had no purchase in this antagonistic climate. Even Robespierre abandoned them. On October 28, 1792, he delivered a speech at the Jacobin Club, *Discours sur l'influence de la calomnie sur la Révolution*. Without mentioning Roland by name (probably to avoid charges of calumniating!), he accused the Minister of the Interior of perpetuating the repressive policies of the Feuillants in 1791. "What will you say when I demonstrate that there now exists a coalition of virtuous patriots, of austere republicans [i.e., the *rolandistes*] who are perfecting the criminal policies of Lafayette and his allies?"[156] He explained the "criminal" nature of these policies. "In [Lafayette's] empire, any word, any writing was [deemed] a crime….All patriots, of which the dungeons were full, knew well that to speak ill of Lafayette was to 'destroy discipline in the military,' to 'favor the forces in Coblentz and Austria,' to 'preach anarchy and overthrow the state.'"[157] According to Robespierre, Roland was a menace to press freedom but also a great abuser of the press, indeed, a calumniator. Whereas in 1791 Robespierre had claimed that the calumnious press was impotent next to probity and virtue, he now acknowledged its power: "Journalists hold the destiny of the people in their hands….They make or break heroes."[158]

At this point, Robespierre did not call for punishing Girondin speech. The contradiction of doing so in a pamphlet aimed at portraying the Girondins as violators of press freedom would have been too flagrant. Instead, he urged his listeners to "observe in silence the incriminating maneuvers [of the Girondins]; let them unmask themselves and become the victims of their own excesses…. A magnanimous and enlightened people will always in good time reclaim its rights and avenge itself for injurious attacks."[159] In the violent context of autumn 1792, Robespierre's allusion to a future vengeance had an altogether more menacing ring than Diderot's "public vengeance" of 1762. During the Old Regime, "public vengeance" amounted to an embargo of esteem. During the Revolution, it amounted to heads on pikes.

Rising intolerance for radical and royalist speech was soon translated into law. On December 4, 1792, and again on March 29, 1793, the National Convention (which succeeded the Legislative Assembly in September 1792) prohibited certain speech.[160] There were important differences in the scope of the legislation passed on those days. The law of December 4 imposed death on "anyone who proposes or attempts to reestablish either the monarchy or any other power that threatens the sovereignty of the people." The law of March 29 reiterated the December 4 law (with some added precisions) but extended it to encompass those who incited the people to pillage and murder. Whereas the December 4 law targeted counterrevolutionaries, the March 29 law targeted both counterrevolutionaries and radicals.

Already in January 1793, the month the king was executed, clashes between radicals and moderates threatened to become lethal. An anti-Jacobin play, *L'Ami des lois*, provoked disturbances at the Comédie-française, renamed the Theater of the Nation. The play depicted Robespierre, Marat, and the sans-culottes as bloodthirsty brigands.[161] Despite the commune's ban and its canons parked outside the theater, spectators clamored for the play's performance, crying out, "Down with the mobs of September 2" (referring to the September prison massacres). The National Convention intervened, reminding the mayor that he had no censorship authority. Tensions over the play ran so high that deputies were forced to postpone debate over the fate of Louis XVI in order to deal with them.[162]

Controversy over *L'Ami des lois* turned on the issues of vengeance, brigandage, and calumny. At the time the play appeared, Jacobins were accusing Roland of calumniating patriots and corrupting public spirit with his propaganda bureau. For their part, the Girondins portrayed radicals as thieves and tried to begin prosecuting those involved in the September Massacres. The position of the Girondins was momentarily weakened by the vote to execute the king, which many Girondins opposed. On January 18, Armand-Guy Kersaint resigned from the Convention, explaining that he could no longer sit next to deputies who condoned the massacres. Outraged, radicals summoned him to justify his remarks, which he qualified, saying that he was referring only to Marat. He invoked the right to free speech and fumed at the hypocrisy of the Convention, which, while forcing him to justify his comments, ignored those of Marat, who had asserted in a recent issue of his newspaper that France would be better off after hanging another 200,000 corrupt men.[163]

Marat did not remain immune from the Convention's ire for long. On February 27, moderate deputies—many Girondins among them—accused him of instigating food riots through his new newspaper *Journal de la République*. The Convention refrained from formally accusing "the Friend of the People" but ordered the Minister of Justice to "proceed against the authors and instigators of the events that occurred yesterday." On the evening of March 9, radicals struck back by ransacking the Girondin presses of Antoine-Joseph Gorsas.[164] The next day, the Convention, after decreeing the establishment of revolutionary tribunals, discussed what kinds of speech crimes should fall within their jurisdiction. An initial *projet de loi* called for prosecuting authors who "mislead the people." Its advocates clearly had Marat in mind. Robespierre tried to have the text rephrased in such a way as to target the Girondins. He proposed prosecuting authors who "denounce...patriots who voted for the death of Capet...and who seek to spark civil war by making Paris appear suspect to the departments."[165] A Girondin cried out, "This is the most odious tyranny....They [the radicals] want to oppress all writers who haven't sold out to the anarchists." Others joined in, "Give us press freedom or give us death!"[166] Despite polarization, deputies struck a compromise. The final wording of the law was sufficiently vague: it criminalized attacks on liberty, equality, and the indivisibility of the Republic, thus giving neither faction legal leverage over the other.

Deputies did not exercise such impartiality on March 29. Initially, they set out to reiterate the December 4 ban on royalist speech, with the added stipulation that the authors of royalist publications would be brought before revolutionary tribunals and executed. The law was intended to unite revolutionaries against counterrevolutionaries, but it ended up pitting revolutionaries against each other. Anti-*maratiste* deputies militated to extend the scope of exceptional justice to encompass radical speech as well. Marie-Joseph Chénier called for imposing the death penalty on anyone who incited the people to murder or to attack property. Aware that this measure targeted him, Marat ran to the podium. "Chénier's proposal...amounts to a blade that cuts two ways, striking both counterrevolutionaries and revolutionaries." A deputy siding with Marat stressed that revolutionary laws and revolutionary tribunals should strike only counterrevolutionaries. In his view, theft and murder were ordinary crimes that could be treated through ordinary justice. The Girondin Charles-Jean-Marie Barbaroux retorted that theft and murder contributed to anarchy, thereby favoring the cause of those seeking to discredit the Revolution and restore the monarchy. Such crimes were thus political, necessitating revolutionary justice. In the end, the Girondins carried the day. The Convention decreed that authors inciting the people to murder or pillage were to be executed if such crimes occurred in the wake of the publication.

With the law of March 29, 1793, revolutionaries crossed the Rubicon, advancing quickly toward the Terror.

In April, the Girondins took advantage of the departure of several radical deputies for the provinces to make their move against Marat. In a recent pamphlet Marat had declared, "The counterrevolution is in the government and in the National Convention."[167] Invoking the Penal Code of 1791, deputies accused him of "degrading the Convention and constituted authority," among other offenses.[168] Efforts to arrest Marat backfired. No sooner was he acquitted than his supporters counterattacked. On May 8, the Commune sent a deputation to the Convention to denounce Brissot's *Patriote français*, in the same terms as the accusation against Marat, "for preaching the degradation of constituted authorities."[169] On the morning of May 31, the department of Paris convoked a joint meeting with the Paris sections to discuss "the means to repel all the calumnies which have been spread against the citizens of Paris."[170] The means employed was the purge of twenty-two Girondin deputies on June 2.

It was in the throes of these events that Thomas Paine wrote to Danton, warning him of the dangers to the besieged Republic of ongoing, unchecked calumny. He explained,

> While the hope remains to the enemy of seeing the Republic fall to pieces, while not only the representatives from the departments but *representation itself* is publicly insulted as it has been lately by the people of Paris…the enemy will be encouraged to hang about the frontiers.…The danger increases everyday of a rupture between Paris and the departments.…The departments did not send their deputies to Paris to be insulted, and every insult shown to them is an insult to the departments that elected and sent them.[171]

Paine may have been naive in thinking that the charges against the Girondins would be dropped, but he was acutely aware of the dangerous impact of calumny on fledgling authorities: "If every individual is to indulge his private malignancy

FIGURE 5.2. Le 31 mai 1793. Courtesy of the Bibliothèque nationale de France, cabinet d'estampes.

or his private ambition, to denounce at random and without any kind of proof, all confidence will be undermined and all authority be destroyed." Unlike the quasi-libertarian Jacobins of 1791, who believed that calumny was sufficiently counterbalanced by the power authorities wielded, Paine brooked no tolerance for it. "Calumny is a species of treachery that ought to be punished as well as any other kind of treachery."

In subsequent months, the Terror gave vent to widespread obsessions with calumny. The Law of Suspects of September 17, 1793, targeted those who "by

FIGURE 5.3. Thomas Paine. Courtesy of the Carnavalet Museum.

T . PAINE .

their conduct, relations, words, or writings show themselves to be the partisans of tyranny and federalism and the enemies of freedom."[172] In a pamphlet intended to reconcile the law with the principle of free expression, Louis-François Ferrières Sauvebeouf began by attributing the great achievements of recent years to the freedom of the press, "It is thanks to press freedom that the French Revolution has achieved the most rapid successes ever in history."[173] He insisted, though, that "there is a moment when the whirlwind of revolution must be controlled."

> The sacred and irrevocable right to petition permits the denunciation of govern-
> mental abuses and even of the representatives of the people [read: the Girondins].
> Each individual has the right to rectify hazarded assertions which may be found
> calumnious: and may the person who makes a career of calumny be removed from
> society![174]

Just as Oudet had confounded individual honor (that of the duc d'Orléans) with the majesty of the nation in 1790, Sauveboeuf confounded it with the revolutionary government.

> The man who obstructs the march of the Revolutionary government through
> calumny…is guilty. No law would dare circumscribe the freedom of the press;
> it is an arm that belongs to all citizens; but isn't it necessary to punish those who
> use this arm to assassinate others, in so far as an honest man puts his reputation
> before his life?[175]

The passage echoed arguments made by Robespierre and Paine in 1793, as well as those advanced by Malouet, Mirabeau, and Oudet in 1790. It chimed with widespread, deep-seated convictions stretching back to the Old Regime about the need to avenge attacks on honor, particularly the honor of authority.

Obsessions with calumny and honor continued shaping politics and legislation during the Terror. On January 23, 1794, the Convention appended the Penal Code with a law that imposed death on anyone found guilty of giving false testimony in a trial concerning a capital offense. In debate on the matter, Jacques-Alexis Thuriot declared, "There is not a single man in the Republic who…does not prefer death to the loss of his honor."[176] Whereas Montesquieu had seen honor as the moral principle of monarchy, and virtue the moral principle of republics, Thuriot insisted that "honor in Republics is dearer than life; those who attack the honor of a citizen must be punished by death."[177] The following day, after the Convention passed further decrees concerning false testimony, Louis-Joseph Charlier proposed expanding the law to include calumny even outside the courtroom. "Honor is the most precious of man's possessions. Will we allow it to be destroyed with impunity by calumny? Undoubtedly not; I demand the death penalty against calumniators."[178] Danton intervened, reminding his colleagues that intentions, not truth, mattered in determining culpability and that, in any case, calumny against officials could serve as a salutary check on their power. He succeeded in getting Charlier's proposal sent to the *comité de législation*, where it stalled.

Still, the will to punish calumniators could not be repressed, even after the liquidation in March and April of the radical *hébertistes*, who wanted to push the Terror further, and the *dantonistes*, who wanted to end it. The law of 18 Floréal, Year II (May 7, 1794), which instituted the Festival of the Supreme Being, was viewed enthusiastically by many clubs and local administrations throughout France as a measure that would confound the Revolution's calumniators, especially those who accused it of atheism. The patriotic club in Serres (department of the Hautes Alpes) characterized the festival as "the only possible dignified response a free people could give to the calumnies of perverted, corrupt men who dare depict us as materialists and atheists."[179] But less dignified responses were possible as well, notably the Law of 22 Prairial (June 10, 1794). It imposed the death penalty on anyone found guilty of "disparaging the National Convention and the republican government," "calumniating patriotism," "spreading false news," "misleading public opinion," "corrupting the public conscience," and "impairing the energy and purity of revolutionary and republican principles."[180]

Although the language of the Prairial Laws, like that of the Law of Suspects, was extreme, both laws amounted to little more than hyperbolic reformulations of legislation passed prior to the Terror. And as we shall see, many convictions for speech crimes during the Terror were based on those earlier laws and constitutional provisions. Still, revolutionaries of the Year II were the ones who actually enforced these laws. They did so to such a horrific extent that in the Terror's aftermath, amnesia set in about the collective origins of it all. Thermidorians blamed a bloodthirsty, calumnious, and conveniently dead Robespierre.[181] For their part, historians have stretched blame to include Jacobins and Jacobin ideology, characterizing them as inherently illiberal. But perhaps the quasi-libertarian Jacobins of 1791 had a clearer sense of the problem. They recognized the persistence of Old Regime punitive reflexes and how the strains of regime change excited them. As Robespierre admitted in May 1791, revolutions were not ideal moments for extending free speech, for too many people harbored grudges for the calumnies spread by the free press.[182] (He believed nevertheless that it was important to try.) His reflections were of a piece with Pétion's comments about revolutions involving "transitional storms" between old and new political forces and Lanthenas's view that press freedom would require a certain thickening of skin and the cultivation of civic consciousness.

In any case, the rapidity with which Jacobin quasi-libertarian views on free speech gave way to obsessions with calumny over the course of the early years of the Revolution is instructive. It suggests that the repression of speech in the Year II sprang from attitudes and reflexes whose origins stretched back further than Jacobinism. They stretched back, in fact, to the Old Regime.

CHAPTER SIX

Oaths, Honor, and the Sacred
Foundations of Authority

When legislators protected the freedom of religious opinions [in 1789], it never
entered their minds to allow all religions to be free, except for one, the religion that
has been the national religion for more than twelve hundred years.
—Deputy-bishops of the National Assembly, October 30, 1790

Exclusionary Dynamics

On the morning of October 21, 1790, the comte de Mirabeau thundered at
the podium in the National Assembly. Debate concerned a measure that would
require the French Navy to raise the revolutionary tricolor flag instead of the traditional white one. In arguing for the revolutionary ensign, Mirabeau excoriated
the opposition in terms that amounted to an accusation of treason.

> I demand a judgment. I insist that it is not only disrespectful or unconstitutional
> to question [the tricolor flag]. I insist that it is profoundly *criminal*. . . . I denounce as
> seditious conspirators those who would speak of maintaining old prejudices. . . . No,
> my fellow deputies, these tricolors will sail the seas; [they will] earn the respect of
> all countries and strike terror in the hearts of conspirators and tyrants.[1]

Mirabeau's incendiary speech riled the opposition, prompting one deputy on
the right, Jean-François-César de Guilhermy, to mutter injurious epithets. Over-
hearing them, Mirabeau's allies demanded Guilhermy's arrest, "for the honor of
the National Assembly."[2] After a vote—and, as evidence suggests, communication between individuals in the Assembly and crowds outside—the deputies
expelled Guilhermy for three days, keeping him under house arrest during that
time. Mirabeau endorsed the measure. Despite having championed the freedom

of expression and the inviolability of deputies the year before, he now reasoned, "It is not fitting for a deputy to sacrifice the portion of respect due to him as a member of this Assembly."[3]

Guilhermy was one of four deputies condemned for speech in the Constituent Assembly in 1790. Three were put under arrest; a fourth was pardoned. Temporary arrests were not the only form of exclusion. In the spring of that year, François-Henri, comte de Virieu was pressured into stepping down as president of the National Assembly for having signed and circulated a declaration protesting a recent decree, thereby violating an oath. To be sure, these exclusions were mild compared to the deadly ones carried out three years later; punishments ranged from three- and eight-day house arrests to three days in prison. Still, they suggest that alongside liberal reforms, illiberal practices were seeping into high politics. Nor was the illiberal nature of these exclusions lost on the deputies of the losing side (in all cases, right-wing deputies). In their view, these exclusions ran counter to the Assembly's professed commitment to free speech. Worse, they had no basis in law. Although deputies had set rules governing Assembly discipline in the summer of 1789, they had not agreed on authorizing arrests of members. A motion calling for the temporary arrest of obstreperous deputies was advanced in June 1790 but was rejected.[4]

What prompted these exclusions in the Constituent Assembly? Few historical studies of the early Revolution acknowledge that they even occurred. These incidents run counter to the prevailing view of the "liberal phase" of the French Revolution. According to this view, national deputies are seen keeping their extremist elements in check, conducting debate "without imputations of disloyalty or treason," and remaining above the fray of popular passions, at least after October 1789.[5] Before then, of course, the storming of the Bastille on July 14, rural attacks on noble property in the following weeks, and the Women's Bread March to Versailles in early October helped progressive deputies push through liberal reforms, notably, the abolition of feudalism and the Declaration of the Rights of Man and of the Citizen. But from late 1789 until September 1791, the high politics of the Constituent Assembly are depicted as just that, *high*. As one historian has recently asserted—and most accounts concur on this point—in this period, "[Popular] terror spread at the bottom without ever contaminating the high reaches of the state," even when it would have been easy and opportune for leaders to exploit it.[6]

But leaders did exploit it. While patriot deputies courted crowds gathered outside the National Assembly in Paris, reactionary deputies capitalized on, even fomented, sectarian agitation in the provinces. Moreover, noble deputies injected their own form of violence, the duel, into revolutionary politics, where it mixed with popular punitive dynamics. In the course of interactions between the National Assembly and society, religion, oaths, and honor played important roles. Deeply engrained in Old Regime culture, religion, oaths, and honor provided familiar idioms for defining the legitimate limits of opposition and customary practices for preventing and structuring conflict. To be sure, these practices and social idioms were not inherently radicalizing forces. During the Old Regime, they had helped affirm allegiances, reinforce hierarchical power relations, and structure patterns of esteem and deference. During the Revolution, however, they polarized politics, lowered tolerance thresholds, and generated punitive, exclusionary impulses. They had markedly illiberal consequences for free speech.[7]

Oaths, Religion, and the Virieu Affair

The first attempt to arrest a deputy in the National Assembly for speech occurred on December 15, 1789. The Assembly was considering whether the Parlement of Rennes had obstructed the Assembly's efforts to reform the justice system (the creation of a system of elected judges was on the agenda). The magistrates had sent a letter to the king asking him to declare where he stood on this issue, a gesture that some deputies construed as undermining the National Assembly's authority. Robespierre denounced the letter as "criminal."[8] The irascible and frequently drunk vicomte de Mirabeau (André-Boniface-Louis Riqueti, not to be confused with his more famous brother, Honoré-Gabriel Riqueti, comte de Mirabeau) insisted that Robespierre was skewing the matter by ignoring key documents concerning the Parlement's communication with the king. The vicomte then belched forth speech "peu mesuré," too offensive, in any case, to be printed in the *Archives parlementaires.*[9] A moment of disorder followed, after which demands were made to have the vicomte expelled from the Assembly for eight days. Barnave pointed out that the Assembly did not have the right to do so, since it had not yet passed a law for dealing with such violations, and the matter was soon dropped.

Another deputy was nearly expelled on January 22, 1790. The matter concerned an insult. During heated discussion about the management of state finances, Jean-Siffrein, abbé Maury blurted out, "I insist that those in this Assembly whom nature has denied all but a *shameful courage.*"[10] This was considered an egregious affront. Indignant, one deputy proposed expelling Maury from the Assembly and having his constituents in Péronne elect another representative. He claimed that, although public opinion was capable of redressing insults against individuals, those against the National Assembly required official, punitive measures, since they amounted to an attack on the representative body in which the nation had invested its honor. If the Assembly failed to command respect and avenge itself, insults would eventually undermine efforts to enforce its decrees.[11]

The comte de Mirabeau agreed that some kind of official reprimand was needed but proposed a more moderate response. He called for censuring Maury. Maury claimed that according to new judicial maxims concerning the separation of powers, the National Assembly could not be both plaintiff and judge. Pierre-Louis Roederer countered by invoking the example of the French sovereign courts, the parlements. In cases of internal wrongdoing, the magistrates had legitimate authority to investigate and adjudicate. Roederer believed this logic should apply to the Assembly, warning that without the authority to enforce internal discipline, nothing would prevent deputies from disrupting meetings. In the end, the Assembly chose to follow the moderate guidelines it had set the previous summer. Mirabeau's motion was accepted. Maury received formal censure, and his behavior was recorded in a *procès-verbal*.

The first instance of an exclusion for speech in the Constituent Assembly occurred on April 27, 1790. On the surface, the affair involved the violation of an oath. At root, it turned on the more profound issues of a national religion, religious freedom, and sectarian strife. On that morning, the Assembly elected the comte de Virieu for its president. Virieu's election was controversial because of his recent protest against the decree of April 13, which put an end to right-wing efforts to declare Catholicism the national cult.[12] Ever since August 1789, the right had sought to secure official exclusive status for their faith. Their aim was, in part, to gain political leverage in order to reduce the impending damage to their interests caused by the Declaration of the Rights of Man and of the Citizen (which declared the freedom of religious opinions) and the abolition of privilege (which put the fate of tax-free Church property into question). Although these reforms had been ratified in 1789, deputies had not yet agreed on how to implement them. When the right was defeated on April 13, Virieu, along with more than three hundred other deputies—that is, between a quarter and a third of the National Assembly—signed a petition protesting the decree. Published a week later under the title *Déclaration d'une partie de l'Assemblée nationale sur le décret rendu le 13 avril 1790 concernant la religion*, it circulated widely, galvanizing resistance to the Revolution and provoking unrest and massacres.

Efforts to oust Virieu from his post as president of the National Assembly began the morning of his induction on April 27. The Jacobin deputy

Charles-François Bouche proposed a motion requiring incoming presidents to repeat the civil oath of February 4, 1790—the day when the National Assembly and the king formally declared their allegiances to the nation, the law, and each other. But Bouche added a clause requiring them to swear that they *had* never partaken and *would* never partake in any protest or declaration that undermined the Assembly's decrees sanctioned by the king or that undermined the respect due to the king or Assembly.[13] The measure, which passed, was clearly intended to challenge Virieu's election.[14]

During his induction, Virieu made no mention of his participation in the protest declaration, but the left pressed the issue. "Who would have thought," asked Alexandre de Lameth, "that the Assembly would choose for its president a member who protested its own laws?"[15] Virieu replied that, since the king had not yet ratified the April 13 decree, his signing of the protest declaration did not constitute a violation of the civil oath.[16] Bouche intervened to remind him that the oath had two components. The first forbade deputies from protesting decrees *sanctioned by the king*. This was the clause that Virieu's defense was riding on. The second forbade dissent that weakened or undermined the honor of the king and National Assembly. He insisted that Virieu was guilty on this count.[17] Charles de Lameth added that, even though Louis had not signed the April 13 decree at the time the *Declaration* appeared, Virieu's involvement was all the more criminal, since it constituted an attempt to coerce the king through the threat of sectarian strife.[18] For Bouche and the Lameth brothers, then, free speech ended where disrespect for authority and threats to public order began. The strongest argument in defense of Virieu was advanced by the abbé Maury, who claimed (rightly) that the inviolability of deputies, declared in the summer of 1789, prohibited anyone except a judge appointed by the National Assembly from ruling on the matter and only after proper investigation.[19] The left, however, persisted, and eventually Virieu's defenders backed down. Virieu resigned from his position as president.[20]

If one considers only what transpired in the Assembly that day, it would seem that the use of the oath to force Virieu to step down as president was an early sign of the inherent intolerance of Jacobins and their obsession with unity; and, indeed, the key left-wing deputies in this affair were members of the Jacobin Club. This interpretation would reinforce the view of revolutionary oath taking as nothing but coercion masquerading as unanimity, the acting out of Rousseau's social contract, with all its illiberal trappings.[21] Yet, we can better appreciate revolutionary oath taking, I believe, by considering its long-standing place in early modern political culture and the contingent problem of distrust provoked by conditions of regime change. Revolutionary oath taking owed much to Old Regime pre-occupations with honor, deference, and allegiance. For centuries, oaths were an important part of corporate and political life.[22] In France, high-ranking office holders came to Versailles to place their hands between those of the king to swear their allegiance to him. In the oaths sworn during coronations, kings promised to uphold the Catholic faith, peace, and justice in the kingdom. They also swore to enforce edicts against dueling—an oath that reveals much about the relationship between oath taking and concerns about violence.[23] Although oaths were commonly sworn throughout France, they were prominent in frontier regions, where conflicting allegiances could readily spark wars.[24] They were also commonly sworn in Enlightenment institutions, such as royal academies.[25]

Ironically, Edmund Burke—no friend of the French Revolution—was sensitive to the importance of trust and allegiance, which oaths were intended to reinforce. Instead of applying his insights to Revolutionary oath taking, he applied them to idealize feudal fealty, which he claimed the Revolution had destroyed. "By freeing kings from fear," he wrote in *Reflections on the Revolution in France*, "fealty [declared through oaths]…freed both kings and subjects from the precautions of tyranny."[26] By "precautions of tyranny," Burke was referring to preemptive violence, such as assassinations or invasions, which grew out of conditions of distrust. Burke failed to see that revolutionary oath taking was also intended to prevent "precautions of tyranny" by cultivating a climate of trust. So, too, have historians who have por-trayed revolutionary oath taking as nothing but the imposition of Enlightenment ideology—the sign of sterile, authoritarian politics.[27]

The oath that brought down Virieu's presidency on April 27 was a modified version of the civil oath of February 4, 1790. The events that led to this oath reveal much about the problems of distrust and violence in a period of abrupt political change. Some historians have argued that revolutionary oaths sought to replace the charisma of the king with that of the nation.[28] Yet, the oath of February 4, which served as the basis for all major revolutionary oaths for the next two and a half years, was initiated by the king himself. It was intended not to eclipse his charisma but to fuse it with the honor and charisma of the nation. Louis swore the oath in a desperate effort to reverse a rapidly deteriorating politi-cal situation. At the beginning of 1790, suspicions about where he stood with regard to the Revolution were pushing France to the brink of civil war. In early January, the king's brother presented himself to municipal authorities in Paris to deny rumors of his complicity in a recently unveiled counterrevolutionary plot to take the king abroad.[29] Days later, violence broke out on the Champs-Elysées between royalist and radical groups within the Paris National Guard. Violence nearly erupted in the Cordeliers district of Paris on January 22 when police came through with an arrest warrant for the radical journalist Jean-Paul Marat (district fury forced the police to withdraw empty-handed). All this, together with reports of rioting in Brittany, Bas-Limousin, and Quercy, convinced the king's advisors, notably Necker and Lafayette, that to stop ongoing entropy, Louis had to position himself publicly with regard to the Revolution.[30] A royal oath sworn before, and to, the National Assembly was devised as a solution.

In his speech before the National Assembly on February 4, the king described, quite accurately, how "the suspension or inactivity of Justice, the dissatisfactions and hatreds that spring from persistent dissensions…combined with a general atmosphere of unrest" were "fueling the anxieties of loyal friends of the Kingdom." To overcome these problems, he swore to "defend and maintain constitutional liberty, the principles of which the general desire [væu général]—at one with my own—has consecrated."[31] Later that day, Marie-Antoinette, descending from the royal carriage with the dauphin, swore before the crowds gathered near the Tuileries Palace that she would raise her son to be loyal to public liberty and the laws of the nation. Inspired by the queen's pronouncements and still under the spell of the king's visit, deputies in the National Assembly devised an oath of their own, requiring it of all members: "I promise to be faithful to the Nation, the Law, and the King, and to maintain with all my power the Constitution decreed by the National Assembly and accepted by the King."[32]

The oath spread quickly throughout France. In Paris, special masses were celebrated to honor it, municipal officials swore it, and zealous individuals forced random pedestrians to repeat it.[33] In the provinces, it was received with equal enthusiasm, accompanied by Te Deums (Catholic hymns) and echoed in the correspondence of local officials to the National Assembly in the following weeks and months. In a world in which justice, administration, and the military were in disarray or mired in conflict, the oath offered hope and reassurance that, with some goodwill, strife could be averted.

But strife was not averted. Within three months, sectarian violence broke out in southern France, fueled in part by intransigent deputies who insisted that their allegiance to God trumped their allegiance to the nation, or that the nation was inseparable from allegiance to a Catholic God. When the left succeeded in blocking the motion to declare Catholicism the national religion on April 13, hundreds of deputies, in a powerful display of defiance, stood up in the Assembly, raised their right hands to the heavens, and swore an oath to God and their religion.[34] The gesture posed the threat of schism—and schism over the issue of religion would unfold in coming months.

A week later, on April 19—the day the National Assembly transferred the administration of Church property to the state—dissenting deputies published their protest declaration, sending it into the provinces, somehow with the Assembly's official seal. The declaration hit a France that was already on the brink of revolt in many places. Not only had fighting among French troops broken out in the North; contest over religion was also heating up in many areas, especially in the Midi.[35] Despite numerous studies on the violence of 1790, most general accounts of the Revolution still ignore or gloss over these incidents, reinforcing the myth of 1790 as the "happy" or "peaceful" year of the Revolution.[36] Yet, the signers of the declaration were neither happy nor naive about the impact their declaration would have.[37] Upon exiting the Assembly on April 12, the abbé Maury was reported announcing that the issue of a national religion had lit the fuse of a political "powder keg."[38] To prevent troubles in Paris, the National Guard was stationed in sensitive locations on the morning of April 13. Aside from minor incidents (angry crowds chased two right-wing deputies through the streets of Paris after one of them had drawn his sword), peace was maintained.[39]

In the Midi, however, the powder keg exploded. The worst incidents occurred in Nîmes, where Protestants, who dominated the National Guard, and Catholics, who controlled the municipal government, clashed. On April 20, 1790—too soon to have received the April 19 *Déclaration* but certainly late enough to have been informed about the scandal in the Assembly on April 13—reactionary Catholics in Nîmes published a pamphlet insisting that Catholicism be declared the official religion of the nation. Less than two weeks later, on May 2–3, violence broke out. The National Assembly was sufficiently alarmed to summon the Mayor of Nîmes, Jean-Antoine Teissier, baron de Marguerittes, who was also a national deputy, to explain his actions, or rather, his suspicious inaction the day Catholics initiated hostilities against Protestants.[40] Marguerittes had been on leave from the National Assembly and was in Nîmes at the time violence erupted. On behalf of outraged deputies, Charles de Lameth tried (but failed) to persuade his colleagues to suspend the inviolability of deputies in order to hold Marguerittes responsible for the violence.[41]

The situation in Nîmes worsened. On June 1, Catholic forces published another provocative pamphlet in which they openly aligned themselves with religious opposition to the Revolution in Alsace, Comminges, Toulouse, Montauban, Albis, Uzès, Lautrec, Alais, Châlons-sur-Marne, and numerous other towns.[42] They claimed that although they had been among the first to denounce the abuses of the Old Regime in 1789, they now wanted to bring the Revolution to an end. They professed their allegiance to monarchical and religious authority, which they believed the Revolution was undermining. Oddly, they justified their resistance to the Revolution by invoking the Declaration of the Rights of Man and of the Citizen, which guaranteed the freedom of religious opinions provided public order was not disturbed. To charges that they themselves were disrupting public order, they responded, "People cannot accuse us of expressing opinions that disturb the public order since our mission is, to the contrary, to reestablish and maintain it."[43] For them, as for many devout contemporaries, "public order" meant not merely the absence of agitation; it referred to a moral order as well, one based on throne and altar. In any case, their intransigence provoked another outbreak of sectarian violence between June 14 and 17, killing more than three hundred.[44]

Throughout the spring and summer of 1790, the National Assembly received a steady stream of denunciations of the declaration of April and the flurry of local pamphlets inspired by it. The municipalities of Arras, Bordeaux, Casteln-audary, Châteauneuf, La Rochelle, Lyon, Lorient, Montbrison, Issoudun, and

FIGURE 6.1. Massacre des patriotes de Montauban. Courtesy of the Carnavalet Museum. Unlike in Nîmes, where hundreds died in sectarian violence, few were actually killed in Montauban.

Tarbes, among others, expressed their indignation and alarm. They warned the Assembly about the destabilizing impact of these tracts, which they were banning and seizing as best they could.[45] Some threatened to prosecute anyone involved in spreading them.[46] Officials in Issoudun and Saint-Martin-en-Ré went so far as to order the public executioner to burn copies of them in front of their respective city halls.[47] Members of the *conseil général* of the commune of Lyon explained why they thought the protest declaration, which they banned, was treasonous.

> Such protests, which might have been considered simply erroneous had they not been publicized, become crimes of lèse-nation the moment that they are published and distributed with the National Assembly's [official] seal to ecclesiastic and religious bodies in order to…renew the flames of religious strife.[48]

The council reiterated the oath of February 4 and declared its determination to bring charges of lèse-nation against anyone involved in undermining the Assembly's decrees or threatening public order.

By summer 1790, even supporters of the protest declaration began acknowledging the dangers of ongoing resistance. In his pamphlet published in July, the deputy François Simonnet, abbé de Coulmiers encouraged supporters of the declaration to desist. He said that, even though he believed Catholicism should be the national religion, public opinion was clearly opposed and ongoing intransigence was threatening public peace.[49] He went so far as to characterize ongoing support for the protest declaration as "criminal."[50]

On July 12, 1790, the National Assembly passed the Civil Constitution of the Clergy. This far-reaching reform nationalized Church property, put priests on the state payroll, made clerical posts subject to local elections, restructured dioceses and parishes around new civil jurisdictions, and required new clergymen to swear an oath based on the civil oath of February 4 (with minor additions). In November, the National Assembly went further, imposing the oath on all clergymen and teachers, threatening to remove them from their offices if they refused. Many historians have criticized the clerical oath of November for being unnecessary, illiberal, and catastrophic for the course of the Revolution. It has been described as "one of the Constituent Assembly's greatest mistakes," producing a crisis of conscience by forcing individuals to choose between their religion and the Revolution.[51]

There is no doubt about the oath's polarizing impact, which has been thoroughly documented.[52] Still, I would stress the significance of struggles over defining the place of religion in the new order even before the Civil Oath was imposed on the clergy. Catholic resistance to religious freedom was indeed threatening the new order, as the sectarian violence of May and June 1790 demonstrates. In their *Exposition des principes sur la Constitution civile du clergé* of October 1790, right-wing bishops in the National Assembly announced their refusal to recognize the Assembly's policies on religion until receiving the pope's views.[53] They explicitly rejected the freedom of religion, claiming that "when legislators protected the freedom of religious opinions [in the Declaration of the Rights of Man and of the Citizen], it never entered their minds to allow all religions to be free, except for one, the religion that has been the national religion for more than twelve hundred years."[54] Historians critical of the clerical oath often mistake the distinction contemporaries made between spiritual and secular domains with the more recent distinction between the public and the private. In most developed democracies, religious freedom is based on the premise that religious convictions have no privileged place in public affairs and cannot serve as criteria for the negotiation or judicial settlement of competing interests. Catholic reactionaries during the Revolution, however, insisted on the distinction between secular and spiritual authority, both of which were public in their minds. They had no intention of seeing religious faith relegated to the private sphere. To the contrary, they wanted Catholicism to be declared the official national cult—the moral essence of "public order," which would justify limiting free expression according to the Declaration of Rights. In light of the clergy's agenda, the clerical oath should be seen not as gratuitous provocation by Jacobins unable to distinguish between public and private spheres, but rather as an attempt to prevent sectarianism from undermining the Revolution's achievements, religious freedom among them. Seen in this light, the clerical civil oaths decreed in July and November 1790, like the rapid rise of Jacobin Clubs throughout France in the spring of 1790, were not so much the cause of religious troubles but responses to Catholic resistance to the Revolution.[55] Given the Church's privileged role in education—there was no universal secular education system yet—the insistence of revolutionaries that the clergy swear allegiance to the new order can be seen as an expression of practical concerns.

Honor in the Revolutionary Dynamic

If oaths were intended to prevent conflict, honor was invoked to structure conflict that was not averted. Honor, which had figured prominently in social and political life during the Old Regime, persisted into the Revolution, becoming imbricated in profound sociopolitical shifts. In his *Honour among Men and Nations*, Geoffrey Best notes that the Revolution marked a decisive turning point in the history of honor.[56] Whereas honor had been based on social hierarchy before 1789, the Revolution democratized it while also fastening it to the sacred concept of the nation. How did this transformation take place? Best attributes it to the rise of Jacobins to power in 1792 and their commitment to Rousseauian notions about virtue and unity within the nation-state. This explanation, I believe, reifies Jacobin ideology and exaggerates its causal role in the radicalization of the Revolution. Like many discursive analyses of the French Revolution, it takes the Jacobin discourse of 1792–1794 as its starting point, confusing effects for causes. It fails to appreciate the way in which honor had already started becoming collectivized in the nation before the Revolution and overlooks how Jacobin discourse itself grew out of interactions between elite politics and popular agitation—interactions inflected by a deeply engrained culture of honor.

During the Old Regime, however, popular and elite cultures of honor were distinct, and elite violence rarely fused with popular revolt. Social and political hierarchy determined legitimate forms of resolving conflicts over honor. With the advent of civil equality in 1789, the system of honor, esteem, and deference was thrown into question. The dignity that had been concentrated in elites, giving them social and juridical privileges, was now recognized to exist among the people. Although revolutionaries did try to maintain hierarchical distinctions, notably, between active and passive citizens (defined by property) and between men and women, the genie was out of the bottle. With the democratization of honor, popular indignation and punitive demands gained legitimacy. Recognizing this, leaders of the left and the right often exploited them to advance their respective causes.

From Libel to Arms: The Frondeville and Faucigny Affair

The first arrest for speech of a deputy in the National Assembly occurred on August 21, 1790. The incident reveals how elite and popular cultures of violence merged in struggles over honor. That morning, the deputy Thomas-Louis-César Lambert de Frondeville distributed a pamphlet he had written to deputies arriving in the Assembly. In it he boasted about the censure he had received a few days earlier in the Assembly for his behavior during discussion of a political affair dating back to 1789. Frondeville's insolence incensed deputies, who declared his pamphlet a punishable insult to the National Assembly. The question was how far to go with the punishment.[57] Debate was heated. Some left-wing deputies declared that the majesty of the nation resided in the national representation; any insult against the Assembly, therefore, amounted to an insult against the entire nation.[58] Maury countered with the argument that there was no law justifying the arrest of a deputy for speech (which was correct). He claimed that perceptions of honor or dishonor belonged to the realm of public opinion, and that it was not for the deputies to decide whether the Assembly's honor had been violated. Invoking Old Regime custom, the left retorted that all corporate assemblies had the right to exercise internal policing and discipline members. But the right insisted that punishment be based on laws, not custom. If the Assembly punished without recourse to a previously declared law, they would be, in the bigoted words of a clerical deputy from Noyon, "worse than the Jews."[59]

The situation became explosive when Barnave declared that if a deputy congratulated himself for the censure he received from the Assembly, then imprisonment was the *least* severe penalty he should expect.[60] This statement implicitly invoked and legitimized punitive violence. The right struck back immediately in the words of Louis-Charles-Amédée, comte de Faucigny-Lucinge, who leapt forward and cried out, "This is all starting to look like an open war by the majority against the minority. There's only one way to settle this … to attack those bastards with sabers in hand."[61] Deputies on the left rose, bracing themselves for combat. Frondeville, panicking, rushed to the podium to try to restore calm. He pleaded guilty and begged the Assembly to punish him, but only him, not Faucigny. (Faucigny, by the way, had been a career cavalryman in the Old Regime.) Frondeville claimed that if, for his defense, a deputy would go so far as to jeopardize the security of the Assembly and declare civil war, then all responsibility should fall on him, and he encouraged the Assembly to overlook Faucigny's call to arms.[62] The Assembly granted the first part of Frondeville's request, condemning him to eight-day house arrest.[63] The remaining problem was what to do with Faucigny. For some deputies, a call to arms was far more egregious than Frondeville's puerile pamphlet. But Guillaume-François-Charles Goupil-Préfelne, who had initiated debate on punishing Frondeville, urged his colleagues to "close [their] eyes" to this incident. Like Roman legislators who believed that parricide was too horrible a crime to even mention, they should pass over the event in silence.

This "oblivion" option was promptly extinguished when a rumor spread throughout the Assembly that the comte de Mirabeau had ordered messengers to inform crowds outside about what had just happened. Mirabeau dismissed the rumor, but he nevertheless admitted that the left had so many supporters, its popularity might turn out to be its greatest weakness if it proved incapable of securing the personal safety of Frondeville and Faucigny.[64] Faucigny must have recognized these risks, for he immediately apologized and declared himself willing to submit to whatever punishment the Assembly wished to impose.[65] The left was reluctant to make a martyr of him and sought ways to downplay the event. The two sides compromised: after formally condemning Faucigny, the Assembly accepted the errant deputy's apologies and pardoned him.[66] In this way, the National Assembly avoided losing face and, in obtaining an apology, assuaged popular punitive sentiments that might have boiled over had Faucigny remained intransigent or gone unpunished.

National Symbols and the Guilhermy Affair

We return to the incident concerning the tricolor ensign in October 1790. The issue had grown out of concerns in Paris about insurrections in Brest, where sailors in the French Navy, recently arrived from Saint-Domingue, had staged a mutiny against their officers. The municipality and the local Jacobin Club got involved, and the situation deteriorated.[67] Between mid-September and mid-October, Brest was in a state of rebellion, no insignificant matter given its vulnerability to British invasion. France was still traumatized by a similar such mutiny in Nancy, which led to a bloodbath that, according to one historian, killed as many as three thousand people.[68] Left-wing deputies suspected Louis's ministers of fomenting reaction in Saint-Domingue (the governor had tried to shut down the new local representative assembly). The mutiny in Brest, they claimed, was nothing but the predictable backlash of the sailors against their reactionary officers. In a controversial motion proposing that the ministers be held responsible for the troubles in Saint-Domingue and elsewhere, left-wing deputies included an article calling for the replacement of the traditional white Bourbon Banner with the revolutionary tricolor ensign.

The rebellion in Brest, along with the smoldering sentiments over the massacre in Nancy, should be kept in mind in assessing Mirabeau's long, incendiary speech. In it, he maintained that symbols were powerful instruments in the hands of patriots and counterrevolutionaries alike and should not be treated superficially.[69] The Brest tragedy, he insisted, demonstrated this. His repeated reference to the white flag as the symbol of counterrevolution infuriated the right. The situation became explosive when he stated that a deputy defending the white flag would have paid for such views with his head had he voiced them just a few weeks earlier.[70] The statement was a thinly veiled threat, and it enraged the right.

In the commotion that followed, Guilhermy was overheard calling Mirabeau a "scoundrel" and "assassin." Guilhermy defended himself, insisting that Mirabeau had insulted deputies by interpreting support for maintaining the white flag as counterrevolutionary.[71] He added that Mirabeau's statements incited sedition by legitimizing popular punitive violence against deputies who supported the Bourbon Banner.

Indeed, the presence of crowds outside the National Assembly could not be ignored. Terrified that he might be implicated in this affair, Maury requested that two officers be sent out into the Tuileries gardens to inform the crowds that he had nothing to do with this incident.[72] A fellow right-wing colleague, Jacques-Antoine-Marie de Cazalès, frowned upon Maury's request, warning that nothing was more dangerous than putting the National Assembly in direct contact with the people.[73] Cazalès added that he had indeed found Mirabeau's speech to be libelous but claimed to have refrained from stopping Mirabeau out of respect for the freedom of expression. This same freedom, he now insisted, should be extended to Guilhermy, even if the Assembly might consider calling Guilhermy to order, as was purportedly done in the British Parliament.[74]

After more wrangling, Roederer boiled the matter down to this: was it tolerable that a deputy call another a scoundrel and assassin?[75] At this point, Mirabeau turned the dispute into a zero-sum duel: "I demand that the Assembly condemn either Mr. Guilhermy or myself. If he is innocent, I am guilty."[76] The majority chose the former option and condemned Guilhermy to three-day house arrest.[77]

In an open letter to his constituents, Guilhermy described the maneuvers against him in the Assembly that day.[78] He claimed that Mirabeau's allies had tossed notes out the windows of the Assembly, informing crowds that he, Guilhermy, had insulted Mirabeau, thus inciting them to avenge the comte. He provided the names of several witnesses (and claimed he could provide thirty more) who had seen individuals scooping up the messages and reading them aloud. He complained that when he and several other deputies tried to alert the Assembly to this dangerous situation, the majority brushed off the matter, claiming that the notes belonged to a journalist whose assistants were picking them up on the other side before carrying them to print shops.[79] Whether the notes were intended for the crowds or the presses, the crowds were clearly being informed (or misinformed) about events going on inside as they unfolded. Maury's panicky request to have officers inform the crowds outside that he had nothing to do with the incident suggests that such communication had occurred and, more significantly, that threats of popular violence were inflecting internal Assembly politics. It is likely that Mirabeau's allies exploited popular punitive sentiments to intimidate the right. In any case, the tactic succeeded in avenging Mirabeau for insults in the absence of legal limits on speech offenses. In the long run, however, such demagogical tactics had dangerous implications. They encouraged conflating the individual honor of deputies with the honor of the nation. They reinforced the idea that popular punitive violence—or the threat of it—might be just.

Duels and Arrests: The Roy Affair

Revolutionaries did no better than their predecessors in curtailing the age-old practice of dueling. Demands that the National Assembly pass strict laws against it were made frequently after 1789, but the odds of eliminating the practice were not great when deputies themselves did not refrain from engaging in it.[80] The duel between Charles de Lameth and Armand-Charles-Augustin de la Croix, duc de Castries, which occurred in November 1790, just a few weeks after Guilhermy's arrest, reveals how personal rivalries could escalate into affairs of state, stirring up Parisian crowds and leading to imprisonment for injurious speech.

The events leading up to the duel began when the vicomte de Chauvigny arrived at the Assembly (escorted by guards) seeking to settle a private matter with Lameth. When Chauvigny challenged Lameth to a duel, Lameth sneered, saying that the duc de Castries must have put him up to it. When news of this remark reached Castries (he was absent from the Assembly that morning), he rushed to the Assembly to challenge Lameth to a duel. The next morning, the two deputies squared off on the Champs de Mars. Lameth, the expected victor, was wounded in the arm.[81]

As deputies discussed the event in the National Assembly, crowds numbering between forty thousand and two hundred thousand (the latter figure was undoubtedly exaggerated) descended upon Castries's *hôtel particulier*.[82] Castries was already notorious for having protested the abolition of noble titles the previous summer and for having led cavalry troops in the suppression of the mutiny in Nancy. After storming the residence in search of him and discovering that he had fled, the invaders ransacked the place, tossing furniture out windows. Upon receiving news about the riot, some deputies applauded, but others scowled them into silence. Alarmed, Maury exhorted the National Assembly to order the municipality to deploy forces to break it up. He also demanded that all such gatherings be treated as lèse-nation and that all who participated in them be corporally punished. Another deputy called for outlawing duels but warned that,

FIGURE 6.2. Duel Lameth-Castries, Bagarre d'hommes du peuple. Courtesy of the Carnvalet Museum. The caption on the left reads, "In the clash of opinions over how to disrupt everything in France, those with opinions are not always in control of their expression. Bloody situations sometimes result." The duel and its tumultuous aftermath are described. The caption on the right reads, "The manner in which ordinary citizens explain their different opinions."

given the present "emotional state" of the deputies, it was not wise to convict Castries now.

That evening, a deputation of National Guardsmen from the section *Bonnes-Nouvelles* arrived in the National Assembly. The guardsmen demanded that Castries be charged with lèse-nation.

> Considering that nothing is *more urgent than to impose public vengeance against those who attack the respect due to the nation's legislators* and considering, moreover, that any further indulgence might embolden the enemies of the Revolution and slow down progress on [drafting] the Constitution, [the battalion of *Bonnes-Nouvelles*] sends its envoys to the Assembly to request, with all due justice, a decree declaring attempts to provoke a national deputy to a duel or to hinder him from carrying out official duties to be a crime worthy of universal indignation and treated as lèse-nation.[83]

The demand met with vigorous applause in the Assembly. On the right, however, a deputy from Angoulême, Antoine-Joseph Roy, chided enthusiastic deputies,

FIGURE 6.3. Pillage de l'hôtel Castries. Courtesy of the Carnavalet Museum.

PILLAGE DE L'HÔTEL DE CASTRIES, F B G. S.ᵗ GERMAIN À PARIS.
le 13 Novembre 1790

saying, "Only villains could applaud such a request."[84] Indignant murmurs spread on the floor, and once again demands for punishment were made. This time the left would not settle for house arrest. They wanted Roy imprisoned.

At this point, the National Assembly had two matters to settle: duels and insults. Barnave drew a causal link between the two, arguing that insults often sparked acts of vengeance and public disorder. "If there is a true means to prevent personal vengeance and to take out of the people's hands the arms they use to attack their fellow citizens, it is to empower the law to stop them.... [The Assembly should] punish insults, and soon people will stop making them."[85] He asked his fellow deputies, who among them had not, at one time or another, been insulted just walking through the Tuileries? An ironic voice, probably from the right, shot back that they had even been insulted from the podium.

Barnave then peppered his injunctions with suspicions about plots. He claimed that counterrevolutionaries were testing the limits of the people's patience by provoking them to violence. Castries's aggression offered Barnave an opportunity to stretch a particular instance of personal animosity into an orchestrated conspiracy.

I am not sure of the exact source of such provocations, but there is clearly a system of provocation directed against good citizens. It seems that conspirators are
seeking to exhaust the people's steadfastness which has been, up to this point, the
source of terror and despair for the country's enemies.[86]

Since Barnave was a leading Jacobin, such speech seems to bear out François
Furet's observations that Jacobins were prone to paranoia. Yet, the right harbored
similar such suspicions. Roy insinuated that some external and malicious force
(on the left) was behind this uprising: "Whether the people acted on their own
initiative or whether they were provoked by..." The left growled, but Roy persisted. "It seems my hypothesis raises complaints; but who here has not remarked
that the enemies of public order have always incited the people to seditious acts,
that there has not been a single insurrection in the realm which has not been
generated by the enemies of the public good."[87]

After both sides vented their suspicions about plots, Virieu spoke up. He said
that it was dangerous to allow the Assembly to be transformed into a Roman
arena, "where the moderate clash of opinions gives way to the violent clash of
passions."[88] To calm tensions in the National Assembly, he thought it was necessary to ban all approbatory and disapprobatory expression by the audience—an
audience, by the way, that was filled with bribed supporters of the left, at least
according to the secret correspondence of Mirabeau.[89] The left howled and
hissed, but Virieu persisted, deploring "in the name of the provinces" the injus-
tice of a few hundred spectators imposing their views on the entire nation.

Further altercations followed. On the right, Louis, marquis de Foucauld de
Lardimalie opposed Roy's arrest on the basis of the inviolability of deputies.[90]
The comte de Mirabeau (who had been the driving force behind the decree
securing the inviolability of deputies in June 1789) countered with biting sar-
casm, humiliating Foucauld and stirring up such indignation that deputies had
to be physically restrained from assaulting him. It appeared now that the left
was as prone to incendiary propos as the right. Mirabeau was, in fact, called to
order by the president of the National Assembly, but the left kept pressing for
Roy's arrest. Barnave emphasized the exigencies of the moment. "I request that,
given the circumstances and the dangerous effects of indulgence, the National
Assembly arrest [Roy]."[91] Mirabeau stretched Barnave's contingent imperative
into universal principle. Much like the leaders of the Committee of Public
Safety in the winter of 1793–1794, he warned that "continued indulgence
will be criminal and fatal.... *La chose publique* [the common, sovereign weal] is in
danger.... You need to impose obedience to legitimate authority throughout the

Empire."[92] He continued his tirade by flattering the crowds who had ransacked Castries's residence.

> Behold, the people: violent but reasonable, excessive but generous; behold, the people even in insurrection: [this is how they act] when a free Constitution has restored in them their natural dignity and they feel this freedom threatened! Those who would judge the people otherwise underestimate and insult it.[93]

These paradoxical pairings reveal the strains involved in trying to exploit and sanitize popular violence. Mirabeau described how "dispassionately" these crowds imposed their vengeance, "destroying [Castries's] house with a kind of order and calm." Those exiting it, he claimed, emptied their pockets so that "no baseness would sully the vengeance they believed to be just."[94] (He said nothing about how things got into their pockets in the first place.) The image of a virtuously restrained but punitive crowd pandered to the rioters as well as to elites who expected legitimate political actors to behave with civility and restraint, their own inability to do so notwithstanding. Mirabeau ended his speech by imploring the deputies to "make an example of how your respect for the law is neither tepid nor feigned...decree that Roy be condemned to prison."[95] His performance must have been spellbinding, for no one refuted him with the fact that no law authorized such arrest.

Discussion then turned to the question of punishment. Various propositions were advanced, ranging from three-day house arrest to eight days in prison. Pierre-Victor Malouet made one last-ditch effort for the right, pushing Barnave's reasoning to its logical conclusion by proposing that, if the National Assembly was going to arrest Roy, it might as well arrest all who insulted deputies in the Palais-Royal, in the Tuileries gardens, and even from the audience of the Assembly.[96] Another deputy on the right, less sarcastic, tried to have Roy's punishment mitigated by citing the Latin proverb *Prima gratis, secunda debet, tertia solvet*, claiming that this was only the second violation of its kind and therefore punishment should be light. The left corrected the count, pointing out that it was the third such incident, following the condemnations of Faucigny and Guilhermy. Roy's offense thus had to be paid in full (*solvet*).[97]

In the end, the majority passed a decree condemning Roy to three days in the Abbaye prison. To avoid provoking further trouble, deputies did not have Roy arrested on the floor, allowing him to present himself at the prison within the following twenty-four hours. Interestingly (and tellingly), now that Roy was free to exit the Assembly on his own, he adopted an apologetic and submissive tone, promising to uphold the Assembly's decision with utmost respect and adding that he was willing to serve as long a sentence as the Assembly wished to impose.[98]

Toward the Terror?

Were these punitive exclusions of 1790 in the Constituent Assembly the beginning of an inexorable slide into the Terror? I think not. First, it appears that no such arrests took place in 1791, despite a close call in January. An arrest did occur in 1792. The deputy Jean-Jacques-Louis Calvet-Méric was thrown into the Abbaye prison for "insulting the French people in the person of one of its representatives."[99] This appears to be an isolated case. Second, although nearly all the excluded deputies of 1790 would emigrate and become active counter-revolutionaries after December 1791 (Virieu, Frondeville, Faucigny, Guilhermy, and Castries), they do not seem to have been so vexed or traumatized by their treatment in 1790 as to flee France as soon as they might have—there was a major wave of emigration in December 1790. They continued participating in Assembly politics for nearly another year before going abroad. Their temporary arrests (or, in the case of Virieu, forced resignation) were not that shocking, since corporate bodies had habitually exercised such disciplinary authority over members.

That said, these exclusions shed light on the cultural dynamics that injected punitive impulses into revolutionary politics. They reveal how oaths, honor, and religion became polarizing forces after 1789. Under stable conditions, the act of oath taking can reinforce allegiances, express the central values of the political order, and strengthen attachments to that order. Indeed, oaths continue to hold an important place in republican political culture today. Under revolutionary conditions, however, oaths served as vehicles for asserting competing notions about the sacred, prelegal foundations of authority. While progressives elevated the nation and sought to place the sacredness of the monarchy and religion within its scope, reactionaries elevated throne and altar over the nation and new civil authorities. In the clash over first principles, politics took on eschatological dimensions, making moderate, middle paths increasingly treacherous. With such inflated stakes, compromise smelled of conspiracy, and opposition took on the hue of heresy or treason.

Revolutionary conditions also radicalized the culture of honor. With the collapse of Old Regime hierarchy, honor became horizontally reconfigured. Elite and popular forms of violence—the duel and rebellion—began fusing into a politically combustible mix. In the volatile economy of coercion and punishment being worked out between authorities and agitating forces, the nation's honor was increasingly invoked. To be sure, Rousseauian conceptions of collective sovereignty were often invoked as well. Ultimately, though, the drive from political representation in 1789 to popular sovereignty and terror in 1792 and 1793 was fueled by calumny, honor, and vengeance—the dynamics of a hierarchical culture unhinged in the throes of democratic transition.

CHAPTER SEVEN

From Local Repression to High Justice

Limits in Action

The people are astir, ready to avenge the nation's majesty, gravely offended.
— Antoine-Joseph Santerre, Commander-in-Chief
of the Paris National Guard, June 20, 1792

The Massacre of Lèse-Nation Prisoners at Versailles

On August 25, 1792, little more than a week before the September prison massacres broke out in Paris, crowds of angry sans-culottes left town. Rumors about their number varied, but by the time they reached their destination, Orléans, they were reported at fifteen hundred.[1] Recruited among the city's sections and the visiting National Guard from Marseilles, they formed into two groups. One was led by Claude Fournier L'Héritier, a former slave driver from Saint-Domingue who had been close to members of the Court before the Revolution, notably Marie-Antoinette and the comte d'Artois. The other was headed by Claude-François Lazowski, son of Polish immigrants and former royal inspector of manufacturing before the Revolution abolished his post. Both men were renowned for their involvement in revolutionary *journées*—Fournier for nearly assassinating Lafayette during the massacre on the Champs de Mars in 1791, Lazowski for his key role in the invasion of the Tuileries Palace in June 1792 and the insurrection of August 10.[2] In the aftermath of the monarchy's overthrow, the Paris sections began clamoring to have the lèse-nation suspects held in the prisons of the Haute Cour nationale in Orléans moved to Paris for trial and execution.[3] The National Assembly was reluctant and postponed responding to their demands. Implacable, the sans-culottes took matters into their own hands. They ordered the transfer of prisoners to Paris and the dispatch of two contingents of volunteers and National Guardsmen to fetch them.[4]

The National Assembly did nothing to stop the expedition. Deputies did not even learn about it until after the contingents had left. Bypassed by events, deputies tried to save face by authorizing the mission. On the twenty-sixth, they ordered troops to be sent to Orléans to "protect" the prisoners.[5] The contingents arrived on August 30, just in time to witness the execution of Duléry—the only prisoner this high court would condemn. Duléry had been accused of recruiting French soldiers to fight with foreign troops. His case differed little from the one against two prisoners acquitted at the beginning of the month.[6] Back then, however, the monarchy had not yet fallen, and vengeance-seeking sans-culottes had not yet descended on Orléans. A national decree passed on the twenty-fifth simplifying judicial procedures and the impending arrival of Parisians who intended to expedite procedures on their own probably influenced the verdict.[7]

After a few days fraternizing with the local clubs and menacing the court, the sans-culottes plucked the fifty-three prisoners from their cells, shuffled them into carriages, and headed for Paris, despite Danton's instructions—he was now Minister of Justice—to take them to Saumur (the prison massacres had just started in the capital). It is not clear whether Fournier, now in charge of the whole operation, simply dismissed these instructions or, as some historians have claimed, Danton secretly sent contradictory orders to have the prisoners brought to Paris.[8] Little matter in the end, since in these turbulent weeks leaders led by following, and the sans-culottes made their stance clear in clamoring, "Paris ou la mort!"[9]

Upon reaching the outskirts of the blood-stained capital on September 8, Fournier received injunctions from Paris authorities to take the prisoners to Versailles. The next day, when they entered Versailles, the convoy was met by the mayor and seething crowds, some of whom had come from Paris to continue purging the nation's enemies. The convoy managed to cross most of the town safely, encountering only hisses. In turning toward an enclosure where the prisoners were to descend from their carriages, the convoy's leaders passed through a gate that was quickly closed behind them, separating them from the prisoners. The crowd closed in on the carriages, despite the efforts of escorts to fend them off. An hour and fifteen minutes later, forty-four lèse-nation prisoners lay dead (nine escaped), strewn across the rue l'Orangerie not far from the Jeu de paume, where the Tennis Court Oath had been declared three years before.[10] The attackers probably did not meditate on this historical irony. Upon finishing with the lèse-nation prisoners, they rushed off to the local prison to continue the slaughter.

Who were these prisoners awaiting trial at the Haute Cour nationale, and what had they been accused of to merit lèse-nation charges? By summer 1792, most were suspected of armed resistance or cooperation with foreign enemies.[11] But the charge of lèse-nation had been elastic enough between 1789 and 1792 to cover expression deemed insulting or calumnious to the political order. On May 3, 1792, the Legislative Assembly brought lèse-nation charges against two notorious journalists, the radical Jean-Paul Marat of *L'Ami du peuple* and the counterrevolutionary Marie-Thomas Royou of *L'Ami du roi*. Both avoided arrest. Royou did so by dying, apparently of natural causes.[12] As for Marat, he had become skilled in the art of dodging arrest warrants through hiding and mobilizing popular support. Despite the dozens of lèse-nation charges brought against individuals for speech and writing between 1789 and 1792, the only two lèse-nation prisoners killed in Versailles whose arrests had anything to do with political expression were Jean-Arnaud de Castellane and Étienne de La Rivière. As Bishop of Mende, Castellane had published antirevolutionary tracts and had organized local resistance to the Civil Constitution of the Clergy. La Rivière had been a justice of the peace in Paris closely aligned with royalists at Court. Ironically, he was arrested for cracking down on libels. Although the Legislative Assembly had enjoined the Minister of Justice to instruct justices of the peace to do precisely this, La Rivière's fatal and factionally motivated mistake was to harass members of the Legislative Assembly's own *comité de surveillance* for complicity in circulating them.

Charges of lèse-nation were not taken lightly, even by Marat's supporters, after August 10. To clear his name before his appointment to the Paris commune's *comité de surveillance* on September 3, a deputation appeared before the Legislative Assembly on his behalf, just as the prison massacres were under way.[13] The deputation demanded the official copy of the lèse-nation charge against him. Intimidated, the Legislative Assembly granted amnesty to all individuals condemned or awaiting trial for press crimes committed since July 14, 1789.[14] Yet, this amnesty hardly marked the dawn of heightened tolerance for the press. To the contrary, repression intensified over the next two years.

This chapter examines how revolutionaries dealt with perceived abuses of free speech from 1789 through the Terror. We have already seen how revolutionary legislation reflected widespread concerns about such abuses. The limits on speech that figured in demands for press freedom in the cahiers de doléances—notably, speech that undermined mœurs, honor, and authority—worked their way into constitutional provisions and the Penal Code of 1791 and were reiterated emphatically in the legislation of the Terror. We have also seen that, even before the passage of such legislation, punitive impulses had already begun pervading revolutionary politics, lowering tolerance and influencing the way deputies punished insults and calumny in the Constituent Assembly. But how did authorities and the courts deal with such speech on the local level? Why did calumny come to be treated as a political crime necessitating extraordinary justice? And how did official action, or inaction, in dealing with alleged speech offenses contribute to the Revolution's radicalization?

Local Policing (1789–1791)

The French Revolution abolished many institutions that had hitherto regulated the world of print: the Lieutenant General of Police in Paris, the intendants in the provinces, the inspectors of the Book Trade, local courts, and the parlements. Much of their authority was transferred to the municipalities in 1789. Yet, Old Regime institutions did not collapse immediately, and their continued existence in the first year of the Revolution helped radicalize politics. For example, although the National Assembly ordered parlementary magistrates to disband on November 3, 1789, those in Toulouse, Bordeaux, Rennes, Rouen, and Metz refused to do so. In the case of Toulouse, the magistrates justified their recalcitrance by stressing how press abuses were threatening public order. On this pretext, they began pursuing revolutionary journalists and circulating (or protecting the circulation of) counterrevolutionary propaganda.[15] In Paris, the Châtelet court was spared immediate abolition when the National Assembly accorded it temporary jurisdiction over lèse-nation affairs, before replacing it with the Haute Cour provisoire in spring 1791. And until their abolition in 1790, some branches of the Book Trade continued inspecting shipments, though their efforts were often frustrated by the irksome intervention of municipal authorities.[16]

Upon what legal basis did the municipalities repress opinions? On August 10, 1789, in the wake of widespread disturbances generated during the Great Fear that seized France in late July and early August, the National Assembly instructed municipalities to monitor and maintain public tranquility, authorizing them to use force if necessary against the "disturbers of public peace."[17] Subsequent decrees repeated this measure over the next two years.[18] In the absence of press laws, municipalities invoked these decrees to justify repressing perceived libels.[19] Yet, even before these decrees were passed, the municipality of Paris had already begun policing print. Ten days after the storming of the Bastille, its *comité provisoire* prohibited the distribution of works that withheld the names of printers (July 24 and 31).[20] The city government also acted upon requests from the districts to regulate the distribution of print by passing ordinances throughout the fall requiring colporteurs to be registered with the police and limiting their number to three hundred, as specified by the Book Trade Law of 1723.[21]

Municipal authorities also tried to intimidate the writers and printers of tracts they took to be incendiary or seditious, summoning them to appear publicly before them. Lacking press laws, authorities hoped that humiliating reprimands would prompt them to mend their ways. Marat was one of the first writers to be summoned before municipal leaders in August and September 1789. In August, he was admonished for his excessive propos after authorities had refused to grant him permission to start his newspaper. Authorities defended their decision on the grounds that since the terms of impending press freedom had not yet been worked out, they could not yet accord such permission. They reproached him for his disrespectful response to their refusal: "We cannot restrain ourselves from condemning the indiscreet pretensions of a citizen who undertakes the task of advancing his own will against the will of an Assembly which the nation has specially honored with its confidence to take care of its interests."[22] Giving Marat a lesson in civic morality, the authorities reminded him that "public happiness rests on the foundations of wisdom, which is at one with moderate conduct, as well as on the subordination of all particular wills to the general will."[23] Marat appears to have imbibed the lesson, though in his own way. Henceforth, he claimed to speak on behalf of the people's will. Doing so, however, did not spare him from being summoned again at the end of September, this time for slandering the municipality's *comité des subsistances*. The mayor, Jean-Sylvain Bailly, asked Marat if he had any concrete accusations to make. The journalist said no, signed a statement attesting to this, and was dismissed.[24] This face-to-face encounter with authorities did nothing to defang Marat. Within days, his denunciations became more virulent. His denunciation of one administrator, de Joly, as we have seen, led to criminal charges against the journalist in early October.

In addition to harassing peddlers and summoning writers and printers to appear before them, municipal authorities also seized incendiary print. The archives of the National Assembly's *comité des recherches* and those of many communes throughout France reveal the frequency of police raids on print shops. In justifying the arrests and bans that often followed such raids, authorities went beyond the imperative of maintaining "public order," even though that was the only justification recognized by the law until August 1791. They stressed the moral dangers of calumnious attacks on the nation, and for several reasons. First, as we have seen, the policing of opinion in eighteenth-century France was considered a vehicle for moral instruction. Acts of repression, therefore, had to convey lessons. Second, the weak legitimacy of new authorities compelled them to explain their motives to the public, certain sectors of which might accuse them of despotism. Finally, in the absence of press laws, public bans functioned as speech acts conveying where authorities thought legitimate limits on public expression would lie once the National Assembly got around to legislating them.

These motivations show through in the repressive measures taken by local authorities in Marseilles in 1791. On March 16, the police arrested Antoine-Julien Floret, the employee of a local merchant, for his propos during a performance of a politically charged play, *Le ballet du déserteur*. Toward the end of the performance, the wealthy spectators in the loges started crying out, "Vive le roi!" (Long live the king!) Patriots in the pit fired back, "Long live the nation, the king no longer exists!" Spotting Floret in his National Guard uniform among the "royalists" in the loges, patriots taunted him. Floret rushed into the pit, where he began strangling one of the patriots.[25]

Had this event occurred ten years later, it is likely that authorities, more stable then, would have presented the incident as nothing more than a disturbance of public order. In 1791, however, officials could not easily ignore its politically combustible potential. They imposed an enormous fine on Floret (five hundred livres) and ordered him to remain in prison until he paid. In reading the lengthy judgment, which was posted throughout the city, one detects the authorities' predicament. To cry out "Vive le roi!" did not constitute a crime, at least not in 1791; after all, France was still a constitutional monarchy. Yet, it was evident that the clash in the theater reflected profound divisions in Marseilles concerning the sacred source of authority. To assert their control over the situation while maintaining the appearance of evenhandedness, officials declared that, in addition to menacing "the people" by descending into the parterre, Floret had insulted the king by crying out "Vive le roi!" They cited the king's proclamation of May 25, 1790, which declared to be "public enemies" those who sought to "disrupt the important work that the National Assembly is undertaking, *in concert with the King*, to secure the people their rights and prepare their happiness." The proclamation also called for punishing all those "who raise doubts as to our intentions."[26] To cry out "Vive le roi!" as a retort to "Vive la nation!" according to the officials, implied that the king was opposed to the nation. The officials thus managed to side with patriots by invoking royal proclamations about the king's commitment to the Revolution. One can appreciate the dilemma such officials encountered after the king's failed attempt to flee France three months later. Henceforth, it would be more difficult to cite royal proclamations to justify punishing royalist speech.

In late May 1790, authorities in Soissons took the occasion of seizing a locally distributed libel to convey where their tolerance threshold lay. The libel, *Lettre d'un français à son ami, du 18 mai 1790*, castigated the National Assembly for usurping both the king and the people. It insisted that national deputies had exceeded their authority the moment they repudiated their imperative mandates (the instructions given to deputies by the primary assemblies that had elected them to the Estates-General). It referred to the Declaration of the Rights of Man and of the Citizen as a "barbarous code" and accused the National Assembly of spreading impiety. Local authorities summoned the printer, reprimanded him, and ordered the pamphlet to be lacerated publicly. Setting guidelines for future repression, they warned that any persons involved in producing and circulating works containing "false maxims that are seditious and prejudicial to the constitution, liberty, or the majesty of the nation" or "injurious to the person of the King or the loyalty of his subjects" would be treated as traitors.[27]

If arrests, bans, and denunciations served as occasions for asserting revolutionary values, this should not obscure the fact that, in many instances, public order was truly threatened by antirevolutionary movements. In Marseilles in the fall of 1789, for example, opponents of the Revolution formed into "circles" that combed the city, seizing copies of the Declaration of the Rights of Man and of the Citizen and attacking those who distributed them.[28] The ability of local officials to deal with agitators—radical and antirevolutionary—was often compromised by their weak command over the police and the military, themselves often divided. The producers of polemical propaganda were well aware of the fissures running through the forces of public order and sought to exploit them. In January 1790, the National Assembly, alarmed by the diffusion of such propaganda among the armed forces, instructed the Minister of War, Jean-Frédéric de La Tour du Pin Gouvernet, comte de Paulin, to investigate the matters and to take appropriate measures. In a long letter dated January 24, the Minister confirmed the deplorable situation. Despite the efforts of commanders, radical and antirevolutionary tracts were circulating in prodigious quantities, exacerbating tensions within the military and National Guard. Animosities between the "aristocratic" and "bourgeois" officers and the lower-class soldiers and guardsmen intensified during the winter, spring, and summer of 1790. Several revolts were averted or quickly contained, but tensions mounted.[29] On August 19, the deputy Michel-Louis Regnaud de Saint-Jean-d'Angély complained about the impact of such tracts, reporting that a naval commander had been nearly assassinated in Toulon during a revolt inspired by them. "It is time that the National Assembly put an end to these disorders. I demand that [its committees] present the *projet de décret* that the Assembly has requested concerning the freedom of the press."[30]

Tensions finally exploded in Nancy in August 1790. Radicals in the royal regiments organized a mutiny that lasted nearly two weeks. National Guard battalions from neighboring regions were called in to crush the revolt. They managed to restore order but only after more than two hundred soldiers were killed. Convicted of lèse-nation, thirty rebels were hanged, forty-one condemned to the galleys, and one broken on the wheel.[31] Many National Guardsmen throughout France sympathized with the revolt and were scandalized by the Guard's repressive intervention. Claims that the National Guard had dishonored itself in Nancy circulated throughout France, exacerbating tensions among the troops.[32]

Some tracts were intended to spark mutinies, persuading soldiers in the lower echelons of the military to abandon their posts or to revolt against their "aristocratic" officers. Such tracts had circulated in Nancy shortly before the revolt.[33] Others stirred up opposition to the Revolution among the officers. In Grenoble, for example, a former *garde du corps*, the sieur de Rival, wrote *Lettre écrite sur le tombeau de Bayard adressée à toute l'armée française*. Rival was arrested and interrogated.[34] Asked why he had written the tract, he claimed to have been troubled by the lack of discipline among the *maréchaussées* (highway troops) and had sought to encourage the soldiers to obey National Assembly decrees. Skeptical, interrogators asked why he had made no mention of such decrees in his pamphlet. Rival skirted the question and brought up the horrors of the October Days affair of 1789 (the Women's Bread March to Versailles) when some of his fellow *gardes du corps* were killed. The interrogators asked why he placed the word "king" before "law" in his pamphlet, suggesting that they detected a seditious hierarchy of first principles; again, Rival provided a convoluted response. In the end, the local authorities forwarded the affair to the National Assembly's *comité des recherches*. They explained, "Having only simple policing powers, we do not have the authority to rule on this affair, which strikes us as a crime of lèse-nation."[35] They added that since the *comité des recherches* had a national vantage point, it was better situated to determine whether this was an isolated incident or part of a broad conspiracy.

With such explosive tensions among the forces of public order in 1790, even bar-room insults between soldiers alarmed authorities. In November 1790, Jean-George-Charles Voidel, the secretary of the *comité des recherches*, instructed municipal authorities in Quimper (Brittany) to investigate and punish a reactionary guardsman who had insulted the National Assembly and the Guard.[36] At a bar in late October, the sieur Rosblat allegedly ridiculed an elderly guardsman sporting medals received for his participation in the Festival of the Federation in Paris the previous July. Rosblat referred to the deputies of the National Assembly as a "fucking mob" and announced that he respected the National Guard uniform about as much as his ass. The municipality contacted Rosblat's commander, who wrote back that there were other men like Rosblat and that the best thing to do would be to send them to Brest and Lorient. The commander assured the municipal officials that in these Breton cities, where revolutionary fervor was greater, "there are 'seminaries' that will be salutary for them."[37]

There is no evidence that Rival and Rosblat were part of counterrevolutionary conspiracies on a national scale, but there is evidence that orchestrated campaigns to spread antirevolutionary propaganda existed. The fact that many such tracts were sent through the postal system with the National Assembly's official seal suggests that there was either corruption within the Assembly's own dispatching service or that opponents of the Revolution had managed to counterfeit the seal. Sometimes, local administrations surreptitiously supported and protected the local networks diffusing these tracts. The emergence of such networks injected the nascent patriotic clubs with a sense of purpose. These clubs made it their mission to monitor the flow of antirevolutionary propaganda (often by storming post offices) and to denounce those responsible for spreading it.[38] In a letter of December 4, 1790, to the *comité des recherches*, the patriotic club in Hesdin (where, incidentally, a military mutiny had occurred the previous April) accused local administrators of colluding with the local Abbaye de Dommartin to spread rumors and pamphlets announcing that Church property would not be sold, contrary to actual decrees. The club claimed that one of the pamphlets, *Le naviget anticyras*, was being distributed through a complex network of administrators and postmen.[39] (The tract was denounced widely throughout France.)[40] According to club members, the profusion of such propaganda emboldened officials to obstruct the sale of Church property, and they cited several instances in which potential buyers were turned away. In explaining why they were sending their denunciation to the National Assembly, they observed that the affair could not be treated locally because the old tribunals were defunct and the new ones had not yet been established.

Discoveries of covert antirevolutionary propaganda networks led many to believe that a nationwide counterrevolutionary conspiracy was afoot. In June 1790, a local *adjutant de chasseurs* in Nice informed the National Assembly about the suspicious behavior of former parlementary magistrates (who had lost their venal positions) and the Bishop de La Fare (who, as we have seen, had given the sermon at the opening of the meeting of the Estates-General in which he had insisted on maintaining Catholicism as the official national cult).[41] These men were seen being escorted by the Prince of Monaco to a local print shop known for producing counterrevolutionary pamphlets. Evidence of a conspiracy to spread counterrevolutionary propaganda was uncovered in Tours in autumn 1790. After receiving complaints from the local patriotic club, officials arrested and interrogated individuals suspected of involvement with a tract entitled *Avis aux vrais français*. The royalist thrust of the pamphlet was unmistakable: "Oh, that the cry of honor be awakened in our souls! In these times of oaths, let us make a sacred one, to swear to prosecute those who participated in the October Days [during which the king and queen were brought to Paris]." It also called for punishing those involved in spreading "infamous broadsides" against the royal family.[42] In his interrogation, the local printer, Marie-François Légier, explained how he came to print this pamphlet. He recounted how he had been awakened at 2 a.m. and taken to the home of Gosselin Dupré, a *ci-devant* canon of the local cathedral. Dupré introduced Légier to some unknown man who, by all appearances, had been traveling. The stranger handed Légier a copy of *Avis aux vrais français*, and Dupré requested Légier to print five hundred copies of it. When Légier hesitated, Dupré reassured him that the ideas in the tract were no different from those expressed in Royou's royalist newspaper, *L'Ami du roi*, printed in Paris.[43] Through interrogating one of Légier's apprentices, officials discovered that Légier had been well aware of the dangers in printing this tract; for when a local National Guardsman came to inspect the print shop, Légier ordered the apprentice to hide the document.[44] (The tract, of course, did not carry the printer's name.) In his interrogation, Dupré identified the midnight stranger as the comte de Saint-Cyr, a former *prévôt*. (*Prévôts* had been abolished in 1789.) Dupré said that Saint-Cyr had reassured them that the freedom of the press gave them the right to produce copies of the pamphlet. In the end, the municipality—which had already refused to deal with local nobles and priests who openly expressed opposition to the Revolution—washed their hands of the affair. They concluded that it involved lèse-nation and forwarded it to the National Assembly.[45]

In some cases, antirevolutionary propaganda was spread by national deputies themselves. At the request of the National Assembly's *comité des rapports* and the *comité des recherches*, officials in Vitré (Brittany) forwarded the letters written by their deputy, Hardy de la Largère. Largère had opposed the Declaration of Rights in the summer of 1789 and was now going underground with his antirevolutionary views. To avoid drawing attention to himself, he sent libels against the National Assembly, with the Assembly's official seal to ensure delivery, to a local notary with instructions to pass them on to the deputy's wife, who, it appears, would distribute them.[46] The notary got cold feet. Deciding that the libels were too dangerous, he turned them over to district officials, who forwarded them to the Assembly's *comité des rapports*.[47]

Six months later, the police in Lyon discovered that their national deputy, Jean-Antoine de Castellas, was sending antirevolutionary tracts to the abbé Boisboissel. On March 23 and 24, 1791, they interrogated Boisboissel and his accomplice, the sieur Gal, and subsequently arrested the abbé. They based these actions on a decree of December 26, 1790, which authorized local officials to pursue "those who threaten public order."[48] At Gal's home, police found a laundry bag full of anti-revolutionary pamphlets and a locked drawer with more copies and some cash.[49] Gal denied any knowledge of them and said that Boisboissel must have stashed them there. The Lyon authorities waited a month before turning the matter over to the local prosecutor. During that time, they collected batches of pamphlets addressed to Boisboissel from Castellas in Paris. The shipments—again, sent with the National Assembly's official seal—included Royou's *L'Ami du roi*, the pope's *Bref du pape* condemning the Revolution, and an *Ordinance de l'Archevêque de Lyon* by the refractory archbishop and comte de Lyon, Yves-Alexandre Marbeouf.

The letters accompanying the shipments of counterrevolutionary propaganda revealed the great secrecy of the operation. Castellas used codes to refer to individuals involved in an elaborate nationwide network seeking to stir up resistance to the Civil Constitutional Clergy.[50] Castellas informed Boisboissel that since the Bishop of Soissons, a vigorous opponent of the Civil Constitutional Clergy, had emigrated, it was all the more imperative to conceal the network: "I feel more than ever now that it is impossible to use the regular channels to communicate this *Ordinance* [by Marboeuf]."[51] In another letter, Castellas wrote that he dared not send the tracts directly to a local bailiff who, apparently, was supposed to distribute them, and he conveyed his hope that Boisboissel would succeed in doing so. "I wait with impatience to hear about the effect these writings have. It will certainly be one of choler."[52]

After compiling a month's worth of compromising letters and counterrevolutionary propaganda, officials bypassed the new district court and sent what it took to be a lèse-nation affair directly to the National Assembly. When the Assembly failed to respond, they turned it over to the district court. The judges decided that since the affair involved a national deputy, it was beyond their jurisdiction. They re-sent the case to the National Assembly and ordered Boisboissel to remain in prison.[53] Finally, in July, the court released Boisboissel "temporarily" on the orders of the Minister of Justice.[54] The case went no further. A few months later, an arrest warrant was issued against Castellas, but he had already fled to England.[55]

The Castellas-Boisboissel affair was one of several in Lyon involving speech and writing between 1790 and 1792. These affairs exacerbated tensions between the municipality, the department, and national authorities. One of the earliest of these affairs involved a pamphlet by J. Imbert-Colomès. As temporary *prévôt* in the summer of 1789 (before the position was definitively abolished), Imbert established a corps of voluntary guardsmen to deal with disturbances in July and August. The traditional *milice bourgeoise* was apparently unable to handle these problems on its own. In establishing the corps, Imbert incurred the ire of both the *milice*, who felt slighted, and the patriots, who criticized him for allegedly recruiting only the sons of wealthy citizens.[56] By February 1790, patriot fury against Imbert boiled over. He was chased from his home, fleeing on rooftops.[57] He soon became active in the counterrevolution, working as an agent for the king's émigré brother, the comte d'Artois.[58] Despite seditious allegiances, Imbert managed to work his way into the new departmental administration. During one of its preliminary meetings in December 1790 (it was not officially installed until January), Imbert began delivering a speech criticizing the Revolution, calling for the dissolution of the National Assembly and the establishment of a new one outside Paris. His colleagues stopped him, warning him that his views were too dangerous, at least for the moment.

Six months later, in June 1791, Imbert had his speech printed up and distributed in Lyon. In the pamphlet, he accused certain national deputies of corruption and of mishandling treasury funds. He also called for transferring the National Assembly to either Orléans or Tours.[59] Scandalized, municipal authorities swung into action, seizing copies of the pamphlet and arresting Imbert. In searching his home, they found several pamphlets that sought to stir up sectarian opposition to the Revolution. They also found the manuscript of the speech, which differed from the printed version. It included the names of the colleagues who had congratulated him for his "courageous" views back in December 1790 while warning him that airing such views would lead to his being "hanged wholesale."[60] In their *procès-verbal*, local officials accused Imbert of calumny for falsely claiming that he had expressed these views at a department meeting.[61] The authorities argued that in refusing to inform his readers that his colleagues had, in fact, stopped him, Imbert implicated them in his seditious opinions. For their part, the departmental administrators denied any complicity, insisting that the speech never took place.[62] The district court acquitted Imbert on the grounds that an inferior administration (the municipality) could not file charges against a member of a superior administration (the department) for actions taken as a public official. This ruling raised suspicions about the neutrality of the court, since it contradicted the fact that nearly everyone, except Imbert, agreed upon, namely, that he had published the tract as a private citizen, not as a public official.

Around the time of the Imbert affair, departmental authorities filed charges against the radical newspaper *Journal de Lyon*.[63] In Marat-like incendiary language, the newspaper had accused the department of, among other things, refusing to deal with a denunciation that the municipality had sent to it of an antirevolutionary libel titled *Franchon*. Although the Minister of Justice supported the department in its denunciation of the *Journal de Lyon*, the district court declared the case to involve lèse-nation and forwarded it to the National Assembly. Clearly, this was the easiest way for the new court to wash its hands of a highly politicized affair that pitted two administrations against each other.[64] Since the National Assembly rarely acted on such affairs from the provinces, there was little reason for the public to believe that it would do anything about this one. The district court's decision to send it to the National Assembly thus raised suspicions among radicals, who believed that the department was teeming with royalists and that the judges of the district court were either cowards or in cahoots with the department.

Relations between the department and municipality of Lyon deteriorated in the winter and spring of 1792. On February 23, a theater in Lyon staged a play that was generating disturbances in many parts of France, *Le club des bonnes gens*. According to the playwright, *bonnes gens* were law-abiding Catholics, and he depicted the president of a patriotic club as an ignorant brute.[65] The play was interpreted by many, especially by spectators in the pit, as a calumnious attack on patriotic clubs and the Revolution. In one scene, as a priest finished his aria, some spectators sang out, "Amen, amen"; others cried out, "Down with the aristocratic priest!"[66] Tensions reached such a pitch that the National Guard was called to the theater to restore order. The municipality banned the play, citing the law that turned over the policing of the theater to the municipalities. The disgruntled actors appealed to the sympathetic department, which reprimanded the municipality for violating the freedom of expression.[67]

Meanwhile, another play, *La forêt noire*, was stirring up more trouble in Lyon.[68] It depicted a band of brigands wreaking havoc in a forest until heroic forces of public order arrested them. In the opening scene, as the brigands were awakened by their leader, a spectator exclaimed, sarcastically, "Vive la nation!" At the end of the play, when the troops arrived on the scene with official orders to destroy the brigands "infecting the forest," a spectator yelled, "Down with the sans-culottes…down with the nation!" The play was clearly intended to excite counterrevolutionary sentiment. The fact that the heroic forces of public order depicted in it were the king's troops and not the National Guard suggested that justice and order were secure only in the hands of royal forces.

Controversy over permitting further performances of the first play, *Le club des bonnes gens*, lasted more than a month. On April 4, the department ordered the municipality to lift its "illegal" ban. The municipality gave in but relieved itself of responsibility for any violence that might erupt.[69] Not long after the municipality conceded, the new Jacobin Minister of the Interior, Jean-Marie Roland, intervened. Roland was allied with several local officials in Lyon. He sided with them and reprimanded the department. He informed the department that he had spoken with the king, who was abreast of the disturbances occasioned by the play in Lyon, and he ordered the department to respect the municipality's initial ban.[70] The department took offense, insinuated that Roland was biased in favor of his friends in the municipality, and took the moral high ground, insisting on upholding the freedom of expression. (Apparently, departmental officials saw no contradiction between their defense of the royalist play and their prior effort to prosecute the patriot journalist of the *Journal de Lyon*.)[71] They also called Roland's bluff, reminding him that only a royal proclamation or a National Assembly decree could overturn a departmental decision.

Like many politically charged plays at the time, *Le club des bonnes gens* aggravated local tensions, pitting spectators against each other and sending shock waves up and down the administrative hierarchy, from the municipality all the way up to the national government. Such plays, much like radical and antirevolutionary propaganda, forced authorities into taking a stand on free speech. In the absence of legal limits on this freedom, they constantly ran the risk of appearing arbitrary. Officials often declared such affairs to be instances of lèse-nation and forwarded them to the National Assembly to avoid incurring local wrath. But the National Assembly, lacking legal definitions for lèse-nation, often did not act on denunciations. Thus, between 1789 and 1792, there was widespread consensus that lèse-nation existed and should be punished, but little was done to accomplish this. The failure of new institutions to satisfy punitive demands undermined their credibility. It also emboldened radicals and counterrevolutionaries, making it increasingly difficult for the center to hold.

Some affairs did make it on to the dockets of the lèse-nation courts. To understand why most of them stagnated there, it is worth examining the political purpose of creating a lèse-nation jurisdiction in the first place: to preempt popular violence.

The Attribution of Lèse-Nation: Mollifying the Furies (1789–1791)

Few disputed the legitimacy of the lèse-nation attribution. The problem was defining it. For Boullemer de la Martinière, the public prosecutor of the Paris commune in charge of dealing with such crimes, lèse-nation was "nothing other than what we used to know and have always recognized as lèse-majesté."[72] For him, Old Regime jurisprudence and classical republicanism were compatible. He claimed that although lèse-majesté first appeared in French law under Louis XI in 1483, its spirit stretched back to ancient Rome, when "this title of majesty belonged to a free people."[73] Likewise, in his *Réveil des principes des loix et des ordonnances sur le crime de lèze-Majesté royale, de lèze-État ou de lèze-Nation* of fall 1789, Charles-Pons-Borromée Sarot drew on laws and ordinances dating from the sixteenth century to justify the revolutionary attribution of lèse-nation. Sarot refuted those who claimed that lèse-nation had no legal basis. "Oh, that people would stop crying that it is absurd to establish a tribunal for crimes of lèse-nation under the false pretext that no laws exist determining its nature, character, or punishment; the ordinances cited [here] demonstrate clearly that they exist for crimes against the State, and the State is synonymous with the Nation."[74] Yet, grounding the majesty of the nation in sacred notions of monarchy, republicanism, the people, state, and nation all at once was more difficult than these authors acknowledged. In the throes of revolution, competing camps elevated certain terms over others, generating a clash over first principles, notably between monarchy and nation.

Jacobins and radicals resisted narrow definitions of lèse-nation. For them, the crime was identifiable by the visceral outrage it evoked, and its egregiousness summoned the moral dictates of natural law, not the technicalities of positive law. Such views show through in a letter sent to the National Assembly denouncing Bayard de La Vingtrie, mayor of Bellême and former subdelegate of the intendant of Alençon.[75] Writing on behalf of furious citizens, a local lawyer of that town accused Vingtrie of embezzling public funds, ordering troops to fire on the people, and slandering the National Assembly. In declaring these crimes "lèse-peuple" or "lèse-nation"—he considered the two synonymous—the lawyer reflected on the nature of this new charge.

> If our legislators, in multiplying infinitely what can be considered a crime of lèse-majesté against the Prince, have maintained the greatest silence about the crime of lèse-nation, this crime is nonetheless one whose punishment does not require preexisting laws.... Although [the requirement of preexisting laws] is valid in matters of positive law, it is not pertinent to matters of natural law.... For all social

institutions there is a [natural] law that resides in all hearts, and this law cries out to us that [La Vingtrie's] actions are criminal.

The lawyer warned that locals would likely take justice into their own hands if deputies did not act. "If the National Assembly refuses to recognize his actions as lèse-nation, it amounts to saying that this criminal category does not exist....It amounts to leaving to the people the burden of imposing its own vengeance."[76]

Several left-wing deputies and journalists shared these conceptions of lèse-nation. In debate on establishing a new lèse-nation court in October 1790, Robespierre distinguished between ordinary and exceptional crimes: whereas positive law was sufficient to deal with ordinary violations of individual rights, attacks on the rights of the nation constituted lèse-nation and required special judicial procedures. According to him, violations of the rights of individuals involved only physical actions and violence. However, since the rights of the nation were grounded in moral forces—laws, rights, and justice—their violation constituted treason. "Whoever should attack the people's freedom, that is, its constitutional laws which ensure the exercise and protection of its rights, is guilty of parricide."[77] For the abbé Maury, such ideas were dangerously vague. Establishing a court for lèse-nation without defining the crime, he insisted, would lead to arbitrariness and despotism.

There were revolutionaries who held views on lèse-nation even more radical than those of Robespierre. In an issue of *Révolutions de Paris* appearing that same month, Louis Prudhomme went so far as to argue against defining lèse-nation at all. This otherwise quasi-libertarian defender of press freedom wrote, "What perils will the social body face if, to punish for lèse-nation, it is necessary to legally define it?" He explained, "Isn't it impossible to classify all the various ways of injuring the political body? If it is deemed necessary to wait for a legal definition, what will become of the people's safety?" Prudhomme accused "aristocrats" of militating for a legal definition of lèse-nation in order to maneuver around it. "They know that, the moment such a law exists, they can conspire without fear, escaping the vengeance of the courts as easily as they escape the surveillance of the [National Assembly's] *comité des recherches*."[78]

Complaints about the lack of a legal definition for lèse-nation were made primarily by moderates, conservatives, and reactionaries. The anonymous author of *Mémoires pour les criminels de lèse-nation*, for example, believed that the act of writing had become more dangerous since 1789. During the Old Regime, writers knew at least whether their works would be considered criminal by submitting them to

FIGURE 7.1. Execution of the sentence handed down by the bourgeois militia of Sivrai (Poitou) in reparation for the insult made against the Nation and the King by the Citizen…of…, who had attached the tricolored cockade to the tail of his dog, which he was condemned to kiss three times. Courtesy of the Bibliothèque nationale de France, cabinet d'estampes.

Execution de la Sentence rendû par la milice-Bourgeoise de Sivrai.
en réparation de l'injure faite à la Nation et au Roi par le C........
de .. .., qui avoit attaché la Cocarde Nationale à la queue de
son chien, dont il fut condamné de baiser 3 fois le derriere.

A.P.

censors before publication. Now, writers were being held accountable according to undefined criteria, for legislators had defined neither "abuses" of free speech, as announced in the Declaration of Rights, nor lèse-nation. Without legal clarification, the new regime risked becoming more arbitrary and despotic than the previous one.

> The Assembly fears that [press freedom]…can become dangerous. It feels the need to restrain this freedom but does not dare declare the abuses that the law should proscribe. It does not pass new laws but allows the new municipalities, clubs, and patriotic associations to impose their own desires.… These municipalities and clubs track down and denounce "the guilty" who will be accused of a crime [lèse-nation] for which no one knows the limits or punishment.[79]

The author insisted that since lèse-majesté had never been adequately defined by law, the National Assembly should never have recognized lèse-nation.[80] Revealing his attachment to the social hierarchy of the Old Regime, the author claimed that charges of lèse-nation were being exploited to conduct class warfare, serving as a pretext to attack those whom "birth, fortune, or public function has placed at the forefront of society."[81]

Radicals also believed lèse-nation affairs were being exploited to conduct class warfare but in an inverse manner. They depicted the Châtelet as a bastion of aristocracy. In its address to the National Assembly in spring 1790, the Cordeliers district cited examples in which the Châtelet acquitted aristocrats while punishing innocent workers and peasants.[82] The district called for the abolition of the Châtelet but not for the abolition of the lèse-nation attribution, which its members conceived of in inflated, metaphysical terms. "What is the crime of lèse-nation? It is to disregard—by will or deed—the rights of the nation."[83] They believed that although lèse-nation had its origins in the old doctrine of lèse-majesté, "the offense is new and requires new spirits who love liberty."[84] The lèse-nation attribution thus served coercive and pedagogical purposes. It described a punishable sedition springing from the moral failings of those "who form within themselves a link in the long and tortuous chain of despotism."[85]

In early 1791, as the National Assembly was preparing the establishment of a new Haute Cour nationale for lèse-nation crimes, right-wing deputies Nicolas Bergasse and Pierre-Victor Malouet warned of the dangers of ongoing legal imprecision.[86] According to Bergasse, "A judge, without fixed rules and positive law, having no other guide than popular terrors, will find himself…punishing those whom, in less stormy moments, he would excuse."[87] Malouet warned that without clear legal definitions, demagogues would exploit proscriptive impulses in the name of "public safety" in order to expand the repressive power of the state.[88] Leaving lèse-nation undefined would, he feared, "produce more victims than [military] conquests."[89] The Assembly's *comité de constitution* presented a long list of lèse-nation crimes, but Bergasse and Malouet insisted that it be short, encompassing only conspiracies against the state; abuses of power by public officials; physical attacks on the king, officials, and representatives; and seditious violence. None of the proposed lists of lèse-nation crimes included abuses of free speech. For Malouet, injurious speech against the king, public officials, or national representatives was to be treated as lèse-majesté and handled by the ordinary courts according to positive law.[90]

Some of the most incisive reflections on lèse-nation—and from a modern perspective, familiar—were those of François de Pange. Pange was among the few who rejected the very notion of lèse-nation. He believed that it would be exploited for purposes as tyrannical as those to which lèse-majesté had been put during the Old Regime. Back then, he explained, lèse-majesté had been distinguished from crimes that threatened the general interest of society and that were treated according to ordinary law by ordinary courts. Since all citizens were now equal before the law, the idea of "lèse"-anything made no sense. All legal violations, he insisted, constituted attacks against the interests of society and were thus to be treated according to ordinary laws by ordinary courts.[91] Pange warned that the concept of lèse-nation would bring popular passions to bear on what should be rational legal judgment, "exciting spirits that might impose their influence on judges, altering their decisions."[92]

Pange recognized why the National Assembly had institutionalized the lèse-nation attribution in 1789, and his insights reveal much about the nature of the revolutionary crisis. Facing chronic agitation, deputies had sought to prevent "misled patriots" from avenging the nation on their own. By giving the Châtelet exclusive jurisdiction over lèse-nation affairs, the Assembly had alleviated the burden of local judges who had such affairs foisted on them by crowds and local factions.[93] These measures had been dictated by circumstances, Pange conceded, but it was now time to sever the links between popular passions and rational justice. The lèse-nation attribution had to be abolished.

The National Assembly never defined lèse-nation. The Constitution of 1791 called for the establishment of a high court to handle affairs involving "public security," but it said nothing about lèse-nation per se. Some historians have taken this as a sign that, despite popular punitive pressures, the Constituent Assembly was truly committed to the rule of law and did all it could to avoid making extraordinary political justice a permanent feature of the new order.[94] It is more likely that the absence of the lèse-nation attribution had to do with the inability of deputies to agree on its definition. In any case, the Penal Code of 1791 specified crimes against "la chose publique" (*res publica*, or the common weal).[95] More significantly, deputies continued invoking "lèse-nation" after September 1791, reinforcing expectations that the high court would hand down convictions. The failure of the court to do so weakened its credibility, not to mention the credibility of the new regime. Meanwhile, punitive desires among royalists and radicals intensified.

Lèse-Nation Affairs and Radicalization

If popular agitation led to the injection of "lèse-nation" into revolutionary politics, authorities were largely responsible for extending its scope to cover speech. In the first year of the Revolution, the charge was brought against Catholic reactionaries, antirevolutionary royalists, and radicals. Despite accusations that the Châtelet was biased, the archives show that, in matters of speech, the court was relatively evenhanded.[96] There were nearly as many affairs against radicals as there were against counterrevolutionaries, and the social profile of most suspects put them in the educated middle or upper-middle classes.

What kinds of speech offenses made it onto the Châtelet's docket? Insults against notable national figures and statements that sought to weaken trust in authorities made up the majority of lèse-nation speech affairs. In March 1790, for example, the magistrates of the Châtelet convicted Pierre Curé for seditious propos and insults against the queen. Curé had been arrested in Bourg-en-Bresse in November 1789 for trying to recruit locals in the Jura to join him in burning down châteaux. He was foreign to the region and claimed to have been sent from Paris by the duc d'Orléans. The *comité des recherches* ordered authorities in Burgundy to investigate the matter.[97] No evidence of the duc's involvement was uncovered, but the affair was nevertheless sent to the Châtelet. Curé was sentenced to publicly apologize, to wear an iron collar for three days, to be branded on his shoulder, to be publicly beaten and thrashed, and to spend the rest of his days in the galleys. Had the Châtelet convicted Curé only for threatening to burn châteaux, the affair might not have attracted the attention of the patriot press. But because the judgment stressed Curé's "criminal insults" against the queen, radicals seized upon the occasion to accuse the Châtelet of violating the freedom of expression by imposing cruel and excessive punishment.[98] In his *Révolutions de France et de*

Brabant, Camille Desmoulins lambasted the Châtelet for sentencing "an ignorant villager" to life in the galleys for having "spoken against the wife of the King—a crime that he has committed along with the rest of France and all of Europe." Desmoulins decried the hypocrisy of the Châtelet, pointing to its recent release of the reactionary journalist François Suleau, who "encouraged the provinces to revolt in a stupid and fanatical address."[99]

Other lèse-nation affairs involved attacks on the majesty of the National Assembly. In March 1790, the mayor of Paris, Jean-Sylvain Bailly, informed the Assembly that he had stopped the circulation of some issues of *Sottises de la semaine*, which contained "disgusting obscenities, atrocious insults against national deputies" and tried to "incite the parlements to revolt."[100] The case was turned over to the Châtelet on March 17. By interrogating the printer's daughter two days later, authorities learned that the authors were Antoine-Jean-Mathieu Séguier, a former barrister at Parlement, his son Armand-Louis Maurice, and André Rolland.[101] By the time the Châtelet got around to prosecuting them, two had fled to Italy, while the third had gone into hiding in Paris. The court stopped pursuing the affair but did not acquit the suspects.[102]

The Châtelet failed to complete most cases. Stymied by numerous political and practical obstacles, the court nevertheless kept the cases open, leaving suspects in judicial limbo, neither acquitted nor condemned. This gave suspects time to mobilize the public in their favor. The magistrates, aware that the Châtelet's days were numbered, often proceeded timidly or not at all, especially when suspects turned out to be journalists or important public figures. This was the case in the affair against Stanislas Fréron, a representative of the commune of Paris and covert journalist of *L'Orateur du peuple*. The affair originated with the commune's outrage at a statement made in the June 1 issue, which claimed that "the aristocracy is amassing over [the people's] heads a treasure of vengeances." The newspaper also announced that the "Austrian Committee" at Court was plotting the king's escape from France.[103]

Fed up with such abuses of press freedom, the public prosecutor of Paris vowed to pursue them, beginning with *L'Orateur du peuple*.[104] After interrogating the printers of the newspaper on June 9, he ordered the arrest of Marcel Enfantin, the presumed journalist writing under the name "Martel." Enfantin confessed that he was Fréron's front man.[105] As other testimony was corroborating this confession, the Cordeliers district weighed in, denouncing the despotism of the commune. The affair now risked turning into a political quagmire. The prosecutor washed his hands of it, forwarding it to the Châtelet as a lèse-nation affair. Emboldened by public support and authorities' cold feet, Fréron confessed his involvement with *L'Orateur du peuple* in a public address in which he also lashed out against the Châtelet, accusing it of repressing patriot journalists and of violating press freedom.[106] Already unpopular for pursuing other lèse-nation affairs, the Châtelet decided to release Enfantin and the printers, but it neither dropped the case nor arrested Fréron.

Several lèse-nation speech affairs turned on the issue of subsistence. Louis-Joseph Noël, James Rutledge, and Julien Poulain-Delaunay were all accused of exploiting subsistence problems to malign authorities. Noël was arrested on October 26, 1789, for reading incendiary pamphlets aloud at cafés, most notably *Le patriote véridique ou vous n'aurez pas de pain*. (Bread revolts had broken out a few days earlier.) Because testimony had been collected secretly, thus violating new judicial procedures, the case was dismissed but was reopened in mid-November. Still in prison at the beginning of December, Noël asked to be released for health reasons. He was eventually released, and the case stalled there. Noël was not acquitted, and his affair was among those transferred to the Haute Cour provisoire in the spring of 1791.

The Châtelet also ended up releasing the chevalier James Rutledge. Of Irish origins, Rutledge was a lawyer and pamphleteer in Paris at the beginning of the Revolution. He, too, was accused of exploiting subsistence problems to insult and slander officials, and his affair stirred up a good deal of controversy in the capital. Rutledge claimed that Necker's *maître de requêtes*, Antoine-Nicole-Waldeck Delassart, had asked him to offer subsidies on the part of the royal administration to Parisian bakers in order to lower the price of bread. At the same time, the commune was offering loans to the bakers. Since subsidies were more attractive than loans, Rutledge encouraged the bakers to accept Necker's offer and refuse the one made by the commune. The commune was outraged by the monarchy's meddling in local affairs, but Necker denied the allegation.[107] Unsurprisingly, Rutledge began bad-mouthing Necker. The commune denounced him to the Châtelet, which charged him for obstructing bread provisions in the capital and for incendiary propos. The Cordeliers district and the journalist Camille Desmoulins came to Rutledge's defense. (They already had axes to grind against Necker.) The affair dragged on for months, providing grist for patriot mills. Emboldened by such support, Rutledge kept up his campaign against Necker through much of 1790, denouncing him to the National Assembly.[108] He started a radical newspaper, *Le Creuset*, in 1791 and produced numerous incendiary and obscene pamphlets. He was arrested along with the *hébertistes* in 1794 and died in prison.

While the Rutledge affair was polarizing politics in the capital, Julien Poulin Delaunay was stirring up trouble in Rennes. Municipal authorities accused this priest of misrepresenting the will of local guilds in a published address to the National Assembly. Delaunay's accomplice, Pierre-Charles Girard, persuaded the masters of several guilds to sign the address without revealing to them its full, incendiary content—at least that is what several masters claimed in their depositions. Believing that the address simply encouraged the National Assembly to deal with the problem of subsistence, the masters were surprised to learn that it accused local administrators of hoarding grain and denounced the National Assembly's economic policies. In the address, Delaunay argued that, although subsistence had been difficult to procure before the Revolution, at least the Church had been able to provide aid to the poor. With the liberalization of the grain market and the seizure of Church property, the poor were now denied this aid. Authorities were particularly scandalized by the final passage of the address, which read, "[The corporations of Rennes] protest that, if you [deputies] do not take care [of the problem of subsistence] as quickly as possible, you will see blood flow everywhere, and you may turn out to be yourselves the first victims of this blight that you have made us suffer for too long."[109] The phrase could have been interpreted, as Delaunay insisted during his interrogation, as a warning made in good faith, not a threat. Still, its menacing tone prompted several masters to retract their names from the address. The authorities held Girard, Delaunay, and their printer responsible. Girard and the printer were eventually released, but Delaunay was charged with lèse-nation. In their accusation against Delaunay, officials conceded that all citizens had the right to express their demands and seek aid from authorities, but that this freedom did not justify "obscure denunciations, unsubstantiated imputations against the holders of public confidence, and actions capable of alienating them from the heart, esteem, and affection of their fellow citizens, denying them the public consideration they need in order to carry out their functions successfully."[110]

The Delaunay affair dragged on for nearly two months before local officials forwarded it to the Châtelet. During a public hearing in Paris in March, Delaunay requested the opportunity to debunk a rumor that he was related to the former governor of the Bastille, whose name he shared.[111] He feared that the rumor would unduly influence the court's judgment. (Undoubtedly, he also feared meeting with the same fate as the governor, whose head ended up on a pike on July 14.) He then requested permission to read a patriotic poem he had written in 1788 against the despotism of the government and the horrors of the Bastille. After indulging Delaunay in this display of patriotic credentials, the magistrates began questioning. They asked him why he had written a tract that misrepresented the

sentiments of the guilds and why he had cast doubt on the integrity of municipal officials. Delaunay responded that he had merely transcribed the complaints
conveyed to him by Girard, that the points made in the address were frequently
expressed by the public, and that he had only criticized the refusal of local officials
to investigate hoarding and had not accused them of hoarding themselves. When
the judges reprimanded him for airing views that undermined public tranquility,
Delaunay retorted that the freedom of expression was meaningless if citizens did
not have the right to complain about their conditions. The case dragged on with
subsequent interrogations of Girard in early May, but the Châtelet abandoned the
affair shortly thereafter.[112] Still, Delaunay was not acquitted.

The lèse-nation affair that did the most to turn the public against the Châtelet was the one against Marat and Danton. After receiving several denunciations
against Marat in the fall and winter of 1789–1790, the Châtelet tried, but
failed, to arrest him on the night of January 9–10. (Marat watched the National
Guard battalions arriving to arrest him from the window of an adjacent residence and recounted the episode in the next issue of his newspaper.)[113] In the
following days, denunciations against the journalist proliferated.[114] On January
15, a magistrate of the Châtelet, André-Jean Boucher d'Argis, appeared before
the commune to denounce Marat's calumnies in a two-hour speech. The commune issued yet another warrant against the journalist, justifying its actions as
entirely compatible with the principle of press freedom. Its *arrêté* explained that
"salutary press freedom does not extend the dangerous right to calumniate with
impunity, that [even in England] authors and printers are held responsible for
the works they spread to the public; and that the Declaration of the Rights of
Man and of the Citizen hardly authorizes writings that breathe sedition, revolt,
and calumny."[115]

The Cordeliers district, where Marat resided, obstructed the municipality's
efforts to arrest the journalist. Danton, president of the district, declared that
the warrants were invalid, since they specified charges against Marat that predated
October 8, 1789, the day that the National Assembly decreed that it would modify criminal jurisprudence, nullifying all prior affairs.[116] The Cordeliers passed
an *arrêté* requiring all arrest warrants concerning citizens of the district to be
approved with a visa by district commissioners before execution.[117] They also
sent a deputation to the National Assembly to protest the measures taken by the
Châtelet and the commune, but the National Assembly refused to receive it and
declared the district's *arrêté* requiring a visa to be illegal.[118] Finally, when Danton
menaced the bailiff at a district meeting, the Châtelet declared this to be an
obstruction of justice and brought charges against Danton as well.

Like most lèse-nation affairs on the Châtelet's docket, those of Marat and Danton remained idle. For unclear reasons, however, the arrest warrant against Danton was reactivated in March.[119] The Cordeliers immediately launched a protest campaign against the Châtelet, circulating an address and petition among the other Paris districts. Most districts supported the Cordeliers, declaring it scandalous, not to mention illegal, to pursue someone for propos made during a political assembly.[120] (The law did, in fact, prohibit this.) Yet, some districts refrained from taking a stand until they had more information. The district of Sainte-Marguerite was one of the few that sided with the Châtelet. Its members reminded the Cordeliers that the Châtelet had a double jurisdiction. Thus, even if positive law did not authorize the court to arrest Danton for statements made during an assembly meeting, the court's jurisdiction over lèse-nation superseded those restrictions.[121]

The Danton affair eroded the little legitimacy the Châtelet had left. After the Malouet press law of July 31, 1790, was repealed in early August, the court stopped pursuing lèse-nation affairs for speech.[122] Its jurisdiction was revoked in October, but the affairs remained on its docket. In April 1791, just as the new Haute Cour provisoire was being installed in Orléans, the court's prosecutor wrote to the Minister of Justice, Delassart, requesting instructions concerning the status of these affairs and a working definition of lèse-nation.[123] Delassart responded, "It is not my responsibility to provide you with an exact definition of lèse-nation crimes. Only the National Assembly can determine this species of crime."[124] In a subsequent letter, Delassart asserted that if the Assembly would have provided a clear definition of the crime at the outset, "the Châtelet would have found itself in less difficult and embarrassing circumstances."[125] At about the same time, Delassart presented the National Assembly with a report on the status of all twenty-three unsettled lèse-nation cases. Many of these affairs involved speech, and he advised the Assembly to drop them. "I fear that the High Court's pursuit of these affairs, which do not appear to constitute lèse-nation crimes, will only contribute to diminishing the horror that this crime should inspire."[126]

The National Assembly agreed. All prior affairs concerning speech, but one, were dropped. The case that remained open was against Trouard de Riolles. On July 13, 1790, Trouard had been caught outside Lyon on his way to Italy carrying antirevolutionary tracts and surveillance reports on public opinion.[127] The reports contained secret codes to refer to figures at Court and in the National Assembly. The affair was sent to the Châtelet in September. The prosecutor determined that a counterrevolutionary conspiracy was clearly afoot.[128] For a while, it seemed that the comte de Mirabeau would be compromised by the affair; the seized correspondence mentioned him frequently. But a document, "found on a part of Trouard where one should least look for it," referred to Mirabeau as a "villain." Mirabeau seized upon this evidence as proof that he was not involved in the conspiracy.[129]

The evidence collected in this affair shed little light on the covert surveillance and propaganda network. However, in his *Histoire de la Révolution* published ten years later, the proud counterrevolutionary, Bertrand de Molleville, the king's naval minister in 1792, described it (or one resembling it) in great detail. He claimed that Delassart and Alexandre de Lameth were deeply involved.[130] It is plausible that Trouard was initially part of this network, had a falling out with superiors, and began working for French counterrevolutionaries operating in Turin. In any case, no one came forward to defend him. Left to defend himself, Trouard and his family wrote frequently to the National Assembly requesting his release. The letters reveal the various strategies lèse-nation suspects adopted in attempts to persuade authorities to release them. At times he complained about his frail health and presented himself as a virtuous father who needed to take care of his family.[131] At other times he took a bolder stance, insisting that the Declaration of Rights allowed him to spread whatever opinions he wanted.[132] Neither approach moved authorities.[133] Due to delays in establishing the Haute Cour provisoire, he remained in prison for months. His son complained to the National Assembly in May 1791 that his father had been unjustly imprisoned without trial for nearly a year.[134] In August, the Haute Cour acquitted him. The *Gazette des nouveaux tribunaux* celebrated the decision, reporting that it was applauded by the people, though it failed to explain why the people would have been so elated.[135] Radicals were furious, for the ruling was handed down during the *petite terreur*, when the patriot press was under siege. In his *Patriote français*, Brissot pointed out the hypocrisy that, while the Haute Cour provisoire released a man found carrying vast quantities of counterrevolutionary pamphlets, patriot writers were being arrested.[136] Once Desmoulins sprang back from the *petite terreur* at the end of August, he criticized the ruling even more bitterly. He claimed that the release of Trouard represented "a thousand times over the degradation of constituted and constituting powers."[137]

Between October 1791, when the temporary high court stopped functioning, and mid-May 1792, when the new, permanent Haute Cour nationale was established, the Legislative Assembly continued exercising its authority to indict, swelling the prisons of Orléans with lèse-nation suspects. In April, it accused a group of counterrevolutionaries in Lozère of "violating the respect due to authorities, publicly insulting the Nation, and conspiring against the Constitution."[138] Jean-Arnaud Castellane, Bishop of Mende, was among them. He was arrested for distributing incendiary pastoral letters and orchestrating local resistance to the Civil Constitution of the Clergy. A month later, news about the mutiny against General Dillon in the North of France reached the National Assembly. In the panic of retreat maneuvers before the invading Austrians, cries of treason spread among the troops, and Dillon was murdered. As we have seen, the Legislative Assembly charged Marat and Royou with lèse-nation, accusing them of having compromised the unity of the troops with their radical and counterrevolutionary messages.

Later that month, the Legislative Assembly charged Étienne de La Rivière, a justice of the peace in Paris, with lèse-nation for summoning members of its *comité de surveillance* for questioning. La Rivière suspected the committee of orchestrating a covert libel campaign against the monarchy. He began his investigation by interrogating Jean-Louis Carra, journalist of the *Annales patriotiques*, who, in a recent issue, had accused the ministers of the navy and of foreign affairs of conspiring with the secret Austrian Committee at Court. Carra confessed to La Rivière that his information came from members of the *comité de surveillance*. When La Rivière summoned these members for questioning, they refused, accusing him of violating the judicial immunity of national deputies. La Rivière responded that he had not issued an arrest warrant, only a summons for questioning, for which there was no immunity. Protecting his colleagues on the committee, Marguérite-Élie Guadet persuaded deputies to combat this encroachment on their inviolability. Astonishingly, he admitted that the committee had used Carra's newspaper to spread unsubstantiated accusations against the royalist ministers, justifying this as a necessary tactic to uncover true counterrevolutionaries. He argued that, even if the committee's conduct constituted a crime—and he thought it did not—only the Legislative Assembly had the right to accuse and arrest deputies. In summoning the committee members for questioning, La Rivière, Guadet insisted, had violated the Constitution, which criminalized the act of undermining constituted authority. On June 2, the Legislative Assembly accused La Rivière of lèse-nation. He soon joined the dozens of prisoners awaiting trial in Orléans. La Rivière, along with Castellane, was among those massacred in Versailles in September.

In the months leading up to August 10, 1792, constitutional monarchy fell apart. The system of checks and balances between the legislative and executive branches had degenerated into a duel of political justice between republicans and royalists.

The Terror

By September 1792 when the First Republic was founded, many of the forces driving France toward the Terror were in place. Speech crimes had been legally defined, and the principle of extraordinary justice had been confirmed. Although the Haute Cour nationale was abolished along with the monarchy, the National Convention assumed jurisdiction of political crimes, exercising it in the trial of Louis XVI before conferring it to revolutionary tribunals on March 10, 1793. Finally, popular vengeance had injected itself into revolutionary politics, where it became conflated with justice. The September Massacres in Paris, Versailles, and other cities put authorities in the position of having to condone popular vengeance (with the risk of abetting it) or condemn it (with the risk of becoming its victims). The dilemma drove a wedge between the moderate and radical factions in the Jacobin Club, leading to the expulsion of some of the former, notably Roland and Brissot. In establishing the revolutionary tribunal in March 1793, Danton summed up its logic to fellow deputies in the National Convention, "Let us be terrible in order to dispense the people from being so!"[139]

The Terror's legal and judicial machinery was put into place over the spring, summer, and early fall of 1793. Over the next year, thousands were arrested for speech crimes throughout France. According to Donald Greer's statistical study, 988 of 2,639 indictments (or 37.5 percent) by the revolutionary tribunal of the department of the Seine (Paris) were for speech and opinion.[140] The proportion of indictments for crimes of speech and opinion was nearly as high in cities along the borders of France (37 percent). Proportions were lower elsewhere, although in places where civil war had broken out, such as the counterrevolutionary Vendée and regions wracked by the Federalist Revolts, indictments were based on laws of sedition and treason. In any case, Paris—the capital of France and cauldron of radicalism—was where the Terror struck at speech most severely. As Greer concludes, "In Paris...the home of the purest Jacobinism, there was no quarter for political heresy."[141]

But does ideological fanaticism sufficiently explain the dynamics driving the Terror's brutal treatment of speech? Some indictments for speech offenses during the Terror do appear to have been inspired by nothing more than a fanatical desire to enforce Jacobin orthodoxy. Take, for example, the case of the hapless Gaspard Magnin. He was overheard making "counterrevolutionary propos and injurious statements against the Supreme Being" during a festival held in its honor in June 1794. Mocking an inscription on an altar to the nation that read, "[The Supreme Being] presides over our happiness," Magnin snorted, "He presides over our destruction."[142] Magnin was fortunate; Robespierre fell before his case was heard. Still, he remained in prison until November, when the post-Terror revolutionary tribunal acquitted him.

Most affairs were more complex. That of Martin Rémi, a winemaker outside Beauvais, is a good example of how laws regarding speech crimes served as pretexts for settling scores having to do with other matters. Rémi was arrested on April 7, 1793, for "counterrevolutionary propos," but the affair stretched back to late summer 1792. Certain individuals "without property" in the community accused Rémi of expropriating land belonging to the commune.[143] The case went to trial, and it seemed likely that Rémi would win, since the commune could not prove that the land was communal and an earlier ruling by a justice of the peace had ruled in Rémi's favor. Rémi's adversaries strengthened their case by accusing him of antirevolutionary propos. He was alleged to have said that "the district administration can wipe my ass" and that the deputies of the National Convention "are a bunch of villains."[144] District administrators found Rémi's propos "seditious and injurious to the representatives of the people." One of Rémi's defenders wrote to departmental officials in the hopes of persuading them to override the district's "calumnious" charges. He pleaded, "An honest man can protect himself from disparaging remarks [*médisance*], but he cannot protect himself from calumny, no matter how upstanding he is, especially when vengeance distills its poison."[145] Even the Committee of Public Safety of the district thought the affair was overblown: "[Rémi's] words were insignificant," the committee insisted in a letter to the public prosecutor, "[since] they were not followed by attempts to seduce or persuade his fellow citizens of his opinion....They were uttered in a state of anger."[146] But the prosecutor was unmoved. In the margins of the committee's letter, he refuted, "Even if the words of malicious individuals do not achieve their ends, they are nonetheless criminal [*coupables*] and merit the severity of the Law."

Rémi's case was sent to the revolutionary tribunal in July, and he was convicted in late October 1793, around the time the Girondins were executed. The tribunal had no need of the recent Law of Suspects, passed in September, to justify the conviction. The Penal Code of 1791 sufficed, specifically, an article under the title "Crimes and Attacks against *Res Publica*."[147] The article dealt mostly with treasonous relations with enemy powers, but it encompassed "actions tending to weaken the loyalty of officers, soldiers, *and other citizens* toward the French nation." The tribunal also invoked the Thouret provisions included in the Constitution of 1791 and the law against calling for the return of monarchy passed on December 4, 1792. According to the published judgment, Rémi was convicted for "propos tending to provoke the degradation and dissolution of the national representation and the degradation of constituted authority" and "for announcing a desire to see the rebirth of the monarchy."

Rémi appears to have been the victim of local struggles over property. There is little doubt that he would have liked to see the Old Regime restored, but there is no evidence that he actively conspired to bring this about. For the tribunal, his intentions—"the desire to see the rebirth of the monarchy"—were sufficient grounds for conviction. Yet, intentions were slippery things. They could as easily be cited as the basis for acquittal. The tribunal's assessment of the intentions of Lathélise and Amaury—the author and printer of pamphlets that virulently attacked Marat and Robespierre—saved the two men. They had been accused of "calumniating the Revolution and its defenders" and of "insulting the national representation in the most injurious terms."[148] The tribunal did find the two men guilty of producing and distributing writings that "degraded [*avilir*] the national representation and constituted authority." The evidence was ample and incontrovertible. However, to the questions "Did Lathélise and Amaury do so knowingly and with criminal, counterrevolutionary intentions?" the tribunal concluded "no."[149] With luck (and perhaps influential connections), they were released in February 1794.

Many suspects of speech crimes were simply malcontents deprived of power or property by the Revolution. Pierre-Claude Janson, a soldier in the republican army, was convicted for "counterrevolutionary propos tending to degrade the national representation and constituted authority and to provoke the return of royalty."[150] He was accused of saying around the time of Marie-Antoinette's execution, "The Convention is a den of thieves, and the Queen is a brave woman." He complained that the Republic, which had destroyed his parents' theater during the brutal reprisal against the federalist city of Lyon, had "stolen his fortune." When a fellow soldier chided him, "One is rich enough in fighting to defend one's country," Janson retorted, "The Republic takes everything and gives nothing." The Republic took his life on 4 Brumaire, Year II.

Like Janson, Gabriel-Charles Doyen was also upset about the execution of the queen, and with good reason: he had been her personal chef and was now unemployed. For some time after the abolition of the monarchy, the National Convention maintained the pensions of Court retainers. In the spring of 1794, after months of not receiving indemnities, Doyen announced that he would go see Robespierre and Saint-Just to demand his back-pay, then join the émigrés. He was executed in early June for "propos favoring the degradation of constituted authority, the destruction of the Republic, and the return of despotism."[151]

Many affairs during the Terror turned on issues of insult, calumny, and honor. Claude Valentin Millin de la Brosse, for example, was arrested in late January 1794 for counterrevolutionary propos. The affair began at a café near the Seine. La Brosse asked another patron, Jacques Germain Joly Braquehaye (an employee of the departmental administration), to borrow the latter's copy of *Le Moniteur* to read an article concerning Constantinople.[152] Upon learning that the Ottomans were throwing their support behind revolutionary France, La Brosse expressed his dismay. Joly remarked that La Brosse must be a "bad citizen" to be disheartened that France had an ally. Insults flew back and forth, and an undercover police agent of the section warned La Brosse that his words could get him into trouble. (The agent did not arrest him at this point.) Enraged, La Brosse challenged Joly to a duel. Officials later said that Joly brushed off the challenge, but La Brosse claimed that Joly had accepted and had given him his address. In any case, La Brosse appeared at Joly's doorstep at eight o'clock the next morning to challenge him to duel at the Luxembourg at eleven. Joly accepted. No sooner had La Brosse turned to leave than he was apprehended by the police.

La Brosse spent several months in prison, where he apparently antagonized the other prisoners, assaulting one of them. Like many suspects arrested in 1793 and early 1794, his case was not heard until June 1794. During his interrogation, he explained that he had challenged Joly to a duel only after Joly had pelted him with relentless "buggers" and "fuckers."[153] (He admitted that he himself had proffered one "fucker," but no "buggers.") The interrogators reminded La Brosse that insults did not justify endangering the life of a patriot, adding that if La Brosse believed that Joly was not a true patriot, he should have denounced him. La Brosse justified himself, quite eloquently, on the grounds of honor: "The laws of honor to which I adhere—not fanatically, but as a former military officer—have not yet been destroyed in the opinions men have of each other." The interrogators alerted him to the dangers of spilling patriot blood at a time when the country needed it for its defense. La Brosse responded, "If it is necessary for patriots to mutually spare their blood for the good of the country, it is no less necessary that they do not abandon their sense of honor." Clearly, La Brosse had noble, individual honor in mind. The revolutionary tribunal put the nation's honor before it. Citing the law of December 4, 1792, they concluded that La Brosse had "spoken words tending to provoke the dissolution of the republican government and the reestablishment of the monarchy," and that he had "menaced, insulted, and outraged … patriots."[154]

Struggles over honor envenomed the politics of the Year II. They fill many pages of the memoirs of Jacques Ménétra, the master glazier in Paris and active sans-culotte, whom we met above. Although his now published *Journal of My Life* offers only sketchy details about this phase of the Revolution, his unpublished, miscellaneous writings provide a fuller picture. The titles he gave to passages concerning the Terror bespeak his obsession with calumny and honor: "My response to the invectives made by the most inept and intolerant man the most contemptible of all men the intriguer Duplessis great plotter [*cabaleur*] formidable denunciator I scorn backbiting and abhor calumny" (his text lacks punctuation).[155] The title of the following section reveals the tendency, already highlighted in this study, to conflate one's individual honor with the honor of the collectivity in order to justify vengeance: "My response to my denunciators the upstanding man has no venom he forgets calumny and does good *My enemies were those of the Republic* and the facts that I will trace will prove the backbiting of my vile calumniators."[156]

Ménétra's journal of the Terror reveals how petty jealousies and slights of honor could escalate into politicized vengeances. During these years, he held various positions of authority in his section. One day he was instructed to round up guards to protect the local granaries from pillage. When the guards under his command complained about the absence of one of Ménétra's friends, Duplessis, Ménétra went looking for him. He found Duplessis at a local café, but the latter refused to help and started insulting Ménétra. Ménétra forcibly dragged him out of the café. Unbeknownst to Ménétra, the other guards had followed him and witnessed the incident. Humiliated, Duplessis began plotting Ménétra's demise. With the help of others, especially the writer Isidore Langlois, Duplessis spread "sarcasms" and "mauvais propos" against Ménétra and tried to have him arrested as a suspect.[157] Langlois libeled him in one of his publications. Ménétra claims that all this calumny nearly cost him his life. A *robespierriste*, he had good reason to worry after the fall of the "Incorruptible," when his enemies, Duplessis and Langlois, gained the upper hand in local politics. (They, in turn, would be hounded after the reactionary movement was crushed in fall 1795.) In any case, Ménétra managed to survive to recount the story.

In reading Ménétra's account, one gets the sense that the politics of the Terror had more to do with a culture of calumny and honor run amok than with ideological commitments. The term "calumny" appears repeatedly, along with terms such as "indignities," "insolence," "spite," and "vengeance."[158] There is nothing in these passages about abstract political principles, aside from the honor of the nation and of the Republic. Even his enemies who became reactionaries after Thermidor appear to have done so for tactical rather than ideological reasons.

Yet, ideas sometimes mattered in affairs concerning the elites, especially writers, as François-Alexandre Suremain discovered. He was convicted for his manuscript "Reflections on the New Constitution given to France by the National Convention," which refuted the new Declaration of the Rights of Man and of the Citizen, article by article.[159] Suremain was initially arrested, however, for entirely different reasons. Like many affairs of speech during the Terror, his grew out of local jealousies. Suremain was an ex-noble and a municipal officer. During elections, a rival, the sieur Descamps, tried to compromise his credibility by stressing his familial connections to émigrés. Several of Suremain's relatives had, in fact, emigrated, including his brother. Suremain won the election anyway, and Descamps ended up in the departmental administration, where he allegedly plotted Suremain's demise. When the National Convention's representative on mission arrived in the region, the department informed him of Suremain's royalist ties. No arrest warrant was issued immediately, but rumors about his impending arrest frightened the municipality into removing him from office. Suremain was initially imprisoned but subsequently put under house arrest after a doctor attested to his poor health. The affair stalled for months, during which time Suremain's supporters, including other municipal officers, wrote on his behalf. Upon the passage of the Law of Suspects in September, the department reactivated the affair. Suremain was imprisoned again and his papers were seized. Among them, the police discovered his tract on the Constitutional Act of 1793. Although he had not published it, Suremain never denied that he had intended to do so.

Suremain's case did not come before the revolutionary tribunal until the following June, the height of the Terror. In its judgment against him, which ran several pages, the tribunal rebutted his tract line by line.[160] They declared Suremain's assertions to be "a string of calumnies" against the Constitution and authorities. They highlighted the passages in which Suremain criticized the Constitution's aims of procuring "collective happiness" and "equality." The ex-noble had insisted that the government should protect only the pursuit of individual happiness, nothing more, and he roundly dismissed the idea of equality and the redistribution of wealth. "To think that inequality of wealth is a disorder which should be destroyed is a sophism." He also took the fact that nearly all European powers were at war with France for evidence of revolutionaries' folly. He concluded, "Can you still believe that the salvation of the people is the true aim of regenerative efforts that have wrought only calamities?"

The revolutionary tribunal concluded that Suremain had "sought to inspire in readers sentiments of hatred for the republican government in criticizing the entire work of the Convention and calumniating the zealous defenders of the rights of the people." Thus, an affair that had initially grown out of personal rivalries and the issue of émigré property provided the revolutionary tribunal, thanks to Suremain's manuscript, an occasion to assert the principles of the Revolution and the legitimate limits of free expression.

There is one point upon which Suremain and revolutionaries agreed. In an early passage of his manuscript, he speculated, "[The current oppression] would never have prevailed if the National Convention—before drafting the Constitutional Act [of 1793]—had taken care of public instruction, had it prepared the French to enjoy happiness by establishing moral principles as the basis of its politics." Many leaders shared Suremain's concern for moral instruction. They recognized the calamitous nature of the punitive dynamics consuming revolutionary politics, and when they were not exploiting those dynamics (often preemptively) or channeling them into judicial institutions (to assert the state's monopoly on punitive violence), they sought to mitigate them through "public spirit" campaigns. They hoped that improved civic morality would dispense them from having to punish speech offenses by preventing those offenses from occurring in the first place. For them, moral regeneration was the antidote to terror.

CHAPTER EIGHT

Policing the Moral Limits
Public Spirit, Surveillance, and the Remaking of Mœurs

Such is the kind of revolution still needed: that of mœurs.
> Jean-Marie Roland, *Lettre du ministre de l'Intérieur
> à la Convention nationale*, September 30, 1792

Quid leges sine moribus vanae proficiunt?
(How useless and vain are the laws without mœurs?)
> Horace, the Third Ode of *Carmina*, cited by François-Xavier Lanthenas,
> *Bases fondamentales de l'instruction publique*, 1793

Without public spirit, no mœurs.
> Dieudonné Thiébault, *Traité sur l'esprit public*, 1797

Public Spirit, the Moral Limits

In the two and a half weeks between the time her father was fired and the time he was recalled and returned from Bâle, France, wrote Anne-Louise-Germaine Necker, fell apart. The future Madame de Staël, in her letter to the Emperor of Sweden of August 1789, recounted, "My father [Jacques Necker, First Minister of Finances] returned on July 27 to find authorities destroyed or confused with new ones…an old nation fallen into a state of infancy rather than youth, a corrupt people clamoring for American institutions, insisting on freedom before establishing public spirit."[1] In a letter eight months earlier, de Staël described France to be in a state of "great agitation" over the upcoming Estates-General. She thought that with the mass of conflicting interests, establishing public spirit would be treacherous. "The French want to establish public spirit amid a thousand particular interests. They believe a Constitution will be born from the clash of competing parties. I hope this will happen, but I tremble for the navigator who tries to guide them through so many obstacles."[2]

194 *The French Revolution*

Three years later, Jean-Marie Roland was the navigator, and bearing out de Staël's presentiment, he crashed upon the reefs of revolutionary politics. As Minister of the Interior, he was accorded 100,000 livres by the National Assembly on August 18, 1792, to cultivate public spirit. His partisan propaganda, we have seen, raised the ire of radicals. In January 1793, as Montagnard deputies were driving him from office for allegedly corrupting public spirit, he published an essay defining it. His definition, which his wife, Jeanne-Marie Phlipon, may have penned, deserves to be cited at length. It echoes much of what was said about public spirit before the Revolution and offers insight into the political crisis of the early First Republic.

> Public spirit is not what people often confuse unthinkingly with public opinion whose flux and partial applications can take on an indefinite variety of forms. What I call public spirit is a natural tendency, imperious toward all that can contribute to the happiness of the country; it is a most profound and religious sentiment which places the interest of our common mother [the nation] above our [particular] interests and inspires in us a fraternal affection for fellow citizens; it prescribes as the most important duty to love one's country, to respect and obey its laws, and to regard as scandalous and punishable all who violate them, undermine them, *or even censure them;* to honor as fathers the magistrates responsible for communicating the laws and executing them; and to recognize as unworthy of belonging to the social body those who isolate themselves, seeking only advantages without contributing to its harmony.[3]

In short, public spirit was "purely moral," involving civic values, patriotism, and social discipline.[4] Like many revolutionaries before and after his ministry, Roland believed that laws and political authority were nothing without moral attachments binding the people to them. He claimed that this moral force was the much-needed antidote to the "calumny…insults, and attacks made against authorities" and the reigning "social fracture."[5] He distinguished public spirit from public opinion, which allowed him to uphold the freedom of expression and of opinion while justifying state efforts to secure the moral foundations of the new regime. Finally, he considered not only revolt but even censure against the laws to be punishable. He viewed such censure as politically destabilizing—a specious assertion in other contexts, but perhaps less so in 1792 when the regime's legitimacy was uncertain.

The Rolands' definition of public spirit also fit with broader conceptions about civic mœurs developed before the Revolution. "Mœurs," we have seen, was a polyvalent term encompassing propriety, customs, and morality. Contemporaries saw them as the foundation of the social and political order. Laws needed to be conformable to mœurs, and mœurs needed to be good for the laws to have any influence. We have also seen that "public spirit" in Enlightenment tracts referred to republican mœurs. At times, public spirit consisted in disinterested reason, at others, heartfelt patriotism. It implied obedience to the law and respect for authorities. Without suppressing individual interests, public spirit placed collective interests above those of the individual. One did not have to subscribe to Rousseau's writings to accept this hierarchy of interests, even if one could find it there; it appeared in the theories of classical, agricultural, and commercial republicanism circulating throughout the Atlantic world.[6] Indeed, as the daughter of an international financier, de Staël's use of the term in 1789 is not surprising. Nor is its institutionalization under Roland's ministry in 1792. For decades Roland had devoted himself to the study of agriculture, commerce, and industry; he traveled often to England and Holland and wrote much about political economy.[7] He had every opportunity to become steeped in ideas about public spirit.

This study has thus far examined the punitive aspects of policing opinion. Repression, we have seen, grew out of engrained cultural reflexes concerning calumny, honor, and authority—reflexes that ran amok under the strains of regime change and the introduction of civil equality. Yet, punishment and proscription were not the only methods revolutionaries adopted in dealing with perceived speech abuses. They also tried to cultivate moral restraints. For them, public spirit served as a normative ideal to guide them in monitoring and disciplining opinion. As a moral norm, public spirit helped them reconcile their policing of opinion with the principle of free speech; for as we have seen, the cahiers de doléances expressed the belief that the enforcement of mœurs, or moral limits, was compatible with press freedom. Although some revolutionaries initially believed that press freedom would vivify public spirit, they soon came to the conclusion that press abuses were undermining it. How were such abuses to be checked? Many militated for legal restrictions and extraordinary justice. Some, however, thought that the government should do more to instill civic values. They imagined that public spirit, once propagated, would dispense with the need for punishment. But the Revolution paralyzed or abolished mœurs-shaping institutions, notably the Church and the guilds, and it provoked tensions over the role of religion in education.[8] The outlandish attempts in 1793 and 1794 to morally regenerate the nation by breaking with all tradition must be understood within the chronology of the Revolution and the failure to secure civic values and social discipline through religion between 1789 and 1792.

Public Spirit before State Intervention: A Solution to Calumny and the Role of Religion

Belief that press freedom would strengthen public spirit did not last long. The comte de Mirabeau expressed this optimism in his 1788 *Sur la liberté de la presse*, an updated version of John Milton's *Areopagitica* (1644). Unlike de Staël, Mirabeau

FIGURE 8.2. Jeanne-Marie Phlipon, Madame Roland. Courtesy of the Bibliothèque nationale de France, cabinet d'estampes.

believed that France's public spirit was strong enough to risk constitutional overhaul and press freedom without sliding into anarchy. Even if agitation occurred, it was better, he insisted, than putting up with an arbitrary press regime.[9] He claimed that the greatest threat to public spirit came from royal ministers who sought to impede communication between groups within society, keeping people divided and exploiting fears of anarchy.[10] Mirabeau's belief in the positive effects of a free press for the improvement of mœurs was echoed in an anonymous pamphlet published in the summer of 1789. Dismissing worries that press freedom would destroy mœurs, the author proclaimed, "Oh, you reactionary supporters of old errors....[By opposing press freedom] you deprive us of the sole means for reestablishing them!"[11]

Most contemporaries felt differently. They believed that unregulated press freedom was contributing to moral decline and civil strife. In January 1790, a legal scholar from Lyon wrote, "If the Nation wants to regenerate its mœurs, reestablish order...and preserve its liberty, it will never do so by permitting the circulation of these dire writings that attack mœurs, blacken the honor of the most virtuous citizens, and destroy the ties between the people and their monarch and the National Assembly."[12] The poet André Chénier agreed. While his radical playwright brother Marie-Joseph Chénier was clamoring for freedom in the theater, André offered more measured reflections on the freedom of the press. "All that is good and bad in this Revolution," he asserted, "can be attributed to writings."[13] Focusing on the bad, he was convinced that hidden, high-powered interests were behind the production of libels. To combat them, he thought that action needed to be taken. Sedition laws, he believed, would suffice to thwart writings that preached insurrection. But to counteract calumnious writings that managed cleverly to remain within the law's limits, readers would need to become more clever themselves. Wise readers, according to Chénier, "observe the reasoning and precepts [of writers], uncovering the interests that motivate them." That is, wise readers discern the moral intentions behind the words on the page. He called upon such readers to "denounce writers as public enemies if their doctrines tend to mislead, reduce, or deteriorate public spirit."[14] (Ironically, the intentions behind his 1793 *Ode à Charlotte Corday*, which celebrated the assassination of Marat, were the grounds for his arrest during the Terror; he was guillotined two days before the fall of Robespierre.)

What was this "public spirit" that André Chénier thought needed to be protected? It was "a certain generalized, practical reason...always in calibrated accordance with public institutions."[15] He stressed the aspects of calm, cool reason rather than fervent patriotism. Still, like Roland, he saw public spirit as a "kind of religion, almost a superstition." It inspired "respect for the law" and an appreciation of the distinction between what belonged to the individual and what belonged to society.[16] For Chénier, free speech was not incompatible with public spirit, but neither did it guarantee that public spirit would flourish. To secure public spirit in France, the popular classes would have to undergo an "apprenticeship of reason."[17]

Even those espousing quasi-libertarian views on free speech in 1791, though they rejected the notion of seditious libel, nevertheless believed that improved public spirit would reduce calumny. Unlike the philosophes of the 1750s and 1760s, who, as we have seen, dismissed the dangers of libels, the quasi-libertarians of the Revolution acknowledged their potential to do harm. The anonymous author of *Discours sur la censure publique et la calomnie patriotique* (1791), for example, criticized Loustalot's and Prudhomme's "calumny is good" precept and declared Camille Desmoulins to be one of the most dangerous calumniators around.[18] Still, the author believed that legal limits were futile. Addressing legislators (he was probably one himself), he wrote,

> You want to find a way to [establish legal limits] for the freedom of the press . . . but it is impossible to find one that would not compromise public liberty; you want at least to know if it is possible to pass a law against calumny, which is truly moral assassination, but the sad reality is that there are few laws that bad citizens cannot abuse, and a law against calumny would only enervate the courage of those who have hard truths to announce to the public.[19]

Like Chénier, this writer believed that the only solution to the problem of calumny was to teach readers to distinguish truth from calumny and to scorn libels. Society needed more Enlightenment and better mœurs. "Virtue and Verity, these are our gods, these are our guides!"[20]

Even the more strident quasi-libertarians thought improved public spirit was needed to counteract abuses of press freedom, though they still entertained the belief that unlimited freedom would force society to become more self-policing and, hence, virtuous. In his second tract on press freedom in 1790, Louis-Félix Guynement de Kéralio claimed that repressive laws would sap public spirit, provoking public indignation of authorities and discouraging citizens from helping authorities track down true calumniators.[21] The absence of repressive laws would have the opposite effect. Citizens would be more inclined to speak out against calumniators.[22] The public would begin policing itself, and public spirit would consequently improve. Unlike André Chénier, who thought that repressive laws were necessary to combat seditious tracts, Kéralio insisted that a self-policing public could better deal with the problem. "Under an arbitrary government, an expressed *seditious intention* alarms only administrators, since they are its sole target. Subjects sit back and watch events like spectators. Under a free government, however, an announced *seditious intention* excites public spirit, alarms the nation, and all citizens are mobilized."[23]

What about writings that whittled away at mœurs? Kéralio thought that the only viable remedy was to establish sound moral principles, "which exist in man's nature, his rights, and the social pact." "It is necessary," he urged, "to discover them, develop them, and spread them through public oral instruction, writings, and a national education system. It is only through these means that one can rectify the general will, alter opinions, and constitute public spirit with regard to mœurs."[24] In short, France needed "more instruction, more mœurs, and more freedom, but fewer laws."[25]

The compelling reason, then, to embark on the intellectual and moral regeneration of society was to secure the most amount of freedom with the fewest legal restrictions. Enlightened moral instruction was imagined to be the antidote to calumny and a civilizing alternative to repression and punishment. But legislators did little about public instruction, besides draw up proposals, conduct surveys, and blather about its importance. Meanwhile, the old system of education fell into disarray. This occurred for several reasons. The expropriation of Church property upon which many schools depended brought about their financial ruin. The Civil Constitution of the Clergy of July 1790 and the pope's rejection of it in the spring of 1791 polarized clerical communities, sending waves of dissension throughout what remained of the education system.[26] Indeed, disputes over the legitimate role of religion in civic instruction were the main reason the National Assembly did so little to reform the education system. Before 1789, as we have seen, mœurs and religion were considered to be overlapping and mutually reinforcing. After 1789, they became increasingly irreconcilable.

The first serious set of education reforms proposed in the National Assembly did not appear until two years into the Revolution. In September 1791, Charles-Maurice de Talleyrand-Périgord, the very deputy-bishop who had supported the expropriation of Church property in the fall of 1789, called for free education for all girls and boys beginning at the age of seven.[27] His proposals were indeed progressive, but not radical. They did not make schooling compulsory and did not require children to remain in school throughout their teens, since most, he believed, were headed for the trades or domestic work. The least progressive aspect of his proposals was his call for Catholic instruction. Criticizing this point, Desmoulins wrote, "A Protestant, Jewish, or Mohammedan father could never send his child to such a school."[28] As it turned out, Protestant, Jewish, and Muslim fathers did not have to make the choice; the proposal was shelved.

Desmoulins's criticism notwithstanding, most early revolutionaries believed that Christian instruction—which usually meant Catholic instruction—was best suited for spreading civic consciousness. We have seen that Jacques Necker, a Protestant, devoted a lengthy publication in 1788 to arguing that civic mœurs depended on religious instruction. Only religion, he insisted, could bind the individual's conscience to the general interest. This view predominated until 1792. Anthanase Auger, a key figure of the Cercle Social, raised the question in his *Catéchisme du citoyen français*: "Why should we submit to the religion of our ancestors?" His response: "In general, religion is the basis of all virtues and *good* mœurs without which laws would be ineffective."[29] Conceding that all societies have sacred beliefs that morally bind individuals together, he emphasized the superiority of Christianity, "whose dogmas are so sublime, whose morality is so pure, and whose outlook is so gentle, uniting all men through bonds of charity."[30] (He did not clarify whether Christianity encompassed Protestantism.)

Still, secular and outright anticlerical positions on education were, if not prevailing, at least discernible in these early years. On August 3, 1789, the eve of the abolition of feudal privileges, François Boissel submitted to the National Assembly his treatise *Le catéchisme du genre humain*. Boissel discussed guiding principles for public instruction, the most important of which was the exclusion of religion. "One must not mix up the principles of sound morality which have human relations as their chief object with religions that have as their chief object people's relationship to the divinity."[31] Boissel did not pull any punches when it came to assessing the history of religious education. "If the ministers of fanaticism have until now preached principles of morality, without ever practicing them, it has been only to gild the knives they put in our hands...to divide us, to arm us against each other."[32] An ardent Holbachian, Boissel repeatedly referred to the Church as a "mercenary, homicidal, and antisocial establishment."

Such statements were clearly intended to shake up prevailing pieties about how religion and mœurs reinforced each other. Yet, it is unclear that many read Boissel's book in 1789. No one made mention of it in the National Assembly until November 4, when a deputy-bishop, smarting over the expropriation of Church property decreed two days earlier, denounced it. The bishop was probably also trying to settle a score for the Assembly's recent lèse-nation accusation against Le Mintier, Bishop of Tréguier, for circulating antirevolutionary pastoral letters.[33] In any case, the deputy Rabaut Saint-Étienne (a Protestant) informed Boissel that his book had been denounced. He confessed that he had not yet read it, but since Boissel had sent him a copy, he felt obliged to warn him.[34] The author promptly wrote to the National Assembly's *comité des rapports*. He claimed that the ideas in his book were over the heads of "the majority of society"—a convenient claim, though probably accurate: no mention of it appears in the more than forty cartons of the *comité des recherches*, otherwise replete with denunciations of "bad" works.[35] In any case, the affair seems to have fizzled out there. A second edition of the work did not appear until 1792, when troubles over religion made Boissel's anticlerical views more appealing.

Debate on the role of religion in educating the masses surfaced in various societies and clubs in 1790 and 1791. In his study of the Cercle Social, the think tank and propaganda machine of the Jacobin Club, historian Gary Kates shows that while some supported a Christian-based civil religion as the basis of moral instruction, others promoted a secular, nation-based one.[36] In a Jacobin Club meeting in September 1791, discussion on this issue occurred following a speech by an engineer from Lyon, Jean-Claude Simonne. Like Boissel, Simonne was fiercely anticlerical. He asserted that the clergy had always been elitist and bent on keeping people in the dark. He called for establishing a national education system devoted to the teaching of, among other subjects, morality and mœurs, two disciplines that he took to be interdependent.[37] His speech was greatly applauded, though one member, a bishop from the Ain, branded it "atheistic" and accused Simonne of "debasing the clergy."[38] The bishop insisted that the club reverse its decision to have it printed. In the end, Simonne had it printed on his own.

In the winter of 1791–1792, as the Legislative Assembly was debating whether to declare war on Austria, tensions mounted over the clergy's privileged role in morally instructing the nation. The Civil Constitution of the Clergy was turning into a disaster, encountering fierce resistance in many parts of France.[39] Despite the abolition of the regular orders of the clergy in the spring of 1790, the National Assembly allowed members to continue living in their convents, monasteries, and seminaries, many of which became hothouses of counterrevolution.[40] According to a deputy in early February 1792, patriots were starting to "mark" them, a sign of imminent bloodletting. Anticipating violence, some departmental officials washed their hands of their responsibility over religious matters.[41] Hopes that the Civil Constitution of the Clergy would reconcile the principles of religion and the Revolution and secure civic mœurs were vanishing quickly.

It was in this context that Charles-Alexandre de Moy, a constitutional priest from the diocese of Saint-Laurent in Paris, wrote *Accord de la religion et des cultes chez une nation libre*. Moy insisted on the equality of all cults and pressed for the creation of an overarching national religion. "As long as the Roman Catholic cult does not take on the same status as all the other cults in the eyes of the nation, the body politic will never enjoy perfect health."[42] Moy, who had won a prize from the Academy of Besançon in 1776 for a discourse on mœurs, was not anticlerical.[43] He insisted on tolerance for all religions, "except of course those that are contrary, not to reason, for that would be expecting too much, but to good mœurs and the constitution."[44] What was this national cult to consist in? He believed that much still needed to be created. He observed that on July 14, 1789, "The French people dared to declare themselves a nation, but the nation did not yet exist."[45] The only festival the nation had was the Festival of the Federation (Bastille Day), and he criticized the use of Catholic rituals in celebrating it. The new religion was to have its own altar, he asserted. At this altar, the papist would stand hand-in-hand with the Protestant, the Protestant hand-in-hand with the Jew. "Everyone will embrace each other."[46] Factions would disappear before this altar as well. "These odious distinctions of aristocrats, democrats, jurors, non-jurors, royalists, republicans, and counterrevolutionaries will no longer exist."[47] Published in early 1792, Moy's pluralist vision of national unity was expressed against the backdrop of factionalism and civil strife. This context, exacerbated by the king's resistance to the Legislative Assembly's religious policies, helps explain Moy's unambiguous resolve: "There is no middle ground.... Either the nation remains entirely Roman Catholic ... or it gives Roman Catholicism no more priv-ileged status than any other cult" and creates its own.[48]

Although Moy's book received official homage from the National Assembly, which forwarded a copy to the *comité d'instruction publique*, it stirred up a barrage of criticism. Jean-Baptiste-Joseph Gobel, Constitutional Bishop of Paris, was among its critics.[49] What must have been Gobel's consternation can be gleaned from an anonymous publication, *Lettre à M. Gobel*. The author begins, "It is said that you are not satisfied with your priest of Saint-Laurent [Moy]." He insisted that Gobel had no reason to reprimand Moy, since the latter's arguments were the logical, if unfortunate, result of the Civil Constitution of the Clergy, which Gobel, a deputy, had actively supported. "If [Moy's] pages are revolting to you, you should blame yourself.... Since you were witness to all the maneuvers employed in the Constitu-ent Assembly to destroy religion, you cannot pretend that this system of irreligion developed by your priest is not what [the Assembly] was seeking to establish all along."[50] Others blamed the constitutional bishops as well. The author of *Épître dédicatoire à M. l'Évêque et les curés constitutionnels de Paris* wrote, "This is the [national] religion of which the abbé Fauchet was the precursor."[51] (The abbé Fauchet had spearheaded the Civil Constitution of the Clergy.) One of Moy's critics succinctly summed up the reactionary view on the matter: "There is only one faith, and thus only one true religion. All others are false. To realize an accord [among all reli-gions] could only be imagined by an extravagant *philosophe*."[52]

By 1792, doubts that the clergy could reliably cultivate civic mœurs and faith in the new regime led some revolutionaries to count on the patriotic clubs and the press instead. In his 1792 *Des sociétés populaires considérées comme une branche essentielle de l'instruction publique*, François-Xavier Lanthenas wrote, "Since it is now recognized that one cannot count on the priests of any sect for the most essential public instruction, it is necessary to find a mode of education appropriate for the teaching of morality—the most important science—and politics, which is simply a branch of the former."[53] Lanthenas lamented the absence of an adequate education system, and he blamed certain deputies of the Constituent Assembly for not having dealt with the issue.[54] He believed that a national education system would eventually be established and would instill civic morality. In the meantime, political clubs and the press were the only viable means to counteract Old Regime prejudices. Combining the two, he proposed that the clubs devote sessions to discussing published works on morality and politics. In calling together people of all religions, the clubs would foster "a cult of reason and law" and bring about a "regeneration of mœurs."[55]

This was, of course, an unrealistic notion of what clubs could do, especially by 1792, when they were succumbing to calumny and factionalism. Declaring war against Austria was the main issue dividing Jacobins. While Brissot and his followers pressed for it, Robespierre and his allies were opposed, arguing (rightly) that war would drain state coffers and exacerbate domestic tensions. They claimed that the truly dangerous counterrevolution was conspiring in the Tuileries, not Coblentz. France needed to clean house, not start a war that would jeopardize the whole Revolution.

But the *brissotins* got their way; France declared war on Austria on April 20, 1792. Still, like their *robespierristes* adversaries, they were aware that counterrevolutionaries at Court and in the *pouvoir exécutif* were trying to sabotage the Revolution. In getting the king to go along with the war (he had his own reasons for doing so), they managed to get Jacobins, specifically, some of Brissot's allies, appointed to ministries. Roland became Minister of the Interior on March 23, 1792. Together with Madame Roland and their assistant, Lanthenas, Roland established a propaganda bureau, thereby launching a nationwide campaign to spread public spirit and regenerate the nation. But instead of securing civic mœurs, they ended up exacerbating the revolutionary culture of calumny.

The Bureau of Public Spirit: Spreading Republicanism, Spreading Factionalism

By the spring of 1792, libels were coming from all parts. The monarchy, the National Assembly, and the refractory clergy were all secretly subsidizing writers to attack their opponents and advance their political agendas. The lèse-nation affair involving Trouard, we have seen, provided incriminating evidence that the Court was involved in covert surveillance and propaganda campaigns as early as 1790. In rummaging through the monarchy's papers after August 10, 1792, the Legislative Assembly's inspectors found documents showing that the *liste civile*—the 25 million livres accorded annually by the National Assembly to the Court to cover the monarchy's public functions—had been spent on counter-revolutionary propaganda.[56] At the same time, the National Assembly's *comité de surveillance* conducted its own libel campaign, purportedly in efforts to expose counterrevolutionaries. For their part, high-ranking ecclesiastics, some of whom were deputies, churned out libels against the National Assembly, sending them through the postal system with the Assembly's official seal and diffusing them through local clerical networks.

It was amid these covert libel campaigns that Roland entered the fray in the spring of 1792. He managed to obtain a monthly six thousand livres of secret funds to cultivate public spirit.[57] One of the first publications he circulated was an attack on Robespierre. It contained the speeches that Brissot and Guadet delivered at the Jacobin Club on April 25, 1792.[58] They appeared at the club to respond to the "vague accusations" and "insults" of the *robespierristes*. Their speeches were fierce, slanderous, full of suspicions. Delivered just days after war was declared, they painted Robespierre and his antiwar faction as traitors. Feigning contempt for the calumnious tactics of his adversaries, Brissot insinuated that *robespierristes* were on the pay of the monarchy's *liste civile* to undermine war efforts and the Revolution. After repeating a series of incriminating rumors, Brissot stopped short of confirming them. "But," he added, "whatever secret aims the *robespierristes* may have," it was clear that "the *liste civile* has the same opinions as the party of M. Robespierre, slanders the [new Jacobin] ministers as he does, and seeks to discredit the National Assembly as he does."[59] For his part, Guadet accused Robespierre of trying to divide the Jacobin Club for months, and he put Marat in the same bucket, depicting *L'Ami du peuple* as Robespierre's personal propaganda tool. (A week later, Guadet persuaded the Assembly to charge Marat with lèse-nation.) These accusations and Roland's circulation of them exacerbated tensions in the Paris club, where Robespierre and his supporters denounced him and Lanthenas as calumniators a week later.[60]

His partisan propaganda notwithstanding, Roland was straightforward about his efforts to shape public opinion. He was frank with local and departmental administrators that he was counting on them, along with the popular societies and patriotic clubs, to "form and manage opinion."[61] In his circular of April 9, he wrote, "It is up to you, Messieurs, to prepare and hasten instruction…and to always surround yourselves with publicity."[62] To counteract the forces of civil strife, Roland insisted, "Domestic peace must be maintained through instruction, opinion, and only as a last resort, by repressive force."[63]

The Rolands and Lanthenas did have some success with their propaganda efforts, at least in undermining the monarchy. In June, Roland sent a strongly worded letter—a threat, really—to the king, warning him against vetoing two measures passed by the Legislative Assembly. When the king did not respond, Roland went public with the letter, reading it before him at a *Conseil d'État* meeting and printing it up afterward. Humiliated, Louis dismissed him along with two other *brissotin* ministers, Clavière and Servan. Since Roland's funds for propaganda came circuitously through his friend Pétion de Villeneuve, mayor of Paris, the antimonarchical presses remained funded throughout the summer.[64] On August 10, when the monarchy was toppled, many throughout France took Roland and Brissot to be the heroes of the day.[65] Roland returned as Minister of the Interior, and on August 18, the National Assembly granted him 100,000 livres to spread

FIGURE 8.3. Surveiller et s'instruire [Monitor and instruct], a patriotic club in Sèvres, outside Paris. Courtesy of the Bibliothèque nationale de France, cabinet d'estampes.

public spirit.[66] Justifying the sum, the deputy Marc-David Alba Lasource insisted that after so much disinformation and counterrevolutionary calumny spread by the *liste civile*, the nation needed "truth."[67] Facing widespread consternation over the fall of the monarchy, revolutionary leaders desperately sought to rally support for republicanism.[68]

Generously funded, the Rolands and Lanthenas now had the opportunity to create on a national scale what they had already helped create in Lyon: a quasi-universal system of public instruction.[69] Having failed during Roland's first ministry to persuade many local officials in France to instruct the people or even to publicize the laws, they redoubled their efforts by setting up their own network of local instructors.[70] These efforts were more successful.[71] Between August and January, they recruited hundreds of *instituteurs du peuple* (teachers of the people) among municipal officers, lawyers, law clerks, justices of the peace, and constitutional priests. These agents distributed and publicly read the works sent by the bureau.

The August 18 decree gave Roland much discretionary authority in deciding what kinds of tracts the French should read.[72] Aside from the publications that legislators instructed the Minister to distribute (and the Rolands sent out quantities tailored to their tastes), he was free to subsidize and circulate what he wished. The Rolands sent out updates on the war, patriotic hymns, and addresses. They also circulated republican-inspired works on moral philosophy.[73] Among the titles listed in the bureau's registers, one finds Lanthenas's investigation into the effects of freedom on health, morals, and happiness—a publication paid for on the very day sans-culottes stormed freely into Paris prisons and massacred the inmates (September 3).[74] The registers record the subvention of several Cercle Social writers, such as Paine, Condorcet, and Nicolas de Bonneville. In addition to books and pamphlets, the bureau continued to subsidize the newspaper founded during Roland's first ministry, Jean-Baptiste Louvet de Couvray's *La Sentinelle*. It also took out a good number of subscriptions of Gorsas's *Courier des départements*, Carra and Mercier's *Annales patriotiques et littéraires*, and Condorcet's *Chronique de Paris*, among others.

The bureau was clearly biased in favor of Roland's friends and allies. Robespierre, Billaud-Varenne, Fabre d'Eglantine, and Marat all claimed to have had their services turned down by Roland's bureau. Given their hatred of Roland, they probably anticipated this response and counted on exploiting it.[75] Still, the Rolands did nothing to improve relations with those to the left of themselves. They continued circulating publications attacking Robespierre, Marat, and other radicals.[76] (One was titled *À Maximilien Robespierre et à ses royalistes*, by Louvet.) In turn, the *robespierristes* expelled Brissot, Louvet, Roland, and Lanthenas from the Jacobin Club in October and November. They also spread their own propaganda through club correspondence and sympathetic newspapers. Meanwhile, radical sections in Paris plastered the city's walls with libels against the *rolandistes* and *brissotins*.

Roland's partisan subsidies cost him dearly, not financially—in five months he spent barely one-third of his budget—but politically. By December criticism of the bureau was spilling over from the Jacobin Club into the Convention, and many provincial clubs joined the chorus.[77] In early November, Marat lambasted Roland, "that con artist" who was flooding the departments with libels against "true patriots."[78] Shortly before the Convention withdrew the bureau's funds in January, Robespierre wrote, "The most extravagant idea that ever entered the heads of legislators was according sums of money for the propagation of public spirit....If [the bureau] is not the most ridiculous invention, one must agree that it is the most dangerous to public spirit and liberty."[79] In an open letter to Girondin deputies, Robespierre wrote, "You did not consult the people when you poured millions of livres into Roland's hands...with the pretext of buying grain and spreading public spirit, that is, starving the people and calumniating the friends of freedom."[80]

In addition to his partisan propaganda, Roland's backhanded treatment of the agents sent out jointly by the *conseil exécutif des ministres* and the Paris commune in late August and early September also riled radicals. These agents, whose missions Roland had approved, were given verbal instructions by the *conseil exécutif* (which had replaced the monarchy's *pouvoir exécutif*) and the commune. Their powers were vast.[81] With enemy troops only a day from Paris, they were instructed to do whatever it took to recruit soldiers and procure military supplies. Shortly after they were sent out, Roland began exploiting complaints from local officials about these agents' intrusiveness, exaggerating it to the National Assembly.[82] Moreover, he issued a circular to provincial administrators in which he included copies of the instructions he had given to his public-spirit agents, passing them off as if they had been given to the war-effort agents as well. The limited powers of his "patriotic missionaries," whose task was "purely moral and one of providing public instruction," were more palatable to local authorities who balked at the requisitions imposed by the war-effort agents. The circular thus gave administrators a convenient but inaccurate basis for evaluating the actions of the war-effort agents. Upon receiving the circular, several administrators had the war-effort agents arrested.[83] Slandered and double-crossed, these agents carried their rage against Roland back to Paris, where it festered in the Jacobin Club, contributing to the growing list of grievances against the Girondins.[84]

Neither side knew when to stop. Throughout autumn 1792, the Girondins kept pouring oil on the fire, depicting the war-effort agents as bloodthirsty

brigands, the counterparts of the *septembriseurs* who committed the prison massacres.[85] For their part, when the Montagnards were not portraying the Girondins
as Feuillants or outright counterrevolutionaries, they turned the growing Girondin obsession with property against their adversaries, vilipending them as selfish
and egotistical at a time when the nation called upon citizens to make sacrifices
for the war. Although Jacobin and Girondin leaders shared many socioeconomic
and political values, when it came to winning over opinion, each side exploited
different sets of public anxieties, carving out distinct forms of republicanism by
caricaturing and demonizing their adversaries, reducing them to the most extreme
elements of their support base.

On January 21, 1793, the National Convention withdrew Roland's public-
spirit funds. No more publicity, no more power: Roland resigned the next day.[86]
His resignation contributed to mounting tensions between Girondins and Jacobins throughout winter and spring. Letters in support of Roland streamed into
the Convention. Officials in Tulle, for example, expressed dismay at his resignation. They assured that "all the writings he sent us, rather than corrupting public
spirit, have contributed to enlightening opinion and making proselytes for the
Republic."[87] But denunciations against him, particularly from Paris, outstripped
support.[88]

In April 1793, while the Girondins were trying to convict Marat, the Montagnard deputy Jacques Brival conducted an investigation into Roland's bureau on
behalf of the Convention's Committee of General Security (*comité de sûreté générale*).
He concluded that Roland had formed a plot to corrupt public spirit. Since
Roland's subvention of the writings of Brissot and the Cercle Social was already
public knowledge, Brival dug deeper into the bureau's correspondence, uncovering evidence of the cynical manipulation of sans-culottes by one of Roland's
Paris-based agents, Gadol. In an attempt to pry sans-culottes of the faubourg
Saint-Antoine away from Marat and Robespierre, Gadol wined and dined them,
showering them with flattery sprinkled with *rolandiste* propaganda. Gadol's reports
were indeed incriminating. In one, he boasted to Roland, "In taking them out to
dinner and fraternizing in such a way to lead them to believe that I admired their
patriotism—and in putting them in a state of frankness and abandon through
wine which allows me to discover everything [they think], it is easy to manipulate
them."[89] The dinners, by the way, were paid for by the Minister.

Those accused of complicity with the bureau had difficulty defending themselves. Roland did not try to refute the authenticity of Gadol's letter; he merely
downplayed it, accused Brival of ignoring other letters, and emphasized how
much he had succeeded in securing republicanism and public order. Challenging

Brival's notion of corruption, Roland insisted that the term denoted the use of public power for private profit. Since he had not enriched himself with bureau funds, and since he used them only to spread peace and patriotism (he failed to mention the subsidized libels against Robespierre), he believed he had done nothing wrong or shameful.[90] For her part, Madame Roland denied to her interrogators that she and her husband had established public opinion bureaus in the provinces.[91] This was a half truth: although there were no bureaus per se in the provinces, they had recruited local agents to receive and circulate the bureau's propaganda. Moreover, in her memoirs written in prison, she admits that Roland sent out smaller quantities of publications ordered by the Convention if he did not find them *"bons."*[92]

Roland never confronted interrogators. He went into hiding after June 2 and fled to Rouen later that summer. Shortly after his wife's execution in November, his body was found along the road outside Rouen, pierced with a sword cane. The government's representatives on mission there proposed that a plaque be installed at the site, letting all posterity know how Roland had "empoisoned public opinion."[93]

Surveillance and the Spread of (Which?) Republican Values: Roland's Public-Spirit Agents at Work

How was the war going without the king? What was going to happen to the king? These were the questions that the French cared most about after August 10, and their unquenchable thirst for news provided Roland with a great current of demand to graft his republican moralizing mission onto. In late August, he sent a group of nine public-spirit agents into the provinces, to which he added another twelve over the next month. These agents had essentially four tasks. They were, first, to distribute the bureau's propaganda; second, fraternize with the locals to stir up support for the war, inform them about political events, and inspire attachments to the Republic; third, set up political clubs where they did not exist and recruit local individuals to serve as public instructors who would continue distributing the bureau's propaganda after the agent left; and fourth, send the Minister reports on the state of public spirit in the places they visited.[94]

In his study on the revolutionary police, Richard Cobb claimed that one of the "golden rules" that Roland's public-spirit agents followed was telling the Minister what he wanted to hear.[95] If one looks only at the opening lines of these reports, this seems to be true; they express perfunctory optimism and flattery. Further into them, however, it becomes difficult to conclude that these agents were telling Roland what he wanted to hear, if for no other reason than it was not clear what he wanted to hear. Republican values were still inchoate. Roland's recruitment of a strangely eclectic group of agents suggests that even he did not have fixed views on republican values, at least not at the time the agents were sent out. The increasingly differentiated positions that Montagnards and Girondins adopted in the course of slandering each other outpaced the republican discourse Roland's own agents were spreading in the field.

Furnished with authorizations, reams of propaganda, and horses, the first wave of public-spirit agents set out for the provinces in late August. The suspicion they frequently encountered was usually offset by the fervent desire for news and their ability to provide it. The agent Clément Gonchon recounted an incident that began when he stumbled upon a brawl outside his auberge in Bar-Le-Duc. Locals were beating two soldiers from Angoulême who had tried to sell their uniforms, calling them cowards and traitors. When Gonchon intervened, the aggressors turned their aspersions on him, calling him a traitor and an aristocrat. He averted further hostilities when he announced who he was—the famous orator from the sans-culotte faubourg Saint-Antoine—and pulled out newspapers and pamphlets from his sack. The rabid wolves were suddenly transformed into happily bleating sheep. "They all embraced me," he reported, before going off to share the news with friends and family.[96]

Gonchon's anecdote contains a good deal of bravado. Still, Roland's agents did not find it difficult to make contacts and recruit local instructors to carry on the bureau's propaganda campaign. Their success owed much to the clout that providing information conferred. Inversely, failure to deliver information—and this was frequent, either because of Lanthenas's ineptitude or obstruction at the post office—could undermine the agent's status and raise anxieties. Working in the Vienne, agent François Enenon complained in mid-October that it had been twenty days since he had received the last shipment of newspapers and propaganda. He worried that without news, particularly about counterrevolutionary perfidy, the situation would take a turn for the worse. "I am convinced that the people have thus far shown patience to put up with misery only because these papers flatter them with the hope of seeing the destruction of those whom they believe are the authors of their misfortune....It is thus important to inform them, otherwise insurrections are to be feared."[97]

For many agents, establishing good public spirit consisted in cultivating a healthy hatred of the monarchy, not abstract republican principles. Gonchon told the bureau flatly, "I have just received a shipment from the Cercle Social Messieurs, and I must say that this is not at all the kind of writing appropriate for present circumstances."[98] He continued, "I cannot distribute instruction books about how to be an apostle of liberty and equality; I need short, energetic readings." He concluded with a request: "Please send me collections of writings about the treason [of the Court]." Reporting from the Ardennes, where people were outraged about the fall of the monarchy, the agent Vassant insisted that news of the king's treachery was the best vehicle for securing republicanism. "I can never have enough writings dealing with Louis's crimes...to advance the cause of the Republic, the very idea of which alarms citizens here."[99] An agent working in Pontoise was also distressed about the lack of public spirit among the people. All he could do, he said, was to hammer them with "detailed accounts of the plots of our enemies, the counterrevolutionary massacres they provoke, and the bankruptcy that they are about to cause us to suffer." Having done this, he sardonically added, "They almost understand now what these words mean: THE COUNTRY IN DANGER."[100] Jean-Robert Buhot seemed to have more luck in the region of the Manche, at least in the cities. He attributed the good state of public spirit to the publications he was distributing, which "made known the crimes of Louis XVI."[101]

What people wanted, then, was news, not ideology. And the news they hankered after was of the sensational sort that made someone look guilty. From the standpoint of the agents, the king's crimes gave meaning and focus to what was otherwise an ungovernable ensemble of fears and frustrations. Such emotions were observed by Guillaume Bonnemant. On his way to Lyon, he ran into several National Guard battalions headed for Paris to help with the war. He tried distributing republican propaganda, but the soldiers rejected it. They wanted news about the war and the generals, and the agent was startled by the comment of one soldier who wanted the nation to appoint General Luckner as king. (General Luckner was close to Lafayette, who had just defected.) Bonnemant noted that they "often had on the tips of their tongues the word 'vengeance.'... 'Yes, we'll go to war, but we will also purge the interior!'" Whom, exactly, did they want to purge? Bonnemant was not sure. Having put their trust in so many different authorities who betrayed them during the past three years, the people now harbored knee-jerk distrust of all authority (certain generals excepted).[102]

For Enenon, there was an even better way to win the people over to the Republic than distributing propaganda: give them food. In a letter to Lanthenas in early September, he observed that the clergy's charity was doing much to corrupt the people's political morality. "The people are forced to turn to a charitable hand for subsistence, and this hand determines their opinion." "I can think of no more powerful way to transform the masses corrupted in the name of the Divinity than to alleviate the misery of the working class.... The least bit of charity performs miracles!"[103] Apparently, Lanthenas and Roland were of different minds about Enenon's reflections. Lanthenas, who had been Roland's close friend since 1778, wrote back an enthusiastic letter. "Your reflections on the ways to win the people's attachment to the Revolution are just and sound.... There is nothing more impera- tive now than to convey that a government that is *by* the people must also be *for* the people...that the aid people can expect to receive will be greater and less humiliat- ing than the insolent charity handed out by their former tyrants."[104] A month later, when propaganda shipments had still not arrived, Enenon wrote that he had begun handing out money. "The misery of some individuals, combined with the zeal of others, demands the greatest generosity."[105] Roland reprimanded the agent:

> Your mission is purely moral; its aim is to instruct and inspire patriotism through the simple means of persuasion, zeal, and example. It does not authorize you to spread liberalities.... Such alms are on your personal account since I did not autho- rize you to hand them out. They tend to distort your mission, buying sentiments that cannot be bought.[106]

Such scruples, of course, had not prevented Roland from using ministerial funds to have Gadol take the sans-culottes of the faubourg Saint-Antoine out for dinner and drinks, as we have seen. Nor does it appear that he reproached Gonchon for his "liberalities" toward the two soldiers whom he had saved from the clutches of a furious crowd; after freeing them from their attackers, Gonchon offered them drinks and gave them each ten francs. What disturbed Roland about Enenon's generosity were the political convictions behind it. Given the emerging Girondin strategy to win the support of the commercial and propertied classes by exploit- ing fears of brigands and associating their Jacobin adversaries with them, Roland refused to entertain the merits of a principled policy of government hand-outs.

One wonders whether Roland would have hired men with the personalities and convictions of Enenon, Gonchon, and the rather curious L.-J. Bailly had he foreseen in late August the kind of republicanism the Girondins would subse- quently espouse. Enenon believed in state welfare; Gonchon capitalized on his fame as a radical orator of the faubourg Saint-Antoine; and Bailly fashioned him- self as a sentimental sans-culotte. Bailly's correspondence with the bureau shows particularly well how radical self-fashioning could square with the Minister's agenda before Girondin-Jacobin divisions became more clearly defined.

The bureau's records contain a copy of Bailly's cover letter to Roland in August. In it, Bailly recounted his life, starting from the very beginning: "I was born into the tears of misfortune," reads the opening line. It appears that his life went downhill from there. His mother died in his infancy, and his father failed to support the family.[107] Amid many "disgraces and indigence," the writings of Jean-Jacques Rousseau offered him solace (not to mention a template for his letter, which reads like *The Confessions*). During his adolescence, he was accepted into an Oratorian college, where he had been told "liberty had taken refuge." Of "independent character," Bailly claimed that his life had taken on its true purpose in 1789, the moment he "abandoned the phantom of freedom to embrace the real thing, 'truth.'"[108] What the Rolands thought of all this is not known, but Bailly's brief autobiography, together with appropriate patronage, was sufficient to secure him the job.

Bailly infused his mission with the same overblown sentimentalism. He cried his way through Jacobin clubs between Paris and the Vendée, moved to tears by demonstrations of the people's patriotism. In Angers, the local club offered him the VIP chair to listen to all that the local patriots had done since August 10. He declined and took a seat on a bench. "The true place for a sans-culotte is among sans-culottes!"[109] He reported that the recent arrests of refractory priests and their imminent deportation to the Canary Islands were having a positive impact on public spirit. He was less enthusiastic about the state of public spirit in Nantes. He observed that the port city had too many egotistical wholesale merchants and slave-traders for patriotism to take root. "The merchants here clamor against the decrees concerning the colonies....The rich, the propertied, and the *bons bourgeois* fear equality like fire, and they scorn sans-culottes. The young men, referred to here as '*comme il faut*,' have established separate societies."[110] The presence of Americans in the city, he observed, made public spirit worse. They "contribute not a little to spreading this arrogant character that they bring with them from America."[111] Bailly bemoaned the fact that the posters hanging throughout the city were mostly commercial advertisements. Few informed the public about the political situation or the progress of the war.

To get a sense of the overall patriotic temperature in the city, Bailly attended a performance of Marie-Joseph Chénier's 1789 box-office hit, *Charles IX ou la Saint-Barthélemy*. The play recounted the events of the Saint Bartholomew's Day Massacres in Paris during the Wars of Religion in 1572 but was replete with allusions to the revolutionary circumstances of 1789. Bailly complained that the audience applauded at all the wrong passages and failed to cheer at the right ones. "In the final scene [just after the Saint Bartholomew's Day Massacres], when Charles IX cries out 'may the heavens strike me down as an example to all kings' the audience was silent." He added, "I could not help thinking that Louis XVI, in the prison of the Temple, would express this same language if he knew how to speak in verse."[112]

Bailly believed that public spirit could be improved in the Vendean country-side by setting up colonies of good sans-culottes in the region. Beyond that, he stressed the need for public instruction. Other patriotic missionaries echoed his view, insisting that civic education would weaken the power of aristocratic and immoral opinion makers. From the Ardennes, the agent Vassant insisted that public instruction was needed to combat the despotic influence of the manufac-turing elite over their workers.[113] For Buhot in the Manche, although public spirit was generally good in the cities, the despotism of refractory priests was prevent-ing it from taking root in the countryside. "We await the establishment of a good education system which will uproot prejudice and fanaticism."[114]

The agents repeatedly encountered local criticism and hatred of Roland, much of it fueled by propaganda coming from Roland's enemies in the Jacobin Club. Indeed, their reports reveal how faction fighting in Paris was seeping out into the provinces, polarizing them. The agent Pierre Lalande reported on the agitation of a local patriotic club in the Vienne upon receiving a circular from the Paris Jacobin Club announcing Brissot's expulsion. The worst part of the circular, according to Lalande, was its calumny of Roland. "This circular slanders you and calls for defiance against all the writings and agents sent by you."[115] The circular claimed that Roland was "seeking to divide and corrupt" the provinces. To calm spirits, the agent reminded the local club members about Roland's heroic defiance toward the king the previous summer. But the political clout that Roland had accrued back then had diminished significantly by fall and winter.

As if the machinations of the Jacobin Club were not enough for Roland's agents to contend with, some found themselves jeopardized by Roland's own actions. The Minister's September 13 circular, which was intended to compromise only the war-effort agents of the *conseil exécutif* and the Paris commune, ended up imperiling the missions of the public-spirit agents as well. The patriotic mission-ary assigned to Brittany, Ignace Doré, was arrested by local officials in Quimper in September, along with two war-effort agents. A fellow missionary, Guérin, was working in a neighboring region and wrote to inform Roland of Doré's arrest. Guérin stated firmly that Roland's circular undermined the efforts of all the patri-otic missionaries in Brittany. "I dare request of you, Monsieur, a little more con-fidence, which is absolutely necessary for us; we are in a territory uncommitted to the Revolution."[116] Two weeks later, local officials informed Guérin that Roland had cancelled his mission. In inspecting this new circular of September 22, Guérin observed that it applied only to agents sent out by the *conseil exécutif*, not those working for particular ministers, as was the case with Roland's public-spirit agents. The officials preferred their own interpretation and forbade Guérin from proselytizing until they received clarification from Roland. A week after having written to Roland without receiving a response, Guérin wrote to Madame Roland, desperate about his situation and imploring her for help and protection.[117]

Attacked by radicals in Paris, at odds with his own agents in the field, Roland recalled the agents in late October. (Several, however, continued working until the end of November, when the Convention officially revoked their missions.) The bureau suffered from internal strains as well. Lanthenas left the Rolands in December and began distancing himself from the Girondins. In January, the bureau stopped subsidizing Girondin writers.[118] The writing was on the wall.

As de Staël had foreseen, establishing public spirit turned out to be treacherous. Certainly, it would have required more money than the 34,000 livres the Rolands spent on the bureau and more time than the bureau's five-month existence. Securing republican mœurs was all the more difficult given the culture of calumny and honor, which had spun out of control. Bequeathed by the Old Regime, this culture intensified in the early years of the Revolution, when traditional mechanisms for regulating it had broken down. Having undermined the Old Regime by 1789 and constitutional monarchy by 1792, it was now spilling over into republican politics, undermining them as well.

Between Pedagogy and Punishment: Civil Censorship

Calumny, vengeance, and purges: there had to be a remedy. At least that is what many deputies, distressed about the deteriorating political climate, sought in 1793. What was needed, they believed, was a way to give vent to public indignation and outrage while disciplining censorious opinions, preventing them from snowballing into calumny and violence. Civil censorship struck some deputies as a viable solution. Whereas Condorcet, we have seen, had opposed institutionalized forms of public censure in 1789, fearing that they would weaken the authority of the legislature, by 1793 it was evident that the legislature was weakened anyway by relentless calumny. It was also clear that radicals would no longer be placated by imprisoning "bad" deputies in the Abbaye for three days or putting them under house arrest for a week, as had been done in 1790. In this polarized, vindictive climate, civil censorship seemed to offer a way to combine republican pedagogy (which was sorely lacking) with restrained forms of punishment.

On January 6, 1793, a deputy from Nantes, François Mellinet, presented a plan to create a censorial committee within the National Convention. Mellinet deplored the calumny and resentments reigning in the Convention and sought a way to discipline the conduct of obstreperous deputies. He prefaced his suggestions with a passage from *The Social Contract*, "The less particular interests are related to the general interest, the more repressive force must increase."[119] The repressive force he envisaged was actually quite mild—milder, in any case, than the force soon to be employed in the Terror. He proposed appointing eighty-three censors on a biweekly basis from among the deputies, one from each department. Responsible for maintaining order, these deputies would be dispersed throughout the Convention floor wearing signs summoning the deputies to "order," reminding them that "you are here to deliberate in the interest of the country."[120] Each evening these censors would meet to discuss which deputies might need to be censured. The following day, the censors would present their conclusions to the Convention, which would vote on whether formal reprimands were warranted. If so, the offending deputies would be formally censured and their local constituents notified. Deputies applauded Mellinet's suggestions and ordered them to be published. It is probable that moderates liked the plan because it would have given them a means to put loud-mouthed factional leaders in their place.

As animosities intensified in the Convention and popular punitive pressures increased throughout the spring of 1793, more proposals for civil censorship were submitted. In early May, the deputy Jean-Pierre Picqué presented his ideas on *La nécessité d'une censure publique*. Picqué envisaged civil censorship as "a complement to moral education," one that would help society discover the "right measure of political mœurs." Picqué called for establishing censorship tribunals "in all the departments, alongside schools and popular societies."[121] These courts would watch over not only the laws and authorities, but all forms of "treason, lesions of the public's majesty," and "denigrations of the national representation."[122] But since the main motivation for erecting censorship tribunals was to escape "the anarchy now menacing us," these tribunals would have to morally regenerate society. Illustrating what Michel Foucault describes as an eighteenth-century shift from spectacular vengeance to more internalized forms of social control, Picqué said that this civil censorship "will not be satisfied, as justice is, to punish the offender; it is necessary that the chastisement changes his heart."[123] The shame generated by the tribunal's ruling, he imagined, would dissuade citizens from violating mœurs. "Man is made in such a way that he fears ridicule more than rigorous punishment."[124] But given contemporary obsessions with calumny, might not the censors' rulings be considered instances of calumny in themselves?

Picqué thought not. The difference between calumny and the occasional erroneous verdict lay in intentions: "The purpose of calumny is to vilify the individual; the purpose of censorship is to correct the individual."[125] Once again, the Convention praised the proposal, ordered it to be printed, and forgot about it.

After the expulsion of the Girondins in June, Léonard-Joseph Prunelle, a deputy from Isère, proposed erecting a "tribunal of public conscience." As he framed the problem, what France needed was "an imposing voice [i.e., an alternative to pike-fisted sans-culottes] which will warn the legislature if it deviates from sound moral principles."[126] He believed that this tribunal would compensate for the lack of institutional checks and balances in the Republic's unicameral system. Prunelle was practical, not utopian. Although he entertained the fantasy that one day citizens would become fully enlightened and politics would become obsolete, he thought this day was still a long way off. In the meantime, society needed to be governed. Laws alone were not sufficient, for two reasons. First, legislators might err. Second, laws could never be expected to govern all of the citizen's myriad actions. One's internal censor, or conscience, needed to fill in where the law failed to do so. To keep legislators in check and incite moral reflection within society, a tribunal of public conscience—a nationalized superego, really—needed to be created. How? Prunelle proposed that local primary assemblies elect judges who would receive addresses, petitions, and denunciations from citizens. If particular laws or a legislator's actions were thought to warrant reprimand, the judges would discuss the matter. The tribunal would be limited to censure, and its conclusions would be preceded with the solemn statement that "all existing laws will be obeyed until they are explicitly repealed or superseded by new laws."[127]

Prunelle assured that this tribunal would have an "excellent impact on public spirit."[128] In prompting society to reflect constantly on rights and duties, it would prevent civic consciousness from flagging and serve as a branch of moral education for both the people and legislators. Its most attractive feature, one surmises, was that it would "forever prevent people from relying on insurrections, the most justified of which are nevertheless accompanied by excesses that offend free, generous, and sensitive souls."[129]

The most elaborate proposal for civil censorship was presented by Lanthenas. In many respects, Lanthenas seems the quintessential revolutionary idealist, fervent in his politics, utopian in his vision. And indeed, his plans for education reform are imbued with what one might call naive optimism. Yet this enlightened theorist of public instruction proved to be politically astute, successfully navigating his way through the treacherous politics of the Terror without losing his head.

After incurring the wrath of radicals for his involvement with Roland's public-spirit bureau, he managed to distance himself from the Girondins in the winter and spring of 1793. He narrowly escaped the purges on June 2. He was saved by Marat, who insultingly scratched him from the list (he was "too insignificant a mind to fuss over"), probably in veiled reciprocity for Lanthenas's opposition to Girondin attempts to purge him in April.[130] In any case, Lanthenas's civil-censorship proposal can be read as a relatively pragmatic solution to the problem of calumny and vengeance. As he envisaged it, civil censorship would reinforce civic norms while channeling vengeful sentiments into mild, pedagogical forms of censure.

Lanthenas began outlining his theories on moral surveillance and civil censorship in March. In the first edition of his *Bases fondamentales de l'instruction publique* (it was republished later that year and again in 1795), he prefaced his proposals with a diagnosis of the problem: a National Convention infected by "reciprocal insults and calumny."[131] He upheld his quasi-libertarian position on free expression of 1791 but conceded that society would be "perpetually unhappy" if it "did not establish the means for protecting citizens from libels and calumny."[132] Civil censorship, for him, was the solution, and he defined it as "nothing other than the Republic's surveillance of general mœurs."[133] He conceived it operating at all levels of government and society. He called for local justices of the peace to produce regular surveillance reports on mœurs. These reports would be sent to the department, where a national commissioner would synthesize them, forwarding his report to a *conseil national de la morale et de l'instruction publique*.[134] This national council would serve as the moral nerve center of the Republic, devising festivals, public instruction, and literary encouragements to improve mœurs.

Lanthenas's civil censorship would also deal with violations of mœurs. He proposed that they pass through a multi-tiered system of "fraternal" censorship. At the bottom level, civil and military administrations would elect internal censors. If fraternal reprimands failed, cases would work their way up through the administrative hierarchy, potentially ending up at the *conseil national*. If the *conseil national* also failed to find an adequate solution through persuasion, the matter would be turned over to the *tribunal national de la censure publique*.[135] This tribunal would be limited to imposing light punishments, the most severe of which included removal from administrative functions, two-year exile, or temporary detention. Lanthenas's plan also called for authorizing the National Convention to send officials, military leaders, deputies, and even writers whose doctrines "undermined republican principles" before this tribunal. In the case of denounced writings, the National Convention could suspend the distribution of the tracts in question until the tribunal issued a verdict.[136]

What guidelines were censors supposed to follow? Lanthenas resurrected the idea that revolutionaries had rejected in the summer of 1789: a declaration of duties. (Duties would appear in the Constitution of 1795.) Any public official or writer who "by incompetence, stubbornness, negligence, or ill will" failed to abide by these duties was liable to censure. However, to prevent calumny, any denouncer found to be motivated by "envy, hate, or self-interest," regardless of any truth in the assertions, would end up receiving the tribunal's censure.[137] Thus, like Condorcet's ideas about legitimate limits on press freedom in 1776, Lanthenas's plan made intentions, not truth, the criteria for distinguishing virtuous denunciation from calumny.

Despite the enthusiastic reception of some of these proposals for civil censorship, none of them were implemented. Ultimately, spiraling calumny and vengeance stymied efforts to establish gentler, civil (and civilizing) forms of censure. During the Directory, Lanthenas lamented this path not taken. According to him, it "would have prevented the great tragedy." "Oh, victims of 31 May [1793]...it would have saved you and your executioners after you! It would have saved all those who were more faulty than criminal."[138] It would have offered, he believed, a way to "remove men harmful to the Republic other than cutting off their heads!"[139]

Public Spirit as Social Science: Thiébault's *Traité sur l'esprit public* and Enlightened Police Surveillance

Lanthenas's remarks appeared in a tract devoted to civil religion, one of many such tracts written during the revolutionary decade. After the fall of Robespierre, republican theorists continued their search for principles and institutions that would ensure peace and stability. As many saw it, the problem was how to secure social discipline and moral attachments to the regime without sacrificing liberty. Public spirit was imagined to resolve this dilemma. Conceptually, it reconciled the policing of public opinion with the principle of free expression.

Dieudonné Thiébault gave these matters much thought. When we last encountered him, he was an Old Regime censor proposing voluntary censorship to protect writers from judicial repression in 1789. Seven years later, he turned his attention to the problem of how to make the nation's mœurs compatible with republicanism—that is, how to secure public spirit. Like many revolutionaries who had reflected on public spirit, Thiébault associated it with such values as truth, freedom, equality, patriotism, mœurs, and respect for laws and property.[140]

Public Spirit, Surveillance, and the Remaking of Mœurs 221

But he went further than most in his analysis, distinguishing public spirit from a host of other "spirits"—*esprit de nation, de parti, de religion, de corps, de sectes,* and *de faction.* Most of these spirits were to be avoided, but "national spirit" held a central place in his sociological schema. In many ways, his treatise can be read as a revolutionary sequel to *De l'esprit des lois,* with "public spirit" substituting for Montesquieu's "general spirit" as the normative standard to which the national spirit was to be calibrated.

For Thiébault, public spirit was not about orthodoxy or doctrine: "Beware of imagining that you can give a veritable code to a people who lack public spirit." It was about harmonizing, strengthening, and improving the opinions circulating in society. It involved cultivating dispositions favorable to the pursuit of enlightenment. In this regard, it chimed with the ideas of Spinoza, namely, that free speech should be limited to statements inspired by the desire to want to use reason, regardless of whether those statements turned out to be reasonable or not. The progress of public spirit, as Thiébault imagined it, involved tacking between mœurs and opinions as they were and mœurs and opinions as they could and should be, regenerated according to universal reason. Public spirit required adapting the truths discovered through reasoned observation and experience to the already existing national spirit. He counseled, "Study the public spirit of your nation: figure out how to discover its tendencies and grasp its direction and movement....Learn to animate it and correct it if necessary; learn to direct it and even change it, but only in as much as it needs changing and as much as it is possible to do so."[141]

What if newly discovered truths clashed with customs and prejudices? In such cases, customs and prejudices were to take precedence. Changing the foundations of public opinion and mœurs was fraught with dangers and needed to be undertaken prudently, even if that meant that geniuses championing useful knowledge would have to bend to erroneous opinions. Here, Thiébault echoed Kant's views on enlightenment, namely, that "a public can only attain enlightenment slowly," and that, for freedom and enlightenment to advance, a people must be allowed to "argue as much as [they] want," but "obey."[142] But whereas for Kant, the people were to obey the sovereign, for Thiébault, they were to obey the reigning opinions held by the nation. He wrote,

> Enlightened men who respect [the nation's] public opinion even after they have ceased believing in it [should not be seen as guilty of] a cowardly and base deference to public authority or a small portion of society....To the contrary, [their] deference is to the general will; it is a sacrifice made for the good of maintaining

the established order; it demonstrates a necessary respect for the whole of society and public mœurs.[143]

For all his conservatism, Thiébault was strikingly progressive. He claimed that societies based on religion were doomed to decline, since they equated change with decadence and corruption and were thus unable to accommodate it. Nations driven by public spirit, however, were capable of advancing toward perfection, since they encouraged constant reassessment of values and opinions, adjusting them in light of new discoveries or circumstances.[144] But securing public spirit—this "moral fluid" running through the social body, as he referred to it—necessitated the policing of public opinion.[145] The institutional practices Thiébault envisaged for vivifying public spirit included surveillance, public instruction, festivals, and literary encouragements. Surveillance was particularly important because the perfection of opinion was predicated on understanding how opinions were formed. To paraphrase his views in the conceptual terms repeated in previous chapters, surveillance involved studying the relationship between public opinion (convictions), *publicized* opinions (publicity), and political action. The fact that this relationship was thought to be in need of study attests to the flimsiness of the boundary posited by Kant and Spinoza, namely, between speech and action. Kant's precept, "Argue as much as you like, but obey," presupposed a clear boundary between speech and action. Years of revolutionary turmoil, however, proved this boundary to be illusory. Publicity mattered. Under revolutionary conditions, it could set off violence and provoke the overthrow of weak regimes. Surveillance was thus intended to help revolutionaries get a handle on the volatile relationship between speech, opinion, and action. As Thiébault insisted, "The kind of inquiry still needed would focus on the relationship between opinion makers and the people…when the former gives an opinion and the latter receives it."[146]

This kind of surveillance is what the public-spirit agents of the Ministry of the Interior had been doing all along, even after Roland's resignation in January 1793. His successors to the Ministry, Dominique-Joseph Garat and Jules-François Paré, continued developing enlightened surveillance.[147] In many respects, public-spirit surveillance amounted to a kind of state-based Republic of Letters. In his instructions to his observers, Garat wrote, "It is necessary that intelligent men, discreet and well intentioned, are spread throughout [the Republic]…that they observe all that goes on, that they study conditions and people [*les choses et les gens*], that they scrutinize local officials, the people, mœurs, and the people's dispositions, that they pay attention to the effect of new laws."[148] Observers were instructed to assess the social impact of publicity, as well as other phenomena, such as the economy, government policies, climate, demography, and war. Under the rubric *la morale*, Garat's agents were to seek answers to several questions: "What is the character of the habitants? How can it be improved? Is there local public instruction? Can the locals teach themselves? Are their mœurs venerated, property respected?"[149] Garat also gave his agents French translations of Adam Smith's *Wealth of Nations* and Arthur Young's *Journey through France*, instructing them to engage critically with these works in light of their observations.[150]

Garat had even greater plans for his enlightened surveillance. In a printed circular to the Committee of Public Safety in late July 1793, he proposed expanding the network of agents, which already included many philosophers, journalists, orators, and men of letters. He also called for broadening agents' tasks, instructing them to observe the kinds of phenomena social scientists, ethnographers, economists, and medical researchers would concern themselves with in the nineteenth and twentieth centuries. He wanted them to investigate the effects of racial mixing, the age at which girls became nubile, and the impact of the new money on public opinion.[151] In short, he sought to do what the Cercle Social had called for in 1790, "[bringing together] useful truths, tying them into a universal system, getting them accepted into national government," only now it was the government itself bringing together useful truths.[152]

Garat was forced to resign before his ambitions could be realized. Accusations similar to those against Roland, namely, that he was using agents for partisan purposes, were made against him.[153] Despite chronic suspicions about what these observers and public-spirit agents were really up to, surveillance continued to expand, becoming a permanent feature of the modern French state. During the Directory, a hierarchy of surveillance institutions, much like the one Lanthenas had proposed, was established: public-spirit reports worked their way up from local observers and national commissioners before arriving on the desks of the Ministers of the Interior and of the Police.

But surveillance had inherent limits, for the relationship between public opinion, publicized opinions, and collective action remained elusive. The writer of one public-spirit report written in Vendémiaire of the Year V eloquently described the elusiveness of this relationship, the study of which constituted the very essence of his job.

> Between news about the army, the taxes that the government is trying to collect, and the quarrels of opinions between Jacobins and royalists, nothing remains that can give a clear idea of what public opinion is. It has been proved that what is called an "opinion" is, for most of the superficial people, nothing more than a

tradition of words that rebound off bodies like sounds producing echoes, passing from mouth to mouth without ever affecting one's spirit with the slightest conviction, circulating by the whims of passions or according to fashionable caprices. *So then, how many echoes does it take to constitute a generalized opinion?*[154]

That is, at what point did publicized opinions become internalized convictions capable of generating political action, perhaps revolt?

Disaggregating Public Spirit and Moral Regeneration from the Terror

According to recent French dictionaries, "public spirit" is dead. The *Dictionnaire historique de la langue française* dates the term's entry into the language to 1790 and says that it has since fallen out of use.[155] This dictionary, along with others, claims that it was synonymous with "public opinion." To be sure, some eighteenth-century contemporaries did use it in this sense. But as we have seen, revolutionaries who reflected on the concept distinguished it from public opinion. Conceptually, "public spirit" gave moral and scientific justification to policing practices aimed at monitoring public opinion and cultivating civic mœurs. However loathed such practices had been during the Old Regime, by the time of the Directory they were recovering a certain degree of legitimacy. Of course, that legitimacy derived from the traumatic experience of the Terror and an awareness of how calumny had contributed to it. For many, policing public opinion through surveillance and moral regeneration was the only viable alternative to terror.

To argue that moral regeneration was not a principal cause of the Terror's violence cannot obscure the fact that public-spirit discourse was invoked to justify that violence. Examples abound. A chilling one appears in *Le glaive vengeur*, a 216-page "gallery" of those executed in Paris—many for speech crimes—compiled by an anonymous "friend of the Revolution, mœurs, and justice."[156] The author presents the Terror as just vengeance against the nation's enemies, even as he insists that republican morality was "the only true and unique religion."[157] A better-known example is Robespierre's speech on political morality delivered in the National Convention on 17 Pluviôse, Year II, which was discussed at the outset of this study. As Marisa Linton argues, Robespierre "tied himself up in ideological knots" trying to reconcile classical republican notions of virtue with the revolutionary practice of terror; the two were not inherently of a piece. His attempt to fuse them, she continues, "owed nothing to the established meaning of virtue and everything to the dilemmas of revolutionary government."[158]

Thus, we should distinguish the origins and mainsprings of the Terror from the language used by contemporaries to justify it, or to try to justify it. The rhetoric of moral regeneration that accompanied top-down terror (the rhetoric of pure vengeance accompanied bottom-up terror) reveals the desperate attempt of leaders to curb popular vengeances by cultivating a spirit of unity and restraint. The stridency with which they invoked this rhetoric attests to the gravity of the situation. Calls to virtue grew increasingly shrill as calumny and vengeance became increasingly unrestrained. At the same time, leaders seeking to secure the state's monopoly on punitive violence drew on this moral rhetoric to dress up state repression in virtuous garb. The masquerade was not convincing, and as soon as enough deputies could unite to outmaneuver Robespierre and the Committee of Public Safety, they did so.

In any case, the policing practices aimed at securing public spirit—namely, the surveillance of public opinion and the spread of civic consciousness—long outlived the debacle resulting from the breakdown of limits on speech and the desperately strident attempts to reestablish them. The Terror ended. The policing of public opinion did not.

Conclusion

Today, everyone agrees that the press must be free, but not everyone attaches the same meaning to this word, freedom.

Pétion de Villeneuve, *Discours sur la liberté de la presse*, 1791

On her way to the scaffold in November 1793, Madame Roland showed remarkable poise, even cheerfulness according to some accounts. Whereas others condemned to the guillotine succumbed to cackling or fits of hysterical laughter (in the morbid wit of *Le glaive vengeur*, they had already "lost their heads"), she appeared entirely "indifferent to her fate."[1] Legend has it that before mounting the guillotine, she fixed her gaze on a statue of Liberty by Jacques-Louis David in the distance and cried out, "Oh liberty, what crimes are done in your name!"[2]

A year earlier, however, Madame Roland and her husband, the Minister of the Interior, believed that liberty without limits made no sense. In their essay on public spirit, they characterized the acts of censuring the law and dishonoring magistrates as crimes worthy of exclusion from the social body. It is doubtful, of course, that they had executions foremost in mind. As their efforts to spread public spirit suggest, they wanted to see civic consciousness raised, not calumniators killed. Still, the bluster of their statements reflected the general climate of intolerance. It expressed the anxieties and frustrations generated by years of unchecked calumny and weak political legitimacy.

This study has examined how the culture of calumny and honor and the problem of free speech fueled such anxieties and frustrations after 1789, contributing to radicalization and terror. I have shown how the advent of free speech in the Revolution's early years disrupted traditional patterns of honor, esteem, and deference. As old mechanisms for dealing with affairs of honor broke down and new ones failed to function, resentments escalated and became politicized. Although institutions for managing honor had failed in the past, notably during the Fronde, the rise of civil equality complicated matters. It forced revolutionaries to rethink legitimate limits on speech at a time when their own legitimacy was uncertain and their ability to command deference and contain violence virtually nil. The Terror reflected their predicament. Pressured to satisfy punitive demands coming from society and factions (lest they themselves become targets), authorities acted on those demands even as they tried to mitigate them through "public spirit" campaigns. If calumny and vengeance drove them into the Terror, civic morality, they hoped, would lead them out.

It is doubtful that revolutionaries' sermons on civic virtue contributed much to ending the Terror. Still, lethal repression for speech and opinion did decline after Robespierre's fall, at least on the official level—a surprising fact given the persistence of draconian laws against calumny. The first such law of the post-Terror period was passed on 12 Floréal, Year III (May 1, 1795). Worried about the influence of returning émigrés, Marie-Joseph Chénier, deputy in the National Convention, called for exiling for life anyone found guilty of disparaging the deputies in speech or writing. Seconding the proposal, Jean-Baptiste Louvet, former Girondin and expert calumniator himself (he had accused Robespierre of royalism in 1792), saw it as the fulfillment of the promise made in 1789. "The law we propose to you today consecrates press freedom *precisely because it represses abuses of this freedom.*"[3] Supported within the Convention, the Chénier Law was attacked without. Among its critics, André Morellet, former philosophe and now pious reactionary, asserted that press freedom had actually been greater before 1789. He observed that when authors had been *embastillés*, as he had been, they could at least get writing done, and he claimed to have completed his treatise on press freedom there in the 1760s. For Morellet, stays in the Bastille constituted penance, not repression. In any case, he rejected both. "In reflecting on the freedom of the press, I could not conceive of any [legitimate] obstacle. I would overturn all the limits. I would establish this freedom *absolutely.*"[4]

Despite overwhelming support by deputies, the Chénier Law was not enforced. Several right-wing journalists were arrested in August of 1795 but were released without trial.[5] Ineffectual, the law nevertheless conveyed the state's low tolerance threshold regarding free expression. So, too, did the new Constitution. Promulgated on 5 Fructidor, Year III (August 22, 1795), it was prefaced by a declaration of rights and duties that made no mention of the right to free expression, although respect for authority figured among the duties.[6] The Constitution did grant press freedom in Article 353 but tempered it with Article 355, which authorized its suspension for up to one year in times of unrest, subject to renewal. Even before article 355 was invoked, the Council of Five Hundred passed a severe press law on 27 Germinal, Year IV (April 16, 1796), calling for the death or deportation of anyone convicted of trying to overturn the Constitution "through words or writings."[7] Two months later, the radical journalist and key figure in the "Conspiracy of Equals," François-Noël Babeuf, was guillotined.

Babeuf's fate was exceptional. Despite severe laws (or because of them), juries in the post-Terror period were reluctant to return guilty verdicts.[8] To counter such inaction, the Directory—the new executive branch composed of five Directors—sought to shift responsibility for repressing press abuses from the courts to the police. In a letter to the Council of Five Hundred in autumn 1796, the Directors complained that rakes were spreading "calumnies against magistrates, corrupting morality and mœurs, empoisoning [public] opinion, and depriving civil servants of the esteem and trust needed to carry out their functions."[9] Acknowledging that "the [current press] laws are ineffective," they recommended "direct and indirect police action." Some legislators shared the Directors' disillusionment with the press. "Though their responsibilities are to improve public morality," Michel Louis Talot observed, "[journalists today] know only how to calumniate, divide, and blacken reputations." Others inveighed against attempts to "muzzle the press," likening them to "those execrable [measures] that led so many writers to the scaffold." One deputy accused the Directors of hypocrisy; after all, had not the government sponsored newspapers "in which each of us has been calumniated in the most indecent manner?"[10] The Council of Five Hundred did eventually pass measures against written calumny, but they were rejected by the Council of Ancients.

Upon the coup of 18 Fructidor, Year V (September 4, 1797), and the purge of royalists from local and national offices, Article 355 of the Constitution went into effect. In the following days, laws were passed banning several newspapers and exiling those involved with them. Again, the laws were subverted. Several proscribed newspapers reappeared under new titles; others went underground. In the end, few journalists were arrested, and none were deported or executed. Paradoxically, the most rigorous repression of journalists during the Directory occurred after the Fructidor laws had been revoked two years later. In September 1799, the Directors ordered the deportation of sixty-five journalists to the Island of Oléron. They justified the measure on the specious retroactive grounds that the journalists in question had not been properly punished when the Fructidor laws had been in effect.[11]

Why, despite draconian press laws, did the repression of speech during the Directory not regain the lethal intensity of the Year II? One reason had to do with the decline of lèse-nation. A demagogic instrument, lèse-nation had helped revolutionaries exploit widespread sentiments of honor, indignation, and vengeance in their effort to seize sovereignty in the early years of the Revolution. After the trauma of terror and civil war, republican authorities had little desire to stoke such volatile passions. For their part, reactionaries never thought "lèse-nation" had any legitimacy in the first place. Nor did Napoleon have use for the term. Although he did much to advance awareness of the nation's honor, he preferred the unifying effect of foreign war to the polarizing effect of political trials. In any case, by the time he came to power in November 1799, the Revolution had transformed the old culture of honor, of which lèse-nation had been a vestigial, transitional concept. Hierarchy and the sacredness of the throne had given way to civil equality and the sacredness of the nation. But the rise of civil equality did not bring about renewed emphasis on individual honor. To the contrary, as historian William Reddy notes, individual honor became increasingly "invisible" after 1795, camouflaged in the language of "self-interest." Reddy attributes this shift to the gendered logic of liberalism; since the liberal principles of 1789 were theoretically universal, the exclusion of women from public life was achieved by naturalizing gendered conceptions of honor and relegating both honor and women to the private sphere.[12] I submit that the sublimation of individual honor in public discourse owed to the traumatic experience of having democratized honor between 1789 and 1794. Contemporaries had good reason after the Terror to worry that affairs of honor might reignite conflict. In any case, as individual honor receded from public discourse, the nation's honor grew, driving the new cult of the nation toward more virulent nineteenth-century nationalism.[13]

Another, more prosaic reason for the decline in lethal punishment for speech offenses after 9 Thermidor lay in the government's improved ability to restrain popular violence.[14] The currents of vengeance that had so easily passed back and forth between the legislature and the streets during the early Revolution, amplifying each other in the process, were now more effectively contained. To be sure, public order remained precarious in many places until 1800, particularly in the northwest and the Midi. But uprisings were less frequent and more often put down, at least in the capital, as the quashing of the Germinal, Prairial, and Vendémiaire uprisings of 1795 (Years III and IV) demonstrated. Those were the last uprisings in Paris during the Revolution.

Still, authorities remained vigilant. Ever worried that a well-timed calumny might set off violence, they created a battery of policing institutions to monitor, manipulate, and suppress the vehicles of public opinion, notably the theater and the press. A political hothouse during the early Revolution, the theater was now watched over by the Ministry of Police, the Ministry of the Interior, and the new municipal policing office, the *Bureau central*. Directors of post offices were instructed to circulate only newspapers authorized by departmental administrations, and police agents were stationed in the post offices of Paris. In requiring postage to be paid by senders rather than receivers, the government facilitated surveillance, concentrating it in cities where newspapers were printed. In 1797, the government imposed an onerous stamp duty on political newspapers; mass cancellations of subscriptions followed. The Ministry of Police set up an office to keep tabs on the press throughout France, and the Central Bureau did much for Paris. Meanwhile, surveillance reports on public opinion streamed into the capital from all parts of France, providing routine reading for high government officials.[15] The government also developed a system of cultural patronage, first through the Ministry of Public Instruction, subsequently through the Interior Ministry's Office of Encouragement, offering enticements to newspapers and theaters that promoted public spirit. Less transparently, the Directors created a *bureau politique*, which produced propaganda that was surreptitiously inserted into progovernment newspapers.[16]

Napoleon expanded upon the Directory's policing policies. On January 17, 1800 (27 Nivôse, Year VIII), the Consulate banned sixty political newspapers in the department of the Seine and fixed the number of authorized newspapers in Paris at thirteen. It passed a decree prohibiting writings considered to be "invectives against the government" or "contrary to the respect due to the social pact, to the sovereignty of the people, to the glory of the Army."[17] A year later, it ensured state surveillance of the circulation of newspapers by requiring all mailed items weighing less than one kilogram to pass through the national postal system, thereby prohibiting alternative modes of diffusion.[18] With the establishment of *préfets* in the departments, surveillance of the press was extended throughout France.[19] Although Napoleon upheld the Revolution's abolition of prepublication censorship for books—"I repeat," he insisted in 1801, "I do not want censorship because I do not want to be responsible for all idiocies appearing in print"—he nevertheless had censors assigned to newspapers once war resumed in 1804.[20] These policies persisted throughout the rest of his reign.

Tocqueville's thesis that the French Revolution accelerated state centralization is clearly borne out by the policing of public opinion in the nineteenth century.[21] But the Revolution also bequeathed a rich legacy of free-speech arguments, including quasi-libertarian ones. "Absolute freedom of the press," which had meant the definitive abolition of prepublication censorship before 1789, now began encompassing the abolition of ex post facto repression as well. Throughout the nineteenth century, demands for unlimited freedom of expression evolved alongside expanded efforts to police public opinion, leading to strained arguments on the part of nineteenth-century officials who tried to reconcile the two. For example, François Guizot's pamphlet *Quelques idées sur la liberté de la presse*, published upon his appointment as General Secretary of the Interior Ministry during the Restoration of 1814, began by extolling the virtues of absolute press freedom. Statements such as "Today we can hazard unlimited freedom without great risk" chimed with liberal aspirations, and indeed, they were intended to win liberals over to the royalist cause. But halfway through the tract, the reader was suddenly thrown back into the world of censorship. The transition is jarring. "However," Guizot wrote, "since many people seem to fear unlimited press freedom, since I would not dare assert that it could be implemented without some drawbacks (produced more by people's fear than by the real effects of it)…and since the spirit of the nation seems to indicate that circumspection is needed," prepublication censorship would have to be implemented.[22] Thanks to his efforts, it was on October 21, 1814.

Guizot rehearsed the arguments with which we have become familiar in this study. The need to prevent anarchy: "In the midst of the collision of so many diverse interests…the government should reasonably want to avoid the appearance of shock and turmoil." The need for exceptional measures in times of transition: "The state of affairs is entirely different at the time a government is founded: if it undergoes a period of misfortune and trouble, if morality and reason are perverted, if passions abound without restraint…license will have to be restrained."[23] Like Thiébault, whose ideas on censorship he shared, Guizot combined conservatism with enlightenment progress. "The aim of [censorship] is to bring the French people to the level on which they can forgo it and enjoy absolute freedom."[24] For Guizot, "absolute freedom" did not mean boundless freedom. Rather, it meant moral and intellectual self-governance, which required the internalization of public spirit and enlightenment. To protect these pursuits from subversion, press freedom, he advised, should be "attempted in a gentle, gradual manner." Implementing it rashly and without moral safeguards, he warned, would jeopardize "tranquility and trust…without which neither good intelligence nor public spirit will flourish in France."[25]

Censorship came and went before the Third Republic definitively abolished it with the press law of July 29, 1881.[26] The law turned out to be the most stable to date (it is still on the books), but it did not abolish restrictions on free speech or the surveillance of public opinion. Calumnious attacks on public officials and seditious speech continued to be considered crimes. In the twentieth century, the law was amended to include bans on hate speech and apologia for war crimes and crimes against humanity.[27] Despite the wide scope of the law's restrictions, legislators sometimes found them insufficient to deal with what they took to be grave threats. In 1893–1894, for example, they overrode one of the law's provisions by legalizing the suspension of trial by jury for affairs involving the anarchist press.[28] Meanwhile, the state continued its surveillance of public opinion and political movements, as the police records of the Third Republic held in the French National Archives amply show.[29]

As repression and surveillance persisted, efforts to morally and intellectually engineer society increased. Indeed, it is telling about the relationship between free speech, republican legitimacy, and civic morality that the press law of 1881 was closely followed by the Ferry Laws, which instituted free, universal, secular, and compulsory education. The passage of these two sets of laws reinforces historian François Furet's thesis that the Revolution of 1789 came to an end only in the early years of the Third Republic.[30] The press would now be (moderately) free and censorship definitively abolished, but the Republic would expand its power to shape minds. What revolutionaries had tried to achieve through declarations of free speech and moral regeneration in the 1790s was now being accomplished through stable press laws and compulsory education.

Although public education may seem unrelated to the problem of free expression, we should not underestimate its long-term contribution to fostering conditions favorable to tolerance and to the notion of a loyal opposition, not only in France but in other democratic societies as well. When the liberal mantra "We agree to disagree" is proclaimed today, it is usually the colorful diversity of disagreements that is celebrated; taken for granted are the institutions and practices that have historically established the "we agree to" part of the formula—or even the "we," as opposed to "us" versus "them." There is no need to idealize universal education or exaggerate its successes to recognize the fact that, by the end of the twentieth century, an important part of the mission of nineteenth-century education reformers had been accomplished. Citizens by and large accepted the fundamental moral premises of liberal democracy.

It was in the luxurious context of political legitimacy and stability during the latter half of the twentieth century that libertarian views on free speech flourished. No longer viewed as merely a vehicle for achieving some higher aim such as virtue or enlightenment, free speech became an end in itself. From this perspective, any and all limits—moral, legal, and regulatory—appeared suspect.

Whereas libertarian arguments in the past had tended to be contingently mobilized by minorities seeking to outflank power, by the end of the twentieth century they became embedded in sophisticated theories and consistent political
positions. To be sure, not all embraced libertarian conceptions of free speech.
Some argued that absolute tolerance was at best naive (because the "marketplace
of ideas" where conflicting opinions are translated into power is itself structured by inclusions and exclusions), at worst dangerous (because indiscriminate
tolerance weakens resistance, favoring the forces of oppression).[31] Nevertheless,
libertarian dispositions gained ground with the rise of the civil rights and youth
movements of the 1950s and 1960s and persisted thereafter, though not always
without controversy. For example, philosopher, linguist, and political activist
Noam Chomsky became renowned for his defense of a Holocaust revisionist in
France, Robert Faurisson, who was fired by the University of Lyon II in the early
1980s.[32] Chomsky claimed to be following Voltaire's precept, "I detest what you
say, but I will defend to the death your right to say it." Actually, Voltaire never
said this. The quote was invented by a twentieth-century biographer of Voltaire,
A. Beatrice Hall. It reflected her convictions more than those of Voltaire, who did
not defend to the death adversaries such as the censored and persecuted Rousseau, whom he considered a traitor to the Enlightenment cause.[33] Indeed, few
eighteenth-century advocates of press freedom would have countenanced Hall's
and Chomsky's position. For them, tolerance ended where the Enlightenment—
and the social, political, and cultural aspirations it encompassed—came under
attack.

By the late 1990s, free-speech debate and analysis focused less on heavy-handed
state repression than on self-censorship and regulations within civil society aimed
at protecting women and minorities from discrimination and hate speech. The
situation changed dramatically at the turn of the twenty-first century. Since
2001, freedom of expression has suffered colossal setbacks in many democratic
societies, including France and the United States. Surveillance, intimidation, and
manipulation of the press are on the rise.[34] In France, the police have stepped
up searches of the homes and offices of journalists and labor-union officials.
In the United States, journalists have been imprisoned for months for failing
to reveal sources or to turn over footage, even for stories never published. Journalists (including one Pulitzer Prize–winning photo-journalist) have been imprisoned abroad by the United States without trial.[35] More insidiously—and in
ways reminiscent of Directorial policies—government propaganda in the United
States is being passed off as genuine journalism: fake reporters invited to news
conferences to ask flattering questions, professional reporters paid by government

agencies to promote their policies, and "video news releases" (VNRs) produced at the behest of state agencies and large corporations and given free of charge to commercial broadcasters, who air them as authentic news reports.[36] Worse, journalists have increasingly become the targets of political violence. More than a dozen reporters and critics of the new Russian regime, which declared freedom of expression in 1993, have been murdered since Vladimir Putin's rise to power, and in the first three years of war in Iraq, more journalists were killed than during twenty years of hostilities in Vietnam.[37] Meanwhile, self-censorship, consolidation of commercial media empires, and the fragmentation of public forums have continued apace in many democratic societies, diminishing the political influence of noncorporate civil society.[38]

Clearly, the twenty-first century has opened inauspiciously for free speech. Yet, if recent trends are to be deplored, it is not clear that those actively engaged in free-speech issues envisage truly *unlimited* freedom. Pétion's observation in 1791 still rings true: "Today, everyone agrees that the press must be free, but not everyone attaches the same meaning to this word, *freedom*."[39] Indeed, the different ways groups prioritize the rights, values, and objectives housed within democracy explain ongoing struggles over legitimate limits on free speech—why some limits are seen as compatible with freedom, even necessary for it to flourish, and others are branded as fetters. Should hate speech, which menaces the individual, or the burning of the flag, which offends patriotic sentiments, be prohibited? Should public schools be free to teach creationism, or should the curriculum be based on secular knowledge? Does the consolidation of commercial media impoverish the public sphere, or are "free" deregulated media markets the best guarantor of a dynamic marketplace of ideas? In debating these issues, each side accuses the other of undermining free speech, even as both sides fold the limits inherent in their respective conceptions of it into other democratic values: individual empowerment, patriotism, religion, secularism, social progress, property, national security, pluralism, the free market.

This study has shown that the values that mattered the most to contemporaries in late eighteenth-century France—honor, religion, and mœurs—shaped struggles over free speech after 1789. But values were not the only factors inflecting those struggles. Circumstances mattered as well. Indeed, I believe that circumstances go far toward explaining the different courses free speech took in the early French and American republics. Both countries, we have seen, believed that press freedom consisted in the abolition of prepublication censorship, and both left the problem of ex post facto accountability for abuses initially unresolved. But the circumstances under which each republic implemented free speech differed immensely. By the time Americans ratified the First Amendment in 1791, they had already rid themselves of their old regime, Britain. Even earlier, when this freedom was written into state constitutions, British rule had already been overturned, and large numbers of loyalists had emigrated. The United States thus benefited from the unifying effect of war and the removal of old forces before tolerance thresholds were put to the test. Events in France unfolded in an inverse manner. Free speech was declared while old and new elites were embattled in an epochal struggle over constitutional foundations. The allegedly pathological obsession of French revolutionaries with unity—the "general will"—reflected the desire, indeed the imperative, to prevent fatal clashes over liberal reforms, especially civil equality, religious freedom, political representation, and the rule of law. Many of these principles were already engrained in American political culture at the time of independence. For the French, they were new.

Another difference in circumstances that helps explain the contrastive outcomes of free speech in France and the United States was the greater degree to which the advent of this freedom in France disrupted customary patterns of honor and deference. Doubtless, Tocqueville exaggerated when, in *Democracy in America*, he claimed that "the prescriptions of honor [are] less numerous" in democracies than in aristocracies; clearly, honor infused early American politics and provoked numerous violent clashes. The fatal duel between Alexander Hamilton and Aaron Burr serves as an illustrative example.[40] Still, the sudden shift in France from hierarchical privilege to civil equality was arguably more vertiginous and unleashed more systemic violence. Had the framers enfranchised slaves and had blacks begun exercising the right to free speech to denounce the injustices of their former tyrants, waves of terror may well have rolled across the early American Republic. Indeed, they did after the Civil War. And as historians of the postbellum South have argued, ritualized racial violence, on the streets and in the courtroom, expressed the anxieties and hatreds of whites who, like many elites during the French Revolution, believed their honor—and hence, their social, economic, and political privileges—to be violated.[41] To be sure, the systemic violence of Old Regime social hierarchy was not as intense as that of American slavery (slavery in the French colony of Saint-Domingue excepted). But then, neither does the judicial Terror in France compare, in brutality and duration, to the decades of terror experienced by blacks in the United States after 1865.

A comparative study of free speech in France and the United States awaits its historian. Much could be learned from such a study, especially if it considered how the principle evolved as it moved through the Atlantic world. In the meantime, I hope that the present study will be seen as offering a useful approach. In examining how old cultural habits persisted in the course of demo-cratic change, I have put legitimate limits on free speech at the center of histori-cal analysis. Often viewed today as mutually exclusive, freedom and limits have been inextricably intertwined in the development of modern democracies, albeit in contingent and contested ways. Stressing the historical importance of limits should not, I would insist, be seen as hostile or unsympathetic to the principle of free expression. To the contrary, ignoring the relationship between freedom and limits impoverishes our ability to recognize the limits that have already been internalized or institutionalized and impairs our capacity to reconcile free speech with other democratic values. Though we may look skeptically upon the ide-als previously advanced to circumscribe free speech—religious virtue and truth (Milton), reason and enlightenment (Spinoza, Kant), republican virtue and public spirit (Robespierre, Guizot)—we should be wary of disassociating free speech from all other values. Robespierre's slide from defending unlimited free speech in 1791 to presiding over the Terror in 1794, much like the United States' slide from espousing the world's most liberal jurisprudence on free speech at the end of the twentieth century to implementing some of the most sophisticated methods of policing opinion at the beginning of the twenty-first, should give us pause. Rather than rejecting limits out of hand, we would do better to examine their history. Doing so puts us in the empowering and ethical position of accept-ing, rejecting, or changing them.

Such an approach is what Michel Foucault called for in one of his last essays, titled after Kant's famous piece, "What Is Enlightenment?" Defending his long-time devotion to the archaeological and genealogical critique of the Enlighten-ment, he concluded, "I do not know whether it must be said today that the critical task still entails faith in Enlightenment; I continue to think that this task requires work on our limits, that is, a patient labor giving form to our impatience for liberty."[42] Patience, however, is not a disposition that abrupt regime changes, such as revolutions, readily afford.

Notes

Introduction

1. AN AF II, carton 45, doc. 44, the letter is dated May 6, 1793.

2. Thomas Paine, *The Genuine Trial of Thomas Paine, for a Libel Contained in the Second Part of Rights of Man* (London: J. S. Jordan, 1792).

3. AN F^7 4432, in [Louis] Mortimer-Ternaux, *Histoire de la Terreur*, 3rd ed. (Paris: Lévy Frères, 1869), 7:310, fn. 1.

4. AN AF II, 45, doc. 44.

5. The Law of Suspects called for the arrest of those who "by their remarks or their writings show themselves to be the partisans of tyranny or federalism and the enemies of freedom." In its ordinance of October 10, 1793, seven of the twelve criteria defined to identify suspects involved speech, including expressing doubts about the Constitution of 1793 and speaking with contempt or derision of authorities, symbols of the law, popular societies, or leaders of the Revolution. See Richard Mowery Andrews, "Boundaries of Citizenship: The Penal Regulation of Speech in Revolutionary France," *French Politics and Society* 7, no. 3 (Summer 1989): 92–93. Inaugurating the most intense phase of judicial repression, the Prairial Law of June 10, 1794, prohibited all "insidious writings" that sought to "disparage the National Convention," "calumniate patriotism," "inspire discouragement," "mislead opinion," and "corrupt the public conscience." John Hall Stewart, *A Documentary Survey of the French Revolution* (New York: Macmillan, 1951), 528–531.

6. Donald Greer, *The Incidence of the Terror during the French Revolution: A Statistical Interpretation* (Cambridge: Harvard University Press, 1935), 85, 152.

7. Jacques Godechot, "La Presse française sous la Révolution et l'Empire," in *Histoire générale de la presse française*, ed. Claude Bellanger et al. (Paris: Presses universitaires de France, 1969), 1:405–569; Mona Ozouf, "Public Spirit," in *Critical Dictionary of the French Revolution*, ed. François Furet and Mona Ozouf, trans. Arthur Goldhammer (Cambridge: Belknap Press of Harvard University Press, 1989), 771–780. Notable exceptions to this interpretation include recent studies by Carla Hesse and Sophia Rosenfeld. Both historians stress how freedom of expression after 1789 generated problems for which revolutionaries sought legal, administrative, and cultural solutions. In her *Publishing and Cultural Politics in Revolutionary Paris, 1789–1810* (Berkeley: University of California Press,

1991), Hesse shows how press freedom generated problems concerning literary property and the profitability of the publishing industry. Rosenfeld focuses on linguistic policies in late eighteenth-century France, showing how intellectuals during the Revolution attributed political turmoil to *les abus des mots*—the misuse or abuse of words. Drawing on Enlightenment ideas about the social implications of language, revolutionaries believed that civil strife could be avoided by clarifying and fixing the meaning of key revolutionary terms, such as *sovereignty, constitution, patriotism,* and *nation.*

8. Alphonse Aulard writes, "The freedom of the press, which is the fundamental principle of public freedom, was maintained until…August 10, 1792, the moment when the besieged country found itself mortally threatened." "La liberté politique," *La Révolution Française,* no. 81 (1928): 369. Ozouf attributes the suppression of free speech to the rise of Jacobins in 1792, "Public Spirit," 771–780.

9. Anne-Louise-Germaine Necker, Baroness de Staël, *Considerations on the Principal Events of the French Revolution,* ed. Duke de Broglie, Baron de Staël (New York: James Eastburn, 1818), 1:173.

10. Jeremy D. Popkin notes, "The freedom of the newspaper press at the start of the Revolution was protected less by positive legislation than by the National Assembly's inability to agree on the terms of an enforceable law." *Revolutionary News: The Press in France, 1789–1799* (Durham, N.C.: Duke University Press, 1990), 170.

11. Michel Foucault, *Fearless Speech,* ed. Joseph Pearson (Los Angeles: Semiotext(e), 2001), 11–24.

12. David Colclough, *Freedom of Speech in Early Stuart England* (Cambridge: Cambridge University Press, 2005).

13. John Milton, *Areopagitica: A Speech of Mr. John Milton for the Liberty of Unlicenced Printing, to the Parlament of England,* in *English Reprints,* ed. Edward Arber (London: Alex Murray and Son, 1868), reprinted again (Philadelphia: Albert Saifer, 1972), vol. 1, 76. See also Stanley Fish, *There's No Such Thing as Free Speech…and It's a Good Thing, Too* (Oxford: Oxford University Press, 1994), 102–119.

14. Jane Kamensky, *Governing the Tongue: The Politics of Speech in Early New England* (New York: Oxford University Press, 1997), 194.

15. Benedictus de Spinoza, *A Theologico-Political Treatise and a Political Treatise,* ed. R. H. M. Elwes (Mineola, New York: Dover Publications, 2004), 259.

16. Immanuel Kant, "An Answer to the Question: What Is Enlightenment?" in *Perpetual Peace and Other Essays,* 3rd edition, trans. Ted Humphrey (Indianapolis: Hackett, 1983), 42, 45.

17. Ibid., 42.

18. William Blackstone, *Commentaries on the Laws of England* (Dublin, 1770), 4:151–152.

19. Cited in Geoffrey R. Stone, *Perilous Times: Free Speech in Wartime, from the Sedition Act of 1798 to the War on Terrorism* (New York: W. W. Norton, 2004), 42. In his *Legacy of Suppression: Freedom of Speech and Press in Early American History* (Cambridge: Belknap Press of Harvard University Press, 1960), Leonard W. Levy argues that Blackstone's definition of press freedom was not challenged until resistance mounted over the repressive articles of the Alien and Sedition Acts of 1798. For refutations of Levy's thesis and alternative

accounts, see Jeffrey A. Smith, *Printers and Press Freedom: The Ideology of Early American Journalism* (New York: Oxford University Press, 1988); Robert W. T. Martin, *The Free and Open Press: The Founding of American Democratic Press Liberty, 1640–1800* (New York: New York University Press, 2001); and William T. Mayton, "Seditious Libel and the Lost Guarantee of a Freedom of Expression," *Columbia Law Review*, 84, no. 1 (Jan. 1984): 91–142. Levy tempered, but nevertheless maintained, his earlier claims in *Emergence of a Free Press* (New York: Oxford University Press, 1985).

20. Thomas Paine, "On the Liberty of the Press," *Complete Writings of Thomas Paine*, ed. Philip S. Foner (New York: Citadel Press, 1945), 2:1010–1011.

21. Stewart, *Documentary Survey of the French Revolution*, 114, my italics.

22. Ibid., 114–115, my italics.

23. De Staël, *Considerations on the Principal Events of the French Revolution*, 1:335.

24. François Furet, "The Terror," in *Critical Dictionary of the French Revolution*, 149. For a discussion of Furet's contribution to the antitotalitarian movement in France in the 1970s, see Michael Scott Christofferson, "An Antitotalitarian History of the French Revolution: François Furet's *Penser la Révolution française* in the Intellectual Politics of the 1970s," *French Historical Studies* 22, no. 4 (Fall 1999): 599–605.

25. The literature on the ideological origins of the Terror is vast. Key works include François Furet, *Interpreting the French Revolution*, trans. Elborg Forster (Cambridge: Cambridge University Press, 1981); several essays in Furet and Ozouf, *Critical Dictionary of the French Revolution;* Keith Michael Baker, *Inventing the French Revolution: Essays on French Political Culture in the Eighteenth Century* (Cambridge: Cambridge University Press, 1990); Lucien Jaume, *Le discours jacobin et la démocratie* (Paris: Fayard, 1989).

26. The "counterrevolution" thesis has been recently advanced in Arno J. Mayer, *The Furies: Violence and Terror in the French and Russian Revolutions* (Princeton: Princeton University Press, 2000); Jean-Clément Martin, *Contre-révolution, Révolution et Nation en France, 1789–1799* (Paris: Seuil, 1998); Darrin M. McMahon, *Enemies of Enlightenment: The French Counter-Enlightenment and the Making of Modernity* (New York: Oxford University Press, 2001); and Peter McPhee, *The French Revolution, 1789–1799* (Oxford: Oxford University Press, 2002).

27. The thesis of circumstances was advanced by Alphonse Aulard in his *The French Revolution: A Political History, 1789–1804*, trans. Bernard Miall (London: T. Fisher Unwin, 1910). Timothy Tackett has developed this argument more recently in "Conspiracy Obsession in a Time of Revolution: French Elites and the Origins of the Terror, 1789–1792," *American Historical Review* 105, no. 3 (June 2000): 691–713; *Becoming a Revolutionary: The Deputies of the French National Assembly and the Emergence of a Revolutionary Culture (1789–1790)* (Princeton: Princeton University Press, 1996); and *When the King Took Flight* (Cambridge: Harvard University Press, 2003).

28. Stewart, *Documentary Survey of the French Revolution*, 206, 209, and 212. See also Tackett, *When the King Took Flight*, 41–45.

29. Edmund Burke, *Reflections on the Revolution in France*, ed. Frank M. Turner (New Haven: Yale University Press, 2003), 73 and 125.

30. This perspective is developed by Jean-Clément Martin in *Violence et Révolution: Essai sur la naissance d'un mythe national* (Paris: Seuil, 2006).

31. The term is my own. "Libertarian" would be anachronistic to describe the more expansive conceptions of free speech appearing in the Revolution's early years. The proponents of what I call a "quasi-libertarian" view of free expression believed that while injured parties should be able to sue for slander in civil courts (strict libertarians would not concede to this), political speech could never be considered criminal.

32. François Furet and Denis Richet, *The French Revolution*, trans. Stephen Hardman (New York: Macmillan, 1970), 97–121.

33. Carla Hesse, *The Other Enlightenment: How French Women Became Modern* (Princeton: Princeton University Press, 2001); Lynn Hunt, *Politics, Culture, and Class in the French Revolution* (Berkeley: University of California Press, 1984) and idem., "The World We Have Gained," *American Historical Review* 108, no. 1 (February 2003): 1–19; James Livesey, *Making Democracy in the French Revolution* (Cambridge: Harvard University Press, 2001); Bernard Gainot, *1799: Un nouveau Jacobinisme?* (Paris: Comité des travaux historiques et scientifiques, 2001); John Markoff, *The Abolition of Feudalism: Peasants, Lords, and Legislators in the French Revolution* (University Park: Penn State University Press, 1996); Isser Woloch, *The New Regime: Transformations of the French Civic Order, 1789–1820s* (New York: W. W. Norton, 1994).

Chapter 1

1. R. R. Palmer, *Twelve Who Ruled: The Year of the Terror in the French Revolution* (Princeton: Princeton University Press, 1973), 275.

2. Maximilien Robespierre, "Rapport sur les principes de morale politique qui doivent guider la Convention nationale dans l'administration intérieure de la République," in Maximilien Robespierre, *Oeuvres de Maximilien Robespierre*, ed. Marc Bouloiseau and Albert Soboul (Paris: Presses universitaires de France, 1967), 10:354.

3. Ibid., 357.

4. Jean-Jacques Rousseau, *The Social Contract and the First and Second Discourses*, ed. Susan Dunn (New Haven: Yale University Press, 2002), book I, ch. 7, 166.

5. Ibid., book II, ch. 5, 177.

6. "Letter to a Member of the National Assembly," in Edmund Burke, *The Correspondence of Edmund Burke*, ed. Thomas W. Copeland (Cambridge: Cambridge University Press, 1958–1978), 6:31–43. See also Darrin McMahon, *Enemies of the Enlightenment: The French Counter-Enlightenment and the Making of Modernity* (New York: Oxford University Press, 2001), 99.

7. Benjamin Constant, Alexis de Tocqueville, and Hippolyte Taine also saw Rousseau as having been at least partially influential in the outbreak and course of the French Revolution; see James Swenson, *On Jean-Jacques Rousseau: Considered as One of the First Authors of the Revolution* (Stanford: Stanford University Press, 2000), 159. For a brief summary of the historiography on the Terror since the nineteenth century, see Patrice Higonnet, "Terror, Trauma and the 'Young Marx' Explanation of Jacobin Politics," *Past and Present*, no. 191 (May 2006): 127–132.

8. François Furet helped renew attention to Rousseau's influence on the French Revolution in *Interpreting the French Revolution*, trans. Elborg Forster (Cambridge: Cambridge University Press, 1981), esp. 30–32. Keith Michael Baker provides a robust version of this thesis in *Inventing the French Revolution: Essays on French Political Culture in the Eighteenth Century* (Cambridge: Cambridge University Press, 1990), esp. 252–306. According to Baker, although revolutionaries inherited several political discourses from the Enlightenment, they ultimately "opted" for the Rousseauian discourse of "will." In September 1789, they adopted a constitutional arrangement that called for legislative stand-offs between the National Assembly and the King to be settled by popular referenda. The *faute à Rousseau* thesis figured in revisionist studies prior to the publication of Furet's influential book, appearing notably in R. R. Palmer, *Twelve Who Ruled*, esp. 19–20. The thesis has been advanced by many political theorists and philosophers since the 1950s, including J. L. Talmon, *Origins of Totalitarian Democracy* (New York: W. W. Norton, 1970); Hannah Arendt, *On Revolution* (London: Penguin, 1990); Reinhart Koselleck, *Critique and Crisis: Enlightenment and the Pathogenesis of Modern Society* (Cambridge: MIT Press, 1998); Karl R. Popper, *The Open Society and Its Enemies* (Princeton: Princeton University Press, 1971), vols. 1–2; Isaiah Berlin, *Liberty: Incorporating Four Essays on Liberty*, ed. Henry Hardy (Oxford: Oxford University Press, 2002); Lester G. Crocker, "Rousseau's *soi-disant* Liberty," in *Rousseau and Liberty*, ed. Robert Wokler (Manchester: Manchester University Press, 1995), 244–266.

9. Timothy Tackett, *Becoming a Revolutionary: The Deputies of the French National Assembly and the Emergence of a Revolutionary Culture (1789–1790)* (Princeton: Princeton University Press, 1996), 304 and throughout. Bernard Manin argues that revolutionaries were inspired by Rousseau's ideas only in vague and general ways. These ideas did not, he argues, serve as prescriptive guidelines for constitution making. "Rousseau," *Critical Dictionary of the French Revolution*, ed. François Furet and Mona Ozouf, trans. Arthur Goldhammer (Cambridge: Belknap Press of Harvard University Press, 1989), 829–841.

10. William H. Sewell, *A Rhetoric of Bourgeois Revolution: The Abbé Sieyès and What is the Third Estate?* (Durham, N.C.: Duke University Press, 1994), esp. 41–108.

11. François Furet, "Rousseau and the French Revolution," in *The Legacy of Rousseau*, ed. Clifford Orwin and Nathan Tarcov (Chicago: University of Chicago Press, 1997), 178. In his earlier work, Furet pulled back from a full-blown *faute à Rousseau* stance but nevertheless claimed that *The Social Contract* had influenced "revolutionary consciousness and practice" and that revolutionaries had tried to implement Rousseau's ideas; see *Interpreting the French Revolution*, 31.

12. Swenson, *On Jean-Jacques Rousseau*; Carla Hesse, "Revolutionary Rousseaus: The Story of His Editions after 1789," in *Media and Political Culture in the Eighteenth Century*, ed. Marie-Christine Skuncke (Stokholm: Kungl. Vitterhets Historie Och Antikvitets Akademien, 2005), 107–128.

13. *Dictionnaire de l'Académie française*, 3rd ed. (Paris: J.-B. Coignard, 1740), 2:373.

14. Daniel Gordon, *Citizens without Sovereignty: Equality and Sociability in French Thought, 1670–1789* (Princeton: Princeton University Press, 1995), 18–24, the quotation is on page 19; Jean Starobinski, "Le mot civilisation," *Le remède dans le mal: Critique et légitimation de*

l'artifice à l'âge des Lumières (Paris: Gillimard, 1989), 11–59; Peter France, *Politeness and Its Discontents: Problems in French Classical Culture* (Cambridge: Cambridge University Press, 1992).

15. Antoine Furetière, *Dictionnaire universel*, cited in Gordon, *Citizens without Sovereignty*, 19.

16. Nicolas Delamare, *Traité de la police où l'on trouvera l'histoire de son établissement, les fonctions et les prérogatives de ses magistrats, toutes les loix et tous les règlements qui la concernent* (Paris: Jean Pierre Cot, 1705), 1:267.

17. Ibid.

18. Ibid., 1:286.

19. La Bruyère, *Les caractères de Théophraste traduits du grec avec les caractères ou les mœurs de ce siècle*, ed. Marc Escola (Paris: Honoré Champion, 1999), 574. See Tzvetan Todorov's discussion of La Bruyère, *On Human Diversity: Nationalism, Racism, and Exoticism in French Thought*, trans. Catherine Porter (Cambridge: Harvard University Press, 1993), 3–8.

20. Robert Shackleton, *Montesquieu: A Critical Biography* (London: Oxford University Press, 1961), 363–377.

21. Throughout most of the work, Voltaire presents the arts, sciences, commerce, and refined manners as inherently civilizing. Paradoxically, though, he concedes that "this spirit of war, murder, and destruction [which has always depopulated the planet] is less pronounced in the character of the people of India and China," and he duly notes that these societies had never declared war on Europe. Yet, these virtues were the cause of their demise: "their very virtue, or gentleness, betrayed them; they have become subjugated [by Europeans]." *Essai sur les mœurs et l'esprit des nations et sur les principaux faits de l'histoire depuis Charlemagne jusqu'à Louis XIII*, ed. René Pomeau (Paris: Éditions Garnier Frères, 1963), 2:808.

22. For a synthesis of the vast literature on politeness and bibliographical orientation, see Benedetta Craveri, *The Age of Conversation*, trans. Teresa Waugh (New York: New York Review Books, 2005), 1–8, 231–262.

23. Anne Goldgar, *Impolite Learning: Conduct and Community in the Republic of Letters, 1680–1750* (New Haven: Yale University Press, 1995).

24. Gordon, *Citizens without Sovereignty*, esp. 129–176.

25. These views were expressed notably in Rousseau's first and second discourses and in *Lettre à d'Alembert*. See *The Social Contract and the First and Second Discourses*, ed. Susan Dunn (New Haven: Yale University Press, 2002). For his letter to d'Alembert, see *Politics and the Arts: Letter to M d'Alembert on the Theater*, ed. Allan Bloom (Ithaca: Cornell University Press, 1968).

26. [François-Vincent Toussaint], *Les Mœurs* (London [Leiden], 1751), vi.

27. Ibid., xii.

28. Charles Duclos, *Considérations sur les mœurs de ce siècle* (Amsterdam:1751), 78–79.

29. Ibid., 65.

30. Ibid., 13–14.

31. Ibid., 30–31, 38, 63.

32. Ibid., 10. Duclos conceded that refined manners might help reinforce morality; by encouraging self-restraint, manners prompted individuals to "reconcile their own interests with the common interest," ibid., 63.

33. Ibid., 72.

34. Ibid., 106.

35. Ibid., 328.

36. Roberto Romani, *National Character and Public Spirit in Britain and France, 1750–1914* (Cambridge: Cambridge University Press, 2002), 1–62.

37. Paul-Henri-Thiry, baron d'Holbach, *La morale universelle* (Amsterdam: M. M. Rey, 1776), 106–107.

38. Ibid., 138.

39. Abbé Guillaume-Thomas-François Raynal, *Histoire philosophique et politique des établissements et du commerce des Européens dans les deux Indes* (La Haye:1776), 1: book 2, 234.

40. Ibid., 1: book 2, 235.

41. Ibid., 1: book 2, 225. Raynal's conception of public spirit echoed ideas that had been developing in Europe ever since Machiavelli. Like Machiavelli, Raynal envisaged citizenship involving military participation, and like James Harrington, he believed that having property (or, in this case, stock in the Dutch East India Company) was necessary to cultivate civic bonds. For a discussion of these philosophical precedents, see J. G. A. Pocock, *The Machiavellian Moment: Florentine Political Thought and the Atlantic Republican Tradition* (Princeton: Princeton University Press, 1975), 383–396.

42. Antoine Lilti, *Le monde des salons: La sociabilité et mondanité à Paris dans le XVIIIe siècle* (Paris: Fayard, 2005).

43. Daniel Roche, *Le siècle des lumières en province: Académies et académiciens provinciaux, 1680–1789* (Paris: École des Hautes Études en Sciences Sociales, 1989), 1:377.

44. Roland Mortier, "Voltaire et le peuple," in *The Age of Enlightenment: Studies Presented to Theodore Besterman*, ed. W. H. Barber et al. (Edinburgh: Oliver and Boyd, 1967), 143, cited in Harvey Chisick, *The Limits of Reform in the Enlightenment: Attitudes toward the Education of the Lower Classes in Eighteenth-Century France* (Princeton: Princeton University Press, 1981), 277.

45. Chisick, *Limits of Reform*, 277.

46. Georges Minois, *Censure et culture sous l'ancien régime* (Paris: Fayard, 1995), 244; François Lebrun, Marc Venard, and Jean Quéniart, *De Gutenberg aux Lumières*, in *Histoire générale de l'enseignement et de l'éducation en France*, ed. Louis-Henri Parias (Paris: Nouvelle Librairie de France, 1981), 2:391–393, 395. For the social impact of education, see Willem Frijhoff and Dominique Julia, *École et société dans la France d'ancien régime* (Paris: École des Hautes Études en Sciences Sociales, 1975).

47. Duclos, *Considérations sur les mœurs*, 30.

48. For a summary of Old Regime censorship, see Raymond Birn, "Profit on Ideas: *Privilège en librairie* in Eighteenth-Century France," *Eighteenth-Century Studies* 4, no. 2 (Winter 1970–1971), 131–168; Minois, *Censure et culture sous l'ancien régime;* Barbara de Negroni, *Lectures interdites: Le travail des censeurs au XVIIIe siècle, 1723–1774* (Paris: Albin Michel, 1995); Daniel Roche, "Censorship and the Publishing Industry," in *Revolution in Print: The Press in France, 1775–1800*, ed. Robert Darnton and Daniel Roche (Berkeley: University of California Press, 1989), 3–26.

49. Gregory S. Brown, *A Field of Honor: Writers, Court Culture, and Public Theater in French Literary Life from Racine to the Revolution* (New York: Columbia University Press, 2002), 209–265.

50. Roche, "Censorship and the Publishing Industry," 14.

51. Roger Chartier, *The Cultural Origins of the French Revolution*, trans. Lydia G. Cochrane (Durham, N.C.: Duke University Press, 1991), 46. Malesherbes also called for lowering the number of print shops in small cities and concentrating them in larger ones to facilitate surveillance, 44, 48. For a discussion of Malesherbes's tenure as Director of the Book Trade, see the introduction to Chrétien-Guillaume de Lamoignon de Malesherbes, *Mémoires sur la librairie; Mémoire sur la liberté de la presse*, ed. Roger Chartier ([Paris]: Imprimerie nationale, 1994).

52. Carla Hesse, *Publishing and Cultural Politics in Revolutionary Paris, 1789–1810* (Berkeley: University of California Press, 1991), 28.

53. The Church saw its policing authority increasingly curbed in the eighteenth century. It could rarely do more than seek the intervention of the police. On one occasion, though, the archbishop of Paris, Christophe de Beaumont, tried to stop the circulation of a work by offering the publisher indemnities to cover the costs of production and foregone profits; see Negroni, *Lectures interdites*, 66–67.

54. Ibid., 201–212.

55. Ibid., 69, 212–218.

56. Isabelle Martin, *Le théâtre de la foire: Des tréteaux aux boulevards* (Oxford: Voltaire Foundation, 2002).

57. Robert M. Isherwood, *Farce and Fantasy: Popular Entertainment in Eighteenth-Century Paris* (New York: Oxford University Press, 1986), esp. 81–97.

58. Gregory S. Brown observes "that theater censorship tended to be personal and episodic rather than bureacractic and systematic," *A Field of Honor*, 211.

59. Jeffrey S. Ravel, *The Contested Parterre: Public Theater and French Political Culture, 1680–1791* (Ithaca: Cornell University Press, 1999), 133–190.

60. Arlette Farge, *Dire et mal dire: L'opinion publique au XVIIIe siècle* (Paris: Seuil, 1992), esp. 27, 70–71, 241–258; Dale Van Kley, *The Damiens Affair and the Unraveling of the Ancien Régime, 1750–1770* (Princeton: Princeton University Press, 1984), esp. 226–265; Lisa Jane Graham, "Crimes of Opinion: Policing the Public in Eighteenth-Century Paris," in *Visions and Revisions of Eighteenth-Century France*, ed. Christine Adams, Jack R. Censer, and Lisa Jane Graham (University Park: Penn State University Press, 1997), 79–103; Durand Echeverria, *The Maupeou Revolution: A Study in the History of Libertarianism, France, 1770–1774* (Baton Rouge: Louisiana State University Press, 1985), 23–24, 113; Shanti Singham, "'A Conspiracy of Twenty Million Frenchmen': Public Opinion, Patriotism, and the Assault on Absolutism during the Maupeou Years, 1770–1775" (Ph.D. dissertation, Princeton University, 1991), 162–215.

61. There were two principal police systems in Paris under the Old Regime. The commissioners attached to the Châtelet and the Parlement seemed to have been better tolerated than were the repressive agents and spy network established in 1708 by the *Lieutenant général de la police*. See Arlette Farge and Jacques Revel, *The Vanishing Children of Paris: Rumor and Politics before the French Revolution*, trans. Claudia Miéville (Cambridge: Harvard University Press, 1991), 48–49, 125–126.

62. Robert Darnton, *The Forbidden Bestsellers of Pre-Revolutionary France* (New York: W. W. Norton, 1995), 233–236; Daniel Roche, *The People of Paris: An Essay in Popular*

Culture in the 18th Century (Leamington Spa: Berg Publishers, 1987), esp. 271–273; Farge, *Dire et mal dire*, esp. 43–89, 225–286; Graham, "Crimes of Opinion."

Many songs sung publicly in Paris during the Old Regime expressed opinions on judicial affairs or incidents at Court. For a list of songs extracted from *Les mémoires secrètes* categorized by the nature of their content between 1762 and 1787, see Rolf Reichardt and Herbert Schneider, "Chanson et musique populaires devant l'histoire à la fin de l'ancien régime," *Dix-huitième siècle*, no. 18 (1986): 136–142. For the repression of singing during the Revolution, see Laura Mason, *Singing the French Revolution: Popular Culture and Politics 1787–1799* (Ithaca: Cornell University Press, 1996), 25.

63. Alan Williams, *The Police of Paris, 1718–1789* (Oxford: Oxford University Press, 1974), 109–111, 329.

64. Ibid., 111. Although we have no comprehensive study of Old Regime police spies, they appear in studies on the repression of public expression in the Old Regime. See Farge and Revel, *Vanishing Children of Paris*, 49; Ravel, *Contested Parterre*, 38, 148, 149; Robert Darnton, *The Literary Underground of the Old Regime* (Cambridge: Harvard University Press, 1982), 41–70. It seems reasonable to assume that the very existence of spies—even if they were not as numerous as contemporaries thought them to be—reflected and contributed to a general climate of vigilance and distrust. This atmosphere would take on pathological proportions after 1789. Brissot provides a good indication of the mind-set he assumed of his readers in 1789. As head of the Paris municipal police committee in late 1789, he enjoined readers of his newspaper *Patriote français* to "spy upon and watch over the hidden traitors who are preparing new catastrophes for us." *Patriote français*, November 21, 1789, cited in Barry Shapiro, "Revolutionary Justice in 1789–1790: The Comité des recherches, the Châtelet, and the Fayettist Coalition," *French Historical Studies* 17, no. 3 (1992): 661.

65. Nicole Herrmann-Mascard, *La censure des livres à Paris à la fin de l'ancien régime, 1750–1789* (Paris: Presses universitaires de France, 1968), 120.

66. Evelyn G. Cruickshanks, "Public Opinion in Paris in the 1740s: The Reports of the Chevalier de Mouhy," *Bulletin of the Institute of Historical Research* (London: Athlone Press, 1954), 27:54–68; Colin Jones, *The Great Nation: France from Louis XV to Napoleon* (New York: Columbia University Press, 2002), 118–119; Joseph Klaits, *Printed Propaganda under Louis XIV: Absolute Monarchy and Public Opinion* (Princeton: Princeton University Press, 1976). For a discussion of censorship and state propaganda in the seventeenth century, see Jeffrey K. Sawyer, *Printed Poison: Pamphlet Propaganda, Faction Politics, and the Public Sphere in Early Seventeenth-Century France* (Berkeley: University of California Press, 1990).

67. Darnton, *Literary Underground*, 62. The police were not the only state authorities to hire these publicists. By the mid-1780s, Mirabeau and Brissot were collaborating with Étienne Clavière, a Genevan speculator who was seeking to undermine the stock-market schemes—and the stocks—of Charles-Alexandre Calonne, Controller General of Finances. For his part, Calonne hired Pierre Augustin Caron de Beaumarchais to mobilize public opinion in favor of inflating stock values, notably, of the Compagnie des Indes. See Robert Darnton, *Gens de lettres, gens du livre* (Paris: Odile Jacob, 1992), 85–98.

68. Farge, *Dire et mal dire*, 146.

69. Louis-Sébastien Mercier, *Tableau de Paris*, new ed. (Amsterdam:1782–1788), 1:186.

70. This François Métra should not be confused with (Louis-)François Métra, who published *Correspondances littéraires secrètes* from Neuwied. For an account of the Paris-based Métra, see Pierre-Marc-Gaston, duc de Lévis, *Souvenirs et portraits, 1780–1789* (Paris: Beaupré, 1815), 183–184; Durand Echeverria, "'The Sale of the Hessians.' Was Benjamin Franklin the Author?" *Proceedings of the American Philosophical Society*, 98, no. 6 (1954): 428.

71. *Les mânes de M. Métra ou ses réflexions posthumes pour guider ses confrères les gobe-mouches des Tuileries, du Luxembourg et du Palais-Royal, sur les reformes à proposer aux États-généraux* (Paris: Tuileries, 1789), title page. For police propaganda, see Williams, *Police of Paris*, 220.

72. *Les Mânes de M. Métra*, 3.

73. Ibid., 3–4.

74. Ibid., 11.

75. For an overview of this literature, see Harvey Chisick, "Public Opinion and Political Culture in France during the Second Half of the Eighteenth Century," *English Historical Review*, no. 470 (February 2002): 48–77.

76. Baker, *Inventing the French Revolution*, 167–172.

77. Darnton, *Literary Underground*, esp. 1–70; see also his *The Forbidden Bestsellers of Pre-Revolutionary France*.

78. Baker, *Inventing the French Revolution*, 252–304; Darnton, *Forbidden Bestsellers of Pre-Revolutionary France*, 177–178. In his introduction to *To Speak for the People: Public Opinion and the Problem of Legitimacy in the French Revolution* (New York: Routledge, 2001), Jon Cowan alludes briefly to the tension between democratic notions of the public and discriminating (even discriminatory) ones during the Old Regime but concludes, like Baker, that the Revolution radicalized because of "revolutionaries' excessive investment in a highly problematic fiction," namely, in "'the people,' the new sovereign," 186.

79. Chartier, *Cultural Origins of the French Revolution*, 169–192.

80. Farge, *Dire et mal dire*, 68.

81. Martin, *Le théâtre de la foire*, esp. 28–51.

82. Thomas Crow, *Painters and Public Life in Eighteenth-Century Paris* (New Haven: Yale University Press, 1985), 175–258.

83. Ravel, *Contested Parterre*, esp. 133–224.

84. Sarah Maza, *Private Lives and Public Affairs: The Causes Célèbres of Prerevolutionary France* (Berkeley: University of California Press, 1993).

85. Chartier, *Cultural Origins of the French Revolution*, 23–37.

86. Ibid., 32–33. Daniel Gordon arrives at similar conclusions in his reading of Morellet, *Citizens without Sovereignty*, 205.

87. Daniel Roche, "Académies et politique au siècle des lumières: Les enjeux pratiques de l'immortalité," in *The Political Culture of the Old Regime*, ed. Keith Michael Baker, in *The French Revolution and the Creation of Modern Political Culture*, ed. Keith Michael Baker (Oxford: Pergamon Press, 1987), 1:335.

88. Dena Goodman, *The Republic of Letters: A Cultural History of the French Enlightenment* (Ithaca: Cornell University Press, 1994), 90–135; Gordon, *Citizens without Sovereignty*, esp. 86–128; and Brown, *Field of Honor*, passim.

89. Jeffrey S. Ravel, "Seating the Public: Spheres and Loathing in the Paris Theaters, 1777–1788," *French Historical Studies* 18, no. 1 (Spring 1993): 173–210.

90. Marcel Le Clère, *Histoire de la police* (Paris: Presses universitaires de France, 1973), 49–50.

91. David Andress, "Social Prejudice and Political Fears in the Policing of Paris," *French History* 9, no. 2 (1995): 202–226.

92. Marcel Le Clère, "Police" and "Police générale," in *Dictionnaire historique de la Révolution française*, ed. Albert Soboul (Paris: Presses universitaires de France, 1989), 848–850.

93. For ongoing use and hatred of spies after 1789, see Andress, "Social Prejudice and Political Fears," 216–217.

94. Louis Pierre Manuel, *La police dévoilée* (Paris: J. B. Garnéry, Year II), 88; for excerpts of Rousseau and Sartine's correspondence, see 88–98.

95. Ibid., preface, 7.

96. Ibid., preface, 9–10.

97. Ibid., introduction, 3–4.

98. Peuchet, *Jurisprudence*, in *Encyclopédie méthodique*, 9: clii.

99. Ibid., 10:543.

100. Ibid., 9: cxxii–cxxiii.

101. Ibid., iv.

102. Ibid., lxxxi.

103. Rousseau, *Social Contract*, book IV, ch. 7, 244.

Chapter 2

1. *Le véritable tableau de la calomnie et le portraict des médisans, exposez en public, par la vertu triomphante du vice; avec un discours moral sur le mesme sujet* (Paris, 1649), 3.

2. François Dareau, *Traité des injures dans l'ordre judiciaire: Ouvrage qui renferme particulièrement la jurisprudence du petit-criminel* (Paris: Nyon, 1775), 5.

3. Daniel Jousse, *Traité de la justice criminelle de France* (Paris: Debure père, 1771), 3:651.

4. *Encyclopédie*, 2:563–564. The authors cite Blaise Pascal.

5. *Le véritable tableau de la calomnie*, 4.

6. For the notion that honor was a kind of spiritual possession, see Laurent Bouchel, *La bibliothèque ou trésor du droit français où sont traitées les matières civiles, criminelles et bénéficiales, augmentée en cette nouvelle édition par Maistre Jean Bechefer* (Paris: Chez Jean Girin et Barthélemy Rivière, 1671 [orig. 1615]), 2:541.

7. *Traité sur la calomnie en forme de lettre à Mr le Chevalier de C**** (Paris: Lesclapart, 1769), 163.

8. Jacques Necker [Jacques-Henri Meister?], *De la morale naturelle suivie du "Bonheur des sots"* (Paris, 1788), 102–103.

9. *Réponse aux instructions envoyées par S. A. S. monseigneur le duc d'Orléans, à ses chargés de procuration dans ses bailliages, relativement aux États-généraux* (1789), 15.

10. Bouchel, *La bibliothèque ou trésor du droit français*, 1:409.

11. *Le véritable tableau de la calomnie*, 3.

12. Dareau, *Traité des injures*, 19. Jousse also stated that vague imputations were to be punished but less severely than calumny, *Traité de la justice criminelle*, 3:583.

13. *Encyclopédie*, 2:563.

14. *Traité sur la calomnie*, 152.

15. Ibid., 136–137.

16. *Le véritable tableau de la calomnie*, 23.

17. *Encyclopédie*, 2:563.

18. Marquis de Sade, *La philosophie dans le boudoir* (London [Paris]:1795), 2:104. These passages were likely inspired by debate in the National Convention in 1795 on calumny and new press laws; see the conclusion below.

19. Philip T. Hoffman, *Growth in a Traditional Society: The French Countryside, 1450–1815* (Princeton: Princeton University Press, 1996), esp. 69–80. John Markoff also stresses the importance of honor in rural life at the end of the eighteenth century in his *The Abolition of Feudalism: Peasants, Lords, and Legislators in the French Revolution* (University Park: Penn State University Press, 1996), passim.

20. David Garrioch, *Neighborhood and Community in Paris, 1740–1790* (Cambridge: Cambridge University Press, 1986), 40.

21. A. Mericskay, "Le Châtelet et la répression de la criminalité à Paris en 1770" (Ph.D. dissertation, Université de Paris I—La Sorbonne, 1984). The author shows that 23 percent of the criminal cases involved *injures* (without attendant violence), 6 percent involved calumny by writing, thus a total of 29 percent or nearly one-third. If one included incidents in which violence accompanied injurious speech, the proportion increases by another 32 percent, for a total of over 60 percent.

22. Nicole Castan, *Les criminels de Languedoc: Les exigences d'ordre et les voies du ressentiment dans une société pré-révolutionnaire (1750–1790)* (Toulouse: Association des Publications de l'Université de Toulouse–Le Mirail, 1980), esp. 159–192, 326.

23. *Encyclopédie*, 8:288.

24. Honor has been treated in much scholarship on the Old Regime, but a synthesis awaits its historian. For a compelling treatment of honor in Tudor-Stuart England, see Mervyn James, *Society, Politics and Culture: Studies in Early Modern England* (Cambridge: Cambridge University Press, 1986), 308–415. For treatments of the political dimensions of honor during the Old Regime, in addition to the titles already mentioned, see William Beik, *Urban Protest in Seventeenth-Century France: The Culture of Retribution* (Cambridge: Cambridge University Press, 1997); James R. Farr, "The Death of a Judge: Performance, Honor, and Legitimacy in Seventeenth-Century France," *Journal of Modern History* 75, no. 1 (March 2003): 1–22; Kristen Neuschel, *Word of Honor: Interpreting Noble Culture in Sixteenth-Century France* (Ithaca: Cornell University Press, 1989); Orest Ranum, "Courtesy, Absolutism, and the Rise of the French State, 1630–1660," *Journal of Modern History* 52, no. 3 (September 1980): 426–451. For discussions of the social dimensions of honor among

the popular classes, see Yves Castan, *Honnêteté et relations sociales en Languedoc (1715–1780)* (Paris: Plon, 1974); David Garrioch, "Verbal Insults in Eighteenth-Century France," in *The Social History of Language*, 2nd edition, ed. Peter Burke and Roy Porter (Cambridge: Cambridge University Press, 1988), 104–119; Steven Laurence Kaplan, *The Bakers of Paris and the Bread Question, 1770–1775* (Durham, N.C.: Duke University Press, 1996), 423–436; Robert Muchembled, *L'invention de l'homme moderne: Sensibilités, mœurs et comportements collectifs sous l'Ancien Régime* (Paris: Fayard, 1988), passim, esp. 65–67, 218–222, 304–310. For honor in the Republic of Letters, see Gregory S. Brown, *A Field of Honor: Writers, Court Culture, and Public Theater in French Literary Life from Racine to the Revolution* (New York: Columbia University Press, 2002); Pascal Brioist, Hervé Drévillon, and Pierre Serna, *Croiser le fer: Violence et culture de l'épée dans la France moderne (XVIe–XVIIIe siècle)* (Seyssel: Champ Vallon, 2002), 239–478. For commercial honor, see John Shovlin, "Toward a Reinterpretation of Revolutionary Antinobilism: The Political Economy of Honor in the Old Regime," *Journal of Modern History* 72, no. 1 (March 2000): 35–66.

25. *Encyclopédie*, 3:438.

26. Hugo Grotius, *De Iure Praedae Commentarius, Commentary on the Law of Prize and Booty*, trans. Gwladys L. Williams (Oxford: Clarendon Press, 1950), 1:362.

27. Arlette Farge, "The Honor and Secrecy of Families," in *A History of Private Life: Passions of the Renaissance*, ed. Roger Chartier, trans. Arthur Goldhammer (Cambridge: Belknap Press of Harvard University Press, 1989), 588.

28. De Lamet and Fromageau (Docteurs de la Maison et Société de la Sorbonne), *Le Dictionnaire des cas de conscience, décidés suivant les principes de la morale, les usages de la discipline ecclésiastique, l'autorité des conciles et des canonistes, et la jurisprudence du royaume* (Paris: Aux dépens de la Compagnie, 1740), 2:1230.

29. Ibid., 1231.

30. Ibid.

31. Dareau, *Traité des injures*, 19–20.

32. Although speech offenses against religion were more reprehensible than those against the sovereign, Dareau explained that only God could adequately avenge himself for lèse-majesté divine. He observed that calumny against the sovereign was punished more vigorously since it threatened the political order and, hence, public peace, *Traité des injures*, 122–123, 126–127.

33. Interestingly, although women appear at the bottom of the social hierarchy, Dareau and Jousse devoted many pages to discussing injurious speech against them. Both jurists pointed out that punishment for speech offenses against women was twice as severe as those against men. Dareau, *Traité des injures*, 294–395, 296; Jousse, *Traité de la justice criminelle*, 3:574.

34. Dareau, *Traité des injures*, 291.

35. Jousse, *Traité de la justice criminelle*, 3:622. The term *vil* referred to persons deemed to be "of low condition, abject, or contemptible, either by the lowness of their birth or the lowness of their sentiments." Persons *infâmes* were those "who are defamed by the Law" (i.e., found guilty by courts) or "by public opinion." See the respective entries for these terms in *Dictionnaire de l'Académie française* (Paris: Veuve de Bernard Brunet, 1762), 2:938 and 1:927.

36. Jousse, *Traité de la justice criminelle*, 3:574.

37. Dareau, *Traité des injures*, 389.

38. Ibid., 20.

39. Jousse, *Traité de la justice criminelle*, 3:608–612.

40. Dareau, *Traité des injures*, 391.

41. Jousse, *Traité de la justice criminelle*, 3:576.

42. Ibid., 3:623.

43. Dareau, *Traité des injures*, 288.

44. Ibid., 292.

45. Ibid., 475–476.

46. Jousse, *Traité de la justice criminelle*, 3:621.

47. Frantz Funck-Brentano, *Les lettres de cachet à Paris, étude suivie d'une liste des prisonniers de la Bastille (1659–1789)* (Paris: Imprimerie nationale, 1903).

48. Funck-Brentano, *Lettres de cachet à Paris*, article 2379.

49. Peter Gay, *Voltaire's Politics: The Poet as Realist* (New Haven: Yale University Press, 1988), 36.

50. Funck-Brentano, *Lettres de cachet à Paris*, article no. 2940.

51. Gay, *Voltaire's Politics*, 36.

52. Dareau, *Traité des injures*, 280–281.

53. Mericskay's study of the Châtelet in 1770 shows roughly 32 percent of affairs on the docket of the *petit criminel* involved affairs of speech offenses accompanied by violence. Speech offenses without violence accounted for 22 percent; "Le Châtelet et la répression de la criminalité à Paris en 1770," table 4.

54. Jacques-Louis Ménétra, *Journal of My Life*, ed. and intro. Daniel Roche, foreward Robert Darnton, trans. Arthur Goldhammer (New York: Columbia University Press, 1986), passim (the broomstick incident is recounted on 156).

55. For struggles within the Republic of Letters, see Dena Goodman, *The Republic of Letters: A Cultural History of the French Enlightenment* (Ithaca: Cornell University Press, 1994), esp. 183–232; for tensions between philosophes and antiphilosophes, see Darrin M. McMahon, *Enemies of the Enlightenment: The French Counter-Enlightenment and the Making of Modernity* (New York: Oxford University Press, 2001); for the pamphlet war during the Maupeou coup, David A. Bell, *Lawyers and Citizens: The Making of a Political Elite in Old Regime France* (New York: Oxford University Press, 1994); Durand Echeverria, *The Maupeou Revolution: A Study in the History of Libertarianism, France 1770–1774* (Baton Rouge: Louisiana State University Press, 1985), 22–24; David Hudson, "In Defense of Reform: French Government Propaganda during the Maupeou Crisis," *French Historical Studies* 8, no. 1 (1973): 51–76; Shanti Singham, "'A Conspiracy of Twenty Million Frenchmen': Public Opinion, Patriotism, and the Assault on Absolutism During the Maupeou Years, 1770–1775" (Ph.D. dissertation, Princeton University, 1991); for the speculation wars, see Robert Darnton, *Gens de lettres, gens du livre* (Paris: Odile Jacob, 1992), 85–98. For the propaganda war over political scandals of the 1780s, in addition to the published work of Robert Darnton, see "Trends in Radical Propaganda on the Eve of the French Revolution (1782–1788)" (D.Phil. dissertation, University of Oxford, 1964).

56. Brown, *A Field of Honor*, 287–321; Sarah Maza, *Private Lives and Public Affairs: The Causes Célèbres of Prerevolutionary France* (Berkeley: University of California Press, 1993), 133–140, 295–310.

57. Robert Darnton holds this view in *The Forbidden Bestsellers of Pre-Revolutionary France* (New York: W. W. Norton, 1995), though the argument appears in much of his earlier work as well. Roger Chartier questions Darnton's thesis in *The Cultural Origins of the French Revolution*, trans. Lydia G. Cochrane (Durham, N.C.: Duke University Press, 1991), 67–91.

Chapter 3

1. Jacques Necker, "Rapport fait au roi dans son conseil, par le ministre de ses finances, le 27 décembre 1788," in *AP*, 1:496 (my italics).

2. On the pamphlet literature of the period, see Ralph Greenlaw, "Pamphlet Literature in France during the Period of the Aristocratic Revolt (1787–1788)," *Journal of Modern History* 29, no. 4 (1957): 349–354; Mitchell B. Garrett, *A Critical Bibliography of the Pamphlet Literature* (Birmingham: Howard College, 1925); and Robert Darnton, "Trends in Radical Propaganda on the Eve of the French Revolution," (Ph.D. dissertation, University of Oxford, 1964). According to Georges Lefebvre, the monarchy had not intended to suspend censorship with its July 5, 1788 decree, but that is how it was interpreted; *The Coming of the French Revolution*, trans. R. R. Palmer (Princeton: Princeton University Press, 1947), 54.

3. Sophia Rosenfeld, "Writing the History of Censorship in the Age of Enlightenment," in *Post-Modernism and the Enlightenment: New Perspectives in French Intellectual History*, ed. Daniel Gordon (New York: Routledge, 2001), esp. 117–123.

4. In a footnote appearing in the original 1733 edition of *Le Temple du goût*, for example, Voltaire denounced the hypocrisy of the censors, but he conceded that censorship did have a legitimate purpose. "Most bad books," he wrote, "are published with approbations full of praises. In doing so, the censors show their lack of respect for the public. Their task is not to say if a book is good, but *if there is something in it against the state.*" *Oeuvres complètes de Voltaire* (Paris: Garnier Frères, 1877), 8:563, n. 1 (my italics). See also Peter Gay, *Voltaire's Politics: The Poet as Realist* (New Haven: Yale University Press, 1959), esp. 66–86.

5. Notable among the philosophes' supporters at Court were the duc de Choiseul, the marquis d'Argenson, and Louis XV's mistress, Madame de Pompidour. In struggling for power and influence, the philosophes also curried the favor of the Directors of the Book Trade and Lieutenant Generals of Police of Paris, Malesherbes and Sartine. Georges Minois, *Censure et culture sous l'ancien régime* (Paris: Fayard, 1995), 188–192.

6. Nicole Herrmann-Mascard, *La censure des livres à Paris à la fin de l'ancien régime (1750–1789)* (Paris: Presses universitaires de France, 1968), 112–123; Carla Hesse summarizes Old Regime licensing in *Publishing and Cultural Politics and Revolutionary Paris, 1789–1810* (Berkeley: University of California Press, 1991), 11–12.

7. Robert Darnton, *The Forbidden Bestsellers of Prerevolutionary France* (New York: W. W. Norton, 1995), esp. 3–21.

8. Herrmann-Mascard, *La censure des livres*, 112–123; Daniel Roche, "Censure," in *Histoire de l'édition française: Le livre triomphant (1660–1830)*, 2nd ed., ed. Roger Chartier and Henri-Jean Martin (Paris: Fayard 1990), 97.

9. Darrin M. McMahon, *Enemies of the Enlightenment: The French Counter-Enlightenment and the Making of Modernity* (New York: Oxford University Press, 2001), 17–53. For Bastille imprisonments of those involved in the print trade, see Roche, "Police du livre," in *Histoire de l'édition française*, 106.

10. Roche, "Police du livre," 99–109.

11. Robert Darnton, *The Literary Underground of the Old Regime* (Cambridge: Harvard University Press, 1982); Gay, *Voltaire's Politics*, 66–86.

12. Arthur M. Wilson, *Diderot* (New York: Oxford University Press, 1972), 332–346.

13. Roche, "Censure," 96–97.

14. Robert Darnton, *The Business of the Enlightenment* (Cambridge: Belknap Press of Harvard University Press, 1979), 9–14.

15. Voltaire, *Dictionnaire philosophique*, in *Oeuvres complètes de Voltaire*, 19:586.

16. Voltaire, *Questions sur les miracles*, in *Oeuvres complètes de Voltaire*, 25:419; David Hume, "Of the Liberty of the Press," *Essays Moral and Political*, 2nd ed. (Edinburgh: A. Kincaid, 1742), 15.

17. *Encyclopédie*, 13:320. In 1789, Jean-Sylvain Bailly, mayor of Paris, invoked this argument to justify policing the theater, *Mémoires de Bailly* (Paris: Baudouin Frères, 1822), 2:286.

18. André Morellet, *Réflexions sur les avantages de la liberté d'écrire et d'imprimer sur les matières de l'administration* (Paris: Frères Étienne, 1775), 37.

19. Ibid., 38; Daniel Gordon, *Citizens without Sovereignty: Equality and Sociability in French Thought, 1670–1789* (Princeton: Princeton University Press, 1994), 199–208.

20. *Encyclopédie*, 9:459. These arguments are derived from Charles de Secondat baron de Montesquieu, *De l'esprit des lois*, ed. Laurent Versini (Paris: Gallimard, 1995), 1: book 12, ch. 13, 313–314.

21. *Encyclopédie*, 9:459.

22. Ibid. (my italics).

23. Ibid. For an example of a death sentence for calumny, see *Arrêt de la Cour de Parlement condamnant Henri Dufrancey et Etienne Virloy, dit La Jeunesse, à faire amende honorable et à être rompus vifs, et François Meunier à faire amende honorable et à être pendu sur place de Grève, pour faux témoignage et calomnie contre Roy de Pierrefitte* (Paris: Imprimerie Grangé, 1755).

24. Wilson, *Diderot*, 471–491.

25. Roger Chartier, *The Cultural Origins of the French Revolution*, trans. Lydia G. Cochrane (Durham, N.C.: Duke University Press, 1991), 53.

26. Ibid., 53–56; Carla Hesse, "Enlightenment Epistemology and the Laws of Authorship in Revolutionary France, 1773–1793," *Representations*, no. 30 (spring 1990), 109–137; Eric Walter, "Les auteurs et le champ littéraire," in *Histoire de l'édition française: Le livre triomphant*, 499–518.

27. Diderot, "Lettre historique et politique adressée à un magistrat sur le commerce de la librairie," in *Oeuvres Complètes de Diderot*, ed. J. Assézat and Maurice Tourneux (Paris: Garnier Frères, 1876), 18:61.

28. Christopher Kelly, *Rousseau as Author: Consecrating One's Life to the Truth* (Chicago: Chicago University Press, 2003), 9–12.

29. Louis Petit de Bachaumont et al., *Mémoires secrets pour servir à l'histoire de la république des lettres en France* (London [Amsterdam?]: John Adamson, 1777 [1781–1789]), 6:290; Keith Michael Baker, *Condorcet: From Natural Philosophy to Social Mathematics* (Chicago: University of Chicago Press, 1975), 34.

30. Keith Michael Baker, *Inventing the French Revolution: Essays on French Political Culture in the Eighteenth Century* (Cambridge: Cambridge University Press, 1990), 117–120, 188.

31. Ibid., 190–197. Necker's reflections on public opinion appeared in his 1784 work, *De l'Administration des finances de la France*.

32. Gay, *Voltaire's Politics*, 310.

33. Dena Goodman, *The Republic of Letters: A Cultural History of the Enlightenment* (Ithaca: Cornell University Press, 1994), 183–232, esp. 201.

34. Colin Jones, *The Great Nation: France from Louis XV to Napoleon, 1715–99* (New York: Columbia University Press, 2002), 288–292.

35. Baker, *Condorcet*, 44–46.

36. Ibid., 35–40.

37. Douglas Dakin, *Turgot and the Ancien Regime in France* (London: Methuen, 1939), 153.

38. Condorcet, *Fragments sur la liberté de la presse* in *Oeuvres de Condorcet*, ed. M.-F. Arago and A. Condorcet O'Conner (Paris: Firmin Didot Frères, 1847–1849), 11:258.

39. Ibid., 258.

40. Ibid., 269.

41. English jurisprudence today follows these principles.

42. Ibid., 276–278.

43. Carla Hesse, "La preuve par la lettre: Pratiques juridiques au tribunal révolutionnaire de Paris (1793–1794)," *Annales: Histoire, Sciences Sociales*, no. 3 (1996): 629–642.

44. Montesquieu, *De l'esprit des lois*, 1: book 12, ch. 12, 391.

45. Ibid., 395.

46. Ibid., 394–395.

47. Condorcet, *Fragments sur la liberté de la presse*, 11:278.

48. Ibid., 297–298.

49. Condorcet, "Lettres d'un gentilhomme à MM. du tiers état," in *Oeuvres de Condorcet*, 9:254.

50. Ibid.

51. Jacques Godechot, "La presse française sous la Révolution et l'Empire," in *Histoire générale de la presse française*, ed. Claude Bellanger, Jacques Godechot, Pierre Guiral, and Fernand Terrou (Paris: Presses universitaires de France, 1969), 1:415; Hugh Gough, *The Newspaper Press in the French Revolution* (Chicago: Dorsey Press, 1988), 17; and Alma Söderhjelm, *Le régime de la presse pendant la Révolution française* (Geneva: Slatkine Reprints, 1971), 49.

52. Malesherbes also wanted barristers to be free to express themselves individually without fear of being banned by their own order. See David A. Bell, *Lawyers and Citizens: The Making of a Political Elite in Old Regime France* (New York: Oxford University Press, 1994), 156–158; Baker, *Inventing the French Revolution*, 117–119.

53. Pierre Grosclaude, *Malesherbes: Témoin et interprète de son temps* (Paris: Librairie Fischbacher, 1961), 662.

54. Chrétien-Guillaume de Lamoignon de Malesherbes, *Mémoires sur la librairie, Mémoire sur la liberté de la presse*, ed. Roger Chartier ([Paris]: Imprimerie nationale, 1994), 302.

55. Jean Egret, *The French Pre-Revolution, 1787–1789*, trans. Wesley D. Camp (Chicago: University of Chicago Press, 1977), 98.

56. Grosclaude, *Malesherbes*, 662.

57. Malesherbes, *Mémoires sur la librairie, Mémoire sur la liberté de la presse*, 306.

58. Ibid., 284.

59. Ibid., 306.

60. Ibid., 282.

61. Ibid., 298.

62. *AP*, 1:551.

63. Ibid., 550.

64. [Dieudonné Thiébault], *Mémoire sur la liberté de la presse, suivi de quelques autres mémoires concernant la librairie*, 27–28.

65. Ibid., 62.

66. Ibid., 63–64.

67. Ibid., 27–28, 88.

68. Ibid., 88–89. For Malesherbes's support of this stipulation, see *Mémoires sur la librairie, Mémoire sur la liberté de la presse*, 307.

69. [Thiébault], *Mémoire sur la liberté de la presse*, 88.

70. Ibid., 105.

71. Ibid., 105–106.

72. Ibid., 106.

73. Ibid., 42–43.

74. Malesherbes, *Mémoires sur la librairie, Mémoire sur la liberté de la presse*, 231.

75. Ibid., 307.

76. Like the *encyclopédistes* who often tempered bold assertations with conventional qualifications, Malesherbes insisted that censors should still refuse approbations for tracts attacking religion and government. Ibid., 231.

77. [Thiébault], *Mémoire sur la liberté de la presse*, 51–52.

78. Ibid., 54.

79. Ibid., 84–85. Thiébault's reasoning chimed with Montesquieu, who held that freedom inhered in the collective opinion a society had about the exercise of its will. "Philosophical freedom consists in the exercise of our will, or at least (if we must refer to all systems) in the opinion we have of exercising our will. Political liberty consists in security, or at least in the opinion we have of security." *De l'esprit des lois*, 1: book 12, ch. 2, 376.

80. Malesherbes, *Mémoires sur la librairie, Mémoire sur la liberté de la presse*, 315, 317.

81. [Thiébault], *Mémoire sur la liberté de la presse*, 71–72.

82. Ibid., 73.

83. Ibid., 112.

84. Ibid.

85. Ibid., 116–117.

86. Ibid., 99–100. Vivian Gruder has shown that book reviews in newspapers could convey highly political messages. The government embedded propaganda in such reviews, and journalists often veiled political criticism of the government in them as well; "Political News as Coded Messages: The Parisian and Provincial Press in the Pre-Revolution, 1787–1788," *French History* 12, no. 1 (1998): 12–13.

87. [Thiébault], *Mémoire sur la liberté de la presse*, 75–76.

88. Ibid., 69.

89. Ibid., 76.

90. Ibid., 76.

91. Ibid., 106–107.

92. *L'Observateur*, no. 4, August 15, 1789.

93. Ibid., no. 7, August 23, 1789.

94. Ibid.

95. J.-P. Brissot de Warville, *Mémoire aux États-généraux, sur la nécessité de rendre, dès ce moment, la presse libre et surtout pour les journaux politiques* (June 1789), 15.

96. J.-P. Brissot de Warville, *Plan de conduite pour les députés du peuple aux États-généraux de 1789* ([May–June 1789]), 20; see also 124–127 and the notes on 19–20.

97. Brissot, *Mémoire aux États-généraux*, 59–60.

98. Ibid., 52.

99. Ibid., 51–52.

100. Ibid., 53.

101. Ibid., 54.

102. Ibid., 53.

Chapter 4

1. Jean Egret, *The French Pre-Revolution, 1787–1789*, trans. Wesley D. Camp (Chicago: University of Chicago Press, 1977), esp. 144–214. For financial tensions, see Robert Darnton, *Gens de lettres, gens du livre* (Paris: Odile Jacob, 1992), 85–98. For ministerial tensions, see John Hardman, *French Politics, 1774–1789: From the Accession of Louis XVI to the Fall of the Bastille* (Harlow: Longman, 1995).

2. *AP*, 1:496.

3. Alexis de Tocqueville, *The Old Regime and the French Revolution*, trans. Stuart Gilbert (Garden City, N.Y.: Doubleday, 1955), 144.

4. Ibid.

5. *Mémoires de la société des Lettres, Sciences et Arts de l'Aveyron*, 17 (1906–1911): 253–281.

6. *AP*, 3:528.

7. *AP*, 2:711.

8. In his study of the cahiers, Roger Chartier cites Sasha Weitman, who shows demands for press freedom in 74 percent of the general cahiers; Sasha Weitman,

"Bureaucracy, Democracy, and the French Revolution" (Ph.D. dissertation, Washington University, 1968). My data show a higher frequency (see below). Roger Chartier, "Cultures, Lumières, Doléances: Les *Cahiers* de 1789," *Revue d'histoire moderne et contemporaine*, 28 (January–March 1981): 89.

9. Jourdan, Isambert, Decrusy, Taillandier (eds.), *Recueil général des anciennes lois françaises* (Paris: Plon Frères, 1821–1833), 21:244.

10. Ibid., 22:273.

11. For a more thorough discussion of methods, see my "Policing Public Opinion in the French Revolution" (Ph.D. dissertation, Princeton University, 2003), appendices A–D, 453–513.

12. For the sake of concision, I use the term *bailliage* to refer to all circumscriptions authorized to send deputies to the Estates-General: *bailliages, sénéchaussées, sièges royales, colonies royales* or *îles, intendances, juridictions royales, gouvernances, pays, prévôtés et vicomtés, principautés,* and, in exceptional cases, *villes* and *villes impériales.*

13. Aix-en-Provence had 113 *bailliages secondaires*, inferior to the *bailliage principal.*

14. The most complete analysis of the cahiers de doléances is Gilbert Shapiro and John Markoff, eds., *Revolutionary Demands: A Content Analysis of the Cahiers de doléances of 1789* (Stanford: Stanford University Press, 1998). Shapiro and Markoff's coding of qualifications to free press demands was not complete enough for my purposes. Moreover, they did not consult the cahiers of the clergy. I would like to thank the authors for sharing their data with me; their approach has inspired mine.

15. Alma Söderhjelm, *Le régime de la presse pendant la Révolution* (Geneva: Slatkine Reprints, 1971). She consulted 464 general cahiers.

16. Ibid., 54.

17. The phrase "la liberté illimitée de la presse" appears in the cahiers of the clergies of Abbeville, Belfort and Huningue, and Lyon and the third estate of Briey but is invoked as dangerous and in need of being regulated. However, the terms *absolue, indéfinie,* and *entière* appear in 61 of the 427 cahiers mentioning the press.

18. If cahiers that called on some higher authority to define regulations and restrictions are added to these 37 cahiers, the ratio rises to 56 of 61.

19. Söderhjelm, *Le régime de la presse,* 59.

20. *AP,* 6:715 (my italics).

21. *AP,* 2:65.

22. *De la liberté de la presse* (July 5, 1789), 27; *Contre la multiplicité et le danger des brochures* (1789), 12.

23. *AP,* 2:708.

24. *AP,* 2:759.

25. *AP,* 3:152. The cahiers of the clergies of Forcalquier and Dieuze also express the view that press freedom already existed.

26. *AP,* 2:91, the clergy of Auch.

27. Ibid.

28. The clergies of Bourges, Chartres, Châteauneuf-en-Thimerais, Étain, Laôn, Semur-en-Auxois, Sens et Sisteron. The citation refers to the cahier of Bourges, *AP,* 6:509. Divorce

was not legalized until 1792. Therefore, the clergy must have been referring to *séparation de corps*, which were legally recognized by the Church before 1792. Rare, *séparations de corps* were sometimes granted in cases of marital conflict and abuse. See Roderick Phillips, *Family Breakdown in Late Eighteenth-Century France* (Oxford: Clarendon Press, 1980), and Suzanne Desan, *Family on Trial in Revolutionary France* (Berkeley: University of California Press, 2004), esp. 33.

29. The clergy of Villefrance-de-Rouergue insisted, "All that spreads and facilitates the progress of enlightenment should be the special object of attention of an order whose principal task…is public instruction." *Mémoires de la société des Lettres, Sciences et Arts de l'Aveyron*, 17 (1906–1911): 253–281.

30. Eight were drafted by the clergy (Amiens-Ham, Angers, Carcasonne, Clermont-Ferrand, Dax, Le Mantes, Metz, Paris [*hors muros*]), one by the nobility (Bourges), and one by the third estate (Libourne).

31. The clergies of Clermont-Ferrand, Metz, and Paris *hors muros*.

32. *AP*, 2:708–709.

33. Notably, in the noble cahiers of Périgueux, Trévoux, and Villefranche-de-Rouergue. The suggestion is implied by the third estate of the Dix Villes Impériales d'Alsace as well.

34. Charles Étienne, ed., *Cahiers de doléances du bailliage de Vézelise*, in vol. 3 of *Cahiers de doléances des bailliages des généralités de Metz et de Nancy* (Nancy: Berger-Levrault, 1930 [series 1907–1946]), 458.

35. Ibid., 396.

36. Ibid.

37. The content code *punir* appears in 23 percent of the cahiers of the clergy, 12 percent of those of the nobility, and 13 percent of those of the third estate. The higher frequency of punitive language over Enlightenment language appears in the cahiers of the clergy and nobility. The opposite tendency holds for the third estate, which expressed Enlightenment arguments in 17 percent of their cahiers. These percentages are based on the total number of cahiers mentioning the press for each order.

38. Camille Bloch, *Cahiers de doléances du bailliage d'Orléans pour les États-généraux de 1789* (Orléans: Imprimerie Orléanaise, 1907), 2:287.

39. L. Jérôme, *Les élections et cahiers du clergé lorrain aux États-généraux de 1789* (Paris-Nancy:1899), 62.

40. *AP*, 4:70 (the third estate of Montreuil-sur-Mer); *AP*, 3:528 (the nobility of Lille).

41. The category *les droits d'autrui* appears in the cahier by the nobles of Mantes, drafted by Condorcet; see Lucien Jaume, *Les Déclarations des droits de l'homme:1789, 1793, 1848, 1946* (Paris: Flammarion, 1989), 89. The third estate of Paris *hors muros* also used the term in a cahier that contained a proposed declaration of rights. The clergy of Autun invoked *les droits d'autrui* in their demand for press freedom; see A. de Charmasse, ed., *Cahiers des paroisses et communautés du bailliage d'Autun* (Autun: Dejussieux, 1985), 357. As will be seen in chapter 8, the clergy of Autun would be sharply divided over the question of a national religion.

42. Condorcet wrote the cahier for the nobles of Le Mantes.

43. Marc Bouloiseau, *Cahiers de doléances du tiers état du bailliage de Rouen pour les États-généraux de 1789*, 2nd ed. (N.p.: Ministère de l'éducation nationale, [1989]), 1: lxiii.

44. Ibid.

45. Ibid., 1:105.

46. Ibid., 1:89.

47. Ibid., 2:71.

48. Ibid., 2:41.

49. Ibid., 1:230.

50. Joseph Fournier, *Cahiers de doléances de la sénéchaussée de Marseille pour les États-généraux de 1789* (Marseille: Imprimerie Nouvelle, 1908), 1–224; the final draft for the city appears on 224.

51. Since many of the cahiers of the Paris districts burned in 1871, it is impossible to verify how press-freedom demands were formulated in all cases. According to an anonymous 1867 study, forty of sixty Parisian districts demanded this freedom. See *Les principes de 1789 et la liberté de la presse. Extraits des cahiers de doléances des trois ordres de toutes les provinces de France* (Paris: Lemerre, 1867). The cahiers of some districts can be cross-checked with the well-cited, post-Commune study by Charles-Louis Chassin, *Les élections et les cahiers de Paris en 1789* (Paris: Jouaust & Sigaux, 1888).

52. Chassin, *Les élections et les cahiers de Paris en 1789*, 2:437.

53. *AP*, 5:282.

54. *AP*, 2:397; *AP*, 3:616; *AP*, 4:94.

55. [Thémines, M. de l'Évêque de Blois], *Instructions et cahier du hameau de Madon* (Blois: J.-J. Masson, 1789), 68–69. Ironically, the bishop's name does not appear on the pamphlet!

56. *Lettre de M. de Calonne...à M. de Thémines, évêques de Blois, sur son ouvrage intitulé: "Instructions et cahier du hameau de Madon"* (London: T. Spilsbury, 1789), 4.

57. *AP*, 2:70; *AP*, 5:326; *AP*, 2:605; *AP*, 3:766; *AP*, 6:191, respectively.

58. *Instructions envoyées par M. le duc d'Orléans pour les personnes chargées de sa procuration aux assemblées des bailliages, relatives aux États-généraux, suivie de délibérations à prendre dans les assemblées* (1789), 6. Several editions of this pamphlet exist with different pagination. I consulted the edition at BNF 8-Z LE SENNE 13396 (7).

59. Louis de La Révellière-Lépeaux, *Plaintes et désirs des communes tant de ville que de campagne* (Angers:1789). The cahier by the clergy of Autun is in Charmasse, *Cahiers des paroisses et communautés du bailliage d'Autun*, 357.

60. Marcel Gauchet, *La Révolution des droits de l'homme* (Paris: Gallimard, 1989), 45.

61. Carla Hesse, *Publishing and Cultural Politics in Revolutionary Paris, 1789–1810* (Berkeley: University of California Press, 1991), 21.

62. Raymond Manevy, *La Révolution et la liberté de la presse* (Paris: Éditions Estiennes, 1964), 13–14. Also see Pierre Rétat and Claude Labrosse, *Naissance du journal révolutionnaire* (Lyon: Presses Universitaire de Lyon, 1989), 9–12. On May 8, the electors of the third estate of Paris issued an *arrêté* protesting the official shutdown of the newspapers of Brissot and Mirabeau.

63. Gustave Le Poittevin, *La Liberté de la presse depuis la Révolution (1789–1815)* (Geneva: Slatkine, 1975), 13.

64. Not all the *américains*, as French deputies inspired by American state declarations were called, submitted proposals without restrictions, and indeed some state constitutions included them. The deputy from Quercy, Gouges-Cartou, after arguing for the necessity of religion and *bonnes mœurs* to preserve the social order, proposed restrictions on speech attacking the official cult (Gallicanism). See Gauchet, *La Révolution des droits de l'homme*, 52.

65. Antoine de Baecque, Wolfgang Schmale, Michel Vovelle, eds., *L'An I des Droits de l'homme* (Paris: Presses CNRS, 1988), 66. Five proposals explicitly forbade attacks on religion (*projets* 5, 17, 19, and 30). Four other proposals mentioned the importance of religion in securing morality and the general social order (*projets* 3, 19, 21, and 24).

66. See articles 5, 6, and 7 in the Declaration of Rights of April and May 1793, as well as articles 6 and 7 in the *Acte Constitutionnel* of June 24, 1793. Article 2 of the Declaration of Rights prefacing the Constitution of the Year III refers to the *droits d'autrui* but does not mention press freedom (see my conclusion). These documents can be found in Jaume, *Les déclarations des droits de l'homme*.

67. For example, the duc de Lévis asserted that "every man has the right to publicize his thoughts in any way he deems fit, under the condition that the law considers necessary for the good of all," *Projet de Déclaration des droits de l'homme et du citoyen*, in Baecque et al., *L'An I des Droits de l'homme*, 235.

68. Articles 11, 12, and 13 in *Déclaration des droits de l'homme remise dans les bureaux de l'Assemblée nationale, par M. Peytion* [*sic*, Pétion] *de Villeneuve, député de Chartres*, in ibid., 275.

69. M. Sallé de Choux, député de Berry, *Projet de déclaration des droits de l'homme en société*, in ibid., 280.

70. M. Gouges-Cartou, *Projet de déclaration des droits*, in ibid., 266–267.

71. See *projets* 19, 21, and 24, in ibid., 266–267, 270–271.

72. *Projet de déclaration des droits de l'homme et du citoyen, par M. Servan, avocat au parlement de Grenoble*, in ibid., 79–80.

73. Ibid., 129.

74. Gauchet, *La Révolution des droits de l'homme*, 138.

75. Le Hoday, *Logographe*, no. 3:78–79, in Baecque et al., *L'An I des Droits de l'homme*, 171–172. Raymond Birn also discusses the debates in the Constituent Assembly over freedom of religion and expression in "Religious Toleration and Freedom of Expression," in *The French Idea of Freedom: The Old Regime and the Declaration of the Rights of 1789*, ed. Dale Van Kley (Stanford: Stanford University Press, 1994), 267–274.

76. Baecque et al., *L'An I des Droits de l'homme*, 171.

77. Ibid., 172–181, 182–183.

78. Birn, "Religious Toleration and Freedom of Expression," 271; Michael P. Fitzsimmons, *The Night the Old Regime Ended: August 4, 1789, and the French Revolution* (University Park, Pa.: Penn State University Press, 2003), 61–63. At this time, audiences at the Comédie-française were clamoring for performances of a banned (and politically loaded) play by Marie-Joseph Chénier, *Charles IX ou la Saint-Barthélemy*; see my "Charles IX and the French Revolution: Law, Vengeance, and the Revolutionary Uses of History," *European Review of History* 4, no. 2 (1997): 127–146.

79. Baecque et al., *L'An I des Droits de l'homme*, 181.

80. Birn, "Religious Tolerance and Freedom of Expression," 265.

81. Gauchet, *La Révolution des droits de l'homme*, 168.

82. Yann Fauchois, "La difficulté d'être libre: Les droits de l'homme, l'Église catholique et l'Assemblée constituante, 1789–1791," *Revue d'histoire moderne et contemporaine* 48, no. 1 (2001): 74.

83. Baecque et al., *L'An I des Droits de l'homme*, 182.

84. Ibid., 183–185.

85. Ibid., 185.

86. Ibid., 186.

87. Ibid.

88. Jacques Necker, *De l'importance des idées religieuses* (Paris: Hôtel de Thou, 1788), 9–10.

89. Keith Michael Baker, "Politics and Public Opinion under the Old Regime: Some Reflections," in *Press and Politics in Pre-Revolutionary France*, ed. Jack Censer and Jeremy Popkin (Berkeley: University of California Press, 1987), 204–246.

90. Necker, *De l'importance des opinions religieuses*, 79.

91. Ibid.

92. Bernard de Brye, "Liberté de la presse et avatars d'un sermon. Recherches sur le sermon prononcé par Mgr. de la Fare, évêque de Nancy, lors de la messe d'ouverture des états généraux, le 4 mai 1789," *Annales de l'est* 32, no. 4 (1980): 291.

Chapter 5

1. *ACP*, 1st series, 1:413.

2. *AP*, 8:512–513; *ACP*, 1st series, 1:413.

3. *ACP*, 1st series, 1:413.

4. Ibid., 436.

5. Ibid., 447. The severity of the sentence so outraged the public that the Commune was compelled to request the *garde des sceaux* to mitigate it. His sentence was eventually commuted.

6. *Journal de Paris*, no. 245, September 2, 1789.

7. Alphonse de Lamartine, *Histoire des Girondins* (Paris: Plon, 1984), 1:482.

8. Jean-Sylvain Bailly, *Mémoires de Bailly* (Paris: Baudouin Fils, 1822), 2:326–345; *ACP*, 1st series, 1:412–414.

9. The informant publicly confirmed the charge against Joly but denied having told the journalist about it. Marat's accusation appeared in *L'Ami du peuple*, no. 26 (1789), in Jean-Paul Marat, *Oeuvres politiques 1789–1793*, ed. Jacques De Cock and Charlotte Goëtz (Brussels: Pole Nord, 1989), 1:240–241.

10. *AP*, 9:454.

11. Raymond Manevy, *La Révolution et la liberté de la presse* (Paris: Estienne, 1964), 18–19.

12. Camille Desmoulins, *Réclamation en faveur du marquis de Saint-Huruge*, 4–5.

13. Ibid., 6.

14. Samoht, *Et moi aussi, je suis patriote: M. le marquis de Saint-Huruge défendu par un homme qui ne le connaît pas*, 4.

15. Ibid.

16. Saint-Huruge, *Mémoire succinct du marquis de Saint-Huruge, sergent dans les Gardes nationales parisiennes au district de Saint-Roch sur sa demande en liberté provisoire, envoyé à MM. des districts de la commune de Paris* (September 10, 1789), 3.

17. AN D XXIXbis, carton 1, doss. 8, docs. 23–24, "Adresse et dénonciation à l'Assemblée nationale du mandement de l'évêque de Tréguier du 14 septembre 1789" and "Registre des délibérations de la chambre de correspondance de la ville épiscopale de Tréguier du 23 sept 1789." Delegates from the cities Lannion, Morlaix, Guingamp, Châtelaudren, Pontrieuxet La Roche-Derrienconvened at Tréguier to draft the denunciation on September 28, 1789.

18. Ibid.

19. *AP*, 9:454.

20. Ibid., 479.

21. Ibid., 474–475.

22. *Révolutions de Paris*, no. 16, October 24–31, 1789, 31.

23. Ibid., no. 14, October 10–17, 1789, 32. Similar arguments can be found in [Michel Thomassin], *Réflexions sur la liberté de la presse* (1790), 3, and Louis-Félix Guynement de Kéralio, *De la liberté d'énoncer, d'écrire ou d'imprimer sa pensée* ([Paris]: L. Poitier de Lille, 1790), 30–31.

24. *ACP*, 1st series, 3:174.

25. Ibid., 179.

26. Laurence Coudart, *La Gazette de Paris: Un journal royaliste pendant la Révolution française (1789–1792)* (Paris: Harmattan, 1995).

27. *Gazette de Paris* [De Rozoi], March 21, 1790 (original emphasis).

28. *Extrait du registre des délibérations de l'assemblée du district des Cordeliers du 19 juin 1790* (Paris: Moromo, 1790), 9 (my italics).

29. *Grande dénonciation de l'arrestation de deux citoyens par le comité des recherches*, 11.

30. *PV*, July 31, 1790.

31. AN D XXIXbis, carton 12, doss. 129, doc. 31, Letter to sieur Cœur, criticizing Malouet's legislative proposal against patriot journalists, August 3, 1790. See chapter 7 below for more on lèse-nation affairs.

32. Baillio, member of the *Société des amis de la liberté de la presse*, admonished Marat in *La lanterne des français*, no. 5, July–August 1790, 35–36; AN D XXIXbis, carton 12, doss. 129, doc. 31.

33. "Sur la liberté de la presse et les Gens de Lettres," in *Le pour et le contre sur la liberté de la presse, par un impartial* (Perlet), 46.

34. Jean-Baptiste-Louis Billecocq, *Dénonciation aux États-généraux du plus cruel fléau de la société, ou de la nécessité d'une loi précise contre les calomniateurs* (Paris:1789), 15.

35. Ibid., 7.

36. Ibid., 4, 6.

37. Louis-Félix Guynement de Kéralio, *De la liberté de la presse* (Paris: L. Potier de Lille), 6.

38. Eugène Hatin, *Histoire politique et littéraire de la presse en France* (Paris: Poulet-Malassis, 1860), 5:66, cited in Alma Söderhjelm, *Le régime de la presse pendant la Révolution française* (Geneva: Slatkine Reprints, 1971), 1:123.

39. *Patriote français*, January 31–February 1, 1790, in Söderhjelm, *Le régime de la presse*, 1:124.

40. *Patriote français*, February 15, 1790, in Söderhjelm, *Le régime de la presse*, 1:126.

41. *L'Ami du peuple*, no. 105, January 22, 1790, 5, in Marat, *Oeuvres politiques*, 1:633.

42. Loyseau complained that his pamphlet had been ignored at the time. See the postscriptum to the second edition: Loyseau, *Lettre de M. Loyseau…à M. de Condorcet, sur le projet de loi contre les délits qui peuvent se commettre par la voie de l'impression* (Paris: Imprimerie du *Patriote français*, 1790), 78.

43. Ibid., n. 15.

44. William James Murray, *The Right-Wing Press in the French Revolution* (Exeter: Short Run Press Ltd., 1986), 96–102; Coudart, *La Gazette de Paris*, 197.

45. Murray, *The Right-Wing Press*, 102.

46. *Révolutions de Paris*, no. 56, July 31–August 7, 1790, 176.

47. Ibid., 167–168.

48. Ibid., 188. In the end, the Châtelet did not formally drop the case.

49. *L'Ami du peuple*, no. 181, August 4, 1790, in Marat, *Oeuvres politiques*, 2:1158.

50. *Journal de Paris*, August 7, 1790, 892–893.

51. Ibid., 893. For another pamphlet making the same argument, see the anonymous pamphlet, *Théorie de la liberté de la presse* (Paris: Imprimerie Pougin, 1790), 1–2.

52. *Patriote français*, August 10, 1790, 2.

53. Ibid.

54. Ibid., August 8, 1790, 4.

55. Ibid., August 7, 1790, 4.

56. [Thomassin], *Réflexions sur la liberté de la presse*, 4.

57. Ibid.

58. Ibid., 6, 8.

59. Ibid., 8.

60. Kéralio, *De la liberté d'énoncer, d'écrire ou d'imprimer sa pensée*, 30.

61. Ibid., 14.

62. Ibid., 19.

63. On May 10, 1791, the National Assembly banned collective petitions, requiring all demands to be submitted by individuals.

64. Robespierre, *Discours sur la liberté de la presse*, in *Société des Jacobins*, 2:399; François-Xavier Lanthenas, *De la liberté indéfinie de la presse, et de l'importance de ne soumettre la communication des pensées qu'à l'opinion publique* (Paris: Imprimerie du *Patriote français*, June 1791), 37.

65. J. Pétion de Villeneuve, *Discours sur la liberté de la presse* (Paris: Imprimerie nationale, 1791), 31. Lanthenas seconded the view, which had been voiced at a recent Jacobin Club meeting, "that calumny is even sometimes laudable and [to be] tolerated." *De la liberté indéfinie de la presse*, 10.

66. Robespierre, *Discours sur la liberté de la presse*, in *Société des Jacobins*, 2:402.

67. Ibid., 408.

68. Pétion, *Discours sur la liberté de la presse*, 26.

69. Lanthenas, *De la liberté indéfinie de la presse*, 26.

70. Ibid., 28.

71. Robespierre, *Discours sur la liberté de la presse*, in *Société des Jacobins*, 2:402.

72. Ibid., 403–404.

73. Ibid., 407–408.

74. Loyseau, *Lettre de M. Loyseau*, 14.

75. Lanthenas, *De la liberté indéfinie de la presse*, 31–32.

76. Pétion, *Discours sur la liberté de la presse*, 10.

77. Lanthenas, *De la liberté indéfinie de la presse*, 31.

78. Civil courts in revolutionary France were not established until summer 1791. The first calumny affair, adjudicated by the civil court of the 2nd arrondissement in Paris on August 5, 1790, was dismissed. The judges declared, "No human power can command thoughts." A. Douarche, *Les tribunaux civils de Paris pendant la Révolution* (Paris: Cerf, 1905), 1: cxcv. In subsequent affairs, the court ruled often in favor of plaintiffs, though few such affairs seemed to have been adjudicated before 1794. In one affair, Brissot filed suit for a defamatory pamphlet, *Réplique à Jacques-Pierre Brissot de Warville par Charles Théveneau Morande*. He won the case on November 26, 1791, and the author of the libel was condemned to pay damages and the costs of printing three hundred copies of the judgment, Douarche, *Les tribunaux civils*, 1:125.

79. Pierre Beaumarchais, *Le barbier de Séville, suivi par Jean Bête à la foire*, pref. Jacques Scherer (Paris: Gallimard, 1982), act II, scene viii, passage by Bazile, 90.

80. Billecocq, *Dénonciation aux États-généraux du plus cruel fléau de la société*, 9.

81. Barry M. Shapiro, *Revolutionary Justice in Paris, 1789–1790* (Cambridge: Cambridge University Press, 1993), 84–99.

82. [J.-B.] Oudet, *Observations de M. Oudet, avocat au Parlement, sur la liberté de dire ou d'imprimer ses opinions, et sur la nécessité d'empêcher ou de réprimer l'abus de l'impression, et de punir les coupables ou les calomniateurs* (Paris: Imprimerie de la veuve Hérissant), 8 (my italics).

83. Ibid., 49.

84. Ibid., 54.

85. AN D XXIXbis, carton 16, doss. 182, doc. 9, Letter by the department of Seine-Inférieur, denouncing an article by Marat that appeared in no. 355 of *L'Abeille politique et littéraire*, January 4, 1791.

86. *AP*, 17:458.

87. Ibid., 450.

88. Ibid.

89. AN D XXIXbis, carton 42, doss. 415[3], doc. 95, *Réquisition de M. le commissaire du roi contre un libelle du sieur Jean-François Lieutaud et ordonnance du Tribunal de district intervenue à ce sujet*, April 20, 1791, 2.

90. Ibid., 6.

91. AN Z³, carton 116, Pièces diverses des six tribunaux.

92. Murray, *The Right-Wing Press*, 95.

93. For Mirabeau's dealings with the Court, see Barbara Luttrell, *Mirabeau* (New York: Harvester Wheatsheaf, 1990), 205–210, 213–247.

94. [Sébastien Brumeaux de Lacroix], *Trahison découverte du comte de Mirabeau* (Imprimerie de Guillaume junior), 3–4.

95. See the third annex in *AP*, 17:459.

96. AN Y 10546.

97. AN D XXIXbis, carton 4, doss. 47, doc. 1, Letter by the prosecutor of the commune of Preuilly, denouncing no. 132 of Mercier's *Annales patriotiques*, February 21, 1790.

98. Ibid., carton 4, doss. 60, doc. 12, denunciation by the substitute prosecutor of the commune of Brest concerning calumnies in the *Gazette de Paris*, April 5, 1790.

99. Ibid., carton 2, doss. 12, doc. 5, *arrêté* by the district of Prémontrés (Faubourg Saint-Germain) denouncing *l'Ami des honnêtes gens ou l'optimiste*, no. 1, to the President of the National Assembly, October 21, 1789.

100. Ibid., carton 12, doss. 128, doc. 31, letter by sieur Lecomte, director of the post office at Richelieu, denouncing the *Gazette de Paris* for carrying seditious views, June 14, 1790.

101. Ibid., carton 6, doss. 81, doc. 16, letter by the mayor of Tarbes conveying the findings of an investigation into efforts to turn the people against the policies of the National Assembly concerning religion, May 21, 1790.

102. Ibid., carton 12, doss. 135, doc. 11, letter by Jean-Baptiste Loir, grenadier of the section Rue Neuve in Lyon, denouncing an issue of *Courrier du Pont du Gard*, September 15, 1790.

103. Ibid., carton 16, doss. 176, doc. 1, letter by the Société des amis de la Constitution in Brest denouncing Mallet du Pan for calumniating the municipal government, December 24, 1790.

104. *AP*, 16:229–232.

105. *Moniteur*, 4:170, June 19, 1790, 660.

106. Ibid., 4:168, June 17, 1790, 643.

107. AMB I 38, doc. 3, "Ordonnance de la municipalité qui déclare séditieux un écrit ayant pour titre *Déclaration et pétition des Catholiques de Nîmes*," June 26, 1790.

108. Ibid. The *Moniteur* shows no trace of the authors having appeared before the National Assembly.

109. AN D XXIXbis, carton 14, doss. 150, doc. 17, "Extrait des registres des délibérations du Conseil municipal," September 7, 1790.

110. Similarly, the mayor of Saint-Brieuc denounced libels "full of calumnies against the King and the National Assembly." Before learning that the Malouet decree had been revoked, he glowed, "I, along with all good citizens of this city, applaud the vigorous and wise measures that the National Assembly has just taken to thwart the license of writers who show themselves to be the enemies of the Revolution." Ibid., carton 11, doss. 116, doc. 24.

111. Ibid., carton 11, doss. 114, doc. 23, letter by the district of Nantua, denouncing a printed letter signed "Louis Brancas, *ci-devant comte de Lauraguais*," August 4, 1790.

112. Ibid., carton 11, doss. 118, doc. 14, "Extrait du registre des délibérations du directoire du département de l'Aube," August 10, 1790.

113. Ibid., carton 15, doss. 159, doc. 6, letter by the mayor of Gy denouncing *L'Ami du clergé et de la noblesse*, October 27, 1790.

114. Ibid., carton 16, doss. 175, doc. 31, letter by the municipality of Montbrison announcing the interdiction of counterrevolutionary publicity, December 21, 1790.

115. Ibid., carton 37, doss. 380, doc. 13, anonymous letter describing the deleterious effects of press freedom, July 2, 1791.

116. *AP*, 29:635.

117. AN D XXIXbis, carton 14, doss. 151, doc. 10, "Délibération des administrateurs du district de la Tour-du-Pin dénonçant une *Lettre pastorale de M. l'Archevêque de Vienne au clergé séculier et régulier et aux fidèles de son diocèse*," September 25, 1790.

118. Ibid., carton 7, doss. 101, doc. 9, letter from the town of Boué denouncing the uncivic propos of sieur Rousseau, June 29, 1790.

119. Ibid., carton 2, doss. 27, doc. 7, letter by sieur Le Buzel concerning a libel circulating in Toulouse, November 18, 1789.

120. Ibid., carton 15, doss. 164, doc. 8, letter by the municipality of Grenoble denouncing *Lettre écrite sur le tombeau de Bayard adressée à toute l'armée française* by M. de Rival, November 7, 1790.

121. Ibid., carton 3, doss. 35, doc. 11, "procès-verbal dénonçant à l'Assemblée nationale un sermon tendancieux de l'évêque de Senez, M. de Bonneval, November 30, 1789."

122. Ibid., carton 7, doss. 104, doc. 7, letter by the municipal officers of Morlaix to the president of the National Assembly, denouncing *Circulaire de M. l'évêque de Léon*, July 16, 1790.

123. Ibid., carton 3, doss. 32, doc. 29, "Délibération de la municipalité de Massiac (Cantal) dénonçant des libelles injurieux pour l'Assemblée nationale," January 14, 1790.

124. Ibid., carton 6, doss. 82, doc. 4, letter from the municipality of Saint-Hilaire-du-Harcouët (Manche) denouncing a libel titled *Adresse aux assemblées primaires du département de Chaâlons*, May 26, 1790.

125. Ibid., carton 11, doss. 118, doc. 18, letter by the patriotic citizens of Perpignan, denouncing efforts by the marquis de Banyuls de Montferré, brother of a national deputy, to stir up opposition to the National Assembly's policies on religion, May 5, 1790.

126. Ibid., carton 33, doss. 342, doc. 11, letter by sieur Varrailhon, "professeur humaniste" in Hautefort (Dordogne), April 13, 1791.

127. J.-B. Duvergier, ed., *Collection complète des lois, décrets, ordonnances, règlements* (Paris: Guyot et Scribe, 1834–1949), 3:114.

128. *AP*, 28:403.

129. Title II, article 19 of the *Organisation de la police municipale et correctionnelle*, in Duvergier, *Collection complète des lois*, 3:252, July 19, 1791. Richard Andrews has argued that these laws were precursors of the Terror. "Boundaries of Citizenship: The Penal Regulation of Speech in Revolutionary France," in *French Politics and Society*, 7 (1989), 93–109.

130. Ibid.

131. *ACP*, 2nd series, 5:485, July 22, 1791; Marat, *Oeuvres politiques*, 6:1021*; Harvey Chisick, *The* Ami du Roi *of the Abbé Royou: The Production, Distribution and Readership of a Conservative Journal of the Early French Revolution* (Philadelphia: American Philosophical Society, 1992), 60–61.

132. *ACP*, 2nd series, 5:485; Chisick, *The* Ami du Roi *of the Abbé Royou*, 61.

133. For a helpful compilation of sources on the "petite terreur," see Marat, *Oeuvres politiques*, 6:1017*.

134. *AP*, 29:631. Title 3, chapter 5, art. 17 of the proposed law. I have italicized the controversial passages.

135. Ibid., 632.

136. Ibid., 633–636.

137. Marat, *L'Ami de peuple*, no. 548, August 26, 1791, 3, in *Oeuvres politiques*, 6:3276.

138. Ibid., 6, in *Oeuvres politiques*, 3277.

139. *Patriote français*, no. 745, April 24, 1791.

140. *AP*, 42:711.

141. Ibid.

142. Ibid., 712.

143. Ibid.

144. Ibid., 711.

145. Ibid.

146. *AP*, 45:117–118; Douarche, *Les tribunaux civils de Paris pendant la Révolution*, 1:237, 296–297.

147. *AP*, 45:118.

148. Armand Gensonné, *Discours de M. Gensonné, député du département de la Gironde, sur la police de sûreté générale; prononcé le 30 mai 1792* ([Paris]: Imprimerie nationale, 1792), 11, 16. Much of Gensonné's plan had been proposed by the deputy M. Français, *Projet de décret sur les troubles intérieurs, lu à l'Assemblée nationale au nom du comité des douze le 5 mai 1792* (1792), 5 and 14.

149. Gensonné, *Discours de M. Gensonné*, 16.

150. Jacques-Pierre Brissot, *Discours de J-P. Brissot, député du département de Paris, sur les causes des dangers de la patrie, et sur les mesures à prendre* (Paris: Imprimerie nationale, 1792), 50.

151. Ibid., 17.

152. Ibid., 6–7.

153. Ibid.

154. Ibid., 11.

155. Brissot was expelled from the club on October 12, 1792 for having calumniated the commune of Paris. *Société des Jacobins*, 4:377–378.

156. Robespierre, *Discours de Maximilien Robespierre sur l'influence de la calomnie sur la Révolution, prononcé à la Société dans la séance du 28 octobre 1792* (Paris: Pierre-Jacques Duplain, October 28, 1792), 17.

157. Ibid., 14–16.

158. Ibid., 12.

159. Robespierre, *Discours… sur l'influence de la calomnie*, 31.

160. *AP*, 54:351; *AP*, 60:698–700.

161. Victor Hallays-Dabot, *Histoire de la censure théâtrale en France* (Paris: Libraire de la Société des Gens de Lettres, 1862), 171–178.

162. G. Charles Walton, "*Charles IX* and the French Revolution: Law, Vengeance, and the Revolutionary Uses of History," *European Review of History—Revue européenne d'histoire* 4, no. 3 (1997): 142–143.

163. *Moniteur*, 15:25, January 25, 1793, 268.

164. Hugh Gough, *The Newspaper Press in the French Revolution* (Chicago: Dorsey Press, 1988), 92.

165. *AP*, 60:65.

166. Ibid.

167. *Moniteur*, 16:105, April 15, 1793, 136.

168. Ibid., 16:106, April 16, 1793, 140; Marat, *Oeuvres de Marat*, 9:6165–6184, esp. 6167.

169. AN F^{1c} III, Seine, 13.

170. AN F^7 4432, cited in [Louis] Mortimer-Ternaux, *Histoire de la terreur*, 3rd ed. (Paris: Lévy Frères, 1869), 7:310, n. 1.

171. AN AF II 45, collection 348, doc. 44. The manuscript letter is in English.

172. *Moniteur*, 17:262, September 19, 1793, 680.

173. Ferrières Sauveboeuf, *Réflexions politiques sur le gouvernement révolutionnaire, la liberté de la presse et les élections par le peuple dans les circonstances actuelles* (Paris: Roblot, [1793–1794]), 4.

174. Ibid.

175. Ibid., 5.

176. *AP*, 83:576–577.

177. Ibid., 577.

178. Ibid., 607.

179. Ibid., 93:492, see also 40 and 418.

180. *Moniteur*, 20:264, 24 Prairial, Year II (June 12, 1794), 697.

181. Ibid., 21: issues dated 3, 5–7, and 9 Fructidor, Year II.

182. *AP*, 29:631.

Chapter 6

1. *AP*, 19:746 (my italics).

2. Ibid.

3. Ibid., 748.

4. For rules governing internal discipline in the National Assembly, see André Castaldo, *Les méthodes de travail de la Constituante: Les techniques délibératives de l'Assemblée nationale, 1789–1791* (Paris: Presses universitaires de France, 1989), 375–380; Michel Duguit, *Le régime disciplinaire des assemblées législatives françaises* (Bordeaux: Imprimerie de l'Université, 1927), 25.

5. Michael Fitzsimmons, *The Remaking of France: The National Assembly and the Constitution of 1791* (Cambridge: Cambridge University Press, 1994), 248; Edna Hindie Lemay and Alison Patrick, eds., *Revolutionaries at Work: The Constituent Assembly, 1789–1791* (Oxford: Voltaire Foundation, 1996), esp. 122; Barry Shapiro, *Revolutionary Justice in Paris 1789–1790* (Cambridge: Cambridge University Press, 1993). In his study of the Constituent Assembly, Timothy Tackett discusses the impact of popular violence on legislators through to October 1789; thereafter, however, popular violence drops out of his analysis; *Becoming a Revolutionary: The Deputies of the French National Assembly and the Emergence of a Revolutionary Culture (1789–1790)* (Princeton: Princeton University Press, 1996). Samuel Scott examines numerous provincial disturbances in 1790 but does not investigate their relationship with national politics; "Problems of Law and Order during 1790, the 'Peaceful' Year of the French Revolution," *American Historical Review* 80, no. 4 (October 1975): 859–888. See also Michel Vovelle, *La chute de la monarchie, 1787–1792* (Paris: Seuil, 1972), 138–139. A noteworthy study focusing on the often underappreciated relationship between popular unrest and high politics in the early Revolution is John Markoff's *The Abolition of Feudalism: Peasants, Lords, and Legislators in the French Revolution* (University Park: Penn State University Press, 1996).

6. Patrice Gueniffey, *La politique de la Terreur: Essai sur la violence révolutionnaire* (Paris: Fayard, 2000), 100.

7. For discussions of the role of honor in revolutionary politics, see Geoffrey Best, *Honour among Men and Nations: Transformations of an Idea* (Toronto: University of Toronto Press, 1982); Pascal Brioist, Hervé Drévillon, and Pierre Serna, *Croiser le fer: Violence et culture de l'épée dans la France moderne (XVIe–XVIIIe siècles)* (Seyssel: Champ Vallon, 2002); Markoff, *The Abolition of Feudalism,* passim; David A. Bell, *The First Total War: Napoleon's Europe and the Birth of Warfare as We Know It* (Boston: Houghton Mifflin, 2007), 84–119.

8. *AP,* 10:591.

9. Ibid.

10. Ibid., 11:286.

11. Ibid.

12. The right tried to make Catholicism the official cult of France on at least two other occasions: August 28, 1789, and February 13, 1790. See Timothy Tackett, *Religion, Revolution, and Regional Culture in Eighteenth-Century France: The Ecclesiastical Oath of 1791* (Princeton: Princeton University Press, 1986), 210.

13. *AP,* 15:295.

14. *Patriote Français,* no. 263, April 28, 1790, 1.

15. *AP,* 15:302.

16. Ibid.

17. Ibid., 303–304.

18. Ibid., 303.

19. Ibid., 304.

20. Ibid., 305.

21. Jean Starobinski, *1789: Les emblèmes de la raison* (Paris: Flammarion, 1973), 81–98; Mona Ozouf, *Festivals and the French Revolution*, trans. Alan Sheridan (Cambridge: Harvard University Press, 1988); Emmet Kennedy, *A Cultural History of the French Revolution* (New Haven: Yale University Press, 1989), 314–315.

22. "Fidelity oaths" were commonly sworn during the Old Regime, in the military, the church, and royal administration. Marcel Marion, "Serment de fidélité," in *Dictionnaire des institutions de la France XVIIe-XVIIIe siècles* (Paris: A. and J. Picard, 1993), 510.

23. Lucien Bély, ed., *Dictionnaire de l'ancien régime* (Paris: Presses universitaires de France, 1996), 1159; Jean de Viguerie, "Les serments du sacre des rois de France à l'époque moderne, et spécialement le 'serment du royaume,'" in *Le sacre des rois: Actes du colloque international d'histoire sur les sacres et couronnements royaux (Reims 1975)* (Paris: Belles Lettres, 1985), 205–215.

24. Daniel Nordman, *Frontières de France: De l'espace au territoire, XVIe–XIXe siècles* ([Paris]: Gallimard, 1998), 415–442.

25. Daniel Roche, *Le siècle des lumières en province: Académies et académiciens provinciaux, 1680–1789* (Paris: École des Hautes Études en Sciences Sociales, 1989), 1:103.

26. Edmund Burke, *Reflections on the Revolution in France*, ed. Frank M. Turner (New Haven: Yale University Press, 2003), 67.

27. Mona Ozouf raises Jean-Paul Sartre's rhetorical question, "Are not all takers of oaths…swearing to perpetuate an unfruitful present?" *Festivals and the French Revolution*, 178. Lynn Hunt has a less pessimistic (though still Rousseauian) view of revolutionary oaths, "The World We Have Gained: The Future of the French Revolution," *American Historical Review* 108, no. 1 (February 2003): 8–11.

28. Lynn Hunt, *Politics, Culture, and Class in the French Revolution* (Berkeley: University of California Press, 1984), 21; Starobinski, *1789: Les emblèmes de la raison*, 81–98.

29. Dom H. Leclercq, *Vers la Fédération (janvier—juillet 1790)* (Paris: Librairie Letouzey et Ané, 1929), 39–41; Barry Shapiro, *Revolutionary Justice in Paris*, 124–174. The plot concerned the Favras Affair.

30. Leclercq, *Vers la Fédération*, 75–76.

31. *AP*, 11:429.

32. Ibid., 432.

33. Leclercq, *Vers la Fédération*, 88. *ACP*, 1st series, 3:692–695, 4:3–6. See also Alexandre Tuetey, *Répertoire général des sources manuscrites de l'histoire de Paris pendant la Révolution française* (Paris: Imprimerie nouvelle, 1890), 1:192–196.

34. *Moniteur*, no. 104, April 14, 1790, 112. Ironically, the motion was advanced by a Jacobin Cathusian monk, dom Gerle.

35. Scott, "Problems of Law and Order in 1790," 864, 871–876.

36. François Furet and Denis Richet, *The French Revolution*, trans. Stephen Hardman (New York: Macmillan, 1970), 97–121.

37. On the night of April 12–13, leaders of the right met at the Capucin convent on the rue Saint Honoré for a nocturnal strategy session. Anticipating defeat in the National Assembly the next day, they drafted a protest petition, procuring more than three hundred signatures of deputies. They intended to present it to the king to compel him to

intervene. If Louis refused, they would publish and circulate the petition throughout France, which is precisely what they did. Camille Desmoulins, *Révolutions de France et de Brabant*, no. 21, 348.

38. *Complot du clergé découvert* (Paris: Imprimerie de Paris [Gorsas], April 14, 1790), 7.

39. *AP*, 12:719–720.

40. Ibid., 15:483–488, esp. 486–487.

41. Ibid., 486.

42. *Nouvelle déclaration et pétition des Catholiques de Nîmes* (Nîmes: June 1, 1790), 4–5.

43. Ibid., 16.

44. Scott, "Problems of Law and Order," 875.

45. AN D XXIXbis, carton 7, doss. 101, doc. 11–12, letters to the National Assembly from the municipalities of Arras and Montpellier, denouncing *Déclaration et pétition des Catholiques de Nîmes*; PV, 10, no. 301, 4 and 19; AMB I 38, doc. 3, "Ordonnance de la Municipalité qui déclare séditieux un écrit ayant pour titre *Déclaration et pétition des Catholiques de Nîmes*," June 26, 1790.

46. AMB I 38, doc. 3.

47. AN DXXIX^bis, carton 6, doss. 94, doc. 9, "Délibération du conseil général de la commune d'Issoudun," June 7, 1790; Tackett, *Religion, Revolution, and Regional Culture*, 212.

48. AN D XXIXbis, carton 7, doss. 98, doc. 2, "Déclaration du conseil général de la commune de Lyon à l'Assemblée nationale," denouncing *Déclaration d'une partie de l'Assemblée nationale sur le décret rendu le 13 avril 1790*.

49. According to John Markoff, roughly one-third of all disturbances in the summer of 1790 were religious in nature; *The Abolition of Feudalism*, 277, 284.

50. François Simonnet d'Escolmiers [Coulmiers], *Motion de l'abbé d'Abbecourt (de Coulmiers), du 1er juillet 1790, sur la déclaration signée d'une partie des membres de l'Assemblée nationale* (Paris: [1790]), 3.

51. William Doyle, *The Oxford History of the French Revolution* (Oxford: Oxford University Press, 1989), 144; Jeremy Popkin, "Not Over After All: The French Revolution's Third Century," *Journal of Modern History*, 74, no. 4 (December 2002): 808.

52. Tackett, *Religion, Revolution, and Regional Culture*.

53. *Exposition des principes sur la Constitution civile du clergé*, 68.

54. Ibid., 65.

55. Michael Kennedy, *The Jacobin Clubs in the French Revolution: The First Years* (Princeton: Princeton University Press, 1982), 152–177 and appendix B, which shows the trebling of clubs between March and June 1790, 362.

56. Best, *Honour among Men and Nations*.

57. *AP*, 18:199.

58. Ibid.

59. Ibid., 200. The priest was probably referring to the biblical account of the condemnation of Jesus by Jewish crowds before the Roman administrator, Pontius Pilate, who reminded the crowd that Jesus had not violated Roman law.

60. Ibid., 201.

61. Ibid.

62. Ibid.

63. Ibid., 202.

64. Ibid.

65. Ibid.

66. Ibid., 203.

67. Ibid., 19:92, 429, and throughout 714–768.

68. Brioist, Drévillon, and Serna, *Croiser le fer*, 448.

69. *AP*, 19:746.

70. Ibid., 745, 746. Mirabeau was likely referring to tensions over the execution of the leaders of the mutiny of National Guardsmen in Nancy.

71. Ibid., 746.

72. Ibid.

73. Ibid., 746–747.

74. Ibid., 747.

75. Ibid., 748.

76. Ibid.

77. Ibid.

78. Ibid., 749.

79. Ibid., 751.

80. Duels occurred between the following deputies: Barnave and Noailles, the vicomte de Mirabeau and Voranzel, Huguet and Montlosier, and Castries and Lameth. The abbé Maury challenged Lofficial to one, but it apparently did not take place. See Castaldo, *Les Méthodes du travail de la Constituante*, 307, n. 89. The comte de Mirabeau was often challenged to duels but showed remarkable skill in dismissing them without jeopardizing his reputation. His oratory prowess and ability to stir up popular support allowed him to humiliate and menace his adversaries from the podium.

81. P. de Croze, "Un duel politique et ses conséquences," *Le Correspondant*, no. 179 (1895): 1128–1134; Auguste Reynaert, *Histoire de la discipline parlementaire* (Paris: A. Durand, 1884), 2:8; Brioist, Drévillon, and Serna, *Croiser le fer*, 451–454.

82. *AP*, 20:414.

83. Ibid., 417.

84. Ibid.

85. Ibid., 418.

86. Ibid.

87. Ibid., 419.

88. Ibid.

89. Honoré-Gabriel Riqueti Mirabeau, *Correspondance entre le comte de Mirabeau et le comte de La Marck*, ed. A. de Bacourt (Paris: Veuve Le Normant, 1851), 2:31. Mirabeau informed La Marck that Lafayette was the source of the bribes.

90. *AP*, 20:420.

91. Ibid., 419.

92. Ibid., 420.

93. Ibid., 421.

94. *AP*, 421

95. Ibid.

96. Ibid.

97. Ibid.

98. Ibid.

99. Ibid., 44:307–308. Earlier that year, on January 25, 1792, demands were made to have Maury imprisoned for insulting the Legislative Assembly's committees, but nothing came of them; ibid., 22:490.

Chapter 7

1. AN C 170, no. 419; AN BB³, carton 19, "Arrêté du conseil du département du Loiret."

2. Paul Huot, *Les massacres à Versailles en 1792: Éclaircissements historiques et documents nouveaux* (Paris: Challamel Aîné, 1869), 12–13. See also the introduction to Claude Fournier l'Héritier, *Mémoires secrets de Fournier l'Américain, publiés pour la première fois d'après le manuscrit des Archives nationales, avec introduction et notes, par F.-A. Aulard* (Paris: Société de l'histoire de la Révolution française, 1890).

3. *Moniteur*, 13:238, August 25, 1792, 518, and August 26, 1792, 527. [Louis] Mortimer-Ternaux, *Histoire de la Terreur* (Paris: Lévy Frères, 1869), 3:360–400.

4. AN BB³, carton 19(5), "Loi du 25 août 1792."

5. Huot, *Les massacres à Versailles en 1792*, 13; J.-B. Duvergier, ed., *Collection complète des lois, décrets, ordonnances, règlements* (Paris: Guyot and Scribe, 1834–1949), 4:362.

6. M. Roussel, "La Haute Cour nationale à Orléans, 1791–1792," in *Le Droit: Journal des tribunaux*, November 13, 1901, 1017–1018.

7. The decree was originally proposed by Armand Gensonné, *Moniteur*, 13:240, August 17, 1792, 533.

8. Mortimer-Ternaux, *Histoire de la Terreur*, 3:358–360.

9. Huot, *Les Massacres à Versailles en 1792*, 15. For corroborating evidence, see AN BB³, carton 19(5), *Rapport de Léonard Bourdon et Prosper Dubail, commissaires envoyés par le pouvoir exécutif auprès de la Haute Cour nationale à Orléans* (Paris: Imprimerie nationale exécutive du Louvre, [September 10], 1792), esp. 13.

10. Huot, *Les Massacres à Versailles en 1792*, 29.

11. Mortimer-Ternaux, *Histoire de la terreur*, 3:360–361; Huot, *Les Massacres à Versailles en 1792*, 7–11.

12. Albert Soboul, ed., *Dictionnaire historique de la Révolution française* (Paris: Presses universitaires de France, 1989), 943.

13. *Société des Jacobins*, 4:255.

14. *AP*, 49:277.

15. Henri Carré, *La fin des parlements (1788–1790)* (Paris: Hachette, 1912), esp. 165–199; Hugh Gough, *The Newspaper Press in the French Revolution* (Chicago: Dorsey Press, 1988), 49.

16. For examples, see AN D XXIXbis, carton 3, doss. 38, doc. 9, "Adresse des libraires et imprimeurs de Nantes protestant, au nom de la liberté d'écrire, contre un ordonnance du siège de police de cette ville qui les soumet à sa juridiction," and carton 11, doss. 115, doc. 2, "Lettre du garde des Sceaux réclamant une réponse du comité des recherches au sujet de la saisie d'un ballot contenant des exemplaires d'une brochure hostile à l'Assemblée nationale."

17. *PV*, 2, no. 46.

18. *Moniteur*, 4:155, June 4, 1790. The decree was passed on June 2. See also the decree of August 16, 1790, Duvergier, *Collection complète des lois*, 1:327–333.

19. For an example of how local authorities invoked these decrees, see AN D XXIXbis, carton 7, doss. 101, doc. 14, "Délibérations de la municipalité d'Alais dénonçant les manœuvres des contre-révolutionnaires dans la ville," April 25 and 28, 1790.

20. *ACP*, 1st series, 1:82.

21. Lise Andries, "Les imprimeurs-libraires Parisiens et la liberté de la presse (1789–1795)," *Dix-huitième siècle*, no. 21 (1989): 251.

22. *ACP*, 1st series, 1:206.

23. Ibid.

24. Ibid., 1st series, 2:103–104.

25. AMM I 1, carton 550, Police des théâtres, "Procès-verbal de la municipalité de Marseille," March 16, 1791.

26. Ibid., Judgment of March 17, 1791.

27. AN D XXIXbis, carton 6, doss. 89, doc. 2, "délibération et lettre de la municipalité de Soissons dénonçant un imprimé contre-révolutionnaire intitulé: *Lettre d'un français à son ami, du 18 mai 1790*," May 31 and June 2, 1790.

28. AN D XXIXbis, carton 1, doss. 4, doc. 3.

29. The minister cited *Avis aux troupes, Mémoire des difficultés pour établir dans les Provinces belgiques différents décrets de l'Assemblée nationale*, and *Réponse à l'avis aux troupes*, ibid., carton 3, doss. 38, doc. 5.

30. *AP*, 18:168.

31. Georges Carrot, *Révolution et maintien de l'ordre* (Paris: S. P. M. and Kronos, 1995), 130–135; Capitaine H. Choppin, *Insurrections militaires en 1790* (Paris: Lucien Laveur, 1903), 95–150.

32. AN D XXIXbis, carton 12, doss. 135, doc. 11, letter by a grenadier in Lyon denouncing a newspaper article criticizing the National Assembly's handling of the Nancy affair, "[What] dangers will the new Constitution face if people take advantage of press freedom to air any views they like, leading people astray with fears about losing this freedom." Officials in Aignay-le-Duc denounced a local who "invented abominably injurious statements against the august National Assembly," in the wake of the Nancy affair. They believed the individual "merited the death sentence" but deferred the matter to the National Assembly; ibid., carton 13, doss. 148, doc. 26.

33. Choppin, *Insurrections militaires en 1790*, 99.

34. AN D XXIXbis, carton 15, doss. 164, doc. 9.

35. Ibid.

36. AN D XXIXbis, carton 15, doss. 167, doc. 7.

37. Ibid.

38. Eugène Vaillé, *Le Cabinet noir* (Paris: Presses universitaires de France, 1950), 219–220.

39. AN D XXIXbis, carton 15, doss. 169, doc. 3, letter by the *Société des amis de la Constitution d'Hesdin* to the National Assembly.

40. Ibid., carton 12, doss. 132, docs. 1–2; carton 12, doss. 135, docs. 6–7; carton 12, doss. 136, docs. 5–6; carton 13, doss. 140, doc. 3; carton 13, doss. 141, doc. 10; carton 13, doss. 146, docs. 8–10.

41. Ibid., carton 6, doss. 93, doc. 10. The author of the letter also complained that local militia leaders prohibited the tricolored cockade, imposing the black one instead.

42. AN D XXIX[bis], carton 14, doss. 154, docs. 6–22.

43. Ibid., doc. 20.

44. Ibid., doc. 14.

45. Ibid., doc. 21.

46. Ibid., carton 32(b), doss. 336, doc. 12.

47. Ibid., carton 15, doss. 168, doc. 6.

48. ADR 26 L, carton 54, first document, dated June 11, 1791.

49. Ibid., carton 54, fourth document, dated June 10, 1791.

50. Ibid., carton 54, see the sixth through eleventh documents.

51. Ibid., carton 54, seventh document.

52. Ibid.

53. Ibid., carton 54, twelfth document, May 3, 1791.

54. Ibid., carton 54, thirteenth document.

55. Edna Hindie Lemay, *Dictionnaire des constituants, 1789–1791* (Paris: Universitas, 1991), 1:175.

56. W. D. Edmonds, *Jacobinism and the Revolt in Lyon, 1789–1793* (Oxford: Clarendon Press, 1990), 45–46.

57. Ibid., 50.

58. Louis Trenard, *La Révolution française dans la région Rhône-Alpes* (Paris: Perrin, 1992), 226–231.

59. AN D XXIXbis, carton 8, doss. 105 B2 I[A], doc. 3, Imbert, *Opinion de M. Imbert de Montbrison, proposée à la session générale du Département de Rhône et Loire, le 11 décembre 1790*.

60. Ibid., carton 8, doss. 105 B2 I[A], docs. 2, 10, "arrêté de la municipalité de Lyon," June 10, 1791.

61. ADR 26 L, carton 54, "Procès-verbal de la municipalité de Lyon," July 24, 1791.

62. AN D XXIXbis, carton 8, doss. 105 B2 IA, docs. 2, 4, *Extrait du registre des délibérations du directoire du département de Rhône et Loire* (Lyon: Imprimerie Bruyset, fils aîné, June 10, 1791); and doc. 7, "Extrait du registre des délibérations du directoire du département de Rhône et Loire," June 13, 1791.

63. ADR 1 L, carton 459, *Arrêté du directoire du département de Rhône et Loire* (Lyon: Imprimerie de Bruyset, 1791).

64. Ibid., "Extrait du régistre des rapports du comité contentieux," November 25, 1791.

65. AN D XXIXbis, carton 9, doss. 105[B7], XXV, doc. 6, "Arrêté de la municipalité de Lyon," March 6, 1792. The playwright was L.-A. Beffroy de Reigny.

66. Ibid., doc. 20, report by municipal officers in charge of theater surveillance in Lyon, February 23, 1792.

67. Ibid., docs. 5, 8 (the actions of the actors are described in a letter by departmental officials and an "arrêté du Directoire du district de la ville de Lyon," dated March 4 and March 12, 1792, respectively).

68. Ibid., doc. 7, report by municipal officers in charge of theater surveillance in Lyon, March 11, 1792.

69. Ibid., doc. 11, "Délibération de la municipalité de Lyon," April 19, 1792.

70. Ibid., doc. 13. The copy of Roland's letter is dated April 24, 1792.

71. Ibid., doc. 15, letter dated April 28, 1792.

72. Boullemer de la Martinière, *Compte rendu à l'assemblée des représentants de la commune, le 11 mai 1790, par le procureur-syndic de la commune, des travaux du parquet depuis le mois d'octobre 1789* (Paris: Imprimerie de Lottin, 1790), 3–4.

73. Ibid., 4.

74. Sarot, *Réveil des principes des loix et des ordonnances sur le crime de lèze-majesté royale, de lèze-état ou de lèze-nation* (Paris: J. Grand), 3.

75. AN D XXIXbis, carton 2, doss. 15, doc. 3.

76. *AP*, 10:513.

77. Ibid., 20:25. For a similar definition, but one limiting the offense to the actions of public officials and powerful figures in society, see Louis-François Jauffret, ed., *Gazette des nouveaux tribunaux* (Paris: Desaint [C.-F. Perlet and L.-P. Couret], 1791), 2:269.

78. *Révolutions de Paris*, no. 68, October 23–30, 1790, 124–125.

79. *Mémoire pour les criminels de lèse-nation*, 5–6.

80. Ibid., 21.

81. Ibid., 20.

82. *AP*, 15:251–255.

83. Ibid., 253.

84. Ibid., 254.

85. Ibid., 253.

86. The high court was decreed into existence on March 5, 1791.

87. Nicolas Bergasse, *Discours sur les crimes et les tribunaux de haute trahison, par M. Bergasse, pour servir de suite à son discours sur l'organisation du pouvoir judiciaire* (N.p., n.d.), 5.

88. Pierre-Victor Malouet, *Opinion de M. Malouet sur les crimes de lèse-nation, sur la responsabilité des ministres et autres agents du pouvoir exécutif* (N.p., 1791), 5.

89. Ibid., 6.

90. Ibid., 7.

91. François de Pange, *Observations sur le crime de lèse-nation* (Paris: Barrois, 1790), 9.

92. Ibid.

93. Ibid., 7.

94. See Patrice Gueniffey, *La politique de la Terreur: Essai sur la violence révolutionnaire* (Paris: Fayard, 2000), 93–98; Roberto Martucci, "Qu'est-ce que la lèse-nation? À propos du problème de l'infraction politique sous la Constituante (1789–1791)," *Déviance et société* 14, no. 4 (1990): 392–393.

95. Carla Hesse, "The Law of the Terror," *Modern Language Notes* 114, no. 4 (September 1999): 708.

96. Of the nineteen cases concerning speech on the Châtelet's lèse-nation docket at that point, eight involved reactionary or ultraroyalist expression, while eleven involved radical expression; see my "Policing Public Opinion in the French Revolution" (Ph.D. dissertation, Princeton University, 2003), appendix E, 497–502.

97. AN D XXIXbis, carton 2, doss. 25, docs. 25–26, investigative documents by Durand, *lieutenant de la maréchaussée de Bourgogne*, November 22–December 22, 1789.

98. *Jugement en dernier ressort, rendu publiquement à l'audience du parc civil du Châtelet de Paris* ([Paris]: Veuve Desaint, n.d.), 1. He was condemned for "incendiary and seditious propos and for criminal propos against the Queen, which are detrimental to the respect due to His Majesty."

99. Desmoulins, *Révolutions de France et de Brabant*, no. 18, 114–115. For the Suleau affair, see Edmond Seligman, *La justice en France pendant la Révolution (1789–1792)* (Paris: Plon-Nourrit et Cie., 1901–1913), 1:236; AN D XXIXbis, carton 3, doss. 29, doc. 3, and carton 12, doss. 138, doc. 8. Suleau was killed during the insurrection that brought down the monarchy on August 10, 1792.

100. AN Y 10506, affair concerning "Les auteurs, imprimeurs et distributeurs d'un journal intitulé *Les sottises de la semaine*."

101. AN Y 13320, interrogation of March 19, 1790.

102. AN Y 10506, affair *"Les sottises de la semaine."* For the statement by the *greffier* Denonvilliers that the Séguiers had departed for Italy and that Rolland was missing, see the document dated July 5, 1790; Alexandre Tuetey mentions the affair in his edited *Répertoire général des sources manuscrites de l'histoire de Paris pendant la Révolution française* (Paris: Imprimerie nouvelle, 1890–1914) but misattributes the documents to AN Y 10504; several of his references to lèse-nation affairs are incorrect.

103. Such rumors were common. Barry Shapiro, *Revolutionary Justice in Paris (1789–1790)* (Cambridge: Cambridge University Press, 1993), 124–147.

104. AN Y 10508, affair "Enfantin," letter by the *procureur syndic* of the Paris commune to Mayor Bailly and municipal officials, June 12, 1790.

105. Ibid., affair "Enfantin," interrogation of June 12, 1790.

106. Ibid., affair "Enfantin," Fréron, *Adresse aux amis de la liberté: Au sujet des vexations exercées contre le sieur Martel, L'Orateur du peuple.*

107. AN Y 10506, affair "Routledge."

108. AN D XXIXbis, carton 12, doss. 130, doc. 1, request made by Rutledge to the *comités des recherches* and *des rapports* to stop the alleged flight of Necker from France.

109. AN Y 10504, affair "Julien Poulain-Delaunay," *Adresse de plusieurs corporations et métiers de la ville de Rennes à Messieurs les députés de la sénéchaussée de Rennes à l'Assemblée nationale.*

110. Ibid., affair "Delaunay," "Minutes du greffe criminel de la sénéchaussée de Rennes," December 14, 1789.

111. Ibid., affair "Delaunay," Interrogation of March 9, 1790.

112. Ibid., affair "Delaunay," Interrogation of May 10, 1790.

113. *ACP*, 1st series, 3:521.

114. Ibid., 521–525.

115. Ibid., 458–459. On January 19, the commune authorized another arrest warrant, ibid., 3:524.

116. *Pièces justificatives, exposé de la conduite et des motifs du district des Cordeliers, concernant le décret de prise de corps prononcé par le Châtelet contre le sieur Marat le 8 octobre, et mis à exécution le 22 janvier 1790* ([Paris]: Momoro, [1790]).

117. *ACP*, 1st series, 3:524–525.

118. AN D XXIX, *comité des rapports*, carton 63, *Journal des débats et des décrets* (Paris: Baudouin, 1789 [*sic*]), January 22, 1790.

119. Shapiro, *Revolutionary Justice in Paris*, 190.

120. AN D XXIX 63; see especially the letter by the district of Petits-Pères, March 19, 1790.

121. Ibid., "Extrait des registres des délibérations de l'Assemblée générale du district de Sainte Marguerite," March 21, 1790.

122. AN BB³, carton 19, letter by Delessart, Minister of Justice, April 21, 1791. For a discussion of the press law, see chapter 5.

123. Ibid., carton 19, doc. 2274 (not all documents are numbered in this series).

124. Ibid., unnumbered doc., no date.

125. Ibid., letter, April 19, 1792.

126. Ibid., letter by Delessart to the president of the National Assembly, April 21, 1790.

127. *Opérations du tribunal de la Haute Cour nationale provisoire, établi à Orléans pour juger les crimes de lèze-nation* (Paris: L. P. Couret, 1791), no. 4.

128. Ibid., 112–113.

129. Seligman, *La justice en France pendant la Révolution*, 1:275.

130. A.-F. Bertand de Molleville, *Histoire de la Révolution de France* (Paris: Guiget et Michaud, 1801–1803), 7:220–223.

131. AN D XXIXbis, carton 13, doss. 146, doc. 14, letter to Charles Voidel, secretary of the *comité des recherches*, September 25, 1790.

132. Ibid., doc. 13, letter by Trouard to Voidel, August 29, 1790.

133. Insisting on the right to press freedom was rarely an effective defense in lèse-nation affairs. The Alsatian "Zipp" discovered this in 1791, *Les opérations du tribunal de la Haute Cour nationale provisoire, établi à Orléans pour juger les crimes de lèze-nation*, no. 3 (1791): 82–83.

134. AN D XXIXbis, carton 28, doss. 278, doc. 21, letter of May 29, 1791.

135. Jauffret, *Gazette des nouveaux tribunaux* 2, no. 34 (August 26, 1791): 122.

136. *Patriote français*, 738, August 17, 1791.

137. Desmoulins, *Révolutions de France et de Brabant*, no. 91, 6.

138. *Décret de l'Assemblée nationale, du 10 avril 1792*, reprinted in *Journal de la Haute Cour nationale* (Orléans and Paris: Chez Jacob l'aîné and Chez Cussac and Mme Lesclapart, 1792), 2:302–303.

139. *Moniteur*, 72, March 13, 1793, 683.

140. Donald Greer, *The Incidence of the Terror during the French Revolution: A Statistical Interpretation* (Cambridge: Harvard University Press, 1935), 152.

141. Ibid., 85.

142. AN W, carton 480, doss. 354, "Judgement du Tribunal révolutionnaire," 15 Brumaire, Year III."

143. Ibid., carton 292, doss. 196, "Aux citoyens Président et membres du District du Directoire du Département de Versailles."

144. Ibid., carton 292, doss. 196, "Extrait du registre des dénonciations et déclaration tenu par la municipalité de Champcueil en exécution de la loi du 26 mars 1793."

145. Ibid., carton 292, doss. 196, "Aux citoyens président et membres du district du directoire du département de Versailles."

146. Ibid., carton 292, doss. 196, "Rapport de comité du Salut public du district de Corbeil."

147. Ibid., carton 292, doss. 196, "Jugement du tribunal révolutionnaire."

148. Ibid., carton 323, doss. 510, "Acte d'accusation du 23 pluviôse an II."

149. Ibid., carton 323, doss. 510, list of questions, no title, no date.

150. Ibid., carton 292, doss. 197, "Jugement qui condamne Claude Janson à la peine de mort."

151. Ibid., carton 369, doss. 823, "Jugement du 1 prairial an II."

152. Ibid., carton 323, doss. 504, "Acte d'accusation."

153. Ibid., carton 323, doss. 504, "Interrogatoire du département de la police de la commune de Paris," 29 nivôse, Year II."

154. Ibid., carton 323, doss. 504, "Jugement du 23 pluviôse an II."

155. BHVP, manuscript 678, 2ème partie, Miscellaneous Writings, folio 79. I would like to thank Daniel Roche for sharing his transcription of these precious documents.

156. Ibid., folio 83 (my italics).

157. Ménétra had been arrested in summer 1792 as a moderate, but this appears to have occurred before his struggles with Duplessis, Langlois, and their faction. Jacques Ménétra, *Journal of My Life*, ed. Daniel Roche and Robert Darnton, trans. Arthur Goldhammer (New York: Columbia University Press, 1986), 223, n. 282.

158. BHVP, manuscript 678, 2ème partie, Miscellaneous Writings, folios 79–93.

159. AN W, carton 369, doss. 823, "Réflexions sur la nouvelle constitution donnée à la France par la Convention nationale."

160. Ibid., "Jugement qui condamne à la peine de mort la veuve Lesclapart, Webert, Suremain, la fille Deblaire, 1 prairial an II."

Chapter 8

1. The king's dismissal of Jacques Necker on July 12 sparked the agitation in Paris that culminated in the storming of the Bastille. On July 16, Louis reinstated him with the

new title "premier ministre des Finances," rather than "directeur général des Finances," the title he had held during prior appointments. "Letter to Gustav III of Sweden, August 16, 1789," in Anne-Louise-Germaine de Staël-Holstein, *Correspondance générale*, ed. Béatrice W. Jasinski (Paris: Jean-Jacques Pauvert, 1962), vol. 1, part 2, 328.

2. Ibid., "Letter to Nils Von Rosenstein," January 21, 1789, 274.

3. Jean-Marie Roland, *Compte rendu à la Convention nationale par Jean-Marie Roland, ministre de l'Intérieur, de toutes les parties de son département, de ses vues d'amélioration et de prospérité publique; le 6 janvier de l'an II de la République française* (Paris: Imprimerie nationale, 1793), 227 (my italics).

4. Ibid., 228.

5. Ibid., 229–230.

6. Roberto Romani, *National Character and Public Spirit in Britain and France, 1750–1914* (Cambridge: Cambridge University Press, 2002); J. G. A. Pocock, *The Machiavellian Moment: Florentine Political Thought and the Atlantic Republican Tradition* (Princeton: Princeton University Press, 1975); for commercial republicanism during the Directory, see James Livesey, *Making Democracy in the French Revolution* (Cambridge: Harvard University Press, 2001). For a recent account of the evolution from classical republicanism to liberal republicanism in the French Revolution, see Andrew Jainchill, *Rethinking Politics after the Terror: The Republican Origins of French Liberalism* (Ithaca: Cornell University Press, forthcoming [2008]).

7. Edith Bernardin, *J.-M. Roland et le ministère de l'Intérieur* (Paris: Société des Études Robespierristes, 1964), 3–4.

8. After the Terror, writers lamenting the abolition of the corporations in 1791 argued that society's mœurs had degenerated ever since. See Antoine-Louis Séguier and Louis-Pierre Deseine, *Mémoire sur la nécessité du rétablissement des maîtrises et corporations* (Paris: Imprimerie de Fain, 1815); *Rétablissez les maîtrises et la France est sauvée* (Paris: Imprimerie de Lerouge, Year V). I thank Allan Potofsky for these references.

9. Honoré-Gabriel Riqueti, comte de Mirabeau, *Sur la liberté de la presse* (Paris: Office technique de Presse, 1939), 54.

10. Ibid., 24–25.

11. *De la liberté de la presse* (1789), 25–26. (BNF Lb39–6787.)

12. Chavanel, *Réflexions sur quelques libelles et sur la liberté de la presse* (January 15, 1790), 3.

13. André Chénier, *Avis au peuple français sur ses véritables ennemis* (August 24, 1790), 15.

14. Ibid., 15–16.

15. Ibid., 16.

16. Ibid., 16–17.

17. Ibid., 49–50.

18. *Discours sur la censure publique et la calomnie patriotique: Lu dans une Société de patriotes* (1791), 6–8.

19. Ibid., 2.

20. Ibid., 10.

21. Louis-Félix Guynement de Kéralio, *De la liberté d'énoncer, d'écrire ou d'imprimer sa pensée* ([Paris]: L. Potier de Lille, 1790), 43–44.

22. Ibid., 18–19.

23. Ibid., 45 (my italics).

24. Ibid., 56.

25. Ibid., 41.

26. R. R. Palmer, *The Improvement of Humanity* (Princeton: Princeton University Press, 1985), 102–104.

27. Ibid., 94–102.

28. Camille Desmoulins, *Révolutions de France et de Brabant,* no. 93, 1–21 and no. 95, 29, in Palmer, *The Improvement of Humanity,* 99.

29. Anthanase Auger, *Catéchisme du citoyen français* (Paris: Crapert), 81–82.

30. Ibid., 86.

31. François Boissel, *Catéchisme du genre humain, dénoncé par le ci-devant évêque de Clermont à la séance du 5* [sic] *novembre 1789 de l'Assemblée nationale* (Paris:1792 [orig. 1789]), 30.

32. Ibid.

33. See the passages by Isaac-René-Guy Le Chapelier in *Moniteur,* 1:83, November 3–5, 1789, 134.

34. Boissel, *Catéchisme du genre humain,* 75.

35. Boissel, *Adresse de l'auteur du "Catéchisme du genre humain," aux utiles et vrais représentants de la nation française* (N.p., n.d), 8. See also his letter to the *comité des rapports,* in *Catéchisme du genre humain,* 79–80.

36. Gary Kates, *The Cercle Social, the Girondins, and the French Revolution* (Princeton: Princeton University Press, 1985), 100–110.

37. Jean-Claude Simonne, *Moyen de rendre les peuples plus libres et heureux, ou idées sur leur éducation* (Paris: Chez Grégoire, 1791), 1–5.

38. *Société des Jacobins,* 3:120.

39. The new clergy needed the registers and documents concerning the churches and congregations, but many of the old clergy refused to furnish them; *AP,* 38:179; Timothy Tackett, *Religion, Revolution, and Regional Culture in Eighteenth-Century France: The Ecclesiastical Oath of 1791* (Princeton: Princeton University Press, 1986), esp. 159–182.

40. Michael L. Kennedy, *The Jacobin Clubs in the French Revolution, The Middle Years* (Princeton: Princeton University Press, 1988), 200.

41. *AP,* 38:178–179.

42. Charles-Alexandre de Moy, *Accord de la religion et des cultes chez une nation libre* (Paris: Garnéry, Year IV [orig. late 1791 or early 1792]), 1.

43. Charles-Alexandre de Moy, *Discours qui a remporté les deux prix d'éloquence...sur le sujet: combien le respect pour les mœurs contribue au bonheur de l'État,* in Académie des sciences, belles-lettres et arts de Besançon, *Procès-verbaux, 1776* (Paris: Le Jay, 1776).

44. Moy, *Accord de la religion et des cultes,* 2. David Bell, *The Cult of the Nation in France: Inventing Nationalism, 1680–1800* (Cambridge: Harvard University Press, 2001), 159–168.

45. Moy, *Accord de la religion et des cultes,* 96.

46. Ibid., 102.

47. Ibid.

48. Ibid., 100.

49. *AP,* 38:365.

50. *Lettre à M. Gobel* (Paris: Imprimerie de Guerbart, 1792), 19–20.

51. *Épître dédicatoire à M. l'Évêque et les curés constitutionnels de Paris* (Paris: February 16, 1792), 5. This work was falsely attributed to Charles-Alexandre de Moy. The abbé Fauchet was a deputy, constitutional bishop, and cofounder of the Cercle Social.

52. *Le petit mot pour rire à M. le curé de Saint-Laurent* (Paris: Imprimerie Guerbart, April 1792), 4.

53. François-Xavier Lanthenas, *Des sociétés populaires considérées comme une branche essentielle de l'instruction publique* (Paris: Imprimerie du Cercle social, 1792), 17–18.

54. Ibid., 1.

55. Ibid., 3, 8.

56. For a list of counterrevolutionary tracts subsidized by the *liste-civile*, see *Huitième recueil de pièces inventoriées chez M. Delaporte, intendant de la liste civile* (Paris: Imprimerie nationale, [1792]). The correspondence between Delaporte and his agents reveal that political newspapers and brochures were being distributed. See *Pièces trouvées dans les papiers de MM. De Montmorin, Laporte, Intendants de la liste civile: Cinquième recueil* (Paris: Imprimerie nationale, [1792]), passim. For further documentation concerning the *liste-civile*, see Maurice Tourneux, *Bibliographie de l'histoire de Paris pendant la Révolution française* (Paris: Imprimerie Nouvelle, 1890), 1:312–315.

57. Claude Perroud, "Roland et la presse subventionnée," *La Révolution française*, no. 62 (1912): 208, 315–316.

58. It is not clear that Roland drew on the funds allotted for propaganda to print these speeches, since he did not actually start receiving them until May 13, 1792. (Ibid., 208.) Regardless, he circulated them throughout France with the Minister's seal; Bernardin, *J.-M. Roland et le ministère de l'Intérieur*, 515. Bernardin also mentions that Roland sent out Brissot's speeches on the war without including Robespierre's speeches.

59. Brissot and Guadet, *Discours de MM. Brissot et Guadet…prononcés à la séance de la Société des amis de la constitution, le 25 avril 1792* (Paris: Imprimerie du *Patriote Français*, 1792), avant-propos and 15–16.

60. *Société des Jacobins*, 3:557–558, 564.

61. BNF, manuscripts, Folio-LB41–5364, doc. 3, "Lettre/circulaire du ministre de l'Intérieur" (handwritten date, April 4, 1792), 3.

62. Ibid., doc. 1, *M. Roland aux administrateurs des départements*.

63. Ibid., doc. 3, "Lettre/circulaire du ministre de l'Intérieur." In a subsequent circular, Roland wrote, "It is only after exhausting the means of persuasion that coercive means should be employed," in ibid., doc. 26, "Le ministre de l'Intérieur aux corps administratifs, du 12 décembre 1792, l'an 1er de l'Égalité et de la République," 3.

64. Perroud, "La presse subventionnée," 211. Kates, *Cercle Social*, 231. Roland's speech appears in *Lettres et pièces intéressantes pour servir à l'histoire du Ministère de Roland, Servan et Clavière* (1792), which was published by the Cercle Social with Roland's secret funds.

65. For example, during the Girondin-bashing session at the Jacobin Club on October 9, 1792, an unnamed member coming from the provinces stated how he and

those in his community had been falsely led to credit Roland for August 10, since the only newspapers they received at the time were Brissot's *Patriote français* and the Girondin review *Chronique du mois*; see *Société des Jacobins*, 4:372.

66. As during Roland's first ministry, this sum was to be drawn from the Foreign Ministry's secret funds given to the Paris commune.

67. *AP*, 48:348.

68. For a list of archival sources concerning protest against August 10, see Alexandre Tuetey, ed., *Répertoire général des sources manuscrites de l'histoire de Paris pendant la Révolution française* (Paris: Imprimerie nouvelle, 1819–1914), 4, items 3747–3815.

69. Antoine-François Le Tellier was officially assigned to run the bureau, but Lanthenas took charge of it (Perroud, "Roland et la presse subventionnée," 320–321). The Rolands and Lanthenas had helped found patriotic societies in Lyon for this purpose. In the period before these societies became widespread in Lyon, local Jacobins had put income restrictions on membership in the club. Although the spread of popular societies might appear to have been inspired by a democratic desire to empower the people, their founders saw them as vehicles for civic instruction and public discipline. See Michael Kennedy, *The Jacobin Clubs: The Middle Years*, 46–47.

70. For Roland's own complaints about the failure of local administrators to instruct the people, see BNF, manuscripts, Folio LB41–5364, docs. 4, 9, and 13.

71. Bernardin confirms Mathiez's assessment of these efforts. Albert Mathiez, *La Révolution et l'Église* (Paris: A. Colin, 1910), 50–51, and Bernardin, *J.-M. Roland et le ministère de l'Intérieur*, 511.

72. Marcel Dorigny, "La propagande Girondine et le livre en 1792: Le bureau de l'esprit public," *Dix-huitième siècle*, no. 21 (1989): 203–215; Anne Kupiec, "La Gironde et le bureau d'esprit public: Livre et révolution," *Annales historiques de la Révolution française*, no. 302 (1995): 571–586.

73. For a list of publications, see BNF, manuscripts, nouv. acq. fr., 22423, doc. 136, "Roland à ses concitoyens."

74. This date is found in Roland's own published account of the bureau's subsidies, in ibid. For accounting errors, see Perroud's thorough auditing of the bureau's expenditures, "Roland et la presse subventionnée."

75. Bernardin, *J.-M. Roland et le ministère de l'Intérieur*, 518; Perroud, "Roland et la presse subventionnée," 321.

76. Anti-Montagnard publications appearing in Roland's books can be found in Perroud, "Roland et la presse subventionnée," 403–409; Dorigny, "La propagande Girondine," 209.

77. For an example, see *Moniteur*, 14:353, December 18, 1792, 760. Municipal administrators in Arras also attacked Roland. For the minister's apology, see BNF, manuscripts, nouv. acq. fr., 22423, doc. 261.

78. *Journal de la République française*, no. 38, November 2, 1792. Marat accused the Girondin deputies of spreading libels against Paris in the departments. He said that these calumnies had been debunked in Paris but that the Girondin manipulation of the postal system was impeding the circulation of good patriot publications, in Marat, *Oeuvres*

politiques, ed. Jacques De Cock and Charlotte Goëtz (Brussels: Pole Nord, 1989–1995), 8:5048.

79. Robespierre, "Lettre à ses commettants," 2nd series, no. 2, in *Oeuvres de Maximilien Robespierre*, ed. Gustave Laurent (Paris: Presses universitaires de France, 1961), 5:210, published around January 10, 1793.

80. Ibid., no. 1, 5:192.

81. The authorizations carried by these agents summarized their duties: "to work with the municipalities, districts, and departments to obtain the requisitions deemed necessary [by the agent] for the safety of the country." Pierre Caron, *Les missions du Conseil exécutif et de la Commune de Paris* (Paris: Presses universitaires de France, 1950), 29.

82. Caron concludes that these war-effort agents seldom abused their authority. Although they had been recruited by the Commune, they were not, according to Caron, radical, poor sans-culottes and should not be confused with the revolutionary armies of the following year. They were generally professionals or men of letters. It appears that Roland, fearful of Parisian radicals, sought to outflank them by shoring up his popularity in the provinces, capitalizing on local resentment against these agents; ibid., 140–145. Richard Cobb debunks the myth, echoed by Caron, of the proto-proletarian sans-culotte of the revolutionary armies, *Armées révolutionnaires: Instruments de la Terreur dans les départements, avril 1793—floréal an II* (Paris: Mouton, 1961), 1:342–361.

83. Caron, *Les missions du Conseil exécutif et de la Commune de Paris*, 51, 53, 66, 113–118, 157–158, 173 (n. 1).

84. *Société des Jacobins*, 4:371; *Compte-rendu au pouvoir exécutif national provisoire* (Paris: September 29, 1792), in AN AF II 412, plaq. 3315, pièce 2, in Caron, *Les missions du Conseil exécutif et de la Commune de Paris*, 119.

85. J.-P. Brissot, *député à la Convention nationale, à tous les républicains de France, sur la Société des Jacobins de Paris* (Paris: Cercle Social, October 24, 1792), 4.

86. Roland complained that his enemies were calumniating him and denied having used the *bureau d'esprit public* to "mislead or enslave opinion"; see "Le ministre de l'Intérieur aux corps administratifs, aux sociétés populaires, à tous ses concitoyens, le 22 janvier, l'an 2ᵉ," in *Moniteur*, 15:25, January 25, 1793, 262.

87. BNF, manuscripts, nouv. acq. fr., 22423, doc. 344. Several such letters are found in this series, from doc. 337 onward.

88. For denunciations against Roland, see Tuetey, *Répertoire general…*, 8, entries 2363, 2373, 2695, and 2794. For Roland's defense during the purge of the Girondins, see entry 2638.

89. AN AD XVIIIᶜ 219, no. 18, *Rapport fait par le citoyen Brival au nom du comité de sûreté générale, relativement aux papiers trouvés chez le citoyen Roland* (Paris: Imprimerie nationale, [1793]).

90. Roland, *Observations de l'ex-ministre Roland sur la rapport fait contre lui par le député Brival* (Paris: P. Delormel, 1793), 4–5.

91. Jeanne-Marie Phlipon Roland, *Mémoires de Madame Roland*, ed. Cl. Perroud (Paris: Plon, 1905), 1:129–130.

92. Ibid., 2:289.

93. Alphonse Aulard, *Recueil des actes du comité de Salut public* (Paris: Imprimerie nationale, 1889–1951), 8:399, letter by Delacroix and Legendre, 23 Brumaire, Year II.

94. AN H¹ 1448, "Instruction Destinée à diriger la conduite des commissaires patriotes envoyés dans les départements." Reproduced in Caron, *Les missions du conseil exécutif et de la Commune de Paris*, 72–74.

95. Richard Cobb, *The Police and the People* (Oxford: Oxford University Press, 1970), 52.

96. AN H¹ 1448, report of September 14, 1792.

97. Ibid., report of October 24, 1792.

98. Ibid., report of September 14, 1792.

99. Ibid., report of October 5, 1792.

100. Ibid., report unsigned and undated.

101. Ibid., report of December 31, 1792.

102. AN F7 3686⁶, report of September 11, 1792. Roland conveyed this view to the National Convention in his *Compte rendu par le ministre de l'Intérieur, en vertu du décret de la Convention nationale* (Paris, September 23, 1792), 14. See BNF, manuscripts, nouv. acq. fr., 7543.

103. AN H¹ 1448, report of September 3, 1792.

104. Ibid., letter of September, 1792.

105. Ibid., report of October 31, 1792.

106. Ibid., letter of November 25, 1792.

107. Ibid., letter to Roland, August 1792.

108. Ibid.

109. AN F1ᵇ II, Vendée, 1, report of October 4, 1792.

110. Ibid.

111. Ibid.

112. Ibid.

113. AN H¹ 1448, report of October 5, 1792.

114. Ibid., report of December 31, 1792.

115. Ibid., report of October 30, 1792.

116. Ibid., report of September 28, 1792.

117. Ibid., letters of October 11 and 17, 1792.

118. Perroud, "Roland et la presse subventionné," 415.

119. *AP*, 56:242.

120. Ibid.

121. Jean-Pierre Picqué, *La nécessité d'une censure publique* (Paris: Imprimerie nationale, [June 1793]), 9, 18.

122. Ibid., 13, 17.

123. Ibid., 11.

124. Ibid., 12.

125. Ibid., 15.

126. L. Prunelle, *Observations et projet de décret sur l'établissement d'un tribunal de la conscience du peuple* (Paris: Imprimerie nationale, 1793), 2.

127. Ibid., 7.

128. Ibid., 3–4.

129. Ibid., 4.

130. *Moniteur*, 16:156, 5 June 1793, 552, covering the session of 2 June.

131. Lanthenas, *Bases fondamentales de l'instruction publique et de toutes constitution libre, ou moyens de lier l'opinion publique, la morale...et le progrès de toutes les connaissances au gouvernement national-républicain* (Paris: Cercle social, 1793), 84.

132. Ibid., 77.

133. François-Xavier Lanthenas, *Censure publique ou nécessité de confier à un certain nombre de citoyens instruits et vertueux choisis et périodiquement renouvelés par la nation, la surveillance des mœurs, et de la morale de l'instruction publique* (Paris: Imprimerie nationale, August 1793), 2.

134. Ibid., 19–20.

135. Ibid., 22–24.

136. Ibid., 36–38.

137. Lanthenas, *Censure publique*, 28.

138. François-Xavier Lanthenas, *Religion civile proposée aux républiques pour lien des gouvernements représentatifs* (Paris: Imprimerie de Commingues, Year VI), 4th edition, n. 1, 50–51.

139. Ibid., 10.

140. Thiébault, *Traité sur l'esprit public*, 343–369. They formed a "first class" of priorities. The second class included encouragements for agriculture, industry, commerce, public instruction, the arts and sciences, and national festivals; see 369–392. I would like to thank Bernard Gainot for the reference.

141. Ibid., 79.

142. Immanuel Kant, "What Is Enlightenment?" in *Perpetual Peace and Other Essays*, 3rd ed., trans. Ted Humphrey (Indianapolis: Hackett, 1988), 42, 45.

143. Thiébault, *Traité sur l'esprit public*, 136.

144. Ibid., 81–84 and passim.

145. Ibid., 67.

146. Ibid., 193.

147. Pierre Caron, *Rapports des agents du ministre de l'intérieur dans les départements (1793–an 2)* (Paris: Imprimerie nationale, 1913), passim.

148. Ibid., 1: v.

149. Ibid., 1: xvi.

150. Ibid., 1: xxv.

151. Ibid., 1: xxx.

152. Claude Fauchet's 1790 opening address to the *Confédération des Amis de la Vérité*, cited in Dena Goodman, *The Republic of Letters: A Cultural History of the Enlightenment* (Ithaca: Cornell University Press, 1994), 290.

153. Caron, *Rapports des agents du ministre de l'intérieur*, 1: xxvi–xxxiii.

154. Alphonse Aulard, *Paris pendant la réaction thermidorienne et sous le Directoire* (Paris: L. Cerf, 1899), 3:477.

155. Alain Rey, *Dictionnaire historique de la langue française* (Paris: Dictionnaire Le Robert, 1993), 1:728.

156. [Du Lac], *Le glaive vengeur de la République française . . . ou galerie révolutionnaire, contenant les noms . . . de tous les grands conspirateurs et traîtres à la patrie, dont la tête est tombée sous le glaive national, par arrêt du tribunal révolutionnaire, établie à Paris . . . par un ami de la Révolution, des mœurs et de la justice* (Paris: Galletti, Year II).

157. Ibid., 200.

158. Marisa Linton, "Robespierre's Political Principles," in *Robespierre*, ed. Colin Haydon and William Doyle (Cambridge: Cambridge University Press, 1999), 49–50.

Conclusion

1. [Du Lac], *Le glaive vengeur de la République française . . . ou galerie révolutionnaire, contenant les noms . . . de tous les grands conspirateurs et traîtres à la patrie, dont la tête est tombée sous le glaive national, par arrêt du tribunal révolutionnaire, établie à Paris . . . par un ami de la Révolution, des mœurs et de la justice* (Paris: Galletti, Year II), 131–132.

2. Gita May, *Madame Roland and the Age of Revolution* (New York: Columbia University Press, 1970), 288.

3. AN AD XVIIIc 334, no. 7, *Rapport et décrets sur le prompt jugement des émigrés trouvés sur le territoire de la République . . . suivi du discours [sur la liberté de la presse] du citoyen Louvet, Représentant du peuple* (Paris: Imprimerie de la République, Year III), 18 (my italics).

4. André Morellet, *Pensées libres sur la liberté de la presse, à l'occasion d'un rapport du représentant Chénier à la Convention nationale, du 12 floréal* (Paris: Maret, [Year III]), 5, 6. Jean-François La Harpe also criticized the law; *La liberté de la presse défendue, par La Harpe, contre Chénier* (Paris: Migneret, Year III).

5. Hugh Gough, *The Newspaper Press in the French Revolution* (Chicago: Dorsey Press, 1988), 124.

6. "The obligations of each individual to society consist in defending it, serving it, submitting to its laws, and *respecting those who are organs thereof*." John Hall Stewart, *A Documentary Survey of the French Revolution* (New York: Macmillan, 1951), 574.

7. Jacques Godechot, "La presse française sous la Révolution et l'Empire," in *Histoire générale de la presse française*, ed. Claude Bellanger, Jacques Godechot, Pierre Guiral, and Fernand Terrou (Paris: Presses universitaires de France, 1969), 1:523.

8. Robert Allen, *Les tribunaux criminels sous la Révolution et l'Empire, 1792–1811* (Rennes: Presses Universitaires de Rennes, 2005), 189–229.

9. *Moniteur*, no. 44, 14 Brumaire, Year V (November 4, 1796), 174.

10. Ibid.

11. Godechot, "La presse française . . . ," 543–544, 547; Gough, *The Newspaper Press in the French Revolution*, 142.

12. William M. Reddy, *The Invisible Code: Honor and Sentiment in Postrevolutionary France, 1815–1848* (Berkeley: University of California Press, 1997). See also Robert Nye, *Masculinity and Male Codes of Honor in Modern France* (New York: Oxford University Press, 1993), and Joan Landes, *Women and the Public Sphere in the Age of Revolution* (Ithaca: Cornell University Press, 1988).

13. For the earlier development of national consciousness, see David A. Bell, *The Cult of the Nation in France: Inventing Nationalism, 1680–1800* (Cambridge: Harvard University Press, 2001).

14. Howard G. Brown, *Ending the French Revolution: Violence, Justice, and Repression from the Terror to Napoleon* (Charlottesville: University of Virginia Press, 2006); see also his "Tips, Traps and Tropes: Catching Thieves in Post-Revolutionary Paris," in Clive Emsley and Haia Shpayer-Makov, eds., *Police Detectives in History, 1750–1950* (Aldershot, England: Ashgate, 2006), 33–60.

15. AN: F⁷ 3065, 3448–3463, 3818–3820. For surveillance in Paris, see the three series edited by Alphonse Aulard, *Paris pendant la réaction thermidorienne et sous le Directoire* (Paris: L. Cerf, 1898–1902), *Paris sous le Consulat* (Paris: L. Cerf, 1903–1909), and *Paris sous le premier Empire* (Paris: L. Cerf, 1912–1923). The three series carry the subtitle *Recueil de documents pour l'histoire de l'esprit public à Paris.*

16. For revolutionary regulation of the theater, see F. W. J. Hemmings, *Theatre and State in France, 1760–1905* (Cambridge: Cambridge University Press, 1994), 55–91; Victor Hallays-Dabot, *Histoire de la censure théâtrale en France* (Paris: E. Dentu, 1862), 143–206. For surveillance and regulation of the press at postal offices, see BP:4 1202, Jean Casnave, Jean Duran, and Alain Tislowitz, "Journaux et écrits périodiques, leur diffusion par la Poste et les éditeurs depuis le XVIIIe siècle," unpublished manuscript (1985), and Eugène Vaillé, *Le Cabinet noir* (Paris: Presses universitaires de France, 1950), 211–337. For the stamp duty, subsidies, and postal surveillance, see Gough, *The Newspaper Press in the French Revolution*, 125–128, 141–142. For cultural patronage and state propaganda, see Carla Hesse, *Publishing and Cultural Politics in Revolutionary Paris, 1789–1810* (Berkeley: University of California Press, 1991), 144–162, and Laurence Walter Stoll, "The 'Bureau politique' and the Management of the Popular Press: A Study of the Second Directory's Attempt to Develop a Directorial Ideology and Manipulate the Newspapers" (Ph.D. dissertation, University of Wisconsin–Madison, 1975).

17. Godechot, "La presse française…," 550–551.

18. BP:4 1202, Jean Casnave et al., "Journaux et écrits périodiques…" The measure was promulgated on 27 Prairial, Year IX.

19. André Cabanis, *La Presse sous le Consulat et l'Empire* (Paris: Société des Études Robespierristes, 1975), 176.

20. Godechot, "La presse française…," 553; Cabanis, *La Presse sous le Consulat et l'Empire*, 166.

21. John Merriman detects a general consolidation and reinforcement of policing during the nineteenth century; *Police Stories: Building the French State, 1815–1851* (New York: Oxford University Press, 2006), esp. 89–117.

22. François Guizot, *Quelques idées sur la liberté de la presse* (Paris: Le Normant, 1814), 25.

23. Ibid., 26, 28.

24. Ibid., 32.

25. Ibid., 31, 51.

26. Claude Bellanger, Jacques Godechot, Pierre Guiral, and Fernand Terrou, eds., *Histoire générale de la presse* (Paris: Presses universitaires de France, 1969), vol. 2, passim.

27. For the original text of the 1881 press law, see J.-B. Duvergier, ed., *Collection complète des lois, décrets, ordonnances, règlements* (Bad Feilnbach, Germany: Schmidt Periodicals GmbH, 1995), vol. 81, 290–324. For the text with subsequent modifications and amendments, see "Loi du 29 juillet 1881 sur la liberté de la presse," http://www.culture.gouv.fr/culture/infos-pratiques/droit-culture/cinema/pdf/1-290781.pdf, consulted on September 20, 2007.

28. Jean-Pierre Machelon, *La République contre les libertés?* (Paris: Presses de la Fondation nationale des Sciences politiques, 1976), 440–447. I would like to thank John Merriman for this reference.

29. For political surveillance in the nineteenth and early twentieth centuries, see AN: F⁷ 12428–12521, 12552–12565, 12842–12847, 12852–12869, 13053–13052.

30. François Furet, *Revolutionary France, 1770–1880*, trans. Antonia Nevill (Malden, Mass.: Blackwell Publishing Limited, 1992 [orig. 1989]).

31. Stanley Fish, *There's No Such Thing as Free Speech…and It's a Good Thing, Too* (Oxford: Oxford University Press, 1994); Herbert Marcuse, "Repressive Tolerance," in Robert Paul Wolff, Barrington Moore Jr., and Herbert Marcuse, *A Critique of Pure Tolerance* (Boston: Beacon Press, 1965).

32. Noam Chomsky, "Free Speech in a Democracy," *Daily Camera* (September 1985), http://www.chomsky.info/letters/198509—.htm, consulted on September 17, 2007.

33. Burdette Kinne, "Voltaire Never Said It!" *Modern Language Notes*, LVIII (Nov, 1943), 354–535. To compromise Rousseau, Voltaire wrote to Genevan authorities signaling the heresies in Rousseau's writings, implying that they should take action. See Christopher Kelly, *Rousseau as Author: Consecrating One's Life to the Truth* (Chicago: University of Chicago Press, 2003), 10.

34. In its 2006 annual index of 168 nations ranked according to their respect for press freedom, Reporters Without Borders put the United States at 53 among 168 countries (along with Botswana, Croatia, and Tonga), down from the rank of 17 in 2002. France also dropped precipitously, ranking at 35 (along with Australia, Bulgaria, and Mali), a decline of 24 points from its rank of 11 in 2002. See http://www.rsf.org/rubrique.php3?id_rubrique=639, consulted on September 20, 2007.

35. For the arrests of Judith Miller (imprisoned for nearly three months), Joshua Wolf (imprisoned for over seven months), Pulitzer Prize–winning photographer Bilal Hussein and Sami Al Haj (held in Guantanamo since 2003), see Reporters Without Borders, "United States—Annual Report 2007" at http://www.rsf.org/article.php3?id_article=20542, consulted September 20, 2007, and Reporters Without Borders, "Letter to Robert Gates on first anniversary of AP photographer Bilal Hussein's arrest" (April 12, 2007), http://www.rsf.org/article.php3?id_article=21681, consulted on September 20, 2007.

36. Frank Rich, "The White House Stages Its 'Daily Show,'" *New York Times* (February 20, 2005), http://www.nytimes.com/2005/02/20/arts/20rich.html?ex=1266642000&en=9245d7b440e36c54&ei=5088&partner=rssnyt, consulted September 20, 2007; PBS, "Government 'News,'" (May 13, 2005), http://www.pbs.org/newshour/bb/media/jan-june05/vnr_5–13.html, consulted September 29, 2007.

37. By October 16, 2006, twelve journalists in Russia had been murdered during Putin's presidency. See the Committee to Protect Journalists, http://www.cpj.org/Briefings/2005/russia_murders/russia_murders.html, consulted September 20, 2007. For the deaths of journalists in Iraq, see the Reporters Without Borders report, "Three Years of Slaughter in Iraq," March 20, 2006, http://www.rsf.org/article.php3?id_article=16793. Both sites were consulted on September 15, 2007.

38. Lawrence Soley, *Censorship Inc.: The Corporate Threat to Free Speech in the United States* (New York: Monthly Review Press, 2002); Cass R. Sunstein, *Republic.com 2.0* (Princeton: Princeton University Press, 2007).

39. Jérôme Pétion de Villeneuve, *Discours sur la liberté de la presse* (Paris: Imprimerie nationale, 1791), 4.

40. Joanne Freeman, *Affairs of Honor: National Politics in the New Republic* (New Haven: Yale University Press, 2002).

41. For how honor figured in the culture of slavery and the post–Civil War treatment of blacks by whites, see Bertram Wyatt-Brown, *Honor and Violence in the Old South* (New York: Oxford University Press, 1986), 154–186; W. Fitzhugh Brundage, *Lynching in the New South: Georgia and Virginia, 1880–1930* (Urbana: University of Illinois Press, 1993), 50–53, 70–71; I would like to thank Glenda Gilmore for her insights on this matter; she stresses the importance of social and economic interests in motivating invocations of honor.

42. Michel Foucault, "What Is Enlightenment?" in *The Foucault Reader*, ed. Paul Rabinow (New York: Pantheon Books, 1984), 50.

Works Cited

Primary Sources

Manuscripts and Archival Sources

Archives Nationales (AN). Series AD XVIII^c, Impressions des Assemblées constituante, législative et de la Convention nationale: cartons 219, 334.

———. Series AF II, Conseil exécutif provisoire et Convention, comité de Salut public. cartons 45, 412.

———. Series BB³, Affaires criminelles, cartons 19, 19(5).

———. Series C, Assemblées nationales. Assemblée législative, papiers de la Haute Cour d'Orléans, carton 170.

———. Series D XXIXbis, Comité des recherches, cartons 1–4, 6–9, 11–16, 28, 32(b)–33, 37, 42.

———. Series D XXIX, Comité des rapports, carton 63.

———. Series F^1b II, Série départementale. Vendée, carton 1.

———. Series F^1c III, Esprit public et élections. Seine, carton 13.

———. Series F⁷ Police, cartons 3065, 3686⁶, 4432.

———. Series H¹ (fond anciens), Administrations locales et comptabilités diverses. Pay d'États, pays d'Élections, Intendances, carton 1448.

———. Series W , Juridictions extraordinaires, cartons 292, 323, 369, 480.

———. Series Y, Châtelet de Paris et prévôté d'Île-de-France. Office de Grandin et prédécesseurs, carton 13320 (minutes, 1777–1791). Chambre criminelle, cartons 10504, 10506, 10508 (a-b), 10546 (lèse-nation affairs).

———. Series Z³, Juridictions spéciales et ordinaires, carton 116.

Archives Départementales du Rhône (ADR). Series 26 L, Tribunaux: Informations, enquêtes, interrogations, décisions, carton 550.

———. Series 1 L, Imprimerie et presse: Surveillance des journaux, carton 459.

Archives municipales de Marseille (AMM). Series I 1, Police des théâtres, carton 550.

Archives municipales de Bordeaux (AMB). Series I, Imprimerie, presse périodique, carton 38.

Bibliothèque nationale de France (BNF). Manuscrits: Nouvelles acquisitions françaises, cartons, 7543, 22423. Folios: LB41–5364, LB41–5365.

Bibliothèque de la Poste (BP). Series 4 1202, Casnave, Jean, Jean Duran, and Alain Tislowitz, "Journaux et écrits périodiques, leur diffusion par la Poste et les éditeurs depuis le XVIIIe siècle," unpublished manuscript (1985).

Bibliothèque historique de la ville de Paris (BHVP). Manuscript 678, Jacques Ménétra, "Journal de ma vie," 2nd part, Misc. Writings, folios 79–83.

Published Sources: Newspapers and Unattributed

L'Ami du peuple, ou le publiciste parisien et impartiel. Edited by Jean-Paul Marat. [Paris]: Imprimerie de Roze, de Marat, 1789–1792.

Arrêt de la cour de Parlement: Qui condamne Henry Dufrancey & Etienne Virloy, dit La Jeunesse, à faire amende honorable & à être rompus vifs: & François Meunier à faire aussi amende honorable, & à être pendu en place de Grève, pour faux témoignage & calomnie contre le nommé Roi de Pierrefite . . . : Du sept février 1755. Paris: Imprimerie Grangé, 1755.

Complot du clergé découvert. Paris and Marseille: Imprimerie de Paris (Gorsas) and Imprimerie de F. Brebion, 1790.

Compte rendu au pouvoir exécutif national provisoire. Paris: 1792.

Contre la multiplicité et le danger des brochures, par l'auteur de l'écrit intitulé: "Je ne suis pas de l'avis de tout le monde." 1789.

De la liberté de la presse. [BNF, LB39–6787]: 1789.

De la morale naturelle suivie du bonheur des sots. Meister Jacques-Herni Necker [*sic*]. Paris: 1788.

Dictionnaire de l'Académie française. 3rd ed. 2 vols. Paris: J.-B. Coignard, 1740.

Dictionnaire de l'Académie française. Paris: Veuve de Bernard Brunet, 1762.

Discours sur la censure publique et la calomnie patriotique: Lu dans une société de patriotes. [Paris]: Veuve Hérissant, 1791.

Épître dédicatoire à M. l'Évêque et MM. les curés constitutionnels de Paris. Paris: 1792.

Exposition des principes sur la Constitution civile du clergé, par les évêques députés à l'Assemblée nationale. Paris: Le Clère, 1801.

Extrait du registre des délibérations de l'assemblée du district des Cordeliers du 19 juin 1790. Paris: Moromo, 1790.

Gazette de Paris. Edited by Barnabe Farmain de Rozoi. Paris: De Bray, 1789–1792.

Gazette des nouveaux tribunaux. Edited by Louis-François Jauffret. Paris: Veuve Desaint (L.-P. Couret et Perlet), 1791.

Grande dénonciation de l'arrestation de deux citoyens par le comité des recherches. [circa 1791].

Huitième recueil de pièces inventoriées chez M. Delaporte, intendant de la liste civile. Paris: Imprimerie nationale, [1792].

Instructions envoyées par M. le duc d'Orléans pour les personnes chargées de sa procuration aux assemblées des bailliages, relatives aux États-généraux, suivie de délibérations à prendre dans les assemblées. 1789.

Journal de la Haute Cour nationale. Paris: Cussac and Mme Lesclapart, 1791–1792.

Journal de la République française. Edited by Jean-Paul Marat. [Paris]: Imprimerie de Marat, 1792–1793.

Journal de Paris. Paris: Quillau, 1789–1790.

Jugement en dernier ressort, rendu publiquement à l'audience du parc civil du Châtelet de Paris. [Paris]: Veuve Desaint.

Lettre à Gobel. [Paris]: Imprimerie de Guerbart, An IV de la liberté [orig. 1792].

Lettres et pièces intéressantes pour servir à l'histoire du ministère de Roland, Servan et Clavière. Paris: Cercle social, 1792.

Les mânes de M. Métra ou ses réflexions posthumes pour guider ses confrères les gobe-mouches des Tuileries, du Luxembourg et du Palais-Royal, sur les reformes à proposer aux États-généraux. Paris: aux Tuileries, 1789.

Mémoire pour les criminels de lèse-nation. [BNF: LB39–4754].

Mémoires de la société des lettres, sciences et arts de l'Aveyron. Vol. 17. Rodez: Société des lettres, sciences et arts de l'Aveyron, 1906.

Mémoires secrets pour servir à l'histoire de la république des lettres en France ... Par feu M. de Bachaumont. 8 vols. London [Amsterdam?]: John Adamson, 1777.

Et moi aussi, je suis patriote: M. le marquis de Saint-Huruge défendu par un homme qui ne le connaît pas. By Samoht. [1789].

Nouvelle déclaration et pétition des Catholiques de Nîmes. Nîmes: 1790.

L'Observateur. Edited by Gabriel Feydel. [Paris]: Garnery et Volland, 1789–1790.

Opérations du Tribunal de la Haute Cour nationale provisoire, établi à Orléans pour juger les crimes de lèze-nation. Paris: L. P. Couret, 1791.

Patriote français. Edited by Jaques-Pierre Brissot [de Warville]. Paris: Buisson, 1789–1791; Paris: Imprimerie du *Patriote français,* 1791–1793.

Le petit mot pour rire à M. le curé de Saint-Laurent. Paris: Guerbart, 1792.

Pièces justificatives, exposé de la conduite et des motifs du district des Cordeliers, concernant le décret de prise de corps prononcé par le Châtelet contre le sieur Marat le 8 octobre, et mis à exécution le 22 janvier 1790. [Paris]: Momoro, [1790].

Pièces trouvées dans les papiers de MM. de Montmorin, Laporte, intendants de la liste civile: Cinquième recueil. Paris: Imprimerie nationale, [1792].

Le pour et le contre sur la liberté de la presse, par un impartial. Imprimerie Perlet, [circa 1790].

Rapport fait par le citoyen Brival au nom du comité de sûreté générale, relativement aux papiers trouvés chez le citoyen Roland. Paris: Imprimerie nationale, 1793.

Réimpression de l'ancien Moniteur, *seule histoire authentique et inaltérée de la Révolution française depuis la réunion des États-généraux jusqu'au Consulat (mai 1789–novembre 1799) avec des notes explicatives.* 32 vols. Paris: Plon Frères, 1850–1854.

Réponse aux instructions envoyées par S. A. S. monseigneur le duc d'Orléans, à ses chargés de procuration dans ses bailliages, relativement aux États-généraux. 1789.

Révolutions de France et de Brabant. Edited by Camille Desmoulins. [Paris]: 1789–1791.

Révolutions de Paris. Paris: Prudhomme, 1789–1791.

Théorie de la liberté de la presse. Imprimerie Pougin, 1790.

Traité sur la calomnie en forme de lettre à Mr le Chevalier de C***. Paris: P. Lesclapart, 1769.

Le véritable tableau de la calomnie et le portraict des médisans, exposez en public, par la vertu triomphante du vice; avec un discours moral sur le mesme sujet. Paris: 1649.

Published Sources: Attributed

Auger, Athanase. *Cathéchisme du citoyen français.* Paris: Crapert, [1791].

Aulard, Alphonse, ed. *Paris pendant la réaction thermidorienne et sous le Directoire: Recueil de documents pour l'histoire de l'esprit public à Paris.* 5 vols. Paris: L. Cerf, 1898–1902.

——, ed. *Paris sous le Consulat: Recueil de documents pour l'histoire de l'esprit public à Paris.* 4 vols. Paris: L. Cerf, 1903–1909.

——, ed. *Paris sous le premier Empire: Recueil de documents pour l'histoire de l'esprit public à Paris.* 3 vols. Paris: L. Cerf, 1912–1923.

——, ed. *Recueil des actes du Comité de Salut public, avec la correspondance officielle des représentants en mission et le registre du Conseil exécutif provisoire.* 28 vols. Paris: Imprimerie nationale, 1889–1951.

——, ed. *La Société des Jacobins: Recueil des documents pour l'histoire du club des Jacobins de Paris.* 6 vols. Paris: D. Jouaust, 1889–1997.

Bailly, Jean-Sylvain. *Mémoires de Bailly, avec une notice sur sa vie, des notes et des éclaircissements historiques.* Edited by François Barrière and Albin de Berville. 3 vols. Paris: Baudouin Frères, 1821–1822.

Beaumarchais, [Pierre-Augustin Caron de]. *Le barbier de Séville, suivi par Jean Bête à la foire.* Preface by Jacques Scherer. Paris: Gallimard, 1982.

Bergasse, Nicolas. *Discours sur les crimes et les tribunaux de haute trahison, par M. Bergasse, pour servir de suite à son discours sur l'organisation du pouvoir judiciaire.*

Billecocq, Jean-Baptiste-Louis. *Dénonciation aux États-généraux du plus cruel fléau de la société, ou de la nécessité d'une loi précise contre les calomniateurs.* 1789.

Blackstone, William. *Commentaries on the Laws of England.* 4 vols. Dublin: Printed for John Exshaw et al., 1770.

Bloch, Camille. *Cahiers de doléances du bailliage d'Orléans pour les États-généraux de 1789.* 2 vols. Orléans: Imprimerie Orléanaise, 1906–1907.

Boissel, François. *Adresse de l'auteur du "Catéchisme du genre humain," aux utiles et vrais représentants de la nation française.* [Circa 1790].

Boissel, François. *Le catéchisme du genre humain, dénoncé par le ci-devant évêque de Clermont, à la séance du 5 novembre 1789, de l'Assemblée nationale.* 2nd ed. Paris: 1792.

Bouchel, Laurent. *La bibliothèque ou trésor du droit français où sont traitées les matières civiles, criminelles et bénéficiales.* "Augmentée en cette nouvelle édition par" Jean Bechefer. Nouvelle édition ed. 3 vols. [orig. 2 vols]. Paris: Jean Girin et Barthlemy Rivière, 1671.

Boullemer de la Martinière. *Compte rendu à l'assemblée des représentants de la commune, le 11 mai 1790, par le procureur-syndic de la commune, des travaux du parquet depuis le mois d'octobre 1789.* Paris: Lottin, 1790.

Brissot de Warville, Jacques-Pierre. *Discours de J.-P. Brissot, député du département de Paris, sur les causes des dangers de la patrie, et sur les mesures à prendre.* Paris: Imprimerie nationale, 1792.

——. *J.-P. Brissot, député à la Convention nationale, à tous les républicains de France, sur la Société des Jacobins de Paris.* Paris: Cercle social, 1792.

——. *Mémoire aux États-généraux, sur la nécessité de rendre, dès ce moment, la presse libre et surtout pour les journaux politiques.* 1789.

———. *Plan de conduite pour les députés du peuple aux États-généraux de 1789.* [May 1789].

Brissot, J.-P., and Margérite-Élie Gaudet. *Discours de MM. Brissot et Guadet...prononcés à la séance de la Société des amis de la constitution, le 25 avril 1792.* Paris: Imprimerie du *Patriote français,* 1792.

Burke, Edmund. *The Correspondence of Edmund Burke.* Edited by Thomas W. Copeland. 10 vols. Cambridge: Cambridge University Press, 1958–1978.

———. *Reflections on the Revolution in France.* Edited by Frank M. Turner. New Haven: Yale University Press, 2003.

Calonne, Charles-Alexandre de. *Lettre de M. de Calonne...à M. de Thémines, évêque de Blois, sur son ouvrage intitulé: "Instructions et cahier du hameau de Madon." Avec la réponse de ce prélat et une seconde lettre de M. de Calonne.* London: T. Spilsbury, 1789.

Caron, Pierre, ed. *Rapports des agents du ministre de l'Intérieur dans les départements (1793–an II).* 2 vols. Paris: Imprimerie nationale, 1913.

Charmasse, A. de. *Cahiers des paroisses et communautés du bailliage d'Autun.* Autun: Dejussieux, 1985.

Chassin, Charles-Louis. *Les élections et les cahiers de Paris en 1789.* 4 vols. Paris: Jouaust et Sigaux, 1888–1889.

Chavanel. *Réflexions sur quelques libelles et sur la liberté de la presse.* 1790.

Chénier, André. *Avis au peuple français sur ses véritables ennemis.* [1790].

Committee to Protect Journalists. "Russia: Thirteen Murders, No Justice." Web page, [accessed 15 September 2007]. Available at http://www.cpj.org/Briefings/2005/russia_murders/russia_murders.html.

Condorcet, Jean-Antoine-Nicolas de Caritat marquis de. "Fragments sur la liberté de la presse." *Oeuvres de Condorcet.* Edited by M.-F. Arago and A. Condorcet O'Conner. Vol. 11, 254–314. 12 vols. Paris: Firmin Didot Frères, 1847–1849.

———. "Lettres d'un gentilhomme à MM. du tiers état." *Oeuvres de Condorcet.* Edited by M.-F. Arago. Vol. 9, 215–259. 12 vols. Paris: Firmin Didot Frères, 1847–1849.

Coulmiers, François Simonnet d'Escolmiers, dit l'abbé d'Abbecourt. *Motion de l'abbé d'Abbecourt (de Coulmiers), du 1er juillet 1790, sur la déclaration signée d'une partie des membres de l'Assemblée nationale.* Paris: [1790].

Dareau, François. *Traité des injures dans l'ordre judiciaire: Ouvrage qui renferme particulièrement la jurisprudence du petit-criminel.* Paris: Parult père, 1775.

De Lamet, and Fromageau (Docteurs de la Maison et Société de Sorbonne). *Le Dictionnaire des cas de conscience, décidés suivant les principes de la morale, les usages de la discipline ecclésiastique, l'autorité des conciles et des canonistes, et la jurisprudence du royaume.* 2 vols. Paris: Aux dépens de la Compagnie, 1740.

Delamare, Nicolas. *Traité de la police, où l'on trouvera l'histoire de son établissement, les fonctions et les prérogatives de ses magistrats, toutes les lois et tous les règlements qui la concernent...* 1st ed. 4 vols. Paris: Jean & Pierre Cot [later volumes: Brunet, Herissant], 1705–1738.

Desmoulins, Camille. *Réclamation en faveur du marquis de Saint-Huruge.* [1789].

Diderot, Denis. "Lettre historique et politique adressée à un magistrat sur le commerce de la librairie." In *Oeuvres complètes de Diderot.* Edited by J. Assézat and Maurice Tourneux. Vol. 18, 7–75. 20 vols. Paris: Garnier Frères, 1876.

Diderot, Denis, and Jean Le Rond d'Alembert, eds. *Encyclopédie ou dictionnaire raisonné des sciences, des arts et des métiers.* 17 vols. Paris [and Neuchâtel]: Briasson [Samuel Faulche], 1751–1765.

Douarche, A. *Les tribunaux civils de Paris pendant la Révolution.* 2 vols. Paris: Cerf, 1905.

[Du Lac]. *Le glaive vengeur de la République française . . . ou galerie révolutionnaire, contenant les noms . . . de tous les grands conspirateurs et traîtres à la patrie, dont la tête est tombée sous le glaive national, par arrêt du tribunal révolutionnaire, établie à Paris . . . par un ami de la Révolution, des mœurs et de la justice.* Paris: Galletti, An II.

Duclos, Charles. *Considérations sur les mœurs de ce siècle.* Introduction and notes by Carole Dornier. Critical ed. Paris: Champion, 2000.

Duvergier, J.-B., ed. *Collection complète des lois, décrets, ordonnances, règlements.* Reprint ed. 149 vols. Bad Feilnbach, Germany: Schmidt Periodicals GmbH, 1995.

Étienne, Charles, ed. *Cahiers de doléances du bailliage de Vézelise.* Vol. 3, 5 vols. Cahiers des bailliages des généralités de Metz et de Nancy pour les Etats-généraux de 1789. Nancy: Berger-Levrault, 1907–1946.

Ferrières Sauveboeuf, Louis-François. *Réflexions politiques sur le gouvernement révolutionnaire, la liberté de la presse et les élections par le peuple dans les circonstances actuelles.* [Paris]: Roblot, [1793–1794].

Français, M. *Projet de décret sur les troubles intérieurs, lu à l'Assemblée nationale au nom du comité des douze le 5 mai 1792.* [Paris]: Imprimerie nationale, 1792.

France. *Procès-verbal de l'Assemblée nationale.* 75 vols. Paris: Baudouin, 1789–1791.

Furetière, Antoine. *Dictionnaire universel, contenant généralement tous les mots français tant vieux que modernes, et les termes de toutes les sciences & des arts.* 2 vols. La Haye: 1694.

Gensonné, Armand. *Discours de M. Gensonné, député du département de la Gironde, sur la police de sûreté générale; prononcé le 30 mai 1792.* [Paris]: Imprimerie nationale, 1792.

Grotius, Hugo. *De Iure Praedai Commentarius: Commentary on the Law of Prize and Booty.* Translated by Gwladys L. Williams and Walter H. Zeydel. 2 vols. *The Classic of International Law.* Oxford: Clarendon Press, 1950.

Guizot, François. *Quelques idées sur la liberté de la presse.* Paris: Le Normant, 1814.

Holbach, Paul-Henri-Deitrich baron de. *La morale universelle ou les devoirs de l'homme fondés sur la nature.* Amsterdam: M. Rey, 1776.

Hume, David. "Of the Liberty of the Press." *Essays Moral and Political.* 2nd ed. Edinburgh: Printed for A. Kincaid, 1742.

Jourdan, Athanase-Jean-Léger, Decrusy, Isambert, Armet, and Taillandie, eds. *Recueil général des anciennes lois françaises depuis 420 jusqu'à la Révolution de 1789.* 29 vols. Paris: Plon and Belin-Leprieur, 1821–1833.

Jousse, Daniel. *Traité de la justice criminelle de France.* Vol. 3, 4 vols. Paris: Debure, 1771.

Jérôme, Léon. *Les élections et cahiers du clergé lorrain aux États-généraux de 1789.* Paris: Berger-Levrault, 1899.

Kant, Immanuel. "What Is Enlightenment?" In *Perpetual Peace and Other Essays.* Translated by Ted Humphrey. 3rd ed. Indianapolis: Hackett Publishing Company, 1988.

Kéralio, Louis-Félix Guynement de. *De la liberté d'énoncer, d'écrire ou d'imprimer sa pensée.* [Paris]: L. Potier de Lille, 1790.

——. *De la liberté de la presse*. Paris: L. Potier de Lille, 1790.

La Bruyère, Jean de. *Les caractères de Théophraste traduits du grec avec les caractères ou les mœurs de ce siècle*. Edited by Marc Escola. Paris: Honoré Champion, 1999.

La Harpe, Jean-François. *La liberté de la presse défendue, par La Harpe, contre Chénier*. Paris: Migneret, An III.

La Révellière-Lépeaux, Louis de. *Plaintes et désirs des communes tant de ville que de campagne.*

Lacroix, Sigismond, ed. *Actes de la Commune de Paris pendant la Révolution*. 1st and 2nd series. 19 vols. Paris: L. Cerf, 1894–1955.

[Lacroix, Sébastien Brumeaux de]. *Trahison découverte du comte de Mirabeau.* [Paris]: Imprimerie de Guillaume junior.

Lanthenas, François-Xavier. *Censure publique ou nécessité de confier à un certain nombre de citoyens instruits et vertueux choisis et périodiquement renouvelés par la nation, la surveillance des mœurs, et de la morale de l'instruction publique*. Paris: Imprimerie nationale, 1793.

——. *Bases fondamentales de l'instruction publique et de toute constitution libre, ou moyens de lier l'opinion publique, la morale... et le progrès de toutes les connaissances au gouvernement national-républicain*. 1st ed. Paris: Imprimerie du Cercle social, 1793.

——. *Bases fondamentales de l'instruction publique et de toute constitution libre, ou moyens de lier l'opinion publique, la morale... et le progrès de toutes les connaissances au gouvernement national-républicain*. 2nd ed. Paris: Imprimerie nationale, 1793.

——. *De la liberté indéfinie de la presse, et de l'importance de ne soumettre la communication des pensées qu'à l'opinion publique. Adressé et recommandé à toutes les sociétés patriotiques, populaires et fraternelles, de l'Empire français*. Paris: Imprimerie du *Patriote Français*, 1791.

——. *Des sociétés populaires considérées comme une branche essentielle de l'instruction publique*. Paris: Imprimerie du Cercle social, 1792.

Levis, M. le duc de. *Souvenirs et portraits, 1780–1789, nouvelle édition, augmentée d'articles supprimés par la censure de Buonaparte*. Paris: Beaupré, 1815.

Linguet, Simon-Nicolas-Henri. *Théorie du libelle, ou, l'art de calomnier avec fruit*. Amsterdam [Paris]: 1775.

Louvet, Jean-Baptiste. *Rapport et décrets sur le prompt jugement des émigrés trouvés sur le territoire de la République... suivi du discours [sur la liberté de la presse] du citoyen Louvet, représentant du peuple*. Paris: Imprimerie de la République, An III.

Loyseau, Jean-René. *Lettre de M. Loyseau... à M. de Condorcet, sur le projet de loi contre les délits qui peuvent se commettre par la voie de l'impression*. Paris: Imprimerie du *Patriote français*, [1790].

Malesherbes, Chrétien-Guillaume de Lamoignon de. *Mémoires sur la librairie; Mémoire sur la liberté de la presse*. Edited by Roger Chartier. [Paris]: Imprimerie nationale, 1994.

Malouet, Pierre-Victor. *Opinion de M. Malouet sur les crimes de lèse-nation, sur la responsabilité des ministres et autres agents du pouvoir exécutif*. [1791].

Manuel, Louis Pierre. *La police de Paris dévoilée*. 2 vols. Paris: J. B. Garnery, An II [1793].

Marat, Jean-Paul. *Oeuvres politiques, 1789–1793*. Edited by Jacques De Cock and Charlotte Goëtz. 10 vols. Bruxelles: Pole Nord, 1989–1995.

Mavidal, Jérôme, and Émile Laurent, eds. *Archives parlementaires de 1787 à 1860: Recueil complet des débats législatifs et politiques des Chambres françaises*. 1st series. 82 vols. Paris: P. Dupont, 1867–1913.

Mercier, Louis-Sebastien. *Tableau de Paris*. Nouvelle édition. 12 vols. Amsterdam: 1782–1988.

Mirabeau, Honoré-Gabriel Riqueti. *Sur la liberté de la presse*. Preface by B. Mirkine-Guetzevitch. Introduction by Philippe Sagnac. Paris: Office technique de Presse, 1939.

Molleville, A.-F. Bertrand de. *Histoire de la Révolution de France*. 14 vols. Paris: Giguet et Michaud, 1801–1803.

Montesquieu, Charles de Secondat baron de. *De l'esprit des lois*. Edited by Laurent Versini. 2 vols. Paris: Gallimard, 1995.

Morellet, André. *Pensées libres sur la liberté de la presse, à l'occasion d'un rapport du représentant Chénier à la Convention nationale, du 12 floréal*. Paris: Maret, [An III].

——. *Réflexions sur les avantages de la liberté d'écrire et d'imprimer sur les matières de l'administration, écrites en 1764, à l'occasion de la déclaration du Roi du 28 mars de la même année, qui fait défense d'imprimer, débiter aucuns écrits, ouvrages ou projets concernant la réforme ou l'administration des finances, etc*. Paris: Frères Estienne, 1775.

Moy, Charles-Alexandre de. *Accord de la religion et des cultes chez une nation libre*. Paris: J.-B. Garnéry, An IV [orig. 1791].

——. "Discours qui a remporté les deux prix d'éloquence au jugement de l'Académie des sciences, belles-lettres et arts de Besançon en l'année 1776 sur ce sujet: combien le respect pour les mœurs contribue au bonheur d'un état, par M. l'abbé de Moy, chanoine honoraire de Verdun et curé de Saint-Laurent à Paris." In Académie des sciences, belles-lettres et arts de Besançon, *Procès-verbaux, 1776*. Paris: Le Jay, 1776.

Ménétra, Jacques-Louis. *Journal of My Life*. Introduction and commentary by Daniel Roche. Forward by Robert Darnton. Translated by Arthur Goldhammer. New York: Columbia University Press, 1986.

Necker, Jacques. *De l'importance des opinions religieuses*. Paris: Hôtel de Thou, 1788.

——. "Rapport fait au roi dans son conseil, par le ministre de ses finances, le 27 décembre 1788." In *Archives parlementaires de 1787 à 1860: Recueil complet des débats législatifs et politiques des Chambres françaises*. Edited by Jérôme Mavidal and Émile Laurent. Vol. 1, 489–498. Paris: P. Dupont, 1867.

NewsHour with Jim Lehrer. "Government 'News.'" Web page, May 2005 [accessed September 29, 2007]. Available at http://www.pbs.org/newshour/bb/media/jan-june05/vnr_5–13.html.

Oudet, [J.-B.]. *Observations de M. Oudet, avocat au Parlement, sur la liberté de dire ou d'imprimer ses opinions, et sur la nécessité d'empêcher ou de réprimer l'abus de l'impression, et de punir les coupables ou les calomniateurs*. Paris: veuve Hérissant.

Paine, Thomas. *The Complete Writings of Thomas Paine*. Edited by Philip S. Foner. 2 vols. New York: Citadel Press, 1945.

——. *The Genuine Trial of Thomas Paine, for a Libel Contained in the Second Part of Rights of Man*. London: Printed for J. S. Jordan, 1792.

Pange, François. *Observations sur le crime de lèse-nation*. Paris: Barrois, 1790.

Peuchet, Jacques. "Jurisprudence: Contenant la police et les municipalités." *Encyclopédie méthodique*. Vols. 9–10. 10 vols. Paris: Panckoucke, 1791.

Picqué, Jean-Pierre. *Nécessité d'établir une censure publique*. Paris: Imprimerie nationale, [1793].

Prunelle, L. *Observations et projet de décret sur l'établissement d'un tribunal de la conscience du peuple.* Paris: Imprimerie nationale, [1793].

Pétion de Villeneuve, J. *Discours sur la liberté de la presse.* Paris: Imprimerie nationale, 1791.

Raynal, Guillaume-Thomas-François. *Histoire philosophique et politique des établissements et du commerce des Européens dans les deux Indes.* 7 vols. La Haye: Gosse fils, 1776.

Reporters Without Borders. "Annual Press Freedom Report." Web page, [accessed 20 September 2007]. Available at http://www.rsf.org/rubrique.php3?id_rubrique=639.

———. "Letter to Robert Gates on First Anniversary of AP Photographer Bilal Hussein's Arrest." Web page, April 2007 [accessed 20 September 2007]. Available at http://www.rsf.org/article.php3?id_article=21681.

———. "Three Years of Slaughter in Iraq." Web page, March 2006 [accessed 20 September 2007]. Available at http://www.rsf.org/rubrique.php3?id_rubrique=639.

———. "United States—Annual Report 2007." Web page, [accessed 20 September 2007]. Available at http://www.rsf.org/article.php3?id_article=20542.

Rey, Alain, ed. *Dictionnaire historique de la langue française.* 2 vols. Paris: Dictionnaire Le Robert, 1993.

Rich, Frank. "The White House Stages Its 'Daily Show.'" *New York Times,* February 20, 2005.

Richelieu, Cardinal de. *Testament politique.* Edited and introduction by Louis André. Preface by Leon Noël. Paris: Robert Laffont, 1947.

Robespierre, Maximilien. "Lettres à ses commettants." *Oeuvres de Maximilien Robespierre.* Edited by Gustave Laurent. Vol. 5, 10 vols. Gap: Louis-Jean, 1961.

———. "Rapport sur les principes de morale politique qui doivent guider la Convention nationale dans l'administration intérieure de la République." *Oeuvres de Maximilien Robespierre.* Edited by Marc Bouloiseau and Albert Soboul. Vol. 10, 350–367. Paris: Presses universitaires de France, 1967.

———. *Discours de Maximilien Robespierre sur l'influence de la calomnie sur la Révolution, prononcé à la Société dans la séance du 28 octobre 1792.* Paris: Pierre-Jacques Duplain, 1792.

———. "Discours sur la liberté de la presse." In *La Société des Jacobins.* Edited by Alphonse Aulard. Vol. 2, 396–411. Paris: Imprimerie nationale, 1791.

Roland, Jean-Marie. *Compte rendu à la Convention nationale par Jean-Marie Roland, ministre de l'Intérieur, de toutes les parties de son département, de ses vues d'amélioration et de prospérité publique; Le 6 janvier de l'an II de la République française.* Paris: Imprimerie nationale, 1793.

———. *Compte rendu le 23 septembre par le ministre de l'Intérieur et dont la Convention nationale a ordonné l'impression, l'envoi aux 83 départements et à l'armée.* Paris: Imprimerie nationale, 1792.

———. *Lettre du ministre de l'Intérieur à la Convention nationale, du 30 septembre 1792, l'an premier de la République française. Imprimée par ordre de la Convention nationale et envoyée aux 83 départements.* Paris: Imprimerie nationale, [1792].

———. "Le ministre de l'Intérieur aux corps administratifs, aux sociétés populaires, à tous ses concitoyens, le 22 janvier, l'an 2ᵉ." *Réimpression de l'ancien Moniteur, seule histoire authentique et inaltérée de la Révolution française depuis la réunion des États-généraux jusqu'au Consulat (mai 1789–novembre 1799) avec des notes explicatives.* 32 vols. Paris: Plon Frères, 1850–1854.

Roland, Jean-Marie. *Observations de l'ex-ministre Roland sur le rapport fait contre lui, par le député Brival.* Paris: P. Delormel, 1793.

Roland, Jeanne-Marie Phlipon. *Mémoires de Mme Roland.* Edited by Claude Perroud. 2 vols. Paris: Plon, 1905.

Rousseau, Jean-Jacques. *Politics and the Arts: Letter to M d'Alembert on the Theater.* Translated, introduction, and notes by Allan Bloom. Ithaca: Cornell University Press, 1968.

———. *The Social Contract and the First Discourses.* Edited by Susan Dunn. New Haven: Yale University Press, 2002.

Sade, marquis de. *La philosophie dans le boudoir, ouvrage posthume de l'auteur de Justine...* 2 vols. London [Paris?]: aux dépens de la Compagnie [*sic*], 1795.

Saint-Huruge, marquis de. *Mémoire succinct du marquis de Saint-Huruge, sergent dans les Gardes nationales parisiennes au district de Saint-Roch sur sa demande en liberté provisoire, envoyé à MM. des districts de la commune de Paris.* 1789.

Sarot. *Réveil des principes des loix et des ordonnances sur le crime de lèze-majesté royale, de lèze-état ou de lèze-nation.* [Paris]: J. Grand, n.d.

Séguier, Antoine-Louis, and Louis-Pierre Deseine. *Mémoire sur la nécessité du rétablissement des maîtrises et corporations.* Paris: Imprimerie de Fain, 1815.

George Shapiro. *The French Revolution Analysis System.* Version 1.3. 1999.

Simonne, Jean-Claude. *Moyen de rendre les peuples plus libres et heureux, ou idées sur leur éducation.* Paris: Chez Grégoire, 1791.

Spinoza, Benedict de. *A Theologico-Political Treatise and a Political Treatise.* Introduced and translated by R. H. M. Elwes. Mineola, New York: Dover Publications, 2004.

Staël, Anne-Louise-Germaine Necker Baroness de. *Correspondance générale.* Edited by Béatrice W. Jasinski. 6 vols. Paris: Jean-Jacques Pauvert, 1960–1993.

———. *Considerations on the Principal Events of the French Revolution.* Edited by Duke de Broglie and Baron de Staël. 2 vols. New York: James Eastburn, 1818.

Stewart, John Hall. *A Documentary Survey of the French Revolution.* New York: Macmillan, 1951.

[Thémines, M. de, évêque de Blois]. *Instructions et cahier du hameau de Madon.* Blois: J. P. J. Masson, 1789.

[Thiébault, Dieudonné]. *Mémoire sur la liberté de la presse, suivi de quelques autres mémoires concernant la librairie.* [1789].

Thiébault, Dieudonné. *Traité sur l'esprit public.* Strasbourg: F. G. Levrault, An VI.

[Thomassin, Michel]. *Réflexions sur la liberté de la presse.* 1790.

Tocqueville, Alexis de. *Democracy in America.* Edited by J. P. Mayer. Translated by George Lawrence. New York: Harper Perennial Modern Classics, 2006.

[Toussaint, François-Vincent]. *Les mœurs.* London [Leiden]: 1751.

Tuetey, Alexandre, ed. *Répertoire général des sources manuscrites de l'histoire de Paris pendant la Révolution française.* 11 vols. Paris: Imprimerie nouvelle, 1890–1914.

Voltaire. "Dictionnaire philosophique." In *Oeuvres complètes de Voltaire.* Edited by Louis Moland. Vols. 17–20. Paris: Garnier Frères, 1878–1879.

———. *Essai sur les mœurs et l'esprit des nations et sur les principaux faits de l'histoire depuis Charlemagne jusqu'à Louis XIII.* Edited and introduction by René Pomeau. 2 vols. Paris: Garniers Frères, 1963.

———. *Oeuvres complètes de Voltaire*. Edited by Louis Moland. 52 vols. Paris: Garnier Frères, 1877–1885.

———. "Questions sur les miracles." In *Oeuvres completes de Voltaire*. Vol. 25, 357–450. Paris: Garnier Frères, 1879–1880.

———. "Le Temple du goût." In *Oeuvres complètes de Voltaire*. Edited by Louis Moland. Vol. 8, 547–580. Paris: Garnier Frères, 1877.

Secondary Sources

Les principes de 1789 et la liberté de la presse. Extraits des cahiers de doléances des trois ordres de toutes les provinces de France. Paris: Lemerre, 1867.

Allen, Robert. *Les tribunaux criminels sous la Révolution et l'Empire, 1792–1811*. Rennes: Presses universitaires de Rennes, 2005.

Andress, David. "Social Prejudice and Political Fears in the Policing of Paris." *French History* 9, no. 2 (1995): 202–226.

Andrews, Richard Mowery. "Boundaries of Citizenship: The Penal Regulation of Speech in Revolutionary France." *French Politics and Society* 7, no. 3 (1989): 93–109.

Andries, Lise. "Les imprimeurs-libraires parisiens et la liberté de la presse (1789–1795)." *Dix-huitième siècle*, no. 21 (1989): 247–261.

Arendt, Hannah. *On Revolution*. London: Penguin, 1990.

Aulard, Alphonse. *The French Revolution: A Political History, 1789–1804*. Translated by Bernard Miall. 4 vols. London: T. F. Unwin, 1910.

———. "La Liberté Politique." *La Révolution française* 81 (1928): 366–378.

Baecque, Antoine de, Wolfgang Schmale, and Michel Vovelle, eds. *L'An 1 des Droits de l'homme*. Paris: Presses du CNRS, 1988.

Baker, Keith Michael. *Condorcet: From Natural Philosophy to Social Mathematics*. Chicago: University of Chicago Press, 1975.

———. *Inventing the French Revolution: Essays on French Political Culture in the Eighteenth Century*. Cambridge: Cambridge University Press, 1990.

———. "Politics and Public Opinion under the Old Regime: Some Reflections." In *Press and Politics in Pre-Revolutionary France*. Edited by Jack Censer and Jeremy D. Popkin, 204–246. Berkeley: University of California Press, 1987.

Beik, William. *Urban Protest in Seventeenth-Century France: The Culture of Retribution*. Cambridge: Cambridge University Press, 1997.

Bell, David A. *The Cult of the Nation of France: Inventing Nationalism, 1680–1800*. Cambridge: Harvard University Press, 2001.

———. *The First Total War: Napoleon's Europe and the Birth of Warfare As We Know It*. Boston: Houghton Mifflin, 2007.

———. *Lawyers and Citizens: The Making of a Political Elite in Old Regime France*. New York: Oxford University Press, 1994.

Bellanger, Claude, ed. *Histoire générale de la presse française*. 5 vols. Paris: Presses universitaires de France, 1969–1976.

Berlin, Isaiah. *Liberty: Incorporating Four Essays on Liberty*. Edited by Henry Hardy. 2nd ed. Oxford: Oxford University Press, 2002.

Bernardin, Edith. *Jean-Marie Roland et le ministère de l'Intérieur (1792–1793)*. Paris: Société des études Robespierristes, 1964.

Best, Geoffrey. *Honour among Men and Nations: Transformations of an Idea*. Toronto: University of Toronto Press, 1982.

Birn, Raymond. "Profit on Ideas: *Privilège en librairie* in Eighteenth-Century France." *Eighteenth-Century Studies* 4, no. 2 (1970–1971): 131–168.

———. "Religious Toleration and Freedom of Expression." In *The French Idea of Freedom: The Old Regime and the Declaration of the Rights of 1789*. Edited by Dale Van Kley. Stanford: Stanford University Press, 1994.

Bouloiseau, Marc. *Cahiers de doléances du tiers état du bailliage de Rouen pour les États-généraux de 1789*. 2nd ed. 2 vols. *Collection de documents inédits sur l'histoire économique de la Révolution française, département de la Seine-Maritime*. Haute-Normandie: Comité régional d'histoire de la révolution française, [1989].

Brioist, Pascal, Hervé Drévillon, and Pierre Serna. *Croiser le fer: Violence et culture de l'épée dans la France moderne (XVIe-XVIIIe siècles)*. Seyssel: Champ Vallon, 2002.

Brown, Gregory S. *A Field of Honor: Writers, Court Culture, and Public Theater in French Literary Life from Racine to the Revolution*. New York: Columbia University Press, 2002.

Brown, Howard G. *Ending the French Revolution: Violence, Justice, and Repression from the Terror to Napoleon*. Charlottesville: University of Virginia Press, 2006.

———. "Tips, Traps and Tropes: Catching Thieves in Post-Revolutionary Paris." In *Police Detectives in History, 1750–1950*. Edited by Clive Emsley and Haia Shpayer-Makov, 33–60. Aldershot, Eng.: Ashgate, 2006.

Brundage, W. Fitzhugh. *Lynching in the New South: Georgia and Virginia, 1880–1930*. Urbana: University of Illinois Press, 1993.

Brye, Bernard de. "Liberté de la presse et avatars d'un sermon. Recherches sur le sermon prononcé par Mgr. de la Fare, évêque de Nancy, lors de la messe d'ouverture des États-généraux, le 4 mai 1789." *Annales de l'Est* 32, no. 4 (1980): 279–317.

Butler, Judith. *Excitable Speech: A Politics of the Performative*. New York: Routledge, 1997.

Bély, Lucien, ed. *Dictionnaire de l'Ancien Régime: Royaume de France, XVIe-XVIIIe siècle*. 1st ed. Paris: Presses universitaires de France, 1996.

Cabanis, André. *La Presse sous le Consulat et l'Empire*. Paris: Société des Études Robespierristes, 1975.

Caron, Pierre. *Les missions du Conseil exécutif provisoire et de la Commune de Paris*. Paris: Presses universitaires de France, 1950.

Carrot, Georges. *Révolution et maintien de l'ordre*. Paris: S. P. M. and Kronos, 1995.

Carré, Henri. *La fin des parlements (1788–1790)*. Paris: Hachette, 1912.

Casnave, Jean, Jean Duran, and Alain Tislowitz. "Journaux et écrits périodiques, leur diffusion par la poste et les éditeurs depuis le XVIIIe siècle." Unpublished, dact. [Bibliothèque de la Poste: 41202]: 1985.

Castaldo, André. *Les méthodes de travail de la Constituante: Les techniques délibératives de l'Assemblée nationale, 1789–1791*. Paris: Presses universitaires de France, 1989.

Castan, Nicole. *Les criminels de Languedoc: Les exigences d'ordre et les voies du ressentiment dans une société pré-révolutionnaire (1750–1790).* Toulouse: Association des Publications de l'Université de Toulouse-Le Mirail, 1980.

Castan, Yves. *Honnêteté et relations sociales en Languedoc (1715–1780).* Paris: Plon, 1974.

Chartier, Roger. *The Cultural Origins of the French Revolution.* Translated by Lydia G. Cochrane. Durham, N.C.: Duke University Press, 1991.

———. "Cultures, lumières, doléances: Les cahiers de 1789." *Revue d'histoire moderne et contemporaine* 28, no. 1 (January–March 1981): 68–93.

Chartier, Roger, and Henri-Jean Martin, eds. *Histoire de l'édition française.* 2nd ed. 4 vols. Paris: Fayard, 1990.

Chisick, Harvey. *The Ami du Roi of the Abbé Royou: The Production, Distribution and Readership of a Conservative Journal of the Early French Revolution.* Philadelphia: American Philosophical Society, 1992.

———. *The Limits of the Reform in the French Enlightenment: Attitudes toward the Education of the Lower Classes in Eighteenth-Century France.* Princeton: Princeton University Press, 1981.

———. "Public Opinion and Political Culture in France during the Second Half of the Eighteenth Century." *English Historical Review,* no. 470 (2002): 48–77.

Chomsky, Noam. "Free Speech in a Democracy." *Daily Camera* (1985).

Choppin, H. *Insurrections militaires en 1790.* Paris: Lucien Laveur, 1903.

Christofferson, Michael Scott. "An Antitotalitarian History of the French Revolution: François Furet's *Penser la Révolution française* in the Intellectual Politics of the Late 1970s." *French Historical Studies* 22, no. 4 (1999): 557–611.

Cobb, Richard. *Les armées révolutionnaires, instrument de la Terreur dans les départements: Avril 1793—floréal an II.* 2 vols. Paris: Mouton, 1961–1963.

Cobb, Richard C. *The Police and the People: French Popular Protest, 1789–1820.* Oxford: Oxford University Press, 1970.

Colclough, David. *Freedom of Speech in Early Stuart England.* Cambridge: Cambridge University Press, 2005.

Coudart, Laurence. *La Gazette de Paris: Un journal royaliste pendant la Révolution française (1789–1792).* Paris: Harmattan, 1995.

Cowan, Jon. *To Speak for the People: Public Opinion and the Problem of Legitimacy in the French Revolution.* New York: Routledge, 2001.

Craveri, Benedetta. *The Age of Conversation.* Translated by Teresa Waugh. New York: New York Review Books, 2005.

Crocker, Lester G. "Rousseau's *soi-disant* Liberty." In *Rousseau and Liberty.* Edited by Robert Wokler, 244–266. Manchester: Manchester University Press, 1995.

Crow, Thomas E. *Painters and Public Life in Eighteenth-Century France.* New Haven: Yale University Press, 1985.

Cruickshanks, Evelyn. "Public Opinion in Paris in the 1740s: The Reports of the Chevalier de Mouhy." *Bulletin of the Institute of Historical Research* 27 (1954): 54–68.

Dakin, Douglas. *Turgot and the Ancien Regime in France.* New York: Octagon Books, 1965.

Darnton, Robert. *The Business of the Enlightenment.* Cambridge: Belknap Press of Harvard University Press, 1979.

——. *The Forbidden Bestsellers of Pre-Revolutionary France*. New York: W. W. Norton, 1995.

——. *Gens de lettres, gens du livre*. Paris: Éditions Odile Jacob, 1992.

——. *The Literary Underground of the Old Regime*. Cambridge: Harvard University Press, 1982.

——. "Trends in Radical Propaganda on the Eve of the French Revolution (1782–1788)." Ph.D. dissertation, Oxford University, 1964.

Desan, Suzanne. *Family on Trial in Revolutionary France*. Berkeley: University of California Press, 2004.

Dorigny, Marcel. "La propagande girondine et le livre en 1792: Le bureau de l'esprit public." *Dix-huitième siècle*, no. 21 (1989): 203–215.

Doyle, William. *The Oxford History of the French Revolution*. Oxford: Oxford University Press, 2001.

Duguit, Michel. *Le régime disciplinaire des assemblées législatives françaises*. Bordeaux: Imprimerie de l'Université, 1927.

Echeverria, Durand. *The Maupeou Revolution: A Study in the History of Libertarianism, France, 1770–1774*. Baton Rouge: Louisiana University Press, 1985.

——. "'The Sale of the Hessians.' Was Benjamin Franklin the Author?" *Proceedings of the American Philosophical Society* 98, no. 6 (1954): 427–431.

Edmonds, William. *Jacobinism and the Revolt of Lyon, 1789–1793*. Oxford: Clarendon Press, 1990.

Egret, Jean. *The French Pre-Revolution, 1787–1789*. Translated by Wesley D. Camp. Chicago: University of Chicago Press, 1977.

Farge, Arlette. *Dire et mal dire: L'opinion publique au XVIIIe siècle*. Paris: Seuil, 1992.

——. "The Honor and Secrecy of Families." In *A History of Private Life: Passions of the Renaissance*. Edited by Roger Chartier. Translated by Arthur Goldhammer. Cambridge: Belknap Press of Harvard University Press, 1989.

Farge, Arlette, and Jacques Revel. *The Vanishing Children of Paris: Rumor and Politics before the Revolution*. Translated by Claudia Miéville. Cambridge: Harvard University Press, 1991.

Farr, James R. "The Death of a Judge: Performance, Honor, and Legitimacy in Seventeenth-Century France." *Journal of Modern History* 75, no. 1 (2003): 1–22.

Fauchois, Yann. "La difficulté d'être libre: Les droits de l'homme, l'église catholique et l'assemblée constituante, 1789–1791." *Revue d'histoire moderne et contemporaine* 48, no. 1: 71–101.

Fish, Stanley. *There's No Such Thing as Free Speech...and It's a Good Thing, Too*. Oxford: Oxford University Press, 1994.

Fitzsimmons, Michael P. *The Night the Old Regime Ended: August 4, 1789 and the French Revolution*. University Park: Penn State University Press, 2003.

——. *The Remaking of France: The National Assembly and the Constitution of 1791*. Cambridge: Cambridge University Press, 1994.

Foucault, Michel. *Fearless Speech*. Edited by Joseph Pearson. Los Angeles: Semiotext(e), 2001.

——. "What Is Enlightenment?" In *The Foucault Reader*. Edited by Paul Rabinow. New York: Pantheon Books, 1984.

Fournier, Joseph. *Cahiers de doléances de la sénéchaussée de Marseille pour les États-généraux de 1789.* Marseille: Imprimerie Nouvelle, 1908.

Fournier l'Héritier [dit l'Américain], Claude. *Mémoires secrets de Fournier l'Américain, publiés pour la première fois d'après le manuscrit des Archives nationales, avec introduction et notes, par F.-A. Aulard.* Introduction by Alphonse Aulard. Paris: Société de l'histoire de la Révolution française, 1890.

France, Peter. *Politeness and Its Discontents: Problems in French Classical Culture.* Cambridge: Cambridge University Press, 1992.

Freeman, Joanne B. *Affairs of Honor: National Politics in the New Republic.* New Haven: Yale Note Bene, 2002.

Frijhoff, Willem, and Dominique Julia. *École et société dans la France d'ancien régime.* Paris: École des Hautes Études en Sciences Sociales, 1975.

Funck-Brentano, Frantz. *Les lettres de cachet à Paris, étude suivie d'une liste des prisonniers de la Bastille.* Paris: Imprimerie nationale, 1903.

Furet, François. *Revolutionary France, 1770–1880.* Translated by Antonia Nevill. Malden, Mass.: Blackwell Publishing Limited, 1992.

——. *Interpreting the French Revolution.* Translated by Elborg Forster. Cambridge: Cambridge University Press, 1985.

——. "Rousseau and the French Revolution." In *The Legacy of Rousseau.* Edited by Clifford Orwin and Nathan Tarcov, 168–182. Chicago: University of Chicago Press, 1997.

——. "Terror." *Critical Dictionary of the French Revolution.* Edited by François Furet and Mona Ozouf. Translated by Arthur Goldhammer, 137–150. Cambridge: Belknap Press of Harvard University Press, 1989.

Furet, François, and Mona Ozouf, eds. *Critical Dictionary of the French Revolution.* Translated by Arthur Goldhammer. Cambridge: Belknap Press of Harvard University Press, 1989.

Furet, François, and Denis Richet. *The French Revolution.* Translated by Stephen Hardman. New York: Macmillan, 1970.

Garrett, Mitchell B. *A Critical Bibliography of the Pamphlet Literature.* Birmingham, Ala.: Howard College, 1925.

Garrioch, David. *Neighborhood and Community in Paris, 1740–1790.* Cambridge: Cambridge University Press, 1986.

——. "Verbal Insults in Eighteenth-Century France." In *The Social History of Language.* Edited by Peter Burke and Roy Porter, 104–119. 2nd ed. Cambridge: Cambridge University Press, 1988.

Gauchet, Marcel. *La Révolution des droits de l'homme.* Paris: Gallimard, 1989.

Gay, Peter. *Voltaire's Politics: The Poet as Realist.* Princeton: Princeton University Press, 1959.

Godechot, Jacques. "La presse française sous la Révolution et l'Empire." In *Histoire générale de la presse française.* Edited by Claude Bellanger et al. Vol. 1, 405–569. 3 vols. Paris: Presses universitaires de France, 1969–1972.

Goldgar, Anne. *Impolite Learning: Conduct and Community in the Republic of Letters, 1680–1750.* New Haven: Yale University Press, 1995.

Goodman, Dena. *The Republic of Letters: A Cultural History of the French Enlightenment*. Ithaca: Cornell University Press, 1994.

Gordon, Daniel. *Citizens without Sovereignty: Equality and Sociability in French Thought, 1670–1789*. Princeton: Princeton University Press, 1994.

Gough, Hugh. *The Newspaper Press in the French Revolution*. Chicago: Dorsey Press, 1988.

Graham, Lisa Jane. "Crimes of Opinion: Policing the Public in Eighteenth-Century Paris." In *Visions and Revisions of Eighteenth-Century France*. Edited by Christine Adams, Jack Censer, and Lisa Jane Graham, 79–103. University Park: Penn State University Press, 1997.

Greenlaw, Ralph. "Pamphlet Literature in France during the Period of the Aristocratic Revolt (1787–1788)." *Journal of Modern History* 29, no. 4 (1957): 349–354.

Greer, Donald. *The Incidence of the Terror during the French Revolution: A Statistical Interpretation*. Cambridge: Harvard University Press, 1935.

Grosclaude, Pierre. *Malesherbes: Témoin et interprète de son temps*. Paris: Librairie Fischbacher, 1960.

Gruder, Vivian R. "Political News as Messages: The Parisian and Provincial Press in the Pre-Revolution, 1787–1788." *French History* 12, no. 1 (1998): 1–24.

Gueniffey, Patrice. *La politique de la Terreur: Essai sur la violence révolutionnaire*. Paris: Fayard, 2000.

Hallays-Dabot, Victor. *Histoire de la censure théâtrale en France*. Paris: E. Dentu, Libraire de la Société des Gens de Lettres, 1862.

Hardman, John. *French Politics, 1774–1789: From the Accession of Louis XVI to the Fall of the Bastille*. Harlow: Longman, 1995.

Hatin, Eugène. *Histoire politique et littéraire de la presse en France*. 8 vols. Paris: Poulet-Malassis, 1859–1861.

Hemmings, F. W. J. *Theatre and State in France, 1760–1905*. Cambridge: Cambridge University Press, 1994.

Herrmann-Mascard, Nicole. *La censure des livres à Paris à la fin de l'Ancien Régime, 1750–1789*. Paris: Presses universitaires de France, 1968.

Hesse, Carla. "Enlightenment Epistemology and the Laws of Authorship in Revolutionary France, 1773–1793." *Representations*, no. 30 (1990): 109–137.

———. "The Law of the Terror." *Modern Language Notes* 114, no. 4 (1999): 702–718.

———. *The Other Enlightenment: How French Women Became Modern*. Princeton: Princeton University Press, 2001.

———. "La preuve par la lettre: Pratiques juridiques au tribunal révolutionnaire de Paris (1793–1794)." *Annales: Histoire, sciences sociales*, no. 3 (1996): 629–642.

———. *Publishing and Cultural Politics in Revolutionary Paris, 1789–1810*. Berkeley: University of California Press, 1991.

———. "Revolutonary Rousseaus: The Story of His Editions after 1789." In *Media and Political Culture in the Eighteenth Century*. Edited by Marie-Christine Skuncke, 107–128. Stockholm: Kungl. Vitterhets Historie Och Antikvitets Akademien, 2005.

Higonnet, Patrice. "Terror, Trauma and the 'Young Marx' Explanation of Jacobin Politics." *Past and Present*, no. 191 (2006): 121–164.

Hoffman, Philip T. *Growth in a Traditional Society: The French Countryside, 1450–1815*. Princeton: Princeton University Press, 1996.

Howard, A. E. Dick. "Legal and Constitutional Protections of Freedom of Speech in the United States." In *Liberty of Expression*. Edited by Philip S. Cook, 79–87. Washington, D.C.: Wilson Center Press, 1990.

Hudson, David. "In Defense of Reform: French Government Propaganda during the Maupeou Crisis." *French Historical Studies* 8, no. 1 (1973): 51–76.

Hunt, Lynn. *Politics, Culture, and Class in the French Revolution*. Berkeley: University of California Press, 1984.

———. "The World We Have Gained: The Future of the French Revolution." *American Historical Review* 108, no. 1 (2003): 1–19.

Huot, Paul. *Les massacres à Versailles en 1792, éclaircissements historiques et documents nouveaux*. Paris: Challamel Aîné, 1869.

Hyslop, Beatrice Fry. *A Guide to the General Cahiers of 1789 with the Texts of Unedited Cahiers*. New York: Morningside Heights, 1936.

Isherwood, Robert M. *Farce and Fantasy: Popular Entertainment in Eighteenth-Century Paris*. New York: Oxford University Press, 1986.

Jainchill, Andrew. *Rethinking Politics after the Terror: The Republican Origins of French Liberalism*. Ithaca: Cornell University Press, 2008.

James, Mervyn. *Society, Politics, and Culture: Studies in Early Modern England*. Cambridge: Cambridge University Press, 1986.

Jaume, Lucien. *Les Déclarations des droits de l'homme: 1789, 1793, 1848, 1946*. Paris: Garnier-Flammarion, 1989.

———. *Le discours jacobin et la démocratie*. Paris: Fayard, 1989.

Jones, Colin. *The Great Nation: France from Louis XV to Napoleon, 1715–1799*. New York: Columbia University Press, 2002.

Kamensky, Jane. *Governing the Tongue: The Politics of Speech in Early New England*. New York: Oxford University Press, 1997.

Kaplan, Steven Laurence. *The Bakers of Paris and the Bread Question, 1700–1775*. Durham, N.C.: Duke University Press, 1996.

Kates, Gary. *The Cercle Social, the Girondins, and the French Revolution*. Princeton: Princeton University Press, 1985.

Kelly, Christopher. *Rousseau as Author: Consecrating One's Life to the Truth*. Chicago: University of Chicago Press, 2003.

Kennedy, Emmet. *Cultural History of the French Revolution*. New Haven: Yale University Press, 1989.

Kennedy, Michael. *The Jacobin Clubs in the French Revolution: The First Years*. Princeton: Princeton University Press, 1982.

———. *The Jacobin Clubs in the French Revolution: The Middle Years*. Princeton: Princeton University Press, 1988.

Klaits, Joseph. *Printed Propaganda under Louis XIV: Absolute Monarchy and Public Opinion*. Princeton: Princeton University Press, 1976.

Koselleck, Reinhart. *Critique and Crisis: Enlightenment and the Pathogenesis of Modern Society*. Cambridge: MIT Press, 1988.

Kupiec, Anne. "La Gironde et le bureau d'esprit public: Livre et révolution." *Annales historiques de la Révolution française*, no. 302 (1995): 571–586.

Lamartine, Alphonse de. *Histoire des Girondins*. 2 vols. Paris: Plon, 1983–1984.

Landes, Joan B. *Women and the Public Sphere in the Age of the French Revolution*. Ithaca: Cornell University Press, 1988.

Le Clère, Marcel. *Histoire de la police*. Paris: Presses universitaires de France, 1973.

——. "Police." In *Dictionnaire historique de la Révolution française*. Edited by Albert Soboul, 848–849. Paris: Presses universitaires de France, 1989.

——. "Police générale." In *Dictionnaire historique de la Révolution française*. Edited by Albert Soboul, 849–850. Paris: Presses universitaires de France, 1989.

Lebrun, François, Marc Venard, and Jean Queniart. *Histoire générale de l'enseignement et de l'éducation. Vol. 2: De Gutenberg aux Lumières*. Series edited by Louis-Henri Parias. 4 vols. Paris: Nouvelle Librairie de France, 1981.

Leclercq, Dom H. *Vers la Fédération (Janvier–juillet 1790)*. Paris: Librairie Letouzey et Ané, 1929.

Lefebvre, Georges. *The Coming of the French Revolution*. Translated by R. R. Palmer. Princeton: Princeton University Press, 1947.

Lemay, Edna Hindie. *Dictionnaire des Constituants, 1789–1791*. 2 vols. Paris: Universitas, 1991.

Lemay, Edna Hindie, and Alison Patrick, eds. *Revolutionaries at Work: The Constituent Assembly, 1789–1791*. With a contribution by Joel Félix. Oxford: Voltaire Foundation, 1996.

Levy, Leonard W. *Emergence of a Free Press*. Chicago: Ivan R. Dee, 2004.

——. *Legacy of Suppression: Freedom of Speech and Press in Early American History*. Cambridge: Belknap Press of Harvard University Press, 1960.

Lilti, Antoine. *Le monde des salons: Sociabilité et mondanité à Paris dans le XVIIIe siècle*. Paris: Fayard, 2005.

Linton, Marisa. "Robespierre's Political Principles." In *Robespierre*. Edited by Colin Haydon and William Doyle, 37–53. Cambridge: Cambridge University Press, 1999.

Livesey, James. *Making Democracy in the French Revolution*. Cambridge: Harvard University Press, 2001.

Luttrell, Barbara. *Mirabeau*. New York: Harvester Wheatsheaf, 1990.

Machelon, Jean-Pierre. *La République contre les libertés? Les restrictions aux libertés publiques de 1879–1914*. Paris: Presses de la Fondation nationale des Sciences politiques, 1976.

Manevy, Raymond. *La Révolution et la liberté de la presse*. N.p.: Estienne, 1964.

Manin, Bernard. "Rousseau." In *Critical Dictionary of the French Revolution*. Edited by François Furet and Mona Ozouf. Translated by Arthur Goldhammer, 829–841. Cambridge: Belknap Press of Harvard University Press, 1989.

Marcuse, Herbert. "Repressive Tolerance." In *A Critique of Pure Tolerance*. Edited by Robert Paul Wolff, Barrington Moore Jr., and Herbert Marcuse, 81–123. Boston: Beacon Press, 1969.

Marion, Marcel. *Dictionnaire des institutions de la France XVIIe-XVIIIe siècles*. Paris: A. and J. Picard, 1993.

Markoff, John. *The Abolition of Feudalism: Peasants, Lords, and Legislators in the French Revolution*. University Park: Penn State University Press, 1996.

Martin, Isabelle. *Le théâtre de la foire: Des tréteaux aux boulevards*. Oxford: Voltaire Foundation, 2002.

Martin, Jean-Clément. *Contre-Révolution, Révolution et Nation en France, 1789–1799*. Paris: Éditions de Seuil, 1998.

———. *Violence et révolution: Essai sur la naissance d'un mythe national*. Paris: Seuil, 2006.

Martin, Robert W. T. *The Free and Open Press: The Founding of American Democratic Press Liberty, 1640–1800*. New York: New York University Press, 2001.

Martucci, Roberto. "Qu'est-ce que la lèse-nation? A propos du problème de l'infraction politique sous la Constituante (1789–1791)." *Déviance et société* 14, no. 4 (1990): 377–393.

Mason, Laura. *Singing the French Revolution: Popular Culture and Politics, 1787–1799*. Ithaca: Cornell University Press, 1996.

Mathiez, Albert. *La Révolution et l'église*. Paris: A. Colin, 1910.

May, Gita. *Madame Roland and the Age of Revolution*. New York: Columbia University Press, 1970.

Mayer, Arno J. *The Furies: Violence and Terror in the French and Russian Revolutions*. Princeton: Princeton University Press, 2000.

Mayton, William T. "Seditious Libel and the Lost Guarantee of a Freedom of Expression." *Columbia Law Review* 84, no. 1 (1984): 91–142.

Maza, Sarah. *Private Lives and Public Affairs: The Causes Célèbres of Prerevolutionary France*. Berkeley: University of California Press, 1993.

McMahon, Darrin M. *Enemies of the Enlightenment: The French Counter-Enlightenment and the Making of Modernity*. New York: Oxford University Press, 2001.

McPhee, Peter. *The French Revolution, 1789–1799*. Oxford: Oxford University Press, 2002.

Mericskay, A. "Le Châtelet et la répression de la criminalité à Paris en 1770." Ph.D. dissertation, Université de Paris-Sorbonne, 1984.

Merriman, John. *Police Stories: Building the French State, 1815–1851*. New York: Oxford University Press, 2006.

Minois, Georges. *Censure et culture sous l'ancien régime*. Paris: Fayard, 1995.

Mortier, Roland. "Voltaire et le peuple." In *The Age of Enlightenment: Studies Presented to Theodore Besterman*. Edited by W. H. Barber et al., 137–151. Edinburgh: Oliver and Boyd, 1967.

Mortimer-Ternaux, [Louis]. *Histoire de la Terreur*. 8 vols. Paris: Lévy frères, 1869.

Muchembled, Robert. *L'invention de l'homme moderne: Sensibilités, mœurs et comportements collectifs sous l'Ancien Régime*. Paris: Fayard, 1988.

———. *La société policée: Politique et politesse en France, du XVIe au XXe siècles*. Paris: Seuil, 1998.

Murray, William James. *The Right-Wing Press in the French Revolution: 1789–1792*. Exeter: Short Run Press, 1986.

Negroni, Barbara de. *Lectures interdites: Le travail des censeurs au XVIIIe siècle, 1723–1774*. Paris: Albin Michel, 1995.

Neuschel, Kristen. *Word of Honor: Interpreting Noble Culture in Sixteenth-Century France*. Ithaca: Cornell University Press, 1989.

Nordman, Daniel. *Frontières de France: De l'espace au territoire, XVIe–XIXe siècles*. [Paris]: Gallimard, 1998.

Nye, Robert A. *Masculinity and Male Codes of Honor in Modern France*. New York: Oxford University Press, 1993.

Ozouf, Mona. *Festivals and the French Revolution*. Translated by Alan Sheridan. Cambridge: Harvard University Press, 1991.

———. "Public Spirit." In *Critical Dictionary of the French Revolution*. Edited by François Furet and Mona Ozouf. Translated by Arthur Goldhammer, 771–780. Cambridge: Belknap Press of Harvard University Press, 1989.

Palmer, R. R. *The Improvement of Humanity: Education and the French Revolution*. Princeton: Princeton University Press, 1985.

———. *Twelve Who Ruled: The Year of the Terror in the French Revolution*. Princeton: Princeton University Press, 1973.

Perroud, Claude. "Roland et la presse subventionée." *La Révolution française*, no. 62 (1912): 206–213, 315–332, 396–419.

Phillips, Roderick. *Family Breakdown in Late Eighteenth-Century France: Divorces in Rouen, 1792–1803*. Oxford: Clarendon Press, 1980.

Pocock, J. G. A. *The Machiavellian Moment: Florentine Political Thought and the Atlantic Republican Tradition*. Princeton: Princeton University Press, 1975.

Poittevin, Gustave. *La liberté de la presse depuis la Révolution (1789–1815)*. Geneva: Slatkine, 1975.

Popkin, Jeremy D. "Not Over After All: The French Revolution's Third Century." *Journal of Modern History* 74, no. 4 (2002): 801–821.

———. *Revolutionary News: The Press in France, 1789–1799*. Durham, N.C.: Duke University Press, 1990.

Ranum, Orest. "Courtesy, Absolutism, and the Rise of the French State, 1630–1660." *Journal of Modern History* 52, no. 3 (1980): 426–451.

Ravel, Jeffrey S. *The Contested Parterre: Public Theater and French Political Culture, 1680–1791*. Ithaca: Cornell University Press, 1999.

———. "Seating the Public: Spheres and Loathing in the Paris Theaters, 1777–1788." *French Historical Studies* 18 (1993): 173–210.

Reddy, William M. *The Invisible Code: Honor and Sentiment in Postrevolutionary France, 1815–1848*. Berkeley: University of California Press, 1997.

Reichardt, Rolf, and Herbert Schneider. "Chanson et musique populaires devant l'histoire à la fin de l'ancien régime." *Dix-huitième siècle* 18 (1986): 117–142.

Rétat, Pierre, and Claude Labrosse. *Naissance du journal révolutionnaire, 1789*. Lyon: Presses Universitaires de Lyon, 1989.

Rich, Frank. "The White House Stages Its 'Daily Show.'" *New York Times*, 20 February 2005, http://www.nytimes.com/2005/02/20/arts/20rich.html?ex=12666420 00&en=9245d7b440e36c54&ei=5088&partner=rssnyt, consulted September 16, 2007.

Roche, Daniel. "Académies et politique au siècle des lumières: Les enjeux pratiques de l'immortalité." In *The Political Culture of the Old Regime*. Edited by Keith Michael Baker. Vol. 1 of *The French Revolution and the Creation of Modern Political Culture*. Edited by Keith Michael Baker. Oxford: Pergamon Press, 1987.

——. "Censorship and the Publishing Industry." In *Revolution in Print: The Press in France, 1775–1800*. Edited by Robert Darnton and Daniel Roche, 3–26. Berkeley: University of California Press, 1989.

——. "Censure." In *Histoire de l'édition française: Le livre triomphant (1660–1830)*. Edited by Roger Chartier and Henri-Jean Martin, 88–98. 2nd ed. Paris: Fayard, 1990.

——. *The People of Paris: An Essay in Popular Culture in the 18th Century*. Translated by Marie Evans and Gwynne Lewis. Leamington Spa: Berg Publishers Limited, 1987.

——. "Police du livre." In *Histoire de l'édition française: Le livre triomphant (1660–1830)*. Edited by Roger Chartier and Henri-Jean Martin, 99–109. 2nd ed. Paris: Fayard, 1990.

——. *Le siècle des lumières en province: Académies et académiciens provinciaux, 1680–1789*. 2 vols. Paris: École des Hautes Études en Sciences Sociales, 1989.

Romani, Roberto. *National Character and Public Spirit in Britain and France, 1750–1914*. Cambridge: Cambridge University Press, 2002.

Rosenfeld, Sophia. *A Revolution in Language: The Problem of Signs in Late Eighteenth-Century France*. Stanford: Stanford University Press, 2001.

——. "Writing the History of Censorship in the Age of Enlightenment." In *Post-Modernism and the Enlightenment: New Perspectives in French Intellectual History*. Edited by Daniel Gordon, 117–145. New York: Routledge, 2001.

Rosenvallon, Pierre. *The Demands of Liberty: Civil Society in France since the Revolution*. Translated by Arthur Goldhammer. Cambridge: Harvard University Press, 2007.

Roussel, M. "La Haute Cour nationale à Orléans, 1791–1792." *Le Droit: Journal des tribunaux*, 11 November–12 November 1901 and 13 November 1901, 1013–1014, 1017–1018.

Sawyer, Jeffrey K. *Printed Poison: Pamphlet Propaganda, Faction Politics, and the Public Sphere in Early Seventeenth-Century France*. Berkeley: University of California Press, 1990.

Scott, Samuel. "Problems of Law and Order during 1790, the 'Peaceful' Year of the French Revolution." *American Historical Review* 80, no. 4 (1975): 859–888.

Seligman, Edmond. *La justice en France pendant la Révolution*. 2 vols. Paris: Plon, 1901–1913.

Sewell, William H. *The Rhetoric of a Bourgeois Revolution: The Abbé Sieyès and What Is the Third Estate?* Durham, N.C.: Duke University Press, 1994.

Shackleton, Robert. *Montesquieu: A Critical Biography*. Oxford: Oxford University Press, 1961.

Shapiro, Barry. "Revolutionary Justice in 1789–1790: The Comité des recherches, the Châtelet, and the Fayettist Coalition." *French Historical Studies* 17, no. 3 (1992): 656–669.

——. *Revolutionary Justice in Paris, 1789–1790*. Cambridge: Cambridge University Press, 1993.

Shapiro, Gilbert, and John Markoff, eds. *Revolutionary Demands: A Content Analysis of the Cahiers de doléances of 1789*. Stanford: Stanford University Press, 1998.

Shovlin, John. "Toward a Reinterpretation of Revolutionary Antinobilism: The Political Economy of Honor in the Old Regime." *Journal of Modern History* 72, no. 1 (2000): 35–66.

Singham, Shanti Marie. "A Conspiracy of Twenty Million Frenchmen: Public Opinion, Patriotism, and the Assault on Absolutism during the Maupeou Years, 1770–1775." Ph.D. dissertation, Princeton University, 1991.

Smith, Jeffrey A. *Printers and Press Freedom: The Ideology of Early American Journalism.* New York: Oxford University Press, 1988.

Soboul, Albert, ed. *Dictionnaire historique de la Révolution française.* Paris: Presses universitaires de France, 1989.

Söderhjelm, Alma. *Le régime de la presse pendant la Révolution française.* 2 vols. Geneva: Slatkine Reprints, 1971.

Soley, Lawrence. *Censorship, Inc.: The Corporate Threat to Free Speech in the United States.* New York: Monthly Review, 2002.

Starobinski, Jean. *1789: Les emblèmes de la raison.* Paris: Flammarion, 1973.

———. *Le remède dans le mal: Critique et légitimation de l'artifice à l'âge des Lumières.* Paris: Gallimard, 1989.

Stoll, Laurence Walter. "The Bureau Politique and the Management of the Popular Press: A Study of the Second Directory's Attempt to Develop a Directoire Ideology and Manipulate the Newspapers." Ph.D. dissertation, University of Wisconsin, 1975.

Stone, Geoffrey R. *Perilous Times: Free Speech in Wartime from the Sedition Act of 1798 to the War on Terrorism.* New York: W. W. Norton, 2004.

Sunstein, Cass R. *Republic.com 2.0.* Princeton: Princeton University Press, 2007.

Swenson, James. *On Jean-Jacques Rousseau: Considered as One of the First Authors of Revolution.* Stanford: Stanford University Press, 2000.

Tackett, Timothy. *Becoming a Revolutionary: The Deputies of the French National Assembly and the Emergence of a Revolutionary Culture (1789–1790).* Princeton: Princeton University Press, 1996.

———. "Conspiracy Obsession in a Time of Revolution: French Elites and the Origins of the Terror, 1789–1792." *American Historical Review* 105, no. 3 (2000): 691–713.

———. *Religion, Revolution, and Regional Culture in Eighteenth-Century France: The Ecclesiastical Oath of 1791.* Princeton: Princeton University Press, 1986.

———. *When the King Took Flight.* Cambridge: Harvard University Press, 2003.

Talmon, J. L. *Origins of Totalitarian Democracy.* New York: W. W. Norton, 1970.

Tocqueville, Alexis de. *The Old Regime and the French Revolution.* Translated by Stuart Gilbert. Garden City, N.Y.: Doubleday, 1955.

Todorov, Tzvetan. *On Human Diversity: Nationalism, Racism, and Exoticism in French Thought.* Translated by Catherine Porter. Cambridge: Harvard University Press, 1993.

Tourneux, Maurice, ed. *Bibliographie de l'Histoire de Paris pendant la Révolution française.* 5 vols. Paris: Imprimerie nouvelle, 1890–1913.

Trenard, Louis. *La Révolution française dans la région Rhône-Alpes.* Paris: Perrin, 1992.

Vaillé, Eugène. *Le Cabinet noir.* Paris: Presses universitaires de France, 1950.

Van Kley, Dale. *The Damiens Affair and the Unravelling of the Ancien Régime, 1750–1770.* Princeton: Princeton University Press, 1984.

———, ed. *The French Idea of Freedom: The Old Regime and the Declaration of the Rights of 1789.* Stanford: Stanford University Press, 1994.

Viguerie, Jean de. "Les serments du sacre des rois de France à l'époque moderne, et plus spécialement le 'serment du royaume.'" In *Le sacre des rois: Actes du colloque international d'histoire sur les sacres et couronnement royaux (Reims 1975)*, 205–215. Paris: Belles Lettres, 1985.

Vovelle, Michel. *La chute de la monarchie, 1787–1792*. Paris: Seuil, 1972.

Wahnich, Sophie. *La liberté ou la mort: Essai sur la Terreur et le terrorisme*. Paris: La Fabrique, 2003.

Walter, Eric. "Les auteurs et le champ littéraire." In *Histoire de l'édition française: Le livre triomphant (1660–1830)*. Edited by Roger Chartier and Henri-Jean Martin, 499–518. 2nd ed. Paris: Fayard, 1990.

Walton, G. Charles. "Charles IX and the French Revolution: Law, Vengeance, and the Revolutionary Uses of History." *European Review of History, Revue européene d'histoire* 4, no. 2 (1997).

——. "Policing Public Opinion in the French Revolution." Ph.D. dissertation, Princeton University, 2003.

Weitman, Sasha. "Bureaucracy, Democracy, and the French Revolution." Ph.D. dissertation, Washington University, 1968.

Williams, Alan. *Police of Paris, 1718–1789*. Oxford: Oxford University Press, 1974.

Wilson, Arthur M. *Diderot*. New York: Oxford University Press, 1972.

Wolf, John B. *Louis XIV*. New York: W. W. Norton, 1968.

Woloch, Isser. *The New Regime: Transformations of the French Civic Order, 1789–1820s*. New York: W. W. Norton, 1994.

Wyatt-Brown, Bertram. *Honor and Violence in the Old South*. New York: Oxford University Press, 1986.

INDEX

Page numbers in **bold** indicate pictures. Other figures or tables are indicated by *italics*.

9 780199 795802